KAINUA
(MARZABOTTO)

CITIES AND COMMUNITIES OF THE ETRUSCANS
Nancy Thomson de Grummond and Lisa C. Pieraccini, series editors

This series was initiated to open discussion and ask questions about what defines an Etruscan city. How did Etruscan cities arise, and what can they tell us about urbanism in ancient Italy? How did Etruscan cities create their own identities, and how are they similar to or different from each other? These queries can be applied to the study of the "Twelve Peoples of the Etruscans," a conventional historical term used in ancient Rome to refer to the most important cities of the Etruscans, the majority of which can be identified today. The aim of this book series is to stimulate and contribute to current vigorous debates concerning Etruscan culture and art, state formation, urban development, and the socioeconomic characteristics of settlements in Etruria.

To understand the major Etruscan cities better, it is also vital to look at the numerous smaller settlements and discuss their similarities to and differences from one another and the larger cities nearby. How can we trace how Etruscan communities developed differently from cities? Did these settlements play a distinctive role in networks of trade in comparison to the large cities? Did smaller communities produce the same arts as their sizable neighbors? Did they worship different Etruscan gods from those of the great cities?

By asking such questions we hope to access the social, religious, economic, architectural, artistic, and civic fabric of each Etruscan city and community. This approach highlights the unique Etruscan contributions to ancient Italy without relying heavily on the traditional methodologies that look to Greece or Rome to explain Etruscan customs, culture, art, and traditions.

ALSO IN THE SERIES:

Anthony Tuck, *Poggio Civitate (Murlo)*
Nancy Thomson de Grummond, *Cetamura del Chianti*
Jacopo Tabolli, ed., *Veii*
Nancy Thomson de Grummond and Lisa C. Pieraccini, eds., *Caere*

KAINUA
(MARZABOTTO)

EDITED BY ELISABETTA GOVI

EDITORIAL COORDINATOR: STEFANO SANTOCCHINI GERG

University of Texas Press
AUSTIN

Copyright © 2023 by the University of Texas Press
All rights reserved
Printed in the United States of America
First edition, 2023

This book has been supported by an endowment dedicated to classics and the ancient world and funded by the Areté Foundation; the Gladys Krieble Delmas Foundation; the Dougherty Foundation; the James R. Dougherty, Jr. Foundation; the Rachael and Ben Vaughan Foundation; and the National Endowment for the Humanities.

Requests for permission to reproduce material from this work should be sent to:
 Permissions
 University of Texas Press
 P.O. Box 7819
 Austin, TX 78713-7819
 utpress.utexas.edu/rp-form

♾ The paper used in this book meets the minimum requirements of ANSI/NISO Z39.48-1992 (R1997) (Permanence of Paper).

LIBRARY OF CONGRESS
CATALOGING-IN-PUBLICATION DATA

Names: Govi, Elisabetta, editor.
Title: Kainua (Marzabotto) / edited by Elisabetta Govi ; editorial coordinator, Stefano Santocchini Gerg.
Other titles: Cities and communities of the Etruscans.
Description: First edition. | Austin : University of Texas Press, 2023. | Series: Cities and communities of the Etruscans | Includes bibliographical references and index.
Identifiers:
LCCN 2022024369
ISBN 978-1-4773-2662-6 (cloth)
ISBN 978-1-4773-2663-3 (PDF)
ISBN 978-1-4773-2664-0 (ePub)
Subjects: LCSH: Etruscans—Italy—Marzabotto—Antiquities. | Etruscans—Italy—Marzabotto—Economic conditions. | Etruscans—Italy—Marzabotto—Religion. | Etruscans—Italy—Marzabotto—Social life and customs. | Etruscan cults. | Excavations (Archaeology)—Technological innovations—Italy—Marzabotto. | Marzabotto (Italy)—Antiquities. | BISAC: SOCIAL SCIENCE / Archaeology
Classification: LCC DG70.M36 K35 2023 | DDC 937/.501—dc23/eng/20220601
LC record available at https://lccn.loc.gov/2022024369

doi:10.7560/326626

CONTENTS

List of Illustrations   ix

Preface   xiii
Elisabetta Govi

Introduction to the Volume: Kainua-Marzabotto, the New Face of the City   xv
Elisabetta Govi

Abbreviations   xvii

A Note on Terminology   xix

Album of Maps   xx

PART I. DISCOVERY AND ARCHAEOLOGY OF THE CITY   1

1. The Role of the City in Nineteenth- and Twentieth-Century Scientific Debate   3
Giuseppe Sassatelli

2. The Etruscan National Museum "P. Aria"   9
Federica Timossi

3. Investigating the City: An Integrated Approach   15
Elisabetta Govi, Andrea Gaucci, Simone Garagnani, and Federica Boschi

PART II. THE PLANNED CITY AND ITS TERRITORY   27

4. Founding and Refounding of the City   29
Elisabetta Govi

5. City and Territory: Trade Routes and Cultural Connections   41
Stefano Santocchini Gerg

6. The Settlement of the Territory 51
Tiziano Trocchi and Paola Desantis

7. Environment, Landscape, and Economy 61
Antonio Curci and Marialetizia Carra

PART III. LIVING IN THE CITY 73

8. Sacred Architecture and Landscape 75
Elisabetta Govi

9. Cults, Rituals, and the Offering System 91
Riccardo Vanzini

10. Writing Practice and Society 99
Andrea Gaucci

11. Household Archaeology and Society 115
Giacomo Mancuso, Chiara Pizzirani, and Bojana Gruška

12. Art and Artisans: Metal Production 127
Giulia Morpurgo

13. From Clay to Vases: Operative Workflow 135
Chiara Mattioli

14. Carved Stone Monuments 145
Giacomo Mancuso

15. A World of Images: Attic Pottery 155
Vincenzo Baldoni

PART IV. DYING IN THE CITY 163

16. Funerary Practices 165
Chiara Pizzirani

17. The Necropoleis: Tomb Structures 175
Chiara Pizzirani

18. The Tombs of Sasso Marconi 183
Matteo Tirtei

PART V. THE END OF THE ETRUSCAN CITY 191

19. The Celtic Period 193
Giulia Morpurgo

20. The Roman Period 201
Alessandro Campedelli

Appendix A: Inscriptions from Kainua-Marzabotto   209
Andrea Gaucci

Appendix B: List of Publications and Excavations   213
Giulia Morpurgo

Appendix C: Chronology of Kainua   217

Bibliography   219
Compiled by Stefano Santocchini Gerg

Index   237

ILLUSTRATIONS

MAPS

1. Italy and the Etruscan territory   xx
2. Etruria Padana   xxi
3. Territory of Kainua and trade routes   xxii
4. Territory of Kainua in the Roman period   xxiii
5. Plan of Kainua   xxiv
6. Plan of Kainua with inscriptions   xxv
7. Plan of Kainua with house types   xxvi
8. Plan of Kainua with manufacturing facilities   xxvii
9. Plan of Kainua in the Celtic period   xxviii
10. Plan of the Acropolis   xxix
11. Plan of the Urban Sanctuary   xxx
12. Plans of the houses of *Regio* IV, 1   xxxi
13. Plan of the necropoleis   xxxii

FIGURES

All the objects indicated in the figures and plates listed here are exhibited in the National Etruscan Museum "P. Aria" in Marzabotto, or stored in its warehouses. The related images were kindly granted by permission of the Direzione Regionale Musei Emilia-Romagna (Regional Museum Direction of Emilia-Romagna).

For the images (drawings, photos, maps) of the excavations carried out by the chair of Etruscology at the University of Bologna and the related findings, the copyright belongs to the University of Bologna Archive.

Otherwise, the place of conservation and copyright are indicated in the captions.

1.1. The Northern Necropolis with the pavilion   4
1.2. Edoardo Brizio with colleagues and students   5
1.3. Plate from the report of excavations conducted by E. Brizio   5
1.4. Participants in the First Congresso Internazionale Etrusco   6
2.1. Etruscan museum in "Villa Aria": room 5, showcase A   10
2.2. First page of the gift deed of the museum and archaeological area of Marzabotto   11
2.3. The former farmhouse at Pian di Misano after the war   11
3.1. Geophysics investigations at Marzabotto by the University of Bologna and partners   17
3.2. Aerial view of the archaeological site of Marzabotto   18
3.3. Geomagnetic map and *Regio* III comparing ARP results and aerial photography   19
3.4. Virtual reconstructions of the city, the Temple of Tinia, and House 1, *Regio* IV, 2   21
3.5. Digital reconstruction of the Temple of Uni   22
3.6. Views of the virtual Kainua   23
3.7. The ArchaeoBIM model of the Temple of Uni   23
3.8. Reconstruction of *plateia* B from the crossroads toward the Temple of Tinia   24

3.9. KAINUA 2017, April 19, 2017, visit to Kainua on the occasion of Giuseppe Sassatelli's seventieth birthday   25

4.1. Wall structures of the northern area of the Temple of Tinia   31

4.2. *Podium*-altar B on the Acropolis   31

4.3. Foundation rite of the city, scheme of ritual actions   34

4.4. *Cippus* engraved with oriented cross-mark, or *crux* (*decussis*)   35

4.5. The Etruscan celestial *templum* superimposed on the city plan   36

5.1. Votive bronze statuettes from Monteacuto Ragazza   42

5.2. Corinthian trade amphora   45

5.3. Ivory lid of a *pyxis*   45

5.4. Sample of bucchero vases from Marzabotto   46

5.5. Sample of decorated local pottery   47

6.1. Pian di Venola, bronze cista with embossed decoration   52

6.2. Cantaiola, bronze *kyathos*   53

6.3. La Quercia, the plateau during the excavations   56

6.4. La Quercia, kiln by the north side of structure 1   58

7.1. Diagram showing the total and minimum number of individuals in the animal remains from House 1 and from the Water Shrine   62

7.2. Pig knucklebones with traces of modification compared with unmodified knucklebones   62

7.3. Cattle metacarpals to manufacture tools   63

7.4. Comparison diagram of number of identified specimens, minimum number of individuals, and meat yield of the main domestic species   64

7.5. Chart showing the main livestock in Iron Age sites in northern Italy   65

7.6. Chart of subsistence economy attested by the study of carpological samples   67

7.7. Chart of the carpological study of environmental plants   68

7.8. Chart of the carpological remains accompanying the infant burial   70

8.1. Schematic plan of the temples of the Urban Sanctuary   78

8.2. Inscribed sherds from the Etrusco-Italic temple of Uni   79

8.3. Head of a marble statue (*kouros*) found near the urban temples   79

8.4. Plan of the Water Shrine   81

8.5. Fragments of architectural plaques from the Urban Sanctuary and the Water Shrine   81

8.6. Votive bronze statuette depicting a woman holding a flower bud   83

9.1. Location of the rituals at the Urban Sanctuary   92

9.2. Ritual offering of two vases discovered in the Temple of Uni   92

9.3. The skeleton of a pig at the time of its discovery   94

9.4. The sequence of the ritual depositions of the bones   95

9.5. Comparison of the ritual found at Kainua to others   96

10.1. Inscribed bronze sheet from *Regio* I, 5   100

10.2. Inscribed cobblestone from *Regio* V, 2   101

10.3. Fragments of inscribed amphoras and pit of the courtyard of House 1   106

10.4. Inscriptions, appendix A, nos. 1–13   107

10.5. Inscriptions, appendix A, nos. 14–29   108

10.6. Inscriptions, appendix A, nos. 30–46   109

10.7. Inscriptions, appendix A, nos. 47–60   110

11.1. Plan of the Archaic house in *Regio* IV, 1   116

11.2. Disposition of the buildings during the early phases of Houses 2 and 5 in *Regio* IV, 1   118

11.3. Virtual reconstructions of the houses in *Regio* IV, 1, and House 1 in *Regio* IV, 2   119

11.4. Diagram of mudbrick walls on stone foundations and surface plaster layer   121

11.5. Reconstruction of a truss-like structure   122

12.1. Blacksmith tongs from *Regio* IV, 1   129

12.2. Fragment of clay mold with the print of a *kouros* head from the "Foundry" of *Regio* V, 5   130

12.3. Bronze *korai* from the votive deposit of the Acropolis   131

12.4. Anatomical *ex-voto* from the Water Shrine   132

12.5. The so-called calibrator from the "Foundry" of *Regio* V, 5   133

13.1. Great Kiln, plan of the main structures   136

13.2. House 1, the main pottery workshops   137

13.3. House 1, photo and cross-section of one of the tiled basins   138

13.4. House 1, photo and plan of the ceramic kilns of the latest phase   139

14.1. Drawing of the molding of the *Podium*-altar D on the Acropolis   146

14.2. Typological comparison of the votive bases from Marzabotto and Bologna   146

14.3. *Stelae* from the shrine of the Eastern Gate with comparisons   147

14.4. Bulb-shaped *cippi* and bases from Marzabotto and Sasso Marconi   149

14.5. The aqueduct on the Acropolis   150

15.1. The old museum of Marzabotto in 1933   156

15.2. Attic black-figure band cup from the Water Shrine   157

15.3. Attic black-figure *stamnos* from the tomb of a female in the Eastern Necropolis   158

15.4. Attic red-figure cup by the Diomedes Painter   160

16.1. V. Levi's excavations plan   164

16.2. Sansoni's plans of the eastern group of tombs in the Northern Necropolis   167

16.3. Brizio's sketch of a funerary area in the Eastern Necropolis   168

16.4. *Cista cordonata* from tomb no. 19 in the Northern Necropolis   169

16.5. Statuette from a candleholder from the Eastern Necropolis   173

17.1. The Northern Necropolis during the nineteenth-century excavations   176

17.2. *Cassone* tombs with a square base   177

17.3. *Cassone* tombs with a rectangular base and with a square base   177

17.4. *Cassone* tombs with a rectangular base   178

17.5. Rectangular tomb with cobblestone walls   180

18.1. Plan and section of the two burials of Sasso Marconi   184

18.2. Some of the grave goods from tomb 1 at Sasso Marconi   185

18.3. Drawing of tomb 2 at Sasso Marconi and a picture made during excavations   188

18.4. Some of the grave goods from tomb 2 at Sasso Marconi   189

19.1. Metallic items of adornment from the Celtic tombs of Marzabotto   195

19.2. Iron swords, spear points, and metal belt from the Celtic tombs of Marzabotto   195

19.3. Sketch of a Celtic tomb from the necropolis discovered at the foot of the Acropolis   196

19.4. Fragments of a bronze mirror with a depiction of Lasa   198

19.5. Fragment of *skyphos* belonging to the Group of Ferrara T. 585   198

20.1. Plan of the remains of the rustic villa of Pian di Misano   204

20.2. Sassatello, plan of the Roman structures   205

PLATES

1. Jewelry from Marzabotto

2. Panoramic view of Kainua in 2014

3. View of the Eastern Necropolis

4. Votive bronze statuette (Apollo?) from the Water Shrine

5. Statuettes crowning a *candelabrum* from the private collection of the Counts Aria

6. Terracotta *puteal* (well curb)

7. Examples of local pottery (jugs)

8. Marble *cippus* from the Eastern Necropolis

9. Janiform Attic red-figure *kantharos* in the form of satyr's and woman's heads

10. Virtual reconstruction of the temples of the Acropolis

11. *Podium*-altar D of the Acropolis

12. Virtual reconstruction of *Podium*-altar B of the Acropolis

13. Virtual reconstruction of the Urban Sanctuary

14. Virtual reconstruction of House 5, *Regio* IV, 1

15. Virtual reconstruction of *Insula* 1, *Regio* IV

16. Digital models of the main buildings overlaid on a panoramic view of the plateau

17. La Quercia, plan of the settlement with indication of the chronological phases

PREFACE

ELISABETTA GOVI

Its optimal conservation has made the city of Marzabotto, whose ancient name was probably Kainua, renowned among the Etruscan cities. Ever since the first archaeological investigations in the middle of the nineteenth century, the site has been compared to Pompeii,[1] because its preservation facilitated the reconstruction of both the entire urban layout and its components (houses, workshops, sacred buildings, tombs). During research in the twentieth century, the city was a focus of scientific debate because of its foundation rite and related structures, which represent extraordinary archaeological traces of the city's founding in the Etruscan ritual, described in Latin literary sources. Today, our available knowledge about the city has been enriched by important new discoveries and the systematic study of old excavations, which have rewarded renewed attention. Thus, Marzabotto deserves to be considered in this series of Etruscan Cities, even if it was set apart from the Tyrrhenian *duodecim populi* to which the series is generally dedicated. This city perfectly embodies the Etruscan model of a founded and planned city, offering a very useful ensemble for comparison with other sites. The idea of writing a book about this city arises from the necessity to summarize the most recent finds, collecting the advances made in the last twenty years of study and research.

Recently other publications have been dedicated to Marzabotto;[2] however, this is the first book on the topic written in English and for a wide international audience. The main purpose is to update our information about the site and at the same time display the study and research methodology, which is integrated, complex, multidisciplinary, and experimental: Marzabotto has therefore been transformed into an exciting laboratory, as the "Kainua Project" demonstrates.[3] This volume shows the results of a study based on a "city-scale" perspective: in this way, cultural phenomena are always analyzed not only from an urban but also from a regional point of view, and can be compared and integrated with what is known about Etruria Padana and its cities and Etruria in its entirety. Thus, the reconstruction of the history of the city aims to present the most complete scenario, despite the total lack of written sources.

This book embodies more than thirty years of research in Marzabotto, conducted by the team from the University of Bologna, first under the direction of Giuseppe Sassatelli and recently under my supervision. Here are displayed the results of the annual excavation campaigns carried out since 1988, and the studies by young researchers, often dedicated to the reassessment of old excavations.

Marzabotto has a long excavation history and, for a long time, was considered a key field of interest for researchers not only of Etruscan studies, but also of urban planning and ancient architecture. From the middle of the twentieth century, after a long period of excavation, a notably different approach was applied by Giuseppe Sassatelli, who, from 1988, carried out uninterrupted investigations with a precise scientific goal that was not limited to merely adding context to our present knowledge. He developed an investigative method based on scientific precision, constantly anchored to the finds and stratigraphic data, and involving a wide multidisciplinary spectrum, indispensable for correct historical reconstruction. Thus, with the excavation first of House 1 of *Regio* IV, 2 and then of the urban peripteral temple of Tinia, he set up an integrated approach, combining multiple perspectives in a graded scale from the individual excavation contexts to the entire urban framework, and avoiding a sector-based vision. From the analysis of building and production techniques to the elaboration of general typologies, and from object data to the interpretation of the historical and cultural phenomena that produced them, this approach is today a consolidated investigative system. The recent "Kainua Project," set up from a wide, interdisciplinary perspective to tackle scientific issues with new, effective instruments, is proof of his success.[4]

My sincere gratitude goes to all the authors for having enthusiastically taken part in this challenge. Special thanks to Stefano Santocchini Gerg for generously helping me in the editorial review; to Anna Serra and Carlotta Trevisanello for the translation of some chapters of the volume; and to Joelle Mary Crowle for the linguistic revision of the entire text.

The work of the archaeologists has been supported over the years by many collaborations within the University of Bologna, in the Departments of Biological, Geological, and Environmental Sciences; of Architecture; of Civil, Chemical, Environmental, and Materials Engineering; and of Physics and Astronomy. My thanks go to all these colleagues.

The research was possible thanks to the ongoing economic support of the University of Bologna, Alma Mater Studiorum, which we thank for having always believed in the Marzabotto project.

My heartfelt thanks also go to the National Ministry of Cultural Heritage and the local preservation offices that, over the years, have directed the museum and the archaeological area, currently the Soprintendenza Archeologia, belle arti e paesaggio per la città metropolitana di Bologna e le province di Modena, Reggio-Emilia e Ferrara (Archaeological, Fine Arts and Landscape Superintendence of Bologna, Modena, Reggio-Emilia and Ferrara) and the Direzione Regionale Musei Emilia-Romagna (Regional Museum Direction of Emilia-Romagna). From the beginning, a close and continual collaboration was created with the University, favoring research in both the field and the laboratory, a connection that has helped the academic growth of many young archaeologists. In fact, some officials from the Ministry of Cultural Heritage that had previously taken part in research on the city have contributed to this publication and so I thank P. Desantis, T. Trocchi, and F. Timossi. This shows the synergy between the parties, an important asset for Italian research.

I am deeply grateful to Nancy de Grummond and Lisa Pieraccini, the editors of the "Cities of the Etruscans" series and to the University of Texas Press for agreeing to include Marzabotto in the editorial project on Etruscan cities, giving us a golden opportunity to describe our findings. Nancy and Lisa supported us, giving valuable advice on the structure of the text and the English translation. To them goes my sincere gratitude.

NOTES

1. Brizio 1887b.
2. Govi 2007; Bentz and Reusser 2008.
3. Garagnani and Gaucci 2017.
4. Garagnani and Gaucci 2017.

INTRODUCTION TO THE VOLUME
Kainua-Marzabotto, the New Face of the City

ELISABETTA GOVI

Ancient sources say nothing about Marzabotto, unlike the other cities of Etruria Padana, the Etruscan Po Valley. Bologna-Felsina, the main center, then the Adriatic harbors Spina and Adria, and Mantua to the north of the Po River, are all referenced in the ancient writers.[1] Livy states that in the Po Valley the Etruscans founded a network of twelve cities, a *dodecapolis*, similar to the one in their homeland (Livy 5.33.9–11).

Kainua was founded sometime in the period from the end of the sixth to the beginning of the fifth century BCE in the Reno Valley, a few kilometers from Bologna (*see map 2*). The settlement was located in an Apennine valley, along a transit route between the Po Valley and Etruria,[2] which naturally orients the city southward, toward the Etruscan territory beyond the mountains (*see map 1*). Marzabotto has always been considered the entrance to the Etruscan Po Valley, the first section encountered before arriving in Bologna, to which it is historically connected. Recent discoveries have proved that smaller settlements were scattered along the Reno Valley to guarantee rest for travelers.[3] Some local productive aspects demonstrate this dual perspective in the city, which appears to be a perfect mixture of northern and southern culture, as shown by the sacred architecture, stone sculpture, and funeral rituals. Therefore, its location and ancient landscape are the perfect starting point for an analysis and understanding of its particular features, which differ even from those of the closest city, Bologna.[4]

The main objectives of this book are to summarize the most recent studies and to analyze the focal points of the research. The discovery of the urban sacred area has given rise to a new view of the city and today its urban form can be fully observed in a different light, one that takes into consideration the geometrical and religious principles behind its foundation.[5] Therefore, Marzabotto constitutes a pivotal case study to approach the logic governing the foundation of cities in Etruria, although the site remains a unique case and finds no direct comparison with any other Etruscan cities, probably because of their limited documentation. Even though the historical reasons remain obscure, due to the absence of written sources, we now know that the foundation, between the end of the sixth and early fifth centuries BCE, was actually a rebirth. Traces of previously inhabited structures were recovered during recent excavations, although they were difficult to locate. Research has been primarily aimed at the analysis of the architecture, production facilities, and material culture in order to define the cultural peculiarities that displayed an interesting mixture between the territories north and south of the Apennines, as previously mentioned.[6] Equally important are analyses of the social, political, and economic organization, emerging thanks to the study of the epigraphy,[7] domestic architecture,[8] and both the domestic and public religion,[9] a recent advancement in research, as well as the selection of imported Greek pottery.[10] The recent edition of the excavation of House 1 of *Regio* IV, 2,[11] has demonstrated the complexity of the city's productive system, highlighting an elaborate economic organization. Despite the dispersion of the grave goods and the scarce documentation, the funerary dimension still provides a useful perspective for the reconstruction of the society and the city's cultural aspects, when subjected to contextual analysis.[12]

As is well known, the city's life span was relatively brief; however, we are now better informed about its Celtic and Roman phases.[13] The result is a renewed comprehensive view, still under development, but certainly enriched by continuing excavation and advances in research, making the study of the city dynamic and ongoing.

NOTES

1. The location of the city of *Melpum*, remembered by Cornelius Nepos (*apud* Pliny, *N.H.* 3.17.125), has also been discussed (see Colonna 1989:13 and n. 25 with references; de Marinis 2007b:268). References to the ancient sources mentioning the Etruscan cities of the Po Valley in Sassatelli 1990.
2. See chapter 5.
3. See chapters 5 and 6.
4. See chapter 7.
5. See chapters 4 and 8.
6. See chapters 12, 13, and 14.
7. See chapter 10.
8. See chapter 11.
9. See chapter 9.
10. See chapter 15.
11. Sassatelli and Govi 2010.
12. See chapters 16, 17, and 18.
13. See chapters 19 and 20.

ABBREVIATIONS

In this volume the abbreviations of journals and series as well as of basic reference works in classical studies are those used by the *American Journal of Archaeology* and listed in *AJA* 104 (2000), 10–24. An updated version is maintained on the website of the *AJA*, currently under http://www.ajaonline.org/submissions/abbreviations.

For other common abbreviations not listed there see the *Archäologische Bibliographie* of the *Deutsches Archäologisches Institut*. Other unlisted journals and series are written in full.

A NOTE ON TERMINOLOGY

The title of the book, *Kainua (Marzabotto)*, incorporates one of the most important discoveries of recent years, the inscriptional evidence that the Etruscans of this site called the city *Kainua* (see chapter 10, especially p. 100; *see figs. 8.2, 10.4*). Just as Etruscan Bologna is normally referred to as Felsina, it is now appropriate to refer to this city by its ancient name, Kainua, along with or in place of the modern Italian name of Marzabotto. The name of the city probably contains a term in which a link with the Greek "*kainon* = new" can be recognized (*see fig. 10.4: nos. 6, 10*). If this suggestive hypothesis is true, the name of the city, *Kainua*, conveys the concept of "new city," which is well suited to its history, recalling other well-known cases, such as the Greek Neapolis and the Italic Nola and Nocera.

The city was founded in the Reno Valley, one of the main routes connecting Etruria with the Po Valley. The territory of the Po Valley had been permanently and extensively occupied by the Etruscans since the ninth century BCE, so that scholars use the definition "Po Valley Etruria" or, more widely, "Etruria Padana," with the adjective "Padana" deriving from the Italian name of the Po River, which crosses the entire territory. By convention the term "Etruria Padana" is used to distinguish this territory from those of "Tyrrhenian Etruria" in central Italy and "Etruria Campana" in the south of the peninsula.

The tradition of studies since the nineteenth century assigned to the urbanism of Kainua-Marzabotto definitions proper to Greek and Roman cities. So the main roads are defined by the Greek *plateia/plateiai* (singular/plural), while the minor ones are *stenopos/stenopoi* (singular/plural); by the Latin instead, the parts of the city defined by the main streets are called *regio/regiones* (singular/plural), and those ones delimited by minor streets are defined as *insula/insulae* (singular/plural). In the maps of the city (*see map 5*) the eight *regiones* are enumerated with Roman numerals (I–VIII) and the *insulae* with Arabic numerals (1–5).

In Etruscan studies, it is conventional to use the Greek names for the vases imported from Greece and also for those locally produced with a Greek shape (*kylix, olpe, kantharos, alabastron*, etc.), but we use also Latin names, such as *dolium*, and common English names, such as "plate."

ALBUM OF MAPS

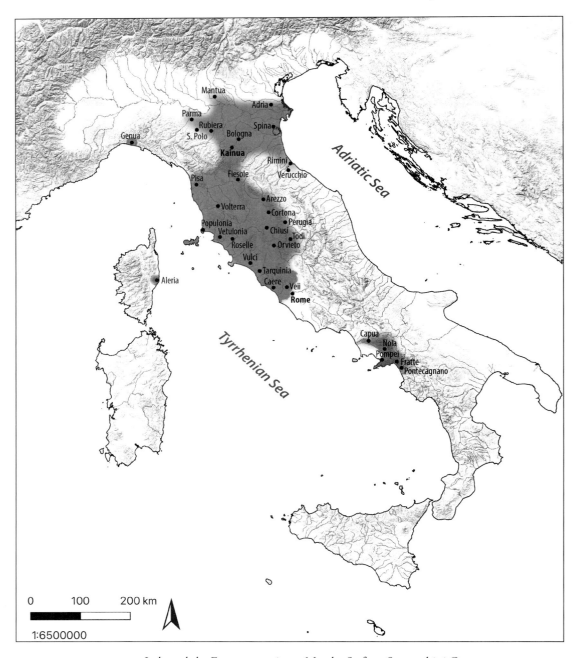

MAP 1. Italy and the Etruscan territory. Map by Stefano Santocchini Gerg.

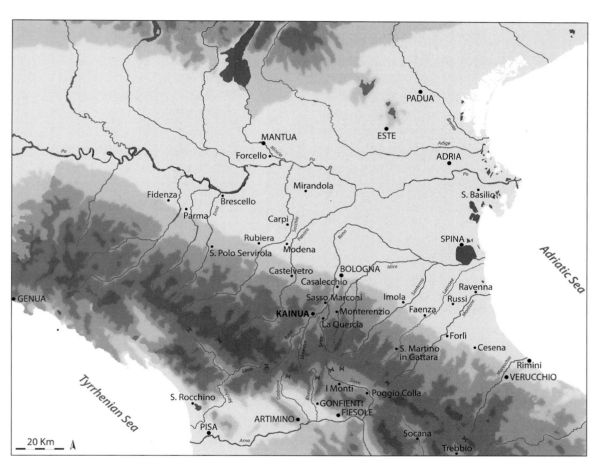

MAP 2. Etruria Padana. Map by Stefano Santocchini Gerg (© L. Cappuccini).

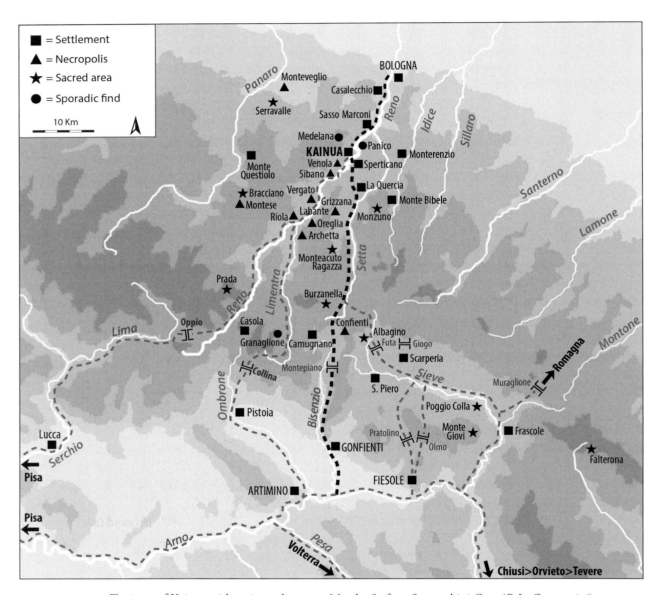

MAP 3. Territory of Kainua with main trade routes. Map by Stefano Santocchini Gerg (© L. Cappuccini).

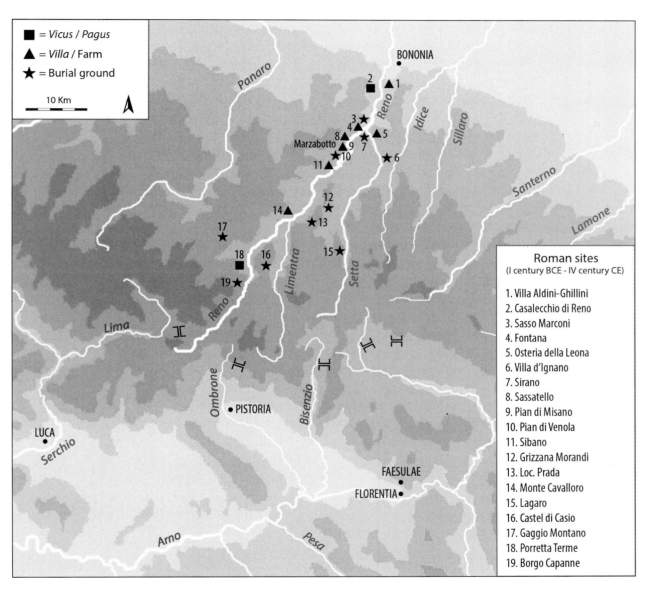

MAP 4. Territory of Kainua in the Roman period. Map by Stefano Santocchini Gerg (© L. Cappuccini).

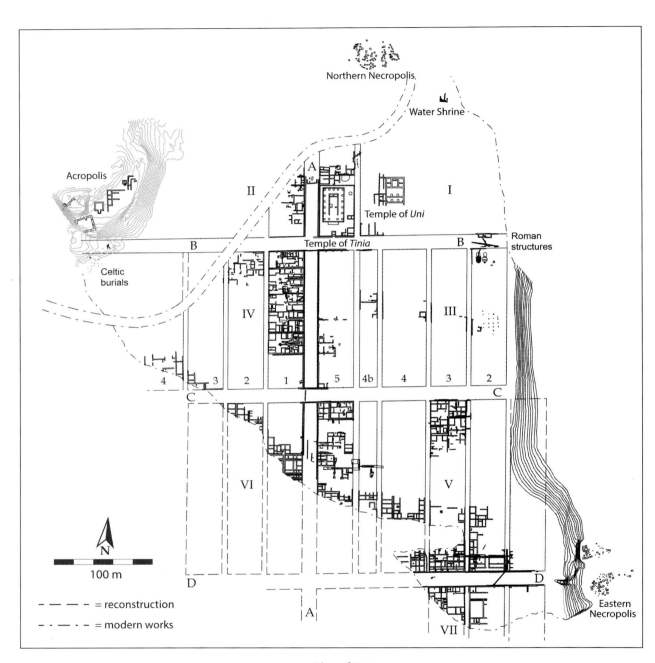

MAP 5. Plan of Kainua.

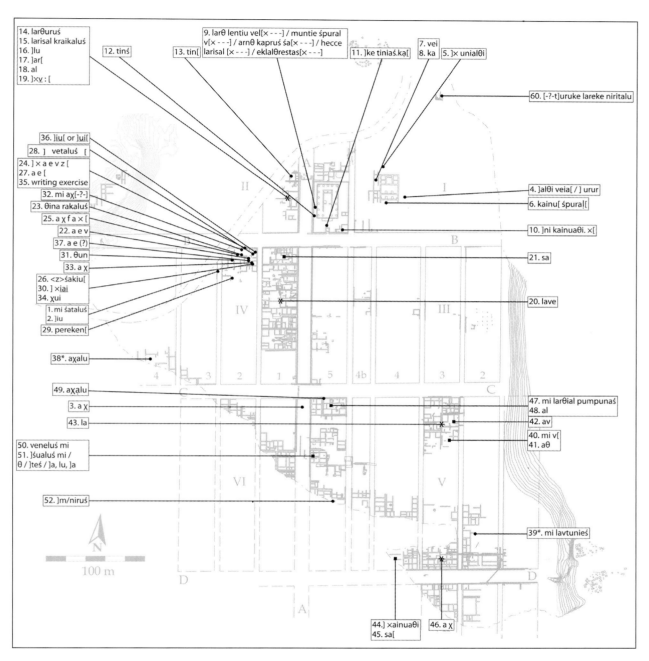

MAP 6. Plan of Kainua with inscriptions: ● = exact spot; ■ = uncertain, inside the building; ✴ = uncertain, in the excavated area. Map by Andrea Gaucci.

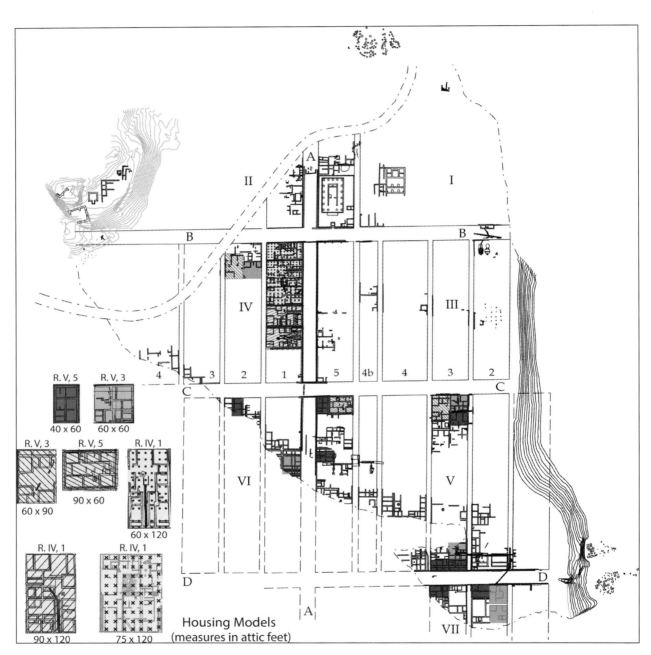

MAP 7. Plan of Kainua with house types. Map by Stefano Santocchini Gerg.

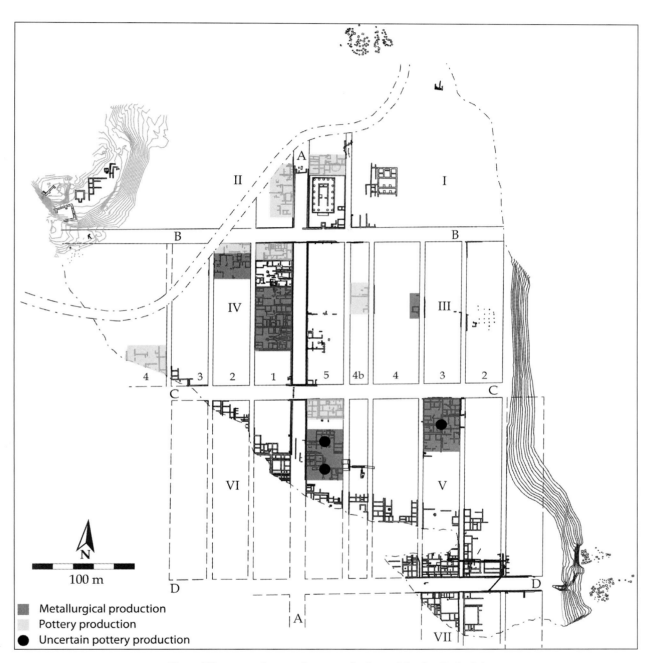

MAP 8. Plan of Kainua with manufacturing facilities. Map by Giulia Morpurgo.

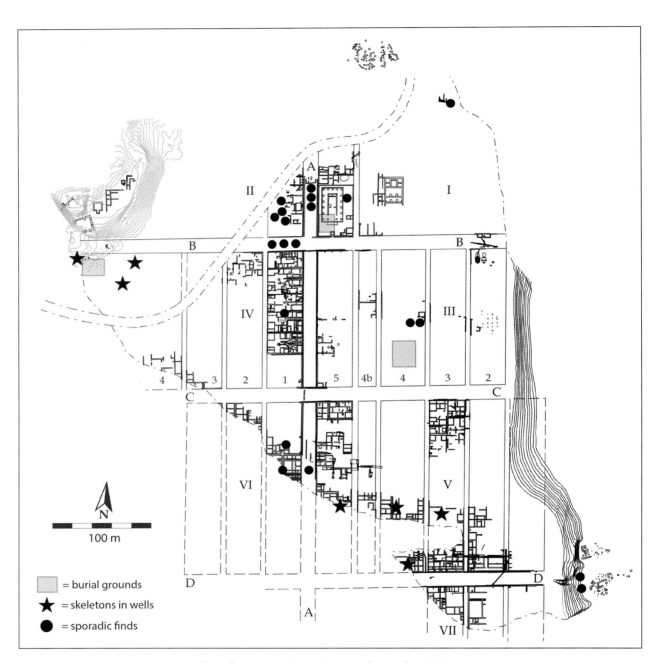

MAP 9. Plan of Kainua in the Celtic period. Map by Giulia Morpurgo.

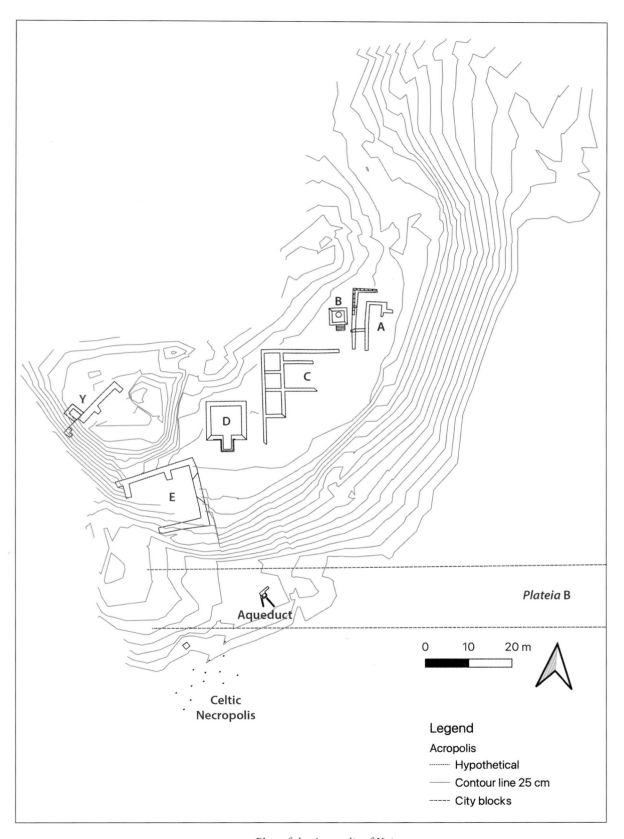

MAP 10. Plan of the Acropolis of Kainua.

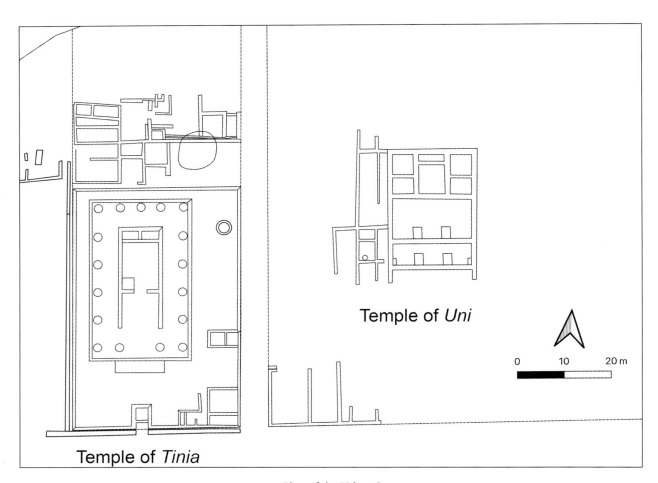

MAP 11. Plan of the Urban Sanctuary.

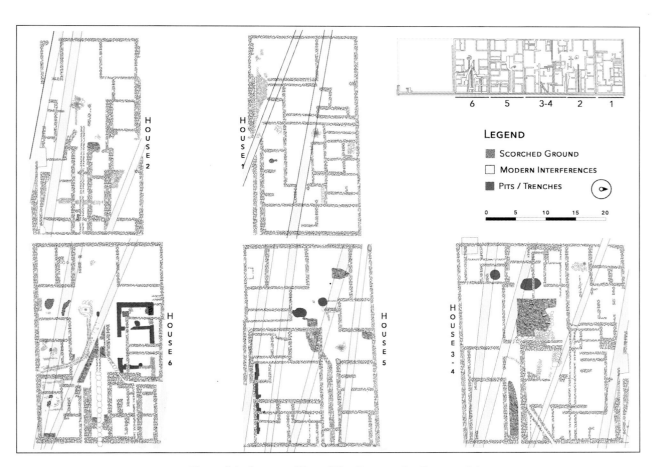

MAP 12. Plans of the houses of *Regio* IV, 1. Drawing by Giacomo Mancuso.

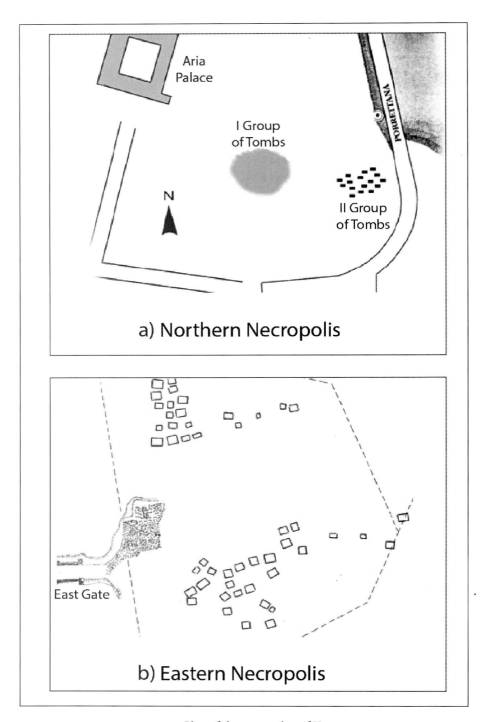

MAP 13. Plan of the necropoleis of Kainua.

KAINUA
(MARZABOTTO)

PART I

DISCOVERY AND ARCHAEOLOGY OF THE CITY

Part I presents the history of the discoveries and studies at Marzabotto, from the nineteenth-century investigations to more current research. In the last twenty years the overall picture of the city has changed, and the study approach is today on a "city-scale," with multidisciplinary and integrated methodologies. Kainua-Marzabotto is, therefore, a laboratory, the ideal space in which to experiment with various methods of archaeological diagnostics. The most ambitious challenge is the contextual approach to the study of objects together with analysis of the city's social complexity.

CHAPTER 1

THE ROLE OF THE CITY IN NINETEENTH- AND TWENTIETH-CENTURY SCIENTIFIC DEBATE

GIUSEPPE SASSATELLI

The first documented mention of the Etruscan city of Marzabotto is in the *Descrittione di tutta Italia* (1551) by Leandro Alberti of Bologna, a monk. In a few clear and effective lines, Alberti describes convincing archaeological remains, which he himself certainly saw, identifying them without hesitation as a city, even though he could not outline its chronology because he found *nessuna memoria di quel luogo* ("no remembrance of that place") in the works of the ancient historians.[1] The imposing extent of the archaeological remains (an entire city) contrasted with the absence of any reference to the place in the ancient authors, a disadvantage at a time when historical sources were considered to be much more important than archaeological documentation.

Perhaps for this reason, Alberti's notice attracted no attention and was completely forgotten, although it appeared during the same period as the extraordinary discovery of the bronze statues of the Chimaera (1553) and Minerva (1552) in Arezzo, and the Arringatore (1566) near Perugia, which provided the impetus for a growing interest in the Etruscans and the birth of Etruscan studies. Its erasure from memory is certainly due as much to the less monumental aspect of the archaeological remains as to the lack of any mention of it in the historical tradition. Moreover, the absence of interest in the site is probably dependent on both its location (its distance from the sea and isolated position on the Apennines) and its short life span (now thought to be just over three centuries).

Interest in the Etruscan city of Marzabotto is closely linked to the complex history of Etruscology, and it is strongly intermingled with the archaeological discoveries that, from the first half of the nineteenth century, brought to light its monuments, materials, and structures. Apart from a few rare and insignificant references after Alberti's discovery, Marzabotto is mentioned again only in the first half of the nineteenth century, because of some important discoveries on the Acropolis and in the Northern Necropolis. Immediately after the ownership transfer of the seventeenth-century villa and its land from the Barbazzi family to Count Aria (1831), the latter undertook renovation work in the park and a large area around the villa. During these operations, the Acropolis buildings and the tombs of the Northern Necropolis were unearthed (*see maps 5 and 13*). This recovery fits perfectly into the "Romantic period" of Etruscan discoveries during the first half of the century, characterized by the desire for adventure and the quest for strong emotional response, rather than real scientific knowledge. Thus, it is no coincidence that the temples of the Acropolis and the tombs of the necropolis uncovered during this renovation were immediately incorporated as decorative elements of the park, along with vegetation, an artificial pond, and atmospheric walkways (fig. 1.1). Sometimes, the structural elements were moved from their original location to more scenic and affecting positions.

The reputation of the location as well as a friendship with Count Giuseppe Aria drew the attention of Giovanni Gozzadini, a prominent figure in Bolognese noble and cultural circles, who conducted several excavation campaigns in the area during the years 1860–1870.[2] Ten years before, Gozzadini had excavated the

FIGURE 1.1. The Northern Necropolis with the pavilion set up for a lunch with the participants in the V Congrès International d'Anthropologie et d'Archéologie Préhistoriques, 1871, during their visit to the Etruscan city. Photo: University of Bologna Archive.

necropolis of Villanova near Bologna and was therefore very interested in research on Etruscans in the Po Valley. At Marzabotto, Gozzadini was convinced that he had found a huge necropolis, probably influenced by his previous excavations in Villanova, but mostly because of the discovery of burials both in the town and on the Acropolis. His interpretation of this as an ancient necropolis is clearly stated in the titles of his two monographs dedicated to the excavations at Marzabotto (Gozzadini 1865 and 1870; *see also plate 1*). This identification was soon overturned by scientific debate and, above all, by the excavations and activities of young Edoardo Brizio, a professor at the University of Bologna from 1876 on (fig. 1.2).[3]

In 1888–1889, Brizio conducted an intense excavation campaign to *rilevare la pianta della città e pubblicare i principali monumenti e specialmente le costruzioni* ("to document the urban plan, and to publish its main monuments and especially their reconstructions"), as seen for example in a reconstruction of the spring and aqueduct system at the foot of the Acropolis (fig. 1.3).

This project was realized during the Italian unification, a delicate moment in Italy's political history. Through the establishment of a General Department for Antiquities and Fine Arts, the State undertook intensive excavation activities throughout the country. The research was conducted as part of a recognized cultural project, aiming not only to recover the historical origins of each urban community, but also to strengthen the new national identity, considering the importance given to the Etruscans as an emblem of Italian identity.[4] During Brizio's campaigns, roads, blocks, sacred areas, and burial grounds were located, allowing the complete reconstruction of the urban plan.

FIGURE 1.2. Edoardo Brizio with colleagues and students at Marzabotto, 1907. Photo: University of Bologna Archive.

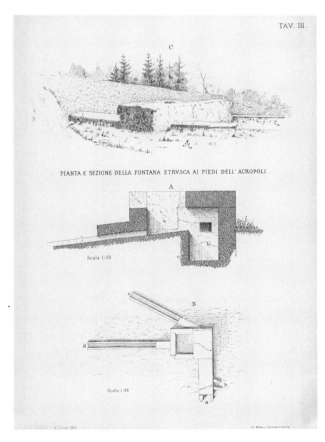

FIGURE 1.3. Plate from the report of excavations conducted by E. Brizio: *Castellum aquae* on slope of the Acropolis. After Brizio 1890: pl. III.

The plan of the city centers on the intersection of two main roads, the *cardo* and the *decumanus*, following the principles of the *limitatio* ritual, considered by the ancient authors to be a typical Etruscan invention, which the Romans later adopted. The most common house plan of Marzabotto has also been correlated with the organization of the Roman *domus*. This erroneous interpretation was due to the importance given to the Roman world as a principal reference in these matters (it appears to be no coincidence that Marzabotto is defined by Brizio as an "Etruscan Pompeii"). Moreover, the analysis also depended on the need to identify an archaeological comparison and confirmation of the orthogonal grid, even by forcing the data, as a model that the Romans had extensively applied in their urban planning. Because of the considerable authority of the proposer, this interpretation of Marzabotto, still the central tenet of the scientific community regarding the site, remained substantially unchanged until the Second World War (fig. 1.4).

During the Second World War Marzabotto was the scene of a horrible massacre perpetrated by Nazi soldiers, and the ravages of the war overtook the local museum, which was destroyed by a mine in 1944 (*see fig. 2.3*). After the war, important advances in the excavation and study of the Etruscan city of Marzabo-

FIGURE 1.4. Participants in the First Congresso Internazionale Etrusco (1928) visiting Marzabotto. Photo: University of Bologna Archive.

tto were achieved by Guido Achille Mansuelli.[5] Information about the city greatly increased during these years, supporting the ongoing interpretation of finds. The main urban structures (roads, houses, workshops, sanctuaries) were identified, leading to a complete historical reconstruction of the city. Thus, its role and relations with the Etruscan Po Valley and with Tyrrhenian Etruria, as well as its manufacturing activities, artistic production, commercial and cultural relations, and the social organization of its inhabitants, were better defined.

Mansuelli's research greatly influenced later inquiries in one important respect. In 1956, a book by F. Castagnoli on Hippodamus of Miletus and the orthogonal city plan (*Ippodamo di Mileto e l'urbanistica a pianta ortogonale*) had questioned the established interpretation of Brizio, stating that Marzabotto's urban planning was not related to the concepts of *limitatio* and the Etruscan axial model, but was instead similar to a layout in widespread use in the Greek world, in particular in the colonial settlements. This assertion meant that the city should be interpreted according to Greek urban planning, and not in the light of Etruscan models (*Etrusca disciplina*), creating an abstract opposition between "Greek" and "Etruscan," and incorrectly exaggerating the amount of Greek influence on Etruria Padana.

G. A. Mansuelli recovered *cippi* at some of the road intersections, and one carrying a *crux* (cross-shaped mark) was discovered in the city center (*see fig. 4.4*). These finds, as well as the discovery of the orientation of the urban plan and the sanctuaries on the Acropolis, helped modern understanding of the city enormously. Mansuelli was indeed aware of elements mentioned by the ancient authors as typical of the Etruscan heritage, such as the axial model and the orientation, which were also inserted in a typical Greek urban form, only later theorized by Hippodamus of Miletus.

However, Mansuelli assigned a subordinate position to the city in relation to the other Etruscan cities of the Po Valley and to Tyrrhenian Etruria in general. Despite the advanced craftsmanship and the significant commercial activity evident at the site, he defined the city as a *città carovaniera* (caravan settlement), emphasizing its cultural and artistic marginality and its overall irrelevance and anonymity in the political and institutional sphere. In this way, the city stands apart from the high status claimed by Mantua and especially by Spina and Felsina, since the former owned a *thesauros* (treasury) inside the sanctuary of Delphi, and the latter was considered the capital city of the region.

At present, thanks to the third phase of studies and excavations, the situation has completely changed.[6] This moment represents the most recent research on the city, in which I was personally involved at the beginning, but which has now been handed over to Elisabetta Govi and her younger collaborators, many of whom are contributors to this publication.[7]

First of all, significant advances in understanding once again concern the urban plan and its interpretation. To consolidate Mansuelli's hypotheses, evidence has been identified that unmistakably leads to the conclusion that the city was founded according to the scrupulous application of the *Etruscus ritus*. Despite its Etruscan foundation, the layout was easily able to integrate Greek influences and urban models. The "Greek city/Etruscan city" dilemma has thus been overcome, by considering both elements as perfectly integrated into the same urban space.

The Greek city model was favored by the Etruscans both for its extraordinary urban potential and for its capacity to absorb, contain, and even strengthen the essential elements of an urban foundation based on Etruscan principles. A similar process is also documented in other fields, such as artistic production and funeral ideology. Therefore, the old interpretation, based on the concept of the prevalence of one of, or contrast between, these two worlds, is outdated. Indeed, the Etruscans' great receptiveness to the Greek world enhanced and underlined their identity and particular nature. This new approach contrasts with the previous one, which regarded Etruscan culture in comparison with external models.[8]

Further, other recent innovations have been introduced, based on new excavations and the valuable review and reassessment of old data. In the first place, a new chronological sequence has been defined for the early stages of the city. New research suggests that the human presence on the plateau was perhaps even older than the middle of the sixth century BCE and has been attested only by sporadic materials, but no structures. This first period was followed by the initial urban planning, already characterized by monumental and important buildings that showed great economic and commercial potential. Then, in the period from the late sixth to the early fifth century BCE, the "new" Kainua was founded as a planned city with a structured grid. The later urban planning appears to substantially continue from the previous one, although some corrections to the grid are recognizable,

due to the strict application of astronomical orientation, a choice that had a strong political significance.

Second, advancements have also been made in the study of domestic architecture, radically changing our knowledge of the matter. In fact, the *atrium* houses of the *Regio* IV, 1, referred to as the *Isolato* Mansuelli, no longer represent the only type of inhabited structures in the Etruscan city, and it has become clear that they were not all compact and immutable. Located on both sides of *plateia* A, the main city road, these houses should be considered dwellings belonging to the upper levels of society that performed important functions as part of the urban community. In the other areas of the city, domestic architecture derives mostly from the aggregation of distinct structures around a large courtyard, recalling the long building tradition of the Late Orientalizing and Archaic periods (e.g., at Acquarossa or Fratte).[9] At a later date, urban planning regulated these different housing structures, via the blocks that dictated a more rigid spatial organization. Houses underwent continuous internal modifications, sometimes radically changing in structure. In conclusion, a large variety of plans and many internal variations can now be identified (*see map 7*), as well as frequent renovations and, sometimes, radical changes in building purpose.

However, the most striking novelties in the research came from the sacred sphere and its political implications.[10] In addition to the previously known temples on the Acropolis, we now have identified two temples inside the city. The oldest is an Etrusco-Italic temple dedicated to Uni, built by the political authorities of the city (*spura*) of Kainua, who took part in a collective rite (a libation, the destruction of the amphora utilized, and its concealment inside the foundations) recalling ancient and almost aristocratic customs. The second is a peripteral temple, a layout that perhaps suggests a receptiveness to the Greek world with strong political significance. This structure was built by *collegia* of officers or priests during a solemn act, recorded on a publicly displayed bronze sheet that refers to more "democratic" customs.

The chronology, the architectural model, and the founding rite point to different meanings and values, which find important similarities in Tyrrhenian

Etruria. At Pyrgi, the "foreign" peripteral temple is the oldest and relates to the tyrant Thefarie, while the newer and larger Etrusco-Italic temple, built according to the "national" model, refers to the civic community. This situation represents exactly the opposite of Marzabotto's evidence, not only because of the chronological sequence. Here, the oldest and smallest Etrusco-Italic temple does not fit into the urban organization of the blocks, even though it influenced the new urban planning, and it was then hidden by the more recent peripteral temple. The latter is much larger and more monumental and is perfectly inserted within an urban block, as if it were the seat of the "highest citizen" (the god Tinia). The political significance of these choices, which is known at Pyrgi, is still uncertain at Marzabotto, even though the more Hellenized architectonic model could hold a message of receptiveness directed to the Greek world, which was strongly interconnected with the history and culture of Etruria Padana.

Even the types of cults present are rich in implications. The close association of Tinia and Uni in the northeast quadrant of the *templum*, in the sector of *summa felicitas*, can be compared once again to Pyrgi. However, in the Temple of Uni at Marzabotto, Vei was also worshiped, a goddess similar to Demeter and, thus, strongly connected to the new and wider social group responsible for the great historical transformations of the whole of Etruria Padana in the period from the late sixth century BCE to the beginning of the fifth century BCE, including the refounding of Marzabotto.

In conclusion, our current interpretation of the city now reflects all the complexity of its urban structure, the abundance of its cultural manifestations, and its political and institutional importance. This reconstruction is completely in contrast with the earlier perception of it as a modest and banal "caravan city." Instead, we should consider Kainua a city in its own right, from an urban, architectural, cultural, and even political point of view. Moreover, this city is perfectly integrated within the historical, cultural, and ideological events of the entire Etruscan world. Another major issue has now emerged and should be considered in future excavations and research in order to find a solution. The political dimension is active and concentrated in the sacred areas, where it exercises and legitimizes its power, but the issue of civic buildings dedicated to public functions, similar to the *agora* of Greek cities or the *forum* in Roman ones, still remains open. The same problem is also recorded in Etruria, where known public spaces are connected to sacred buildings (Ara della Regina in Tarquinia, the Temple of Apollo in Pontecagnano). The only exception seems to be the elliptical building at Vigna Parrocchiale in Cerveteri, which is an isolated case and whose function is partly obscure.[11] Thus, we can only hope that future excavations of the large area in front of the Uni temple in Marzabotto will offer more elements to help us solve this major issue, which concerns the whole Etruscan world and has important historical implications.

NOTES

1. An overview on studies and excavations through 1983 in Sassatelli 1983.
2. On the Aria family and its connections with the Etruscan city, see Bragadin 2009.
3. Sassatelli 1984.
4. The issue has been discussed thoroughly. See Sassatelli 2020.
5. On Guido Achille Mansuelli, see Sassatelli 2002a and Sassatelli 2006.
6. The various issues mentioned and summarized here are extensively discussed in the chapters of this book.
7. I chose to write only this small part of the entire volume precisely to give the idea of a full and integral handover. This decision has been a great source of satisfaction on a personal level and it will give many other results to the research on the Etruscan city.
8. On the relation between Greeks and Etruscans, see Sassatelli 2014; Sassatelli 2017c; and Sassatelli 2019.
9. Govi 2016:196.
10. In particular, see Govi 2017b and Sassatelli 2017b.
11. See Sassatelli 2019.

CHAPTER 2

THE ETRUSCAN NATIONAL MUSEUM "P. ARIA"

FEDERICA TIMOSSI*

The Etruscan National Museum in Marzabotto, more properly called "Museo Nazionale Etrusco 'Pompeo Aria' e area archeologica di Kainua," is located at Pian di Misano and includes both a museum and an archaeological site. At present it is part of the Direzione Regionale Musei Emilia-Romagna (Regional Museum Direction of Emilia-Romagna), a local office of MiC (Ministero della Cultura), the Italian Ministry of Cultural Heritage. The origin and development of this museum are closely related to the discovery of the Etruscan city of Kainua and its ongoing exploration.

According to the Italian historian Leandro Alberti (1479–1552), in his volume *Descrittione di tutta Italia*, by the middle of the sixteenth century CE ancient artifacts had already been found in the area now known as Pian di Misano. However, the first significant findings of Etruscan remains and objects date back to 1831, when the Aria family bought the estate.

Between 1839 and 1841, as a result of agricultural and gardening work, Etruscan tombs and a votive deposit were found on the grounds of the estate. These tombs formed the Northern Necropolis (*see map 5*); the votive deposit, rich in bronze artifacts, was discovered on the slopes of a hill referred to as the Acropolis because of the sacred buildings uncovered there in 1856. All these discoveries became a private collection from which the modern museum would develop. In that period "Villa Aria," an eighteenth-century mansion owned by the Aria family and located on the hill northwest of Pian di Misano, housed the entire private collection.

Official archaeological excavation of the site only started in 1862, under the supervision of the famous archaeologist Giovanni Gozzadini[1] and at the request of the owner, Count Giuseppe Aria. At the same time, the Count bought many ancient artifacts found in the valley of the river Reno to enlarge his collection. He also arranged for news of the Etruscan findings at Pian di Misano to be published in several local newspapers. In 1864 the collection of Etruscan artifacts was moved from the first to the second floor of the Villa, filling five large rooms. Exploration of the area continued until 1889 and, over time, Edoardo Brizio,[2] professor of archaeology at the University of Bologna, succeeded Giovanni Gozzadini as supervisor of the research. The recovery of the Eastern Necropolis and Celtic tombs and several digs in the urban area date from this period.

In 1871, the first international presentation of the discoveries from Marzabotto was held during the V Congrès International d'Anthropologie et d'Archéologie Préhistorique in Bologna (*see fig. 1.1*). On this occasion, scholars visited the Aria estate and saw the Etruscan artifacts and structures firsthand. During this conference Gaetano Chierici, director of the paleontological museum in Reggio Emilia, was the first to suggest that the findings in Marzabotto were related to an inhabited area and not simply a necropolis.[3]

In 1886 Count Pompeo Aria hired Brizio again, this time to revive his private collection. Brizio organized the artifacts into five rooms, by typological order, aim-

---

*Direzione Regionale Musei Emilia-Romagna / Regional Museum Direction of Emilia-Romagna

FIGURE 2.1. Etruscan museum in "Villa Aria": room 5, showcase A, organized by E. Brizio and opened to the public in 1887. Etruscan bronzes and Greek painted vases. Photo: Direzione Regionale Musei Emilia-Romagna.

ing to show their chronological and morphological evolution. Room 1 housed architectural artifacts, the reconstruction of two Celtic burials, and an Etruscan tomb in travertine, along with Etruscan tombstones and grave goods. In room 2 there were human bone remains and carved bones. Room 3 displayed Etruscan pottery from both the inhabited area and the necropoleis. Room 4 held Villanovan, Roman, and Celtic findings. Finally, room 5 contained the finest pieces in the collection: Etruscan bronzes, Greek painted vases, and other valuables, including glass paste, alabaster jars, gold jewelry, and gems (fig. 2.1).

Brizio wrote a guide, *Guida alle antichità della Villa e del Museo Etrusco*,[4] to illustrate the collection, which was followed in 1887 by a scientific pamphlet, "Una Pompei etrusca a Marzabotto nel Bolognese."[5] In the same year, on October 20, the museum was opened to the public. The event received considerable press coverage at the time, and many authorities and scholars attended the ceremony. Among the guests was Giosuè Carducci, who, in 1906, would become the first Italian poet to win the Nobel Prize for Literature.

In 1911 the most valuable items, especially gold objects that had been among the Etruscan grave goods, were stolen from the collection in "Villa Aria." These items have never been recovered and represent an important scientific and patrimonial loss.

About fifty years after its first opening, Adolfo Branca Aria donated the museum and the archaeological site to the Italian government. In 1933 he signed the gift deed, which mentions the foresight of Count Giuseppe Aria, who in 1831 had already understood the historical and scientific importance of the Etruscan artifacts and remains found on his estate. It is thanks to the Count and his son, Pompeo Aria, that these findings were first preserved and protected. Two restrictive clauses in the gift deed established that the collection would be dedicated to Pompeo Aria and that the finds would be left in Marzabotto (fig. 2.2).[6]

So, in 1938, the collection was moved to a former farmhouse near the archaeological site, owned by the Italian government, and which still forms part of the museum today. However, due to the start of World War II, the reopening of the museum was postponed. In 1944, the building was heavily damaged and all the archaeological artifacts stored there were either lost or ruined (fig. 2.3).

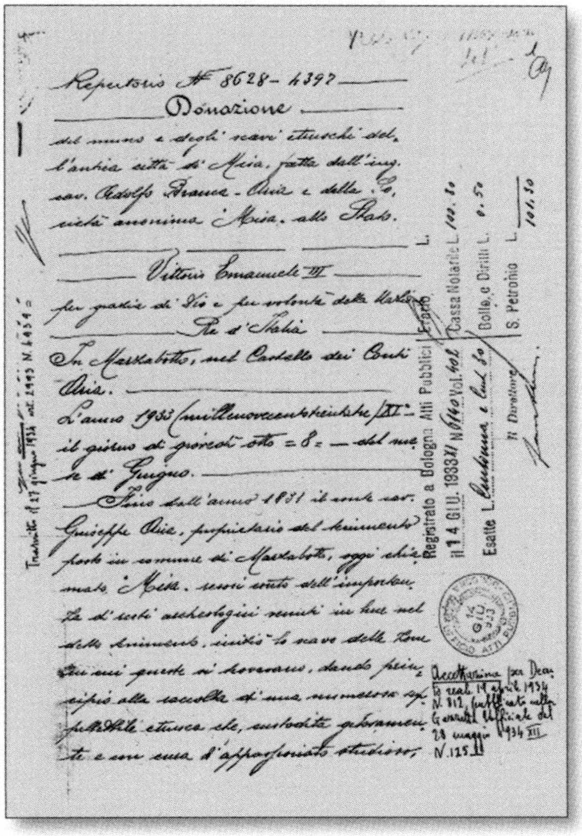

Repertorio N. 8628-4397

Donazione

del museo e degli scavi etruschi del-
l'antica città di Misa, fatta dall'ing.
cav. Adolfo Branca-Aria e dalla Società anonima "Misa" allo Stato.

Vittorio Emanuele III
per grazia di Dio e per volontà della Nazione
Re d'Italia

In Marzabotto, nel Castello dei Conti
Aria.
L'anno 1933 (millenovecentotrentatre) XI°
il giorno di giovedì otto =8= del me-
se di Giugno.
Fino dall'anno 1831 il conte cav.
Giuseppe Aria, proprietario del tenimento
posto in comune di Marzabotto, oggi chia-
mato "Misa", ...
... archeologici venuti in luce nel
detto tenimento, ...
... una numerosa sup-
pellettile etrusca che, custodita ...
te e con cura d'appassionato studioso,

Registrato a Bologna Atti Pubblici il 14 GIU. 1933 XI N. 6140 Vol. 40
Esatte L. ...
Cassa Notarile L. 100.50
Bollo e Diritti L. 0.50
S. Petronio L.
101.50
Il Direttore

FIGURE 2.2. First page of the gift deed of the museum and archaeological area of Marzabotto from Adolfo Branca to the Italian government, dated June 8, 1933. Photo: Direzione Regionale Musei Emilia-Romagna.

The latter are still displayed in the first room of the modern museum as a memento.[7] Thanks to Paolo Enrico Arias, then local superintendent for the Italian Ministry of Cultural Heritage, the museum was reopened in 1950: the collection was housed in two rooms and displayed the damaged artifacts alongside objects that had been kept in a secure warehouse during the conflict, such as Etruscan bronzes and Greek painted vases.

The first reorganization of the museum dates to 1958: Guido Achille Mansuelli,[8] formerly archaeological superintendent of Emilia-Romagna and then professor at the University of Bologna, collected artifacts from the necropoleis in room 1 and findings from the Acropolis and the urban area in room 2. A lot of the finds had been discovered during the nineteenth-century exploration of the necropolis and the inhabited area; due to the lack of topographical information, these artifacts had to be organized into typological sections. The didactic system also included illustrations and photographic records from the archaeological excavation and described Marzabotto in the context of the Etruscan civilization. Afterward,

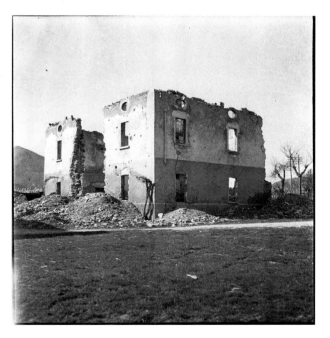

FIGURE 2.3. The former farmhouse at Pian di Misano after the war. Photo: Direzione Regionale Musei Emilia-Romagna.

Mansuelli wrote a new guide to illustrate the museum and the archaeological area, entitled *Guida alla città etrusca e al Museo di Marzabotto* (1971).[9]

From 1950 until today the collection and its repositories have increased, thanks to several archaeological excavations carried out by different institutions, such as the Soprintendenza Archeologica dell'Emilia-Romagna, the University of Bologna, the École Française de Rome, and the universities of Bonn and Regensburg.[10]

In the 1970s the museum was still housed in the former farmhouse near the archaeological area, which was rebuilt after the war. During this period, the building was enlarged and a new wing was added. Mansuelli once again organized the new exhibition and panel installation, together with Anna Maria Brizzolara, Sandro De Maria, Giuseppe Sassatelli, and Daniele Vitali, at the time graduate students and thereafter university professors. Giuseppe Sassatelli directed the excavation and studies by the University of Bologna in the Etruscan city of Marzabotto between 1988 and 2014. The museum collection was enriched by artifacts found during excavations in the archaeological area from 1950 onward. In that period, the archaeological finds were organized into three rooms. Room 1 was divided into two sections: the first showed the history of the museum and archaeological excavations in Pian di Misano; the second displayed burial grave goods and tombstones from the two Etruscan necropoleis. Room 2 also contained two separate themes: sacred areas and production activities. The new wing formed room 3 and held Etruscan artifacts from craft and domestic contexts, along with Celtic and Roman finds from the archaeological area. The aim of the new display was to describe the historical events at Pian di Misano through the excavations of ancient artifacts during a century of archaeological research. In this way the Etruscan finds maintained their importance, due to their abundance and scientific significance, within a chronological path from the Aeneolithic to the Roman age. The sections dedicated to the Etruscan city were organized in topographical order, in order to enhance the correlation with domestic, craft, and funerary remains visible in the archaeological site. Also included were two Etruscan tombs with their grave goods that had been discovered a few years earlier in Sasso Marconi, 10 km north of Marzabotto in the valley of the river Reno (*see map 3*). The inauguration of the new exhibition space took place on November 4, 1979.[11]

Finally, the museum was enlarged in the early 2000s, when the south wing was built. Its ground floor included two new exhibition rooms: room 4 was dedicated to archaeological finds from the whole valley of the river Reno; room 5 was made ready for an enlargement of the collection. The second floor contained a wooden platform and a classroom, dedicated to honorary inspector Sergio Sani, who helped Paolo Enrico Arias and assisted in several excavations conducted by the Superintendence.[12]

In 2020 the panel installation was modernized, thanks to a partnership between MiC (Ministry of Culture)[13] and the University of Bologna.[14] As a result, the museum now consists of five rooms and is closely connected to the archaeological area. At the entrance, seven panels welcome the public to the archaeological site, with an introduction to the Etruscan city of Kainua, an itinerary through the archaeological area and the museum, an overview of the Etruscan civilization, and a timeline of the ancient Italian peninsula, from 900 BCE to 30 BCE. Room 1 is divided into two sections: the first describes the museum and excavation history from the nineteenth century until today; the second displays grave goods and tombstones from the Northern and Eastern necropoleis. There are also two panels dedicated to the Etruscan afterlife and the custom of symposium, from the ancient Greek expression for "to drink together." Room 2 also has two sections. One displays artifacts from everyday life in Kainua: stone, bronze, or lead weights used in trade; clay spools, spindle-whorls, and loom-weights for working at the loom, spinning wool, and weaving textiles; metalworkers' tools; coarse and fine Etruscan pottery, including a bucchero ware jug. The remaining part of room 2 presents findings from the sacred areas: the small sanctuary outside the city built near a spring, now close to the archaeological site parking area; the hill of the Acropolis, which housed temples, altars, and, on its slopes, a rich votive deposit; and the two sacred areas dedicated to the god Tinia and goddess Uni, the most important deities of the Etruscan pantheon, from the northeastern part of the city. The latter were discovered thanks to ongoing archaeological excavations by the University of Bologna over the last few decades, under the supervision of Giuseppe Sassatelli and Elisabetta Govi, whose investigations also led to the identification of the Etruscan name of the city, Kainua. The first section of room 3 displays the Etruscan urban area: domestic architecture, water management, and pottery or bronze workshops. Remains of the earliest settlement at Pian di Misano, dating back to the first half of the sixth century BCE, are also to be found here. Room 3 ends with the Celtic and Roman findings at Pian di Misano. The most significant Celtic evidence is grave goods from burials dating to the fourth and third centuries BCE; during the first century BCE, a Roman farmhouse was established in the northeastern sector of the archaeological site. Room 4 leads out of Pian di Misano into the valley of the river Reno. There are, for example, grave goods found in Pontecchio Marconi, which dates back to a period from the eighth and seventh centuries BCE, during the Villanovan age. Also, the two Etruscan tombs discovered in Sasso Marconi are still displayed here. These provide a model for the grave goods found in the necropoleis of Kainua, most of which were lost or destroyed during World War II. Thirteen panels arranged on the archaeological site complete the description, ensuring a close correlation between the site and the artifacts preserved in the museum.[15]

The future development of the collection is strictly related to room 5, which is at present equipped to hold temporary exhibitions, but is actually designed to house some of the ancient objects stored in the museum's vaults.

NOTES

1. Gozzadini 1870.
2. Sassatelli 1984:381–400.
3. Vitali 1984:282–283; Morigi Govi 1994; Sassatelli 2015: 9–38.
4. Brizio 1886.
5. Brizio 1887b.
6. Aurigemma 1933:43–50; Lippolis 2001:197–198; Anzalone and Gaucci 2019:329–330.
7. Lippolis 2001:203–210.
8. Sassatelli 2006:5–13.
9. Mansuelli 1959a:180–182; Mansuelli 1966.
10. Sassatelli 1970:53–71; Massa Pairault 1997; Lippolis 2001:231–267; Sassatelli and Govi 2005a; Govi and Sassatelli 2010; Bentz and Reusser 2010b; Govi 2017b:145–179.
11. Brizzolara et al. 1980:99–100; Brizzolara and De Maria 1980:60–74; Sassatelli 1980b:51–66; Mansuelli et al. 1982.
12. Govi 2007:78–80; Bragadin 2009; Anzalone 2019:12–15; Anzalone and Gaucci 2019:329–350.
13. Direzione Regionale Musei Emilia-Romagna and Soprintendenza ABAP per la città metropolitana di Bologna e le province di Modena, Reggio Emilia e Ferrara.
14. Department of History and Cultures, chair of Etruscology and Italic Archaeology.
15. Anzalone and Gaucci 2019:329–350.

CHAPTER 3

INVESTIGATING THE CITY
An Integrated Approach

ELISABETTA GOVI, ANDREA GAUCCI,
SIMONE GARAGNANI, AND FEDERICA BOSCHI

CITY-SCALE RESEARCH
Elisabetta Govi

Marzabotto has a long excavation history.[1] What does it mean to investigate a city such as Marzabotto today? What are the most modern research perspectives and the most effective tools?

First of all, the constant presence and long-term commitment of the University of Bologna in Marzabotto favored the application of a "city-scale," and even a "regional-scale," approach. In this context, each aspect was widely analyzed, enhancing both the city's distinctive characteristics and its comparison with the homogenous territory of the Etruscan Po Valley. Since 1988, this approach has been undeniably visible in the study of the local pottery, which has now been gathered together to create a huge database that collates all the city finds and relates them to other finds from the territory.[2] Archaeometric analysis has established the origin of the raw materials, the clay, and the techniques used in the production of the different ceramic classes,[3] making it possible to demonstrate that black-gloss pottery was locally produced,[4] an absolute innovation in the research field that confirms the presence of high-level workshops in the city and allows the identification of imports. The same archaeometric approach has been applied to other archaeological materials, such as metal objects, which had a strong relationship with the metal workshops in the city,[5] and marble sculptures, distinguishing between Greek imports and Etruscan production made with stone from northern Etruria.[6] A multidisciplinary research method has also been applied to the reconstruction of the ancient landscape, considering both the natural and the urban environment. An indispensable study of the bioarchaeological finds showed the productive economy of this flourishing city in a landscape characterized by forests and hill country, where pig farming was prevalent, as in other cities of the Etruscan Po Valley.[7] At present, new data comes from the analysis of the offerings found in the multiple sacred areas of the city.[8] As for the material culture, in the study of a city investigated mostly in the nineteenth and twentieth centuries, the most ambitious challenge is to analyze and comprehend the objects within their context and their function, considering both limited and lost documentation. This contextual approach to the study of objects was extremely useful when applied to Attic pottery, especially for the finds from the necropoleis,[9] the epigraphic documentation,[10] and the local ceramic production,[11] aspects that are now analyzed within the residential, sacred, and funeral areas.

Unlike in the past, more recently various competencies have been applied to the anthropic and constructed landscape, aiming to define the city's urban and architectonic features. On a city-level scale, there is the systematic collection and study of old excavations carried out in the city sectors (the "Great Kiln" in *Regio* II, the "Mansuelli Block" in *Regio* IV, 1, the "Eastern Gate," the necropoleis, the Water Shrine; *see map 5* and appendix B with bibliography on parts of the city) as well as recent investigation of House 1 of *Regio* IV, 2[12] and the Urban Sanctuary of *Regio* I.[13] This data collection revealed a rich scenario on which it was possible to base our analysis of the city; for example, the phase before the foundation of the city is now much more clear thanks to the retrieval of relevant information in all excavation contexts. In addition, an in-depth knowledge of all excavation sectors has made it possible to analyze diachronically the local production, differentiated according to the sacred, domestic, and funerary contexts.

Moreover, geophysical surveys have been conducted in the unexcavated sectors: the results were exceptional and have helped to identify the functions of these areas (see next section). For example, such work made it possible to locate houses in *Regio* III, 5 that are exactly the same as on the opposite "Mansuelli Block" (*Regio* IV, 1), that is, they are characterized by the same type of inner structure, possessing the unique features of these sector buildings located on *plateia* A and understood to have been inhabited by elite members of the community. The plan and extension of these houses facing onto the main road of the city (*Regiones* III and IV) are quite similar to the Roman *domus*, with the long corridor, the lateral *fauces*, a large porticoed courtyard with the central *impluvium* open to the *compluvium*, and finally the *tablinum* open to the court.

The ground plan is now better defined, allowing us to completely reconstruct the city in Virtual Reality, aiming for pinpoint accuracy and taking into account many still unresolved issues (*see plate 16*).[14] Metric and geometric analysis was applied to urban planning.[15] For the first time, various residential models were identified in the city, located within blocks based on their social functions, an aspect never fully investigated in Marzabotto until now (*see map 7*).[16] The residential architecture appears to embody the city's social complexity together with its material culture and epigraphic documentation.[17] In fact, it is now possible to recognize different house types in the city and, on the basis of their position in the urban grid, their inner arrangement and their architectonic configuration, and, with the help of epigraphy, we can assume the social status of their inhabitants. Moreover, thanks to the copious information on the sacred areas now available, the city has also been analyzed from a religious point of view, on the assumption that its internal sacred structure is based on astronomy and rituals: this approach, never applied to Marzabotto, should explain the *templum*, meaning the arrangement of the sacred areas in the city, for example, the position of the temples and their cults in relation to the "sacral geography."[18] The results are in full correspondence with what we know about Etruscan religion. This field of study is more common in anthropological city analysis,[19] which can be appreciated in Marzabotto, while it is more difficult to apply to other Etruscan areas, due to the complex and more eventful history of the settlements.

The enlarged and interdisciplinary view adopted in recent years has led to the development of a new field of research about the architecture and the building reconstruction. The monumentalized space has been thoroughly examined, including not only a study of each context and its building phases,[20] but also a typological and metric analysis of the structures and their reconstruction.[21] This has been accomplished thanks to both traditional means (the description of Vitruvius, a comparative analysis with other buildings from Etruria) and innovative approaches, such as ArchaeoBIM, a method applied to Marzabotto's buildings that merges archaeology, architecture, and engineering (see the third section, below). Unlike the past, each ancient structure was examined in all its parts, including the materials and the building methods, to reconstruct the original as accurately as possible. We now also have a better sense of the ancient economic considerations around the construction of a building.

These multidisciplinary and integrated methods could be used in different ways to define present and future research, an approach made possible thanks to the opportunity given by the University of Bologna. Marzabotto-Kainua is, therefore, a laboratory, the ideal space in which to experiment with various methods of archaeological diagnostics.

BENEATH THE SURFACE: GEOPHYSICS AND NONINVASIVE SURVEYS AT KAINUA
Federica Boschi

As often happens with the most important and the longest-known archaeological sites, the Etruscan city of Marzabotto-Kainua has repeatedly been the subject of experiments with geophysical prospecting

FIGURE 3.1. Geophysics investigations at Marzabotto carried out by the University of Bologna and partners. Photos, clockwise: a moment during the Summer School of 2008, students with Michel Dabas (CNRS, Paris) working with GPR (Ground-Penetrating Radar); geomagnetic survey by University of Bologna; electromagnetic test; ARP (Automatic Resistivity Profiling) survey led by Geocarta Inc.

methods and noninvasive survey techniques. And as frequently occurs, these investigations, repeated over time with increasingly advanced techniques and instruments and prompted by new methodologies and renewed lines of research, have each provided significant new data sets for the characterization of the buried palimpsest and its hidden archaeological and geological features.

After the first successful electrical resistivity applications led by S. Verger and A. Kermovant in 1994, demonstrating the potential gains from this specific technology,[22] the University of Bologna has carried out several geophysical survey campaigns since 2007, aiming at complete coverage of the city and employing a combination of different techniques to assess their performance according to specific targets and the local geology (fig. 3.1).[23] As well as the research objectives, these activities also had important educational purposes, as demonstrated by the 2008 edition of the International Summer School, "Seeing Beneath the Soil—*In profondità senza scavare*," that was held on the site, and by the field labs for students that were part of the geophysical and topographical surveys carried out between 2007 and 2011.[24] Over the years, the Etruscan town has become an authentic experimental "site-school" and remarkable results have been achieved through all the main methods of noninvasive investigation of the subsoil, contributing to the currently known outlines of the ancient cityscape, the street network, and urban planning. From these,

FIGURE 3.2. Aerial view of the archaeological site of Marzabotto.
Photo: Federica Boschi, aerial survey, August 2011, late afternoon.

inferences can also be made about both the functional purpose of some areas and the natural environment.

The integrated approach on which this research project is based includes an analysis by aerial photography, although this particular technique is not very useful for this specific location, given that the grass covering the terrace of Pian di Misano is poorly suited to the formation of visible traces of subterranean structures. In spite of this, aerial surveys were organized in collaboration with the Air Club Francesco Baracca of Lugo (Ravenna), which flew over the site in a four-seater aircraft guided by an experienced pilot, with one or two archaeologists on board as photographers. While confirming the poor effectiveness of this technique for interpreting what might lie in the local subsoil, the flyovers have enabled the acquisition of images that are useful for the documentation and monitoring of this archaeological area (fig. 3.2). Although the geological properties of the soil, which is predominantly silty and clayey, and the lack of cultivation of the land in recent times do not make the site ideal for aerial photography, they do provide an ideal context for geophysical applications.

Surveys and tests conducted with resistivity (traditional along profiles; Ohm Mapper; ARP technology), ground penetrating radar, electro-magnetometry, and geomagnetic methods (Overhauser; cesium and potassium gradiometer) each make their own contribution and have their own level of effectiveness in relation to the context and the archaeological target of the investigation. Furthermore, the combination of different techniques has enabled multireading of the site, providing an overall description of the physical properties of each hidden structure and its archaeological interpretation. Indeed, from the totality of the resistivity measurements emerges the picture of buried stratification where the archaeological deposit lies within the first meter from the surface; the deposit is characterized by medium–high values of resistivity, ranging between 300 and 550 Ohm, and thus matching the profile of the remains of wall foundations. The next levels further down are more conductive layers, likely the silty and clayey soils of the alluvial terrace holding the settlement, and then, lower still, are more resistive concentrations related to sands and gravelly lenses of fluvial deposition. By contrast, measurements show rather low average values of magnetic susceptibility (+/−8 nT/m), consistent with the building materials and techniques used in above-ground structures and infrastructure. The most complete and detailed picture of the still-buried urban area comes from integrated high-resolution large-scale mapping, achieved via a resistivity ARP system[25] (by Geocarta Inc.) and a geomagnetic survey employing an optically pumped potassium gradiometer, which was led by the Laboratory of Geophysics at the University of Bologna (fig. 3.3).

These surveys show the whole of the regular street network, consisting of a system of main and secondary roads, and make it possible for researchers to update existing information about the urban layout to a high degree of accuracy, a long-standing focus of research at the University of Bologna.[26] The communication routes are perfectly detectable and measurable on the geophysical map, which reveals a 15 m width for the main streets (*plateiai*) and a 5 m width for secondary roads (*stenopoi*). The exclusive use of nonmagnetic local cobblestones in the construction of the roads explains why the road system is less well-defined, though still recognizable on a geomagnetic map.

FIGURE 3.3. On the lower right: geomagnetic map by the Laboratory of Geophysics, University of Bologna (photo: Federica Boschi); on the left: detail of *Regio* III compared with the ARP (Automatic Resistivity Profiling) results and what is visible via aerial photography (photo: Federica Boschi, aerial survey, September 2011).

On the other hand, the magnetic survey has provided insights into the functional organization of the urban space. In fact, the southern sector of the town (*Regio* V) stands out on the gradiometric map because of the prevalence there of strong magnetic contrasts, suggesting the presence of buried furnaces and a large metalworking complex, which have also been confirmed by artifact collection during a field-walking survey.[27] In addition, geophysical evidence has revealed that Block 5 of *Regio* III was entirely occupied by residential units, clearly recognizable in the mapping through their shapes and dimensions, with well-articulated extensions marked by dividing walls.[28]

From the large-scale resistivity mapping we also acquire significant data toward the description of the natural environment and the general landscape setting within which the settlement grew. Indeed, the resistivity maps referring to 1 and 1.70 m depths reveal the presence of an ancient paleo-channel of the Reno River beneath the archaeological layers, suggesting a transformation of the landscape by fluvial activity before the Etruscan occupation.

DIGITAL METHODOLOGIES AND THE VIRTUAL CITYSCAPE: RECONSTRUCTING LOST REALITY AT KAINUA
Andrea Gaucci and Simone Garagnani

Archaeology has a tendency to rely on graphic reconstruction to achieve a deeper understanding of what has been lost. Such reconstructions can be very accurate or provide purely a synthetic overview. Although Virtual Archaeology has been strongly influenced by points of view too often limited to its role as a means of visual restoration, the reconstruction of archaeological landscapes should be able to produce a duality in which being either creator or user in a virtual space helps us to understand the construction of the real archaeological space. Obviously, this interactivity/visualization approach, a key element when the discipline was conceived, requires a large number of specialists in archaeology and digital technologies.[29]

Some of the advantages deriving from the use of digital models in field archaeology include the systematic collection of data from different sources,[30] the easier dissemination of analyses and contents,[31] and the visual clarification of complex forms,[32] together with the possibility of simultaneous work on the same contexts by scholars and physical operators in different places.[33] In recent years, the rapid development of new technologies has created a need to integrate these new methods into carefully designed research projects with multiple purposes, primarily focused around three fundamental and interrelated fields: preservation, knowledge acquisition, and dissemination.[34]

The development of Kainua, which almost came to a halt with the abandonment of the town, offers the full range of necessary data for identifying the original urban environment. Therefore, over the years Kainua has been a test case for developing documentation techniques that foster research on the evolutionary path from traditional survey methods to digital models. Virtual reconstructions have already been produced in the context of past projects directed by G. Sassatelli on the Etruscan city between 2000 and 2010 (fig. 3.4).[35] Since 2014 the potential for interdisciplinary research on the site has led to the birth of the "Kainua Project," which merges the fields of archaeology, architecture, engineering, and computer science, aiming at the virtual reconstruction of the ancient city as a whole.[36]

The reconstruction of the digital cityscape started from the Digital Terrain Model (DTM). Thanks to a survey of the Acropolis using terrestrial laser-scanning techniques and the open fields in the lower town using digital photogrammetry through Unmanned Aerial Vehicles (UAV) technologies, a multiscalar DTM of the archaeological area was designed and embedded in the existing Reno Valley DTM.[37]

Primary and secondary urban roads with public and private sewers form the infrastructural platform on which the digital models of all the buildings were later placed. Geophysical surveys, together with excavation data, led to the formulation of an interpretative scheme of the buildings' modules and their layout within the blocks, re-creating wide areas of the city according to detailed criteria (fig. 3.6).[38]

The virtual models of buildings and the urban environment reference the age of greatest development of

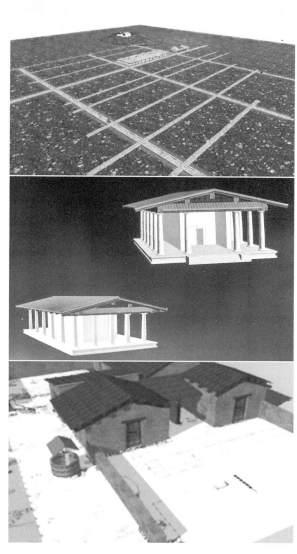

FIGURE 3.4. (a) A first attempt at the virtual reconstruction of the Etruscan city of Marzabotto (after Sassatelli and Taglioni 2000); (b) virtual reconstruction of the Temple of Tinia (after Sassatelli and Govi 2005), front and rear façades; (c) virtual reconstruction of House 1, *Regio* IV, 2 (after Beltrami 2010).

the city, which dates back to the fifth century BCE.[39] The interdisciplinary nature of the interpretative process has involved the entire complex of studies contributing to the understanding of the context and the building materials (i.e., palaeobotany, archaeometry, geophysics, archaeozoology).

During the "Kainua Project," a specific process called Building Information Modeling (BIM) and its tools were applied to justify the architectural choices made by the ancient builders, and to make hypotheses about the appearance and purposes of the Temple of Uni (fig. 3.5), among other structures located in the town.

A key goal of the BIM process is to enhance the synergy and cooperation between the different competencies involved in the project, which aims to digitally convert ancient architectural structures to create three-dimensional digital archives.[40] BIM has also stimulated experimentation in the field of cultural heritage, primarily with the aims of preservation and management, some of the many uses of this technology that are listed in the literature.[41] The application of BIM to preserved structures assumes a noninvasive process, based on data collection and digital acquisition. Therefore, the resulting parametric model, which collects all this information, is potentially the digital analogue of the real structure, not only from a geometric point of view (quantitative data), but also considering all the information it can contain (qualitative data).

A very different methodological approach within the BIM environment concerns the reconstruction of structures that are partially or no longer preserved. BIM testing applied to the archaeological field mainly concerns "lost" structures, such as those of Kainua, namely traced in negative, such as spoliation trenches or wall remains, mostly foundations. In order to better distinguish this scenario from the features of BIM applied to existing buildings, starting from different premises, it was decided to refer to the process adopted with the term "ArchaeoBIM." The application of ArchaeoBIM in this case is even more significant, because a reflection on the Etruscan temple as a three-dimensional building—with all the issues that this entails, and taking into account the state of preservation, limited to its foundations—is rarely encountered in scientific literature.[42] More generally, while the virtual reconstruction of buildings in archaeology is now a shared practice, some serious considerations regarding construction techniques are more difficult to resolve, especially for the Etruscan world, where wood and clay were the main materials.

These digital models, when considered in their form of structured index to facilitate access to information, can surely be considered as the most intuitive and direct medium to understand places and spaces; however, several important criticalities in their conventional adoption could arise, such as the absence of a recognized and universal standard in data collection, an absence particularly felt in the discipline of archaeology.

Ultimately the ArchaeoBIM process tested in Kainua was not meant to be an approach aimed solely at the scientific reconstruction of places. It was an iterative process that allowed a convergence of methods to present a synthesis of knowledge regarding complex archaeological assets as a result of the complementarity of the disciplines involved. The customized ArchaeoBIM process, proposed as the interaction between figures working in different research fields, was designed to study the temple through the language of an ArchaeoBIM model, the exact digital equivalent of the building as it would be in a real domain. Different kinds of information merged into models generated by the conscious aggregation of "smart digital elements," that is, building components embedding self-awareness of their own geometric, material, and behavioral values, able to relate to each other in compliance with precise construction rules as hypothesized by scholars, then simulated by models.

The Temple of Uni's ArchaeoBIM model was produced by investigating semantics and morphology, largely following Vitruvian rules, but the only element that could be acquired with surveys was the foundation plan. A hypothetical reconstruction, consisting of precise metrics for the elevations and sections, was generated, beginning from the foundation walls with the assignment of strict parametric constraints for architectural elements. Proportions were validated according to Vitruvius, even if in similar Etruscan buildings some dimensions were close enough, but not completely respected.[43] Beginning from the known literature—the Vitruvian precepts concerning the proportions and plan of an Etrusco-Italic temple—Uni's ArchaeoBIM models tried to mimic all the physical characteristics of the building materials as recovered by the findings, including their known use and availability on site, along with the study of static

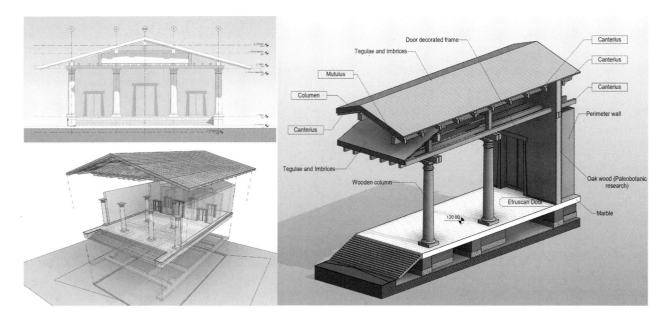

FIGURE 3.5. Digital reconstruction of the Temple of Uni using an assembled BIM model; components are connected following standard construction practices, according to the literature existing on Etruscan buildings and construction techniques. An ArchaeoBIM model easily collects information on materials, components, performance, and geometric morphology in order to share data with those involved in research on the monumental architecture at different levels.

FIGURE 3.6. (a) View from the zenith of the virtual Kainua; (b) view of the Realtime Virtual Environment from southeast; (c) view of the lower city from the Acropolis. The transparent buildings represent the lost part of the city, ruined by erosion.

FIGURE 3.7. The ArchaeoBIM model of the Temple of Uni imported into an RTR (Real-Time Rendering) environment to produce graphic visualization of the inferred reconstruction.

forces carried out to assess the actual strain expressed in the construction. Later, to better validate the Temple of Uni reconstruction, a structural model had to be produced beginning from the architectural one, in order to evaluate the performance of components and materials, to understand if they could have been used as proposed in the ArchaeoBIM reconstruction. The impressive roof, for example, was modeled in its wooden components, named *mutuli*, *cantherii*, and *templa*, to make some hypotheses regarding a complex framework made of crossed beams with rafters inclined 16 degrees from the horizontal, as recommended by Vitruvian treatises.

Beginning from the Vitruvian indications concerning the proportions, and the volumetric design and distribution of the Etrusco-Italic temple, Uni's digital models tried to mimic all the physical characteristics of the building materials, their use according to the known literature, and their availability on site, along with the study on loads and static forces carried out to assess the actual strain expressed in the construction.

The methodology proposed and tested was also applied to the urban scale, moving out from the architectural one: through forms of interactivity and simulations of physical, environmental, and astronomical conditions, the virtual model of the city let us formulate important considerations about historical and social issues, thus putting us at the forefront of the debate about Virtual Archaeology.

In this way, most of the *Regiones*, at least those for which our knowledge of shape and function was plausible enough, were modeled to recreate a realistic Etruscan urban environment, authoring shapes with 3D state-of-the-art modeling software: three-dimensional models were then accurately placed on the DTM (fig. 3.6).

The next step was the insertion of the various models in the urban plan, which thus allowed us to define the critical issues related to the use of spaces and the relationship between the buildings, in accordance with this previously identified objective. Indeed, the visual analysis of the buildings inside the virtual environment allows us to evaluate the criteria for organizing and monumentalizing public spaces, highlighting the issues that can be solved thanks to archaeological investigation. This is the case, for example, regarding the accessibility of the Acropolis from *plateia* B, overcoming a steep slope of 11 m in height, or the reasons that led to the concealment of the Temple of Uni by the more recent Temple of Tinia in the important perspective of the crossroads between *plateiai* A and B (fig. 3.8).[44]

In this way, a virtuous circle is triggered, leading to the continuous implementation of the model, thanks to the acquisition of knowledge, as a result of the questions raised by the model itself.

Digital models, however, were also the foundation of an updated system dedicated to the comprehension of the archaeological area by a wider, nonspecialized audience, mainly onsite. ArchaeoBIM models were easily prepared to be visualized in a Real Time Rendering (RTR) environment (fig. 3.7), based on software dedicated to Virtual Reality (VR) application development. This further use could lead to the production of simple immersive visualization apps, developed especially for museum visitors or people who would like to visit the archaeological site in Marzabotto through virtual remote tours using common devices such as tablets or smartphones.

At present, a user-friendly system, based on stationary immersive views of the virtual model to be used on long visits (fig. 3.9), such as Panoramic Virtual Reality, compensates for the lack of appropriate markers and effective computational resources for Augmented Reality, which was another option but is still not fully viable, in order to reach a wider audience for the dissemination of the outcomes of this long-running research work.[45]

NOTES

1. See chapters 1 and 2.
2. Mattioli 2013. For an update on the city of Spina, see Mattioli forthcoming; for further reflections on pottery productions at Kainua, see Mattioli 2022.
3. See chapter 13. Recently, attention has focused on hand-modeled vases (Braga, Tirtei, and Trevisanello 2022).
4. Gaucci 2010; Gaucci 2022.
5. Govi et al. 2006; Chiarantini et al. 2010. See chapter 12.
6. Sassatelli and Mancuso 2017. See chapter 14.
7. Curci 2010.
8. See chapters 8–9.
9. Baldoni 2009; Baldoni 2011; Baldoni 2012; see chapters 15, 17.
10. See chapter 10.
11. See chapter 13.

FIGURE 3.8. Reconstruction of *plateia* B from the crossroads, looking east toward the Temple of Tinia.

FIGURE 3.9. April 19 KAINUA 2017 session, dedicated to a visit to the site on the occasion of the seventieth birthday of Giuseppe Sassatelli (far right).

12. Govi and Sassatelli 2010.
13. See Govi 2017b; Govi 2018a.
14. See Govi 2017c and Gaucci 2017.
15. Baronio 2017.
16. Govi 2016; see chapter 11.
17. Sassatelli 1994a; Gaucci and Sassatelli 2010; see chapter 10.
18. Gottarelli 2005; Govi 2017b.
19. Govi 2017c.
20. See the conclusions of the editors in Govi and Sassatelli 2010:291–310.
21. For the Temple of Tinia in the urban area, see Baronio 2012.
22. Verger and Kermovant 1994.
23. For the research led by the University of Bologna see Govi 2014a and Govi 2017b.
24. During the research and educational activities organized between 2007 and 2009, the new surveys coordinated by the University of Bologna have benefited from the valuable collaboration of Geocarta© Inc. (promoter of the ARP survey over the whole site in collaboration with the So.Ing company), the University of Siena (with the involvement of the LAPeTLab of the Department of Historical Sciences and Cultural Heritage, and the Centro di GeoTecnologie in San Giovanni Val d'Arno), the University of Denver (CO, USA) and the Becker Archaeological Prospections (Beuberger, Germany). For preliminary considerations on the results see Govi 2014a and Boschi 2016. On the Summer School and labs see also Giorgi 2009.

25. On the Automatic Resistivity Profiling (ARP©) system, see Dabas 2009. The results and maps derived by the ARP survey in Marzabotto are edited in Govi 2014a:92.

26. Within the vast bibliography produced by the *équipe* of Bologna see in particular Sassatelli and Govi 2005a; Lippolis 2005 and Govi 2017b on the cityscape and open urban issues.

27. Sassatelli and Govi 2005a.

28. On the interpretation of the ARP data in *Regio* V see also Govi 2014a:93; Govi 2016.

29. An overview on the topic appears in Garagnani et al. 2021.

30. Foni et al. 2010.

31. Scopigno and Dellepiane 2017.

32. Pintus et al. 2016.

33. Soler et al. 2017; Inglese et al. 2019.

34. Garagnani and Gaucci 2020.

35. Sassatelli and Taglioni 2000; Sassatelli and Govi 2005b:29, pl. 3; Beltrami 2010.

36. See the contributions about the "Kainua Project" in Gaucci and Garagnani 2017.

37. Gaucci, Garagnani, and Manferdini 2015.
38. See chapter 4.
39. Gaucci 2017.
40. Fai et al. 2011.
41. Krider and Messner 2013.
42. Garagnani, Gaucci, and Govi 2016; Garagnani, Gaucci, and Gruška 2016a.
43. Garagnani, Gaucci, and Govi 2016; Garagnani, Gaucci, and Gruška 2016a.
44. Gaucci 2017; Govi 2017c.
45. Garagnani 2017.

PART II

THE PLANNED CITY AND ITS TERRITORY

Part II presents the history of Kainua-Marzabotto, within a broader view of the entire Reno Valley, in which first the settlement was founded and then the city. The chapters deal with the issue of the foundation rite, the urban layout, and the population dynamics through time, with attention to the surrounding territory and the economic and commercial role of the city. An important focus is the reconstruction of the ancient landscape and the subsistence economy.

CHAPTER 4

FOUNDING AND REFOUNDING OF THE CITY

ELISABETTA GOVI

The most recent excavations and the systematic studies of the material culture have made it possible to gain greater insight into the problem of the building phases of the city, which over decades of research on the site were reconstructed as follows:[1]

- Marzabotto I, the settlement of huts dating to the sixth century BCE
- Marzabotto II, the planned city, built in the early fifth century BCE
- the Celtic phase, datable to the fourth century BCE
- the Roman phase, to which belongs a small farm of the first century BCE to the first century CE, equipped with facilities for processing and working clay

Our overall understanding has changed a lot, and the history of this settlement is now understood in more detail, both in chronological terms and also regarding the complexity of the historical phenomena. The initial phases of the inhabited area are now clearer, and the very end of the city cannot be linked simply to the arrival of the Celtic people, but rather to a change in the economic and commercial conditions from which Marzabotto drew its wealth.[2] Even the Roman phase today takes on a different configuration in the light of excavations carried out in the Urban Sanctuary of *Regio* I, the ruins of which were probably reused as building material, worked both on-site and in the vicinity, in *Regio* III.[3]

In the light of new evidence and recent studies, the chronological sequence for Marzabotto can therefore be reconstructed in more nuanced form as follows:[4]

- Marzabotto I, perhaps corresponding to the pre-urban hut settlement (first half of the sixth century BCE?)
- Marzabotto II, coinciding with the earliest urban formulation of the settlement (middle to last decades of the sixth century BCE)
- Marzabotto III, the orthogonal city (from the end of the sixth or beginning of the fifth century to the middle/end of the fourth century BCE)
- the Celtic phase (end of the fourth to the third century BCE)
- the Roman phase (first century BCE to first century CE)

BEFORE THE PLANNED CITY

Traces of occupation of the plateau during the Bronze Age have emerged from the most recent excavations,[5] but they are still too limited to allow us to make any hypothesis. The subsequent phase of the early Iron Age is not documented at the moment,[6] but there is no lack of individual tombs and settlements in the territory around Marzabotto.[7] The picture of the oldest population is therefore still incomplete.

Even the village of huts, defined as Marzabotto I, today appears rather problematic. Its existence was assumed on the basis of the nineteenth-century discovery of hut paving in the southern area of the city, under the walls and roads of the fifth century BCE.[8]

E. Brizio reports having discovered thirteen huts and having verified that the materials corresponded exactly to those used in the city. The dimensions of these alleged huts were between 3.5 and 4.5–5 m and the depth of the layers at which they were found between 50 and 90 cm. Before his excavations, other traces of huts had been identified, for example, below *plateia* A, but no data was kept on these. Quite a few questions still remain about these structures, which could be interpreted as pits, filled to ground level during the construction of the city in the fifth century BCE.[9] It is worth noting that these finds are all concentrated in the southern sector of the city, which was investigated in the first excavations during the nineteenth century, when there was not much knowledge of the chronological phases of Marzabotto, and several hut floors had been brought to light during excavations in the wider Po Valley territory.[10] Even the most recent finds, such as the three hut floors in *Regio* III[11] and the hut and annexed structures of *Regio* V, 2,[12] are questionable, due to the absence of chronologically significant materials and structural details, for example, no post holes have been mentioned. In the same way, the presence of a hut in the northern area of the city appears to be very dubious, verified only through a small dig. The structure, uncovered among the cobblestones of the ancient riverbed, is documented by very few materials, whose dating to the early Iron Age is highly questionable.[13]

Although the housing structures assigned to the first half of the sixth century BCE are therefore completely uncertain, there is no lack of materials from that phase that attest the initial human presence on the plateau, however organized. From the first half of the sixth century BCE there are a few Middle Corinthian (*skyphos* and *aryballoi*), Etrusco-Corinthian (*alabastron*), and Ionic vessels from the first half of the sixth century BCE,[14] to which can be added a fragment of a figured Laconian krater, dating to the second quarter of the sixth century BCE,[15] a rare and valuable piece found in the Water Shrine.[16] To these imports can be added the well-known ivory *pyxis* lid of North Etruscan production, found in the well of *plateia* D (*see fig. 5.3*),[17] and some bucchero pottery (*see fig. 5.4*), recovered in a pit filled to ground level, conventionally defined "*strato del VI*" (layer of the sixth century BCE), in *Regio* V, 3.[18] These sporadic items therefore clarify the early occupation of the plateau, as a stage of the trans-Apennine route (*see map 3*). Around the middle of the sixth century BCE there is a significant increase in imported materials,[19] both Greek ceramics and bucchero vases, and it is evident that this phenomenon is connected to a permanent settlement on the plateau, of which significant traces have recently been found. Excavations by the University of Bologna in the northern area of the Tinia temple (*Regio* I, 5) have brought to light wall structures belonging to this settlement that date to the second half of the sixth century (fig. 4.1).

These walls are characterized by a construction technique different from those of the later city, and by a divergent orientation of 3 degrees in a southeasterly direction. The walls of the planned city are built on top of these previous structures, and the materials found in the layers that cover them date to the last decades of the sixth century BCE.[20] After much effort, and despite the scarce evidence left under the wall foundations of the city, this first inhabited area is better known today. Traces of cobbled streets found below *plateia* A, and the divergent orientation of 3 degrees northwest of *plateia* D and of the Eastern Gate (*see map 5*), later included in the urban grid, suggest an already complete settlement, organized and autonomous, with craft and sacred areas.[21]

In fact, at the northern edge of the plateau, near a natural spring, there is a sanctuary (the Water Shrine) that hosted an important cult, judging by the votive materials, such as some bronzes and Attic black-figured vases of great value and rare distribution in Etruria Padana, as well as Siana cups and Little Master cups.[22] Among these, there is an "extra-large" band cup (*see fig. 15.2*), attributed to the Group of Rhodes 12264 and dating to 520 BCE, with warriors playing dice, a theme that scholars have always linked to historical or literary origins and considered a bearer of political values. Recently this iconography has been read, instead, as a ritual interpretation, accounting for the find context of the cup at Marzabotto—the Water Shrine—where the scene, with undoubted reference to the civic values, was probably read as an act of div-

FIGURE 4.1. Northern area of the Temple of Tinia; the wall structures dating to the second half of the sixth century BCE are highlighted by diagonal lines.

ination.[23] The small sanctuary could therefore have played an important role in the foundation of the first settlement and the restructuring of the city.

During this early phase on the hill of the later Acropolis, there was already a sacred structure: *Podium*-altar B (fig. 4.2), with a central well, and likely tied to chthonic cults (*see plate 12*). This well is a *mundus*, dedicated to *Dis Pater*, who in the sources is linked to the foundation of cities. The sources refer to a god, Mantus (Servius, *ad Aen.* 10.199), homologous to the god Śuri of the Tyrrhenian area,[24] implying that the Etruscans of the Po Valley called this god Mantus instead of Śuri. The foundations of cities in Etruria Padana could be dedicated to Mantus, and it is possible that the name of Mantua/Mantova derives from this god. Confirmation of the existence of this god comes from an inscription mentioning *Manth*, found in a *bothros* (votive pit) in the sanctuary at Pontecagnano. Despite the lack of information about the materials recovered during the

FIGURE 4.2. *Podium*-altar B on the Acropolis, second half of the sixth century BCE. After Govi 2007:21.

nineteenth-century excavations, we know that a tiled basin for water was located near the staircase of Altar B, now missing, and that a large quantity of animal bones, thrown in as offerings, were found in the well.

Therefore, it is not inconceivable that the first settlement was founded according to a rite centered on the *mundus*. It is worth noting that subsequent constructions of the temples of the planned city almost conceal this altar, which remains behind the great Temple C and next to Temple A, meaning that it was barely visible to those who climbed the Acropolis.

Traces of structures earlier than the peripteral temple in the Urban Sanctuary suggest that even here there was already a sacred building, but the lack of material does not allow us to go beyond this hypothesis. Walls and materials datable to the last decades of the sixth century BCE have been found in the large craft workshops of the city, demonstrating continuity of use, just as a building lying under the fifth-century BCE walls of House 6 of *Regio* IV, 1 has a rectangular tripartite plan and front porch, and is flanked by another structure (*see fig. 11.1*).[25] The housing typology recalls plans known in Tyrrhenian Etruria during the sixth century BCE, such as at Acquarossa, but the roof decoration system of this house at Marzabotto is unknown. The materials recovered during the excavation date to the last decades of the sixth century BCE.

Although poorly documented, this early settlement already shows a complex organization[26] and urban characteristics that do not change with the refounding of the planned city at the beginning of the fifth century BCE. In fact, continuity in the use of space (residential, artisanal, sacred, funerary) suggests that the same community is renewing itself, and there is no break between this town and the next city, not even in the chronology of the imported materials/goods, which attest a gradual and uninterrupted growth, starting from the third quarter of the sixth BCE and with an increase at the end of the century.[27]

The problem of the origin of this settlement still remains, since the population of the Reno Valley at this time was scarce and does not seem sufficient to form an organized community,[28] while it is clear that the reason that leads to the foundation is its location along the route connecting Bologna to northern Etruria, which would ensure active trade. Certainly the appearance of imports in Marzabotto around 540 BCE goes hand in hand with the flowering of the whole of Etruria Padana (*see map 2*), during a phase in which preexisting centers, such as Bologna, were restructured, while settlements and cities were founded *ex novo* at strategic points for trade with the Greek world (Spina; Adria is now reorganized) and with the trans-Alpine world (Forcello di Bagnolo San Vito).[29]

Previously, for this general reorganization of the Po Valley territory, a phenomenon of colonization from the south—specifically from central Etruria[30]—was assumed, a hypothesis that has been questioned by G. Sassatelli, who instead imagines a local population with a preeminent role in Bologna, as shown by onomastics, which have local characteristics.[31]

In conclusion, the history of the town of Marzabotto during the sixth century BCE still awaits refinement with respect to the precise chronology of its foundation, for which it will be necessary to study in-depth all the most ancient findings, and also regarding its topographical and urban configuration. While the settlement of huts cannot be confirmed, it is now clear that, around the middle of the sixth century BCE, there was a settlement on the plateau that already had all the urban characteristics and that, on a social and cultural level, showed notable development, as demonstrated by the materials imported from Greece, which are valuable and sometimes quite rare. Henceforth, Marzabotto was an integral part of the most active Etruscan trade routes.[32]

THE REFOUNDING OF THE CITY

In the period from the end of the sixth through the beginning of the fifth century a new city was founded at Kainua-Marzabotto.

In the absence of sources, it is not easy to determine which historical events preceded the town becoming a monumental city. The city, rebuilt with a notable organization and according to a foundation rite that reflected the religious principles of the *Etrusca disciplina*, could have been the result of deep political, social, and economic transformations. The community was renewed, thanks to new social and political forces and flourishing commercial activities, with a design meant to give the city a new face.[33] Certainly, there was substantial continuity in the functions of the residential, craft, and sacred spaces, with a qualitative leap in urban planning and architecture. Something similar can also be seen in Bologna, which, towards the end of the sixth century BCE, restructured the city acropolis and necropolis into monumental forms. In fact, the role of the capital of Etruria Padana was almost certainly decisive in the founding and refounding dynamics of Marzabotto. The city was only a few kilometers from Bologna and represented a stopping point on the Apennine itinerary (*see map 3*). Due to its position in the Reno Valley, its urban characteristics and monumental architecture were certainly visible from a considerable distance. Marzabotto therefore appears to present a preview of Bologna and the other cities of the Po Valley, to which it constitutes the gateway for those coming from the south.

The ancient name of the city is probably revealed by some Etruscan inscriptions recently discovered at Marzabotto that contain an inflected term in the locative case, *kainuathi*. The link with the Greek "*kainon* = new" has been recognized (*see fig. 10.4: nos. 6, 10*),[34] therefore the name of the city, *Kainua*, could convey the concept of "new city," refounded.

Recent studies have been able to establish more precisely the chronology of the foundation of the new planned city. The excavations carried out on the road near House 1 of *Regio* IV, 2 give us an opportunity to date the *stenopos* of the westernmost sector, as some fragments of Attic vases dated between the end of sixth and the beginning of the fifth century BCE and other evidence were found in the preparation level of the road.[35] This chronology is also confirmed by the results of previous excavations[36] and now in the investigation of the Etrusco-Italic temple in *Regio* I, 4. The Urban Sanctuary reveals a foundation rite that, through an inscription, can be placed at the end of the sixth century BCE (*see fig. 8.2*).[37] Kainua-Marzabotto provides us the opportunity to investigate the phenomenon of the foundation of a city by examining both the ritual and religious structures and the concrete implementation of the scheme on the ground.

THE FOUNDATION RITE

The city of Kainua-Marzabotto is the result of a ritual foundation that can be reconstructed on the basis of archaeological evidence and with the help of Latin sources which, as is well known, transmitted the principles of the foundations created by the *Etruscus ritus*. The urban grid is based on a system of four road axes that are 15 m wide (called in the Greek vocabulary *plateiai*), onto which the smaller streets (called *stenopoi*), 5 m wide, are grafted (*see map 5*). The grid is oriented according to the cardinal points and originated from the observation of solar movement, here influenced by the profile of the mountain that surrounds the plateau.[38] On the hill that houses the city's Acropolis there is an *auguraculum*, a platform from which the priest-augur would have performed a ritual at the time of the foundation. According to Festus (*De verborum significatione*) there had to be two different sites for the rite of *inauguratio*, and two people linked by a *stipulatio*, one located on the *auguraculum*, looking eastward, the other in the center of the *templum*, looking southward.[39] In figure 4.3, we have attempted to diagram the actions of the priest-augur on the Acropolis at Marzabotto. He had to look toward the southeast, along a diagonal line whose ends would coincide with the rising of the sun at the winter solstice and with sunset at the summer solstice.

At the midpoint of this diagonal alignment the geometric center of the city was set, indicated on the ground by a stone with an engraved *crux* (fig. 4.4), oriented on the cardinal points, which was then ritually buried under the roadway, as well as other landmarks found at the intersections of the roads.[40] At the end of the ritual action the priest-augur, facing southwest, defined the other diagonal line, corresponding with the sunset of the winter solstice and the sunrise of the summer solstice, and thus he fixed the four points of the rectangular layout of the city (fig. 4.3: no. 4).

That the *cippi* (markers) were thus placed therefore attests that the city's rite of foundation was based on

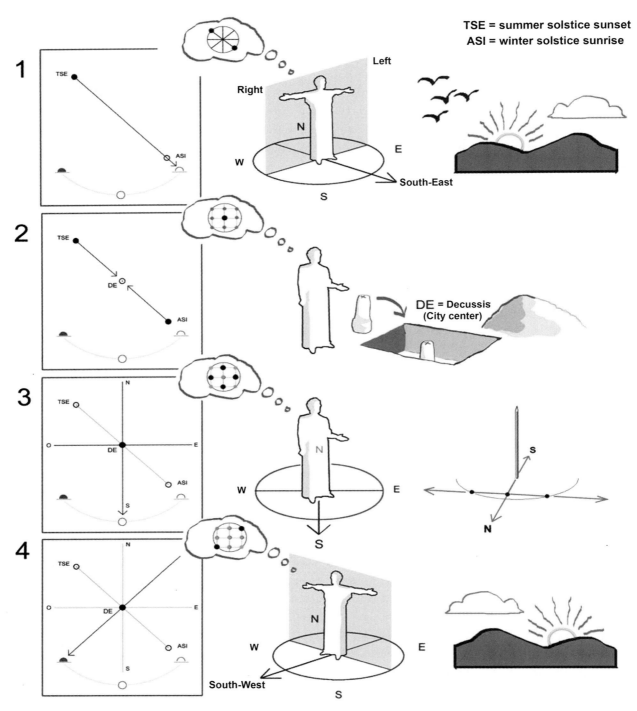

FIGURE 4.3. Foundation rite of the city, scheme of ritual actions. After Gottarelli 2013.

FIGURE 4.4. *Cippus* engraved with oriented cross-mark, or *crux* (*decussis*) (top); during excavation (bottom).

raculum must have stood, have revealed the presence of structural features pointing to a monumental layout of this higher area of the hill.[41] The recent virtual reconstruction of the city has allowed us to appreciate how the visual connection between the *auguraculum* and the *cippus* with the *crux* at the center of the urban grid was kept unhindered.[42]

The definition of the astronomical axes corresponding to the roads and, consequently, the rectangular urban shape, with its interior divided into eight *regiones*, was then based on this diagonal alignment. A landslide in the southern sector of the plateau, caused by the erosion of the Reno River, does not allow us to evaluate the extension of the southernmost *regiones* and the actual extension of the city.

THE URBAN LAYOUT

The urban layout was therefore not the result of a theoretical and perfect geometric design, but the translation on earth of astronomical and religious principles adapted to the place. For the Etruscans those same principles regulated the division of celestial space by dividing the divine seats; the corresponding concept in the Latin language relates to the *templum* = divided and consecrated space. The city, a reflection of divine space, was therefore its ideal image, and this is embodied in an extraordinary way, not only by the astronomical and solar orientation, but also by the layout of the temples, conceived together with the urban plan (fig. 4.5). The "geography of the sacred" seems to respect the celestial seats of the gods, according to the reconstruction of the *templum* based on Latin sources and on the Liver of Piacenza.[43]

As the result of an extraordinary plan based on religious principles, the city of Marzabotto, the symbolic image of a sacred space, is a perfect example of the interconnection between the divine and the human sphere.[44] No other Etruscan city seems to be so coherent in its internal articulation, suggesting that Marzabotto was a unique creation, almost an experiment. Actually, the regular urban plan of the other newly founded cities in Etruria and the Po Valley implies that all were standardized by these urban and religious principles, but our lack of knowledge of their

principles of essential importance within the *Etrusca disciplina*, such as orientation and *limitatio*. The *cippus* with the incised cross, bearing evidence of projection onto the ground of the heavenly *templum*, confirms that the town's foundation arose from the enactment of a purely Etruscan rite. According to Livy's renowned passage about the *inauguratio* of King Numa (1.17–18), the augur performed the *spectio* (ritual viewing) facing the east or, as in this case, southeast. Being up on the Acropolis, the augur could look across the whole plateau below, where the second seat can easily be identified as the point where the *cippus* engraved with a *decussis* was buried. Thus, an astronomical correlation between the solar *templum* and the urban layout has been established. Recent soundings on the terrace dominating the Acropolis, where the *augu-*

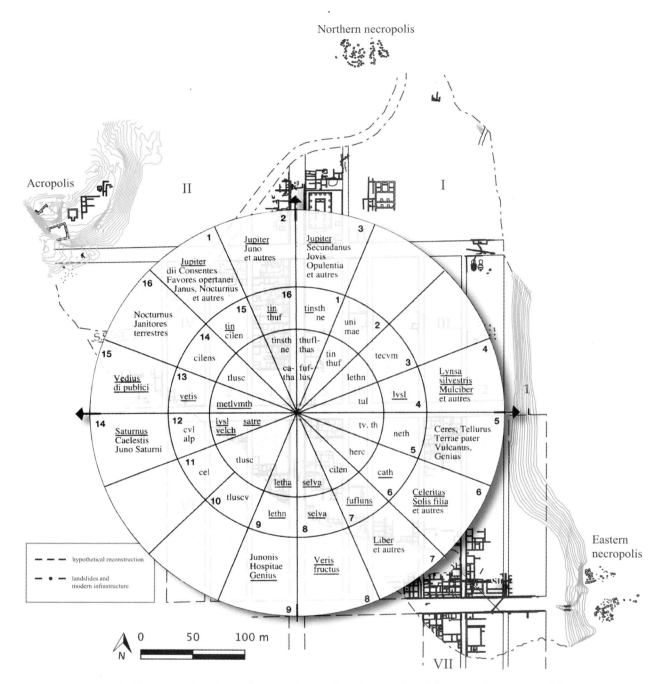

FIGURE 4.5. The Etruscan celestial *templum* superimposed on the city plan. After Govi, Pizzirani, and Gaucci 2020.

articulation does not allow us to fully evaluate the phenomenon.

The city was planned according to a rational system, using a unit of measurement corresponding to the Attic foot, which is 29.6 cm, as documented in other cities of Etruria and Latium, and also hypothe-

sized in the construction of the residential and sacred buildings of the city.[45]

The three east–west *plateiai* are 15 m wide and are 144 m (between B and C) and 179 m (between C and D) apart from each other. The subdivision into *regiones* is determined by the *stenopoi* that define blocks that are 35.6–36.2 m wide. But in the eastern half of the city the logic of division is different (the blocks here measure 36, 18, 45, and 35.5–36 m), probably due to the organization of *Regio* I, where we find the urban temples of Tinia and Uni (*see map 5*). The metrology analysis conducted on the city found that, at the foundation level, the *plateiai* measure 50 feet (= 14.8 m), the *stenopoi* 16 (4.74 m), and the standard width of the *insulae* is 121 feet (35.82 m), while the length is 485–486 feet (= 143.56–143.86 m) in the north (*Regiones* III–IV) and 605–606 feet (= 179.1–179.38 m) in the south (*Regiones* V–VI). At the level of building construction these measurements probably became round numbers.

The complex water supply and disposal system is also the result of rational planning: wide, deep channels at the edges of the roads, with a paved bottom and covered with flat cobblestones, ensured the flow of water from the city by exploiting the natural slope of the plateau; flowing into them were the internal channels of the houses that disposed of waste water from the wells, dug near the central courtyards and protected by clay parapets (which were decorated in bas-relief in the houses of the city's elite); an aqueduct built at the foot of the Acropolis at a source, with a collection tank and with three arms directed toward different points of the city (*see fig. 14.5*), ensured the constant flow of water, especially to the craft workshops.[46] This advanced system not only testifies to a civic organization that also could guarantee its maintenance, perhaps including magistrates in charge of managing the city's water, but could also reflect a ritual dimension linked to the foundation of the city: perhaps the tracings of furrows in the ground that delimited the streets then became water channels. Certainly, the construction of a well with a cobblestone lining up to 7–8 m deep was a very demanding operation with religious implications, sinking into the depths of the earth in search of groundwater.[47]

The houses, inserted into the rigid geometric grid of the blocks, were built in fixed dimensional modules adapted to rationally divided spaces.[48] A recent analysis of the houses discovered up to now and traceable on the basis of geophysical prospections allows us to recognize a variety of plans, thus excluding uniform colonial-type domestic buildings (*see map 7*).[49]

From the smallest module (just over 200 square m) we move on to building blocks of 300 square meters and more, up to the large "*atrium* houses," characterized by the aggregation of distinct buildings around a central courtyard with a well.[50] This type of house, which can reach 900 square meters, is located along the main road axis, *plateia* A, and must have belonged to the city elite.

The general framework of domestic architecture therefore highlights a complex social articulation, as well as the importance of production activities, present throughout the city. From small kilns for the production of vases to extensive structures that document the entire clay and metal workflow, the urban layout appears to be characterized by a lively artisan dynamism (*see map 8*).[51] Today this is even more evident, following the discovery of two monumental temples, known to have been built thanks to local workshops specializing in the production of roofing elements and architectural decoration. There are also votive objects and molded stone bases, used as supports for the bronzes left by the devotees. Therefore, solely artisan districts are not recognized, while the known workshops overlook large streets, thus inserting themselves into the residential fabric.

The city plan therefore followed cosmological and religious principles that created a precise geometric layout. The implementation of this layout, inhabited by its citizens, and the consequent division of internal spaces (streets, blocks, and public and private areas), introduced elements that reveal undeniable comparisons with the Greek world. In fact, in the same period in Greece and Magna Graecia, geometric principles were developing that had an effect on town planning,[52] as demonstrated by the recent interpretation of the layout of Neapolis, organized in a circular structure with the Temple of the Dioscuri at its center.[53] Marzabotto reveals just how close the intercultural dialogue was, as shown precisely by the use of the Greek foot in the planning of the entire city and its buildings.

The city plan is therefore divided according to rigid geometric principles, but the occupation of the spaces follows a different logic. The first factor that influenced the choices is a topographical one, since a hierarchy of road axes emerges, as already hypothesized by G. A. Mansuelli, who recognized the ritual character of the founding act.[54] On *plateia* A we find elite houses that do not appear in any other area of the city, except perhaps for the building of *Regio* V, 2 overlooking *plateia* D, defined by E. Brizio as *Domus Lautuni*, which poses many problems of interpretation. The extraordinary size of the courtyard and the rooms,[55] as well as the presence of an inscribed weight found in the well, have led to the hypothesis of a public use for this building,[56] which contained an extraordinary level of furnishings, with complex water infrastructures,[57] the use of stone blocks for the walls and for the foundations, and clay covering elements for the well and for the columns.

Another factor is the function of the buildings, given the productive vocation that some areas show from the first phase of construction, as seems to happen in the workshop-houses excavated by the École Française de Rome in *Regio* V, 3, or in the manufacturing areas defined in the literature as the "Great Furnace" and the "Foundry," facing *plateia* A.[58]

But the factor that more than any other seems to govern the dynamics of the organization of the living spaces is a sociopolitical one, certainly difficult to evaluate on the basis of the materials recovered during the excavations, when known. So, it is precisely the planimetric-spatial analysis that leads us to the identification of a sector of the city, overlooking *plateia* A, that was occupied by the family groups that held power and whose members probably played important civic roles. In fact, among the houses of the city elites located in *Regio* IV, 1 and in the opposite block (*Regio* III, 5), those with the front on *plateia* A of about 22 meters exactly equal the area of the peripteral urban temple, measurable as 35.50 × 21.92 m, corresponding to 120 × 75 Attic feet. Therefore, these houses occupy an area equal to that of the house of the god Tinia, which is inserted in a regular urban block as if it were the home of an individual citizen, representing the god of the city.[59] Of course, the monumental dimension of the earthly seat of the god, ritually oriented to the south, canceled this equation between the temple and the houses of eminent citizens, which, however, originated at the design level and was therefore ideologically highly significant.[60] Thus, today we can hypothesize the existence of a structured and articulated civic body, as also expressed in the text of the inscribed bronze sheet found during the excavation of the Urban Sanctuary (*see appendix A, no. 1; fig. 10.1*).[61] Eminent citizens are mentioned in relation to the construction of a building, perhaps the city magistrates, whose houses overlooked *plateia* A.

It is already known that the *plateiai* of Marzabotto have similar dimensions, yet they seem to have had differing levels of importance and different functions. *Plateia* B now appears to be a sacred road connecting the city to the Acropolis, and a virtual reconstruction allows us to evaluate the ancient perception of this visual, conceptual axis, a connection allowing for religious processions, which wound through the city to the Acropolis during civic festivals. Furthermore, the virtual reconstruction of the city has also revealed a specific problem, still unresolved, of the relationship between *plateia* B and the Acropolis, which is 11 m higher.[62]

The distinctive characteristics of Marzabotto's urban layout are therefore the extraordinary width of the roads, suitable for commercial activities and civic festivals; the impact of the sacred areas, with temples located at strategic points, corresponding to the divine seats and clearly visible within the city; the mixing of residential and craft activities; and the great houses-workshops.

However, some unsolved problems remain. Unfortunately, we do not know if there were any city walls, but there certainly must have been some form of delimitation of the civic space, precisely because the city came into being according to the principle of the *templum*, a delimited, consecrated space. Furthermore, the "Eastern Gate" implies a demarcation, and it is probable that every *plateia* had an access with a formal gate. The Northern Gate does not exist; it is only a reconstruction of the roadway of the *stenopos*. It has been suggested that an *agger* (earthwork) and a big channel delimited the northern sector with a curvilinear development that would have followed the circular geometric shape within which the city's quadrangle is placed.[63] Were such hypotheses to be confirmed, the geometric principle on which the urban layout was based would appear clearer, and the comparison with

Neapolis, founded at exactly the same time, would be more significant.

There is also the question of clarifying the development of *Regio* III, which would appear to be empty, though geophysical explorations have revealed residential structures in the southern sector, so the problem is still unresolved. Deeper excavations could help to counteract the impression of emptiness in this part of the city, facing onto the sacred area of *Regio* I. Regarding *Regio* III, the public space of the square (the *agora* of the Greek city) is still unknown, an aspect that is generally not documented in Etruscan urbanism, but the excavations in the area in front of the Etrusco-Italic temple will clarify its existence in relation to the Urban Sanctuary, the hub of city life. Recently M. Torelli reviewed the hypothesized cases of Etruscan settlements with an *agora/forum* (Tarquinia, Roselle, Cerveteri, Populonia), assuming that at Marzabotto it did not exist, since the two temples in the urban area are both delimited by walls.[64] The alleged lack of an *agora* would mean that the city did not have its own political autonomy and magistrates, of whom in fact there is still no trace in the epigraphical documentation. But what has so far been observed of the urban structure, the architectural articulation, and the attestation of the institutional term **spura* in the inscriptions found in the Urban Sanctuary, particularly those that played a role in the foundation rites, leads us to believe that Marzabotto was a politically autonomous city with its own territory.

In conclusion, according to the theoretical approach, the city thus reflects a very high level of central planning and coordination between buildings and spaces, since formality and monumentality are applied here through a common orientation of streets and buildings, axiality, the symmetrical arrangement of buildings, and the logic of access points and internal networks.[65]

NOTES

1. Malnati and Manfredi 1991:132–134; Govi 2007:9–10; Bentz and Reusser 2008:30. The problem of the chronology of the different phases, rather confused in the tradition of studies, is addressed in Govi 2014a:103–109.
2. See chapter 19.
3. See chapter 20.
4. Govi 2014a:102–109; Govi 2016:210–211. The hypothesis of an urban settlement dating back to the sixth century BCE is already speculated in Malnati 1987; Forte 1993b:462–463.
5. Bentz and Reusser 2008:30–31; Cattani and Govi 2010.
6. Some *fibulae* and pins datable to the eighth–seventh centuries BCE have been found in much more recent contexts of the city and may refer to accumulations of bronze material (Trocchi 2010:201; see chapter 5, in particular note 28).
7. See chapter 6.
8. Brizio 1890:326–329; Malnati 1987:125–129, with plan of the findings (fig. 82), to be integrated with the hut found in the northern sector of the city (Poppi 1971); Malnati and Manfredi 1991:132–133.
9. Govi 2016:207–208. Doubts are also expressed in Mansuelli 1965b:247.
10. Not by chance one of the hut pavings at Marzabotto has been recognized by G. Chierici during a visit (Govi 2020).
11. De Maria et al. 1972.
12. Tripponi 1971:228–230.
13. Poppi 1971. During the excavations carried out in the northern sector of *Regio* V, 3, traces of a hut were found, connected to a well, and materials of the Villanovan and bucchero tradition are cited (Massa Pairault 1997:63), but even in this case the discovery remains doubtful.
14. Lippolis 2000; see chapter 15.
15. Baldoni 2015:117–118.
16. See chapter 8.
17. Desantis 2009.
18. Malnati 1987; Forte 1993b; Forte 1993a; and chapter 5.
19. See chapter 15.
20. Govi 2016:205–207.
21. A first review of the evidence referable to the settlement of the sixth century BCE is in the doctoral thesis of M. Forte (Forte 1993b), now on academia.edu. Govi 2014a:104; Govi 2016:207–209.
22. Baldoni 2015. See chapters 8, 15.
23. Baldoni 2017; Iozzo 2018.
24. Sassatelli 1989–1990; Colonna 2006:141.
25. Forte 1993b:300–370; Calastri et al. 2010:43–44; Govi 2016:208–209. See chapter 11.
26. A first settlement at the beginning of the sixth century that evolves in an urban sense in the second half of the century was hypothesized in Malnati 1987:128–129.
27. For Attic pottery see Baldoni 2009:244–245 and chapter 15.
28. Sassatelli 1989a:22–23. See chapter 6.
29. Sassatelli 1989a:29–30; Sassatelli 1990:58–60; about urbanism in Etruria Padana see Govi 2014a; Govi 2015b.
30. G. A. Mansuelli, in Mansuelli et al. 1982:100. Of the

same opinion Malnati 1987:128; Malnati and Manfredi 1991:134; Lippolis 2000:105.

31. Sassatelli 1990. See chapter 10.
32. See chapter 5.
33. Govi 2017b; Sassatelli 2017b.
34. G. Sassatelli, in Sassatelli and Govi 2005b:47–55 and see the discussion at pp. 319, 322–324, 329–330. See chapters 8, 10.
35. Govi 2010b:199.
36. Sassatelli and Govi 2010:291–295.
37. See chapter 8.
38. Gottarelli 2013.
39. See Sassatelli 1989–1990.
40. About the foundation rite of Marzabotto see Sassatelli 1989–1990; Sassatelli and Govi 2010; Gottarelli 2013; Govi 2014a:97–102; Govi 2017c:89–93.
41. See chapter 8.
42. Gaucci 2017:106.
43. See chapter 8.
44. Govi 2017c; Govi et al. 2020.
45. Baronio 2017; Govi 2016; Govi 2017c.
46. Sassatelli 1991a.
47. Pizzirani 2014:78.
48. See chapter 11.
49. Govi 2016.
50. Gaucci 2016.
51. See chapters 12 and 13.
52. Lo Sardo 1999.
53. Longo and Tauro 2016.
54. Mansuelli 1962a:21–22.
55. Brizio 1890:317–326. He investigates only the western half of the block (the excavation was then completed in the twentieth century: Tripponi 1971), and hypothesizes an extension of the house equal to the width of the *insula* and the length to one third of the block. The courtyard is 19 × 27 m wide, while the vestibule is 4 × 17.5 m and the rooms overlooking the courtyard are 6.80 × 6.80 m.
56. Sassatelli 1994a:15–18, no. 1.
57. Brizio 1890: pl. VI; Jolivet (2011:74–75) underlines the uniqueness of this structure, perhaps an aristocratic home with comparisons in the Palazzo di Gonfienti or a public building.
58. Morpurgo 2017.
59. G. Sassatelli, in Sassatelli and Govi 2005b:47.
60. A planimetric and ideological relationship between the *atrium* house and the Etrusco-Italic temple has been stressed several times, as has the religious matrix in the analogous conformation between *pars antica* and *pars postica* (Prayon 2010:23).
61. See chapter 10.
62. Govi 2017b; Gaucci 2017.
63. Gottarelli 2005; Malnati and Sassatelli 2008.
64. Torelli forthcoming.
65. Smith 2007:8–12.

CHAPTER 5

CITY AND TERRITORY
Trade Routes and Cultural Connections

STEFANO SANTOCCHINI GERG

Kainua lies on the Apennine piedmont on a large alluvial terrace of about 30 hectares formed by a bend in the Reno River.[1] Albeit not navigable in ancient times since it has a shallow torrential habit, with slopes and obstacles that prevented its ascent, there is no doubt that the course of the river represented the main point of reference for the route that connected the Po Valley to Etruria, which passed over the ridge or along the middle height of the hillside.

Kainua is, in fact, the only large urban center in the Apennine sector, and the first encountered when arriving from Tyrrhenian Etruria, making it a true gateway to the Po Valley (*see maps 1–2*). Its strategic position signals its main function in reference to settlement choices at the base of the population "system" of Etruria Padana.

THE *CHORA* OF KAINUA AND THE TRADE ROUTES

The predominantly mercantile and artisanal vocation of Kainua is attested by the relatively limited extent of its *chora*, the "countryside" (*see map 3*). The agropastoral activity carried out in its territory was not extensive and intended for export, but probably limited to internal livelihood needs.[2] It is not easy to identify the portion of the territory directly attributable to the Etruscan city, but some clues may help. Among these, the most useful is its material culture, in particular the characteristics of ceramic production, votive bronzes (especially those of the "Marzabotto Group"),[3] and the typology of the tombs and funerary memorials.

The analysis of these objects[4] suggests that the boundaries of the *chora* controlling the Reno and adjacent valleys must have coincided, to the north, with the village of Sasso Marconi, which was surrounded by some groups of tombs[5] marked by burial stones of the same type used as identity markers in Kainua (see chapter 18). The dominance of this strategic site was fundamental in ensuring the control of the Reno–Setta confluence and the road bottleneck created by the cliff overhanging the village. Continuing north, and before arrival in Felsina, lies the important center of Casalecchio di Reno, active since the Villanovan period and which, at the same time as Marzabotto (at the end of the sixth century BCE) took on a more urban shape, with streets and orthogonal channels.[6] Here, however, we are already outside the sphere of influence of Kainua and under that of Bologna, as evidenced by one horseshoe-shaped *stele* from its necropolis, a type completely absent in Marzabotto, where only funerary *cippi* were used.

Kainua probably controlled the entire Reno Valley to the south, down to the current border with Tuscany, as proved by the mid-sixth/mid-fourth century BCE villages of Monte Bargi (Camugnano) and Poggio Gaggiola (Casola, Castel di Casio) and discoveries in Castellina (Granaglione) and Burzanella (Camugnano). The upper Reno and Limentra valleys are connected, via the Collina Pass (932 masl) and the Ombrone River, to routes that led directly to the province of Pistoia and, via the Montepiano Pass (700 masl, the watershed between the basins of the Setta and Bisenzio) and following the course of the Bisenzio itself, to the centers of the province of Prato, among which the city of Gonfienti stands out. Founded in the second half of the sixth century BCE at the foot of the Calvana Mountains and not too far from the confluence of the Bisenzio with the Arno, this urban center has an orthogonal layout like Marzabotto. The two cities must therefore have represented the cornerstones of the main route connecting the Po Valley and northern Etruria between the late sixth and fifth centuries BCE.

The other fundamental route connecting with Tyrrhenian Etruria, particularly active from the Villanovan and Orientalizing periods, had to be a little further east to take advantage of the Reno/Setta/Sambro system. Traveling through the Futa Pass (903 masl) or the Giogo (882 masl), it was possible to reach the Mugello Valley and Fiesole, while through the Montepiano/Crocetta Pass (817 masl) one can again reach the plain of Sesto Fiorentino and Prato.

Extensions sent out by Kainua for the control of this strategic route toward Mugello can be identified in the "post station" of La Quercia (first settlement entering the Setta Valley, inhabited from the late sixth until the fourth century BCE)[7] and, on the southern border, in the town associated with the necropolis of Confienti near Castiglione de Pepoli and in the nearby votive deposit of Montorio/Monzuno (at the confluence of the Sambro with the Setta) and the even more famous and southern one of Monteacuto Ragazza straddling the Setta and Brasimone valleys. Here an important sacred area consisted of a 4 × 4 m stone enclosure with a well in which votive offerings were found, including fourteen bronze human figurines. The two best known, of excellent workmanship, represent a *kouros* and a *kore* and were most likely produced by a workshop in Tyrrhenian Etruria (fig. 5.1).

The inscription on a tall stone *cippus* found in the enclosure mentions an offerant named *Larth Veiane* and seems to refer to the city of Veii.[8] The recently discovered sacred area of Albagino[9] near Firenzuola represents one of the first Tuscan sites along this route. Consequently, the fourteen bronze statuettes found there are all stylistically very close to those of the "Marzabotto" and "Serravalle" groups (excluding a Late Archaic *kouros* that has ties to Rome and central-southern Latium).

Toward the east, the control of the city probably ceased before the Idice Valley, as the sixth–fifth century BCE settlement of Monterenzio, located on the ridge between this and the Sillaro Valley, seems to suggest. While exhibiting similarities with the Etruscan culture of Marzabotto, that of Monterenzio Vecchio seems closer to the Umbrian world.[10]

The territorial influence of Kainua to the west probably included the upper course of the Panaro and part of the Samoggia Valley, as evidenced by the villages of Monte Questiolo (near Zocca) and the necropoleis of Monteveglio to the north and Montese to the south. Kainua's control of the sites in the Panaro and Samoggia valleys appears more nuanced, however, as shown by the bronze figurines of Castello di Serravalle and the well-known sacred area of Lake Bracciano, near Montese. These statuettes indeed represent evolutionary variants of the "Marzabotto Group," probably influenced by samples from the Modena and Pistoia areas, and for this reason are called the "Serravalle" and "Montese" Groups.

At the center of the *chora* of Kainua is where, as expected, most of the traces of settlements and their ne-

FIGURE 5.1. Votive bronze statuettes of offerants from Monteacuto Ragazza, ca. 480 BCE. Inv. nos. MCABo 27816, 27820. Bologna, Civic Archaeological Museum. Courtesy of Museo Civico Archeologico, Bologna.

cropoleis can be found. These might be single farms (such as the one founded at the end of the sixth century BCE near the present cemetery of Sperticano) or arranged in groups, as evidenced by the (scattered or funerary) finds at Medelana, Panico, Pian di Venola, Sperticano, and Sibano. All these villages are located in the municipality of modern Marzabotto. They were preferably situated on terraces at the bottom of the valley near the left bank of the Reno and were therefore suitable for agro-pastoral activities intended to supply the city of Kainua. The villages a little further south, such as those related to the necropoleis of Raimondi/Vergato, Grizzana Morandi, Riola, and Archetta/Vimignano, must have had a similar function.

Some of the sites mentioned here (and others not cited)[11] are made up of votive deposits and sacred areas in which the most frequent donation is represented by bronzes of the "Marzabotto Group." These deposits, scattered along all the routes through the Apennine area, as well as representing places of worship for the travelers' protection, can also be considered "outposts" of the city of Kainua, which thus was able to place a sort of "seal" over its territory.

As stated, the real extent of the *chora* of Marzabotto is a complex and not yet fully clarified problem, especially since most of the sites mentioned here are known solely from surveys or bits of information from a rather limited literature. Only future excavations and research will be able to answer the question, although it is clear that an organized territory had to exist, if only because its urban and fully structured community defines itself as the *"spura"* of Kainua,[12] that is, as a city with its own political and institutional autonomy, which implied the control of a jurisdictional area.

CULTURAL CONNECTIONS

From this dense network of routes between the two areas straddling the Apennines, active since the Villanovan age (and earlier), a multiplicity of short and long-range material and cultural connections arise.[13] Contacts toward the south with the towns of the Arno Valley were particularly intense, evidence of a real "*koinè* of the northern Apennines"[14] and, through these, with all the major cities of Tyrrhenian Etruria. The routes seen so far were only those to the south, but Kainua was perfectly inserted into a wider "Etruria Padana system" of medium and wide-ranging routes, controlled by Bologna and linked with the northern regions of Italy and the trans-Alpine world on the one hand and, through the ports on the Adriatic, with the Greek world on the other. In addition to the main north–south axis that exploited the Reno Valley up to Felsina, there was also an east–west axis, which, through the adjacent valleys, joined a route through the foothills that linked Kainua to Romagna on one side and western Emilia on the other.

Regarding the aforementioned cultural connections resulting from the importation of raw materials and finished products, as a first case we can indicate that of the marble of the Apuan Alps, because it allows us to add in another route not mentioned until now. Through the tributary of the Reno called Limentra di Sambuca, or through the Prunetta branch of the Reno itself, one can reach the Pistoia area. Then, going through the Oppio Pass (821 masl) and following the course of the Lima, one can reach the Serchio Valley, which led directly to the major centers of the district of Pisa and the rich marble deposits of the Apuan Alps. Old and new research[15] on the types of marble used in Marzabotto shows that, in addition to Greek marble, many of the local monuments are made of Apuan marble. These include all the tombstones in the form of a bulb/pinecone (including the known one with a square base adorned with ram protomes; *see fig. 14.4d*),[16] indicating a complex network of connections with Pisa that even involved the workshops of Volterra and Chiusi. The spread of bulbous stones perfectly follows the route of Apuan marble into Etruria Padana, as shown by samples from the necropolis of Archetta (located, significantly, at the confluence of the Limentra into the Reno), Raimondi near Vergato,[17] Marzabotto, Sasso Marconi, and, finally, Bologna.

This route is also important because it had to follow the "*via etrusca del ferro*" (Etruscan iron road) connecting with the mining region of Etruria and its rich veins of iron, copper, and other metals. The participation of Volterra and Chiusi in this network of relationships demonstrates that the trade routes were numerous and complex, since from Vetulonia and Populonia it was possible to reach Pisa and then to go up the river Arno to reach the district of Fiesole. But there were internal routes through Volterra and the Era or Pesa valleys and internal byways, such as that of the Ombrone Valley connecting with the Chiusi area. From Chiusi and the other cities of central Etruria, the Tiber route connected to the southern metropolises, while by going up through the Chiana Valley and Arezzo (passing the ford of Florence) one can reach Fiesole and then the Po Valley. The mining region of Etruria was also connected, by sea and land, to the major centers of southern Etruria, thus explaining the complex network of relationships that, through Kainua, connected Felsina to the major centers of Etruria.

Along the "Etruscan iron road" both raw materials and finished products arrived in Kainua. Extant grave goods include rich sets of bronze vases intended for the symposium, such as *situlae, stamnoi, simpula,* and *kyathoi,* as well as mirrors and *candelabra* with precious crowning statuettes (*see plate 5 and figs. 16.5; 18.2h*). Alongside imported vases, preferably from Vulci (the most important Etruscan bronze manufacturing center) and internal Etruria, a thriving local industry began toward the late sixth century BCE.[18] Marzabotto is, in fact, in the ideal intermediate position between the metal routes from the south and the northern ones that brought trans-Alpine tin from areas such as the German Erzgebirge. The foundries of Kainua therefore began to produce bronzes for the local market and, above all, for export throughout northern Italy and the Celtic world, whose demand for luxury productions during the fifth century BCE was constantly growing, as shown by the richest burials in central-northern Europe.

As mentioned, mainly raw materials such as metals and marble arrived in the Po Valley from the south. Marbles, especially the Parian variety, also came from Greece, thanks to Athenian merchants who docked at the ports of Adria[19] and later Spina. It is no coincidence that only Greek marble is found in Spina, and both types in Felsina, while in Kainua—as one might expect—Apuan marble prevails. Abundant Attic ceramics and Greek wine and oil amphoras[20] arrived in Spina, mainly in exchange for the cereals produced in the fertile Po Valley. From the mid-sixth century BCE onward there was a marked increase of Attic ceramics that reached Marzabotto via the internal routes of the Po Valley. From here such pottery was probably redistributed toward the south, helping to satisfy the massive demand of the Etruscan metropolises for prestigious ceramics. One part of these goods was destined for the northern Etruria market, as the Attic ceramics of Gonfienti seem to suggest.[21] For the Greek amphoras, instead, the routes were slightly different: while in the center of Forcello near Mantova there are thousands of sherds of transport amphoras,[22] the numbers at Kainua are clearly lower and probably denote a use limited to domestic consumption. The small urban center of Forcello, strategically located at the confluence of the Mincio with the Po, must have been a freight sorting center for Greek wine destined for export to the rich Celtic market, as indicated by the large deposits produced by the crushing of amphoras, whose contents were poured into wooden barrels. Analysis of the transport amphoras found in Marzabotto,[23] however, reveals the high economic capacity and the varied taste of its community, as attested by the chronological and typological variety of the amphoras, including Corinthian A and B, North Aegean, Chiote, Solokha I, and Samo-Milesian (fig. 5.2).

Some rare Corinthian and Etrusco-Corinthian ceramic imports from the first half of the sixth century BCE[24] indicate a certain degree of frequentation of the plateau and therefore the early inclusion of Kainua in the flow of Greek ceramics from Tyrrhenian Etruria and from here conveyed to Felsina.[25] The centers of the district of Fiesole must have been included in these streams, as evidenced by a well-known ivory *pyxis* (fig. 5.3),[26] found in the well of *plateia* D at Marzabotto and most likely produced by a workshop of the middle Arno Valley during the Late Orientalizing period.

We have to wait until about 540 BCE, however, to find a conspicuous increase in imports from Athens,[27] flanked by a smaller quantity of Laconian, Chalcidian, and East Greek productions, probably conveyed by Athenian merchants. Little is known of this first occupation of the Pian di Misano,[28] but the presence of these imports, including very refined examples (*see figs. 15.2–15.3*), such as the Siana cups, those of the Little Masters, and the parade cups, helps to demonstrate that even before the foundation (or refoundation)[29] of the end of the sixth century BCE, Marzabotto was a trade center of some importance. Already from the first imports of figured ceramics, it is also clear that they were not considered luxury goods, but that the "world of images"[30] they conveyed was fully understood and functional in relation to the communicative needs of the urban elite, both in the funerary and the sacred/residential sphere.

Further evidence of this first urban phase of the second half of the sixth century BCE, the so-called Marzabotto II,[31] is also the growing flow of imports from Tyrrhenian Etruria, mostly represented by bucchero.[32] These are mainly symposium shapes, deriving above all from the districts of Chiusi and Orvieto. These productions, since the late sixth century BCE, had influenced the beginning of a local production that includes chalices, *kantharoi/kyathoi*, *kylikes*, and carinated cups (fig. 5.4).

The latter have many affinities with the products of the middle Arno Valley. Among these, the carinated cups with an externally enlarged rim, emphasized by one or two grooves, very close to local taste, are found until the fourth century BCE and therefore had a remarkable and enduring success.[33] The other drinking vases mentioned had a shorter lifespan, limited to the second half of the sixth through the first decades of the fifth century BCE. Evidently local taste, rather than referring to the vases more linked to the Tyrrhenian tradition, preferred drinking cups of the local tradition, such as cups/bowls and small jars/beakers. The chalice, which continues to be widespread—albeit to a lesser extent—in Marzabotto and the rest of the Po Valley, is an exception. This anomaly is explained because the chalice is adapted to local shapes, losing the classic decoration with three grooves on the lip and opening the basin, to meet and merge with the Villanovan and Orientalizing tradition of stemmed plates.[34]

Of particular interest are the aforementioned Etrusco-Corinthian imports and the subsequent ones of Etruscan figured ceramics and with ornamental

FIGURE 5.2. Corinthian trade amphora, 580–540 BCE. After Govi 2007:60.

FIGURE 5.3. Ivory lid of a *pyxis* in form of chariot with human figures, horses, and felines, 620–580 BCE. After Govi 2007:10.

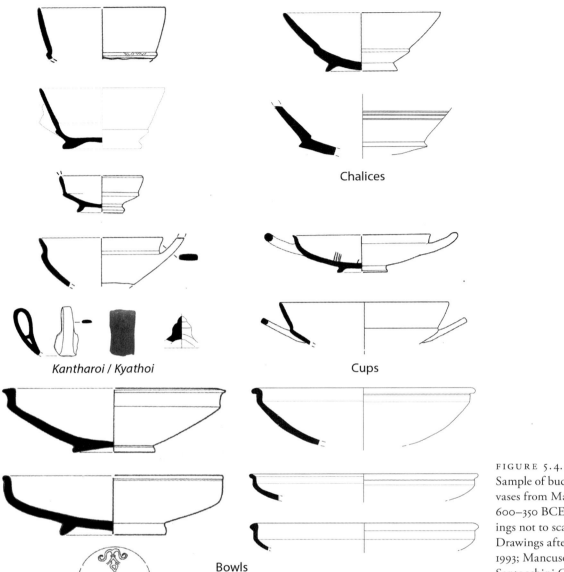

FIGURE 5.4. Sample of bucchero vases from Marzabotto, 600–350 BCE (drawings not to scale). Drawings after Malnati 1993; Mancuso 2022; Santocchini Gerg 2022.

friezes (such as the "Pattern Class Vases"[35] of Orvieto and Chiusi), which inherit their subsidiary decorative tradition. Widespread in the second half of the sixth century BCE both in the Po Valley and in the middle Valdarno,[36] these fine ceramics provided the model for the birth, in this milieu straddling the Apennines, of the class of fine ware with linear decoration (the most widespread, defined "*ceramica etrusco-padana*" north of the Apennines).[37] The fine-ware pottery of Etruria Padana accepts not only linear geometric motifs such as lines, stripes, bands, and waves, but also the characteristic tongue/pod shapes (*linguette/baccellature*) and some palmettes and rosettes typical of Late Archaic figured and painted pottery with ornamental motifs from internal Etruria. Not only are all these decorative elements accepted, but also their compositional syntax.[38] More particular motifs, such as the tridents and the series of sinuous ornaments (spirals, volutes, and S-shaped motifs) are also characteristic and widespread above all in Emilia and in the middle Valdarno; the tree pattern (*alberello/ramo secco*) directly refers to the district of Chiusi.[39] The tableware that most frequently adopts these ornamental friezes is made up of *oinochoai*, *ollae/stamnoi*, mortar basins, and beakers (fig. 5.5).

This point invites us to consider them as part of an alternative and more everyday symposium set than the sumptuous ones in bronze or Attic ceramics. The *oinochoai*/jugs are very significant, in particular the trefoiled and oblique beak ones, which present the richest decorations in the entire Po Valley repertoire. They best exemplify the close connections with central-northern Etruria, not only in the decoration, but also in the shape itself. We can, in fact, observe that they derive from a long and noble tradition recalling bronze jugs[40] produced along the Vulci–Orvieto–Chiusi axis in the second half of the sixth century BCE.[41] It is possible that some of the fifth-century BCE trilobate Po Valley jugs also imitate Attic models. This is less important since these Attic *oinochoai* are mainly produced for the Etruscan market and imitate in turn (for the Etruscan clientele) the jugs of the same tradition,[42] as shown by their chronology, not prior to the second quarter of the fifth century BCE.

As a final chronological and emblematic case study, we can mention the importation of black-gloss ceramics,[43] which once again underline the strong, enduring connections with the territories of Chiusi and Volterra, that is, with the main centers connecting to central Etruria and the mining region. Alongside examples in Attic black-gloss we find imports from Volterra and Chiusi, from the Late Archaic period—with examples of Etruscan black-figure ceramics from Marzabotto and other Po Valley centers[44]—until at least the end of the fourth century BCE. These imports also influenced the birth of a local production that began in the second quarter of the fifth century BCE, imitating Attic models, but inserting influences from the Tyrrhenian and local traditions. The phenomenon becomes particularly evident around the middle of the fourth century BCE, when imports of Attic ceramics almost completely cease,[45] and imports from Chiusi and—above all—from Volterra significantly increase. The wide diffusion of the black-gloss and overpainted ceramics of Volterra shows that their main market was, in fact, the Po Valley,[46] with Kainua playing a strategic intermediary role in transmission to the north. Particularly interesting are the figured and overpainted ceramics of the second half of the fourth century BCE,[47] which see Marzabotto still participating in wide-ranging networks that connect the Etruscans and the new La Tène culture groups of the Po Valley with the district of Fiesole, Volterra, and other cities of central and southern/Tiberine Etruria.

All these connections demonstrate a certain vitality of the Reno/Setta[48] route at this chronological stage, that is, the phase in which the main route moves further east, along the Idice Valley and the Etruscan-Celtic centers of Monterenzio and Monte Bibele.[49] Furthermore, if we consider that the black-gloss productions of Volterra during this advanced phase seem to incorporate formal and decorative influences from the Po Valley, one could suggest the hypothesis that trans-Apennine artisans moved to northern Etruria as

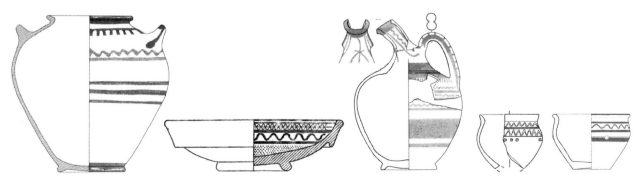

FIGURE 5.5. Sample of decorated local pottery: *olla*, basin, jug, and beakers, 500–350 BCE. After Santocchini Gerg 2013: fig. 5.

a result of Gallic pressure.⁵⁰ These new interpretative ideas could thus throw new light on the destiny of the populations of Etruria Padana in the Late Iron Age.

CONCLUSIONS

All the data presented here show that Kainua's *spura* is a complex and very specific socioeconomic reality, whose material culture, as summarized here, presents traits that refer to internal and southern Etruria on the one hand, and to Bologna and other centers of the Po Valley on the other. As mentioned, the main connections to the south are linked to two areas in particular: the district of Fiesole and through this to inland Etruria with Chiusi and Orvieto, and to the mining region of Etruria through the territories of Pisa and Volterra. In addition to the obvious supply of metals, Kainua is linked to this area—for example—by the common tradition of funerary *cippi*, distinctive markers of the sepulchral landscape and community identity. The material culture, in particular ceramic production, is instead more linked to the first area. These links are particularly evident starting from the Late Orientalizing period, when the new figurative culture of Chiusi focuses on the Orientalizing bestiary syntactically organized in a paratactic sense and on overlapping registers. This form will profoundly influence the language of the main artistic manifestations of northern Italy, such as the *situlae* art and the stone sculptures (first the Orientalizing ones and then the Felsinian *stelae*).⁵¹ In the Archaic and Late Archaic periods, as mentioned above, the imports of bucchero and ceramics that were figured or decorated with ornamental motifs look to Chiusi and Orvieto. Both classes had strong influences in local ceramics, in particular in the decorative apparatus of the most widespread and identifying production of the Po area, the "*ceramica etrusco-padana.*"

This openness to the Tyrrhenian world, even its most distant southern area, is well represented by the dimension of the sacred,⁵² with the two monumental urban temples and the five on the Acropolis, which compete in shape and size with the most famous sanctuaries of Tyrrhenian Etruria. In fact, it is necessary to move to Vulci and Cerveteri to find the best architectural comparisons. Such care and political-economic commitment cannot be explained only by the hospitality and prayer needs of the numerous travelers and merchants who stopped in the city, but had to imply and underline a precise institutional program of self-representation of the *spura*, a real "monumental" political manifesto of community and identity values.

This peculiarity is demonstrated also by inscriptions. In fact, these are mainly in the northern writing system, but with many influences of southern Etruria writing practices, different from the other centers of Etruria Padana.⁵³

Obviously, Kainua also looks to the north, being part of the "political system" that managed the commercial traffic that involved the major centers of Etruria Padana, in which Felsina plays a leading role. In this sense the funerary organization of Kainua is paradigmatic. The material and ideological composition of its grave goods shares the system of values of the leading groups in Bologna,⁵⁴ while the sepulchral landscape decisively departs from it. In Marzabotto it is dominated exclusively by burial *cippi* that refer to northern Etruria, taking on opposite forms (almost in a political sense) compared to those of Bologna, where the figured funerary *stelae* prevail.

Evidently its strategic pivotal position between these southern and northern worlds has profoundly influenced and characterized its cultural features, so much so that Kainua can no longer be defined as a simple outpost dependent on Felsina. Looking at two different worlds, Kainua demonstrates an autonomy that only the most recent studies are highlighting,⁵⁵ and which is perfectly reflected in its *spura* structure, a politically organized community equivalent to the *civitas*.

NOTES

1. Reduced to the current ca. 20 hectares due to the river bend, which caused the landslide of part of the plateau, including about a third of the ancient city.
2. See A. Curci and M. Carra, chapter 7 of this volume.
3. Colonna 1970; Brizzolara 2001.
4. The study of the population of the district of Marzabotto was based above all on the accurate topographical study

by M. Tirtei (Tirtei 2011–2012), to which reference should be made for all the sites mentioned below. See also Millemaci 1999 and T. Trocchi in chapter 6 of this volume.

5. See M. Tirtei, chapter 18 of this volume.

6. Ortalli 2002.

7. See P. Desantis, chapter 6 of this volume.

8. It is possible that the traditional interpretation referring to Veii is to be reconsidered, as the palaeography of local tradition and other clues seem to suggest (cf. A. Gaucci, chapter 10 of this volume).

9. Nocentini, Sarti, and Warden 2018.

10. Guerra et al. 2009.

11. See Miari 2000; Govi 2007:16–18; Tirtei 2011–2012.

12. See the two inscriptions where the term is attested (A. Gaucci in appendix A, nos. 6 and 9).

13. See Millemaci 1999; Sani 2009a; Santocchini Gerg 2012; Chellini 2013; Santocchini Gerg 2015; Cappuccini and Fedeli 2020; and T. Trocchi, in chapter 6 of this volume. For a first picture of the settlement of Prato-Gonfienti, whose excavation and study are ongoing, see Perazzi and Poggesi 2011.

14. Cf. Santocchini Gerg 2022 and the other papers in Cappuccini and Gaucci 2022.

15. Sassatelli 2017a, III, 1; Sassatelli and Mancuso 2017.

16. For the marble sculptures of Marzabotto see G. Mancuso, chapter 14 of this volume.

17. The burial stones of Archetta and Podere Raimondi, in particular the first, could be made of local sandstone, which is however evidence of this route and its control by Kainua.

18. See G. Morpurgo, chapter 12 of this volume.

19. The oldest imports of Attic ceramics from Adria date back to the second quarter of the sixth century (Giudice 2004: fig. 14).

20. Baldoni 2009; Desantis 2001; Lippolis 2000. For the amphoras from the residential area of Spina see also Sciortino 2012, with a list of over a hundred sherds of amphoras of a type not too dissimilar from those from Marzabotto, including oil Corinthian A, wine Corinthian B (the majority, with 57 percent of the total), Chiote, north Aegean, and Greco-italic amphoras.

21. Baldoni 2022; Millemaci and Poggesi 2004.

22. De Marinis 2007a.

23. De Marinis 2010; Desantis 2001; Sacchetti 2012.

24. Lippolis 2000:109–110.

25. It is probable that the Greek imports of the first half of the sixth century BCE arrived in the Po Valley through northern Etruria, where Ionic, Corinthian, and Laconian vases are attested. It is not excluded that part of these already arrived from the Adriatic market, in coastal towns such as Numana and Adria (see Baldoni 2022).

26. Desantis 2009.

27. See Baldoni 2009 and his essay in chapter 15 of this volume.

28. In addition to the aforementioned *pyxis* and Corinthian imports, also a large batch of dozens of bronze *fibulae* datable to the eighth–seventh centuries (most of them to the Late Orientalizing periods) attests this early phase (see Trocchi 2010 and Santocchini Gerg 2018:32–33n64).

29. See E. Govi, chapter 4 of this volume.

30. See V. Baldoni, chapter 15 of this volume.

31. See E. Govi, chapter 4 of this volume.

32. Malnati 1993; Forte 1993b; Santocchini Gerg 2022; and some unpublished sherds in Mancuso 2022.

33. Santocchini Gerg 2022.

34. Santocchini Gerg 2022.

35. See Schwarz 1979 (and Gaucci 2022 for Marzabotto). For the examples of the Po Valley see also E. Govi in Govi 2003, who had the merit of having first suggested the dependence of the local fine ware on these productions. This hypothesis was later confirmed by recent studies (see next note). Among the rare imports of the Pattern Class vases, in addition to those of Bologna, the cases of San Martino in Gattara in the Apennines of Ravenna and San Polo in the district of Reggio Emilia (Govi 2003:64) are very significant. In fact, these two finds perfectly outline the other two main connecting routes between northern Etruria and the Po Valley. The first follows the Tiberine route to Mugello and from here to Romagna, while the second one leads from the mining region of Etruria to western Emilia, via the Serchio/Secchia system (see Santocchini Gerg 2012; Santocchini Gerg 2022).

36. Cf. Santocchini Gerg 2012; Santocchini Gerg 2013; Santocchini Gerg 2022; Pelacci 2017.

37. See Mattioli 2013 and her essay in chapter 13 of this volume.

38. Santocchini Gerg 2013.

39. Santocchini Gerg 2013 and p. 531 for the "dry branch" (*albero secco*) motif, which I believe could be the stylized evolution of a palmette (cf. Santocchini Gerg 2013: fig. 6), as well exemplified by the production of Chianciano (Paolucci 2000: fig. 32–33).

40. In particular, the *Schnabel-* and *Plumpekannen* and the more average ceramic jugs of the Donati A type (Donati 1993).

41. See Mattioli 2013:284; Santocchini Gerg 2013:497.

42. In particular the Attic *oinochoai* form VII (see Donati 1993:251–263).

43. For further information, see Gaucci 2010; Gaucci 2022.

44. Govi 2003; Gaucci 2022.

45. Baldoni 2009:243–246.

46. See Gaucci 2010:54.

47. See Gaucci 2022.

48. The vitality, especially of the Setta Valley, during the fourth and third centuries BCE is demonstrated by the village of Monteacuto Ragazza and the necropolis of Confienti (see

T. Trocchi in chapter 6 of this volume). For similar considerations see also Morpurgo in chapter 19 of this volume.

49. Gottarelli 2017.
50. Cf. Gaucci 2022.
51. See Santocchini Gerg 2021 for the Orientalizing *stelae* and Govi 2015a for the Felsinian *stelae*.
52. See Govi 2017b and her essay in chapter 8 of this volume.

53. Cf. Gaucci in chapter 10 of this volume.
54. However, some significant differences with Bologna and Spina in the use of some vases, especially the Attic ones, can be noted (cf. chapter 16 of this volume).
55. Cf. chapters 1 and 4 of this volume.

CHAPTER 6

THE SETTLEMENT OF THE TERRITORY

TIZIANO TROCCHI* AND PAOLA DESANTIS**

THE TERRITORY
Tiziano Trocchi

The remarkable dynamism of the Reno Valley since the Iron Age is closely linked to the historico-cultural panorama in which the evidence relating to this territory is found.[1] At the beginning of the first millennium BCE, the entire Po Valley was subject to a complete transformation of its settlement structure, due to the progression of Etruscan expansion over most of the region, with Bologna-Felsina as the main center in Emilia.

The Reno, like its neighboring valleys, clearly belongs to the Bolognese sphere of influence (*see maps 2–3*). Already between the ninth and eighth centuries BCE, the early appearance in Bologna of a proto-urban center, characterized by a complex and organized plan,[2] determines the subsequent occupation of the surrounding territory, including the Apennine valleys. The settlement had a dual purpose: the exploitation of agro-pastoral resources and the establishment of safe communication and trade routes toward the Tyrrhenian area. Among these, the Reno Valley certainly played a leading role, partly because of its close proximity to the new Bologna-Felsina urban center, and partly due to the considerable extension and accessibility of the valley at different heights, both at low altitudes, where it was also widely exploited for agriculture and pastoralism, and along the ridges. The ridge routes, in particular, with their connection to the neighboring valleys of the Reno River tributaries, could easily connect the main north–south direction with both the western Etruria Padana, developing along the Samoggia[3] and Panaro valleys,[4] and, on the opposite side, the eastern valleys of the Savena and Idice rivers (*see map 3*).

As part of a gradual expansion, with Bologna as the driving force,[5] in an initial period defined as the first half of the eighth century BCE, mainly the lower and mid-valley levels were occupied. First of all, we find the crossroads settlement of Casalecchio di Reno. In fact, due to its strategic position between the urban area of Felsina and the communication route of the Reno Valley, it would, for a long time, remain a center of primary importance, both for exchanges with Tyrrhenian Etruria and for the development of crafts and production relating to metals and ceramics.[6] Alongside this settlement, there are reports of cremation finds datable to the first half of the eighth century BCE in Pontecchio Marconi, Sasso Marconi, and the town of Canovella, near Marzabotto.[7]

It is from the second half of the eighth century BCE onward that the gradual occupation of the Reno Valley experiences a new and more consistent development. In fact, starting from this phase and up to the seventh century is when the most important residential and funerary evidence in Casalecchio di Reno is found. It is in this area that aristocratic groups of

---

*Soprintendenza Archeologia, belle arti e paesaggio per la città metropolitana di Bologna e le province di Modena, Reggio Emilia e Ferrara; Archaeological, Fine Arts, and Landscape Superintendence of Bologna, Modena, Reggio Emilia, and Ferrara.

**Direzione Regionale Musei Emilia Romagna; Regional Museum Direction of Emilia Romagna.

high cultural and economic status settled, with artistic production closely linked to contemporary Bolognese evidence.[8]

Proceeding southward, the remains, all of a sepulchral nature, belonging to the period of the second half of the eighth and the seventh centuries BCE gradually become denser and of a rich level. In particular, still in the lower valley, we find the Orientalizing tombs from S. Biagio, 2 km south of Casalecchio di Reno, with a wooden coffin and rich grave goods including bronze and ceramic vessels.[9] Even the center of the Reno Valley is now enriched with settlements placed around the Marzabotto area. We refer in particular to the nucleus of graves found in Sperticano,[10] but above all to the necropolis of Pian di Venola, which indicates occupancy already in the first half of the eighth century BCE and continuity up to the seventh century BCE.[11] From this locality there are grave goods of the highest quality, again including bronze and ceramic vases (fig. 6.1).

These represent a clear Bolognese cultural matrix, highlighting increasingly solid infiltration along the valley by groups linked to Bologna, who preferred to settle in strategic points like this one, located at the entrance of the Venola Valley and easily usable as a means of reaching the western Etruscan sector, starting with the Samoggia Valley.

Within the context of the settlement dynamism described, there is also a series of finds in the upper Reno Valley. Its population is not of high density, but highlighted by small nuclei of tombs or simple traces of frequentation, indicating a constant and early interest in this territory and its potential, both for settlements and for trade routes. Mention can be made of four settlements, represented by the nuclei of Monteacuto Ragazza, at the place where the well-known Etruscan sanctuary would later rise, and of Montovolo Serra de' Coppi, Poggio della Gaggiola, and Monte della Croce. These settlements are located on high ground, and are designed to control roads that were perhaps already in use for commercial purposes, as alternative routes or as routes intersecting the main one. In fact, the first two sites can be connected to a possible ridge route to the east of the Reno River, reaching today's Pistoia territory to the south, through Treppio and the Fontana

FIGURE 6.1. Pian di Venola, Tomb A, bronze cista with embossed decoration in overlapping registers with quadrupeds and equine protome friezes, 675–650 BCE. Photo: SABAP Bologna Archive.

Taona Pass, and going halfway up to Sperticano in the north, to reach the mid- and lower valley sites. The other two centers—Poggio della Gaggiola and Monte della Croce—could well have controlled routes along the valley floor, since they were positioned on opposite sides of the Reno River, basically in visual contact with each other.

This brief overview (*see map 3*) suggests the early formation of an itinerant settlement network along the Reno Valley, integrating settlements of the mid- and lower valley with centers on higher ground, strategically placed to constitute a system capable of controlling and managing exchanges between Tyrrhenian Etruria and the Po Valley.

When examining the developments from the second half of the sixth century, we need to narrow down our field of observation. Regarding the settlement arrangements of the Reno Valley, the essential phenomenon during this phase, within the general reorganization of the Etruscan territories of the Po Valley,[12] is the rise of the great Etruscan city in Marzabotto. The importance of this foundation is well known, with its multiple and complex socioeconomic and cultural implications, linked to the role of nearby Felsina. Here we will limit ourselves to considering the evidence relating to the upper Reno Valley and its area (*see map 3*).

In this context we should first mention some graves, found in the nineteenth and the twentieth centuries near the valley floor at Riola[13] in the locality of Cantaiola, on the left bank of the Reno, and Archetta on the right, shortly after its confluence with the Limentra River. The grave goods—especially the two bronze spool *kyathoi* of Cantaiola (fig. 6.2)—were certainly of a quality comparable to the funerary deposits of Marzabotto during the fifth century BCE.

To these we can add some information on Etruscan tombs at Oreglia, a grave found in Vimignano, also dating back to the fifth century BCE, and a bronze statuette of remarkable craftsmanship discovered in the locality of Prada. These findings already show that the upper valley was actively involved in trade, now firmly controlled by Kainua. The two centers located near Riola are significant evidence of this. They are clearly placed in control of a crucial crossroads for exchanges between two valleys (the Limentra and the Reno) which opened the route, through the Collina Pass and the Ombrone Valley, to the Tyrrhenian side, corresponding to the current territory of Pistoia. This settlement dynamic, which shows a strong link between the territory and the urban center located in the middle of the valley, clearly supported the development of local communities of considerable economic status, as evidenced by funeral rites with an urban flavor that were fully inserted into the *koiné* of Etruria Padana.

Also, in this phase, other secondary or alternative traffic routes were flanked by the *Via della Valle del Reno*. Among these, the route offered by the Setta Valley must have played a leading role, since it has yielded a series of finds from the period from the end of the sixth to the beginning of the fourth century BCE. These discoveries indicate the development, also on this slope, of a complex network of secondary routes, mainly along the river and stream valleys.[14] First, we are aware of at least three deposits of votive bronzes.[15] The first nucleus of seven small bronzes comes from the locality of Montorio, on the ridge between the Setta and the Sambro, its left tributary. A second group of two statuettes, one of which is a female with a mantle and *tutulus* hat, comes from the vicinity of the present-day town of Burzanella, located in the valley of the Brasimone stream, a left tributary of the Setta River. A third group of bronzes is believed to have been found[16] in the church of Castiglione dei Pepoli. All the cases cited are specimens pertaining to the well-known class of Etrusco-Italic schematic human-shaped *ex-votos*, collected in the "Marzabotto Group."[17] They generally date to the period from the end of the sixth to the end of the fourth century BCE and result from a standardized production, intended for medium- to long-range marketing. The data on the early presence in the Setta Valley is confirmed by the presence of the well-known settlement of Sasso Marconi[18] in a position of control of the confluence be-

FIGURE 6.2. Cantaiola, Riola di Vergato, bronze *kyathos*, around 450 BCE. Bologna, Civic Archaeological Museum. Courtesy of Museo Civico Archeologico, Bologna.

tween the Reno and Setta. Further evidence consists of the discovery of a large settlement in the Setta Valley, at the locality of La Quercia, which developed at the same time as the main phases of expansion of the city of Kainua, which will be discussed further later in this chapter.[19]

The role of this sector is further clarified if we consider the later findings from Confienti, along the upper Setta Valley at the confluence with the Brasimone stream. These are two graves recovered in 1881 during the construction of the valley floor road.[20] The location of the site, reported in archival documents, has allowed us to hypothesize that the two tombs were part of a larger burial ground. The latter must have belonged to an inhabited area, perhaps placed at the top of the small promontory between the two rivers, in a position of control in both directions. The materials discovered are exceptional for their high quality, as well as for the wide chronological period to which they can be assigned,[21] from the middle of the fourth to the beginning of the third century BCE. In this period, a community with considerable economic capacity and a high cultural level must have settled in this locality, judging by the funerary rituals.

The central position of the area between the upper Reno Valley and the Setta Valley is finally highlighted by the location of the important Etruscan sanctuary of Monteacuto Ragazza. This site was accidentally identified in the late nineteenth century and investigated several times, first under the direction of G. Gozzadini and then by E. Brizio.[22] Well-known evidence was recovered here, relating to a sanctuary active at least from the sixth century BCE. The documentation of the first excavations reveals the presence of a place of worship, structured as an hypethral enclosure open to the sky. Inside, a sacred well has been identified, in which fourteen votive bronze statuettes were recovered.[23] Seven of these belong to the category of schematic bronzes, possibly produced locally, while another five, dating from the first or second quarter of the fifth century BCE, are to be attributed to an average level production in northern Etruria. The two most prominent examples of the group are the two largest offering figures, a male and a female (*see fig. 5.1*). They are considered products of remarkable quality, representative of the Late Archaic stylistic trends present in northern Etruria at the beginning of the fifth century BCE.[24] Some carved stone bases come from the proximity of the well. One of these can perhaps be attributed to an altar, and the others interpreted as supports for *ex-votos*, as well as a sandstone *cippus* with a votive inscription in the Etruscan language, dating back to the first half of the fifth century BCE.[25]

More recent research conducted at Monteacuto Ragazza[26] has unearthed the presence of residential buildings, dating to the period from the middle of the fourth to the second half of the third century BCE. Therefore, the prevalent sacred function can be attributed to the oldest period of the site, from the sixth to the middle of the fourth century BCE, alongside the role of controlling the territory and the trade routes at that time. Later, this function would have at least in part fallen into disuse, leading to the intentional burial of the bronzes in the sacred well and its closure—leaving room for an inhabited area, with masonry buildings. It is no coincidence that this change in the settlement modality of Monteacuto, albeit in a substantial cultural continuity, occurs at the same time as the aforementioned flourishing of the Confienti settlement, located not far away, on the Setta Valley floor.

The context outlined above leads us to think that the Setta Valley route, in use for some time, probably flourished from the fourth century BCE and enjoyed a certain prosperity at least until the end of the third century BCE, with new settlements in a strategic position to control the trade routes. This route could easily have led across the Futa Pass to the Fiesole area and, by means of the Bisenzio Valley, through the Montepiano Pass to the Prato area, where the Etruscan center of Gonfienti, which developed from the second half of the sixth century BCE, is well known.

The enhancement of an alternative route to the Reno Valley—at least in the upper part—must surely be related to the crisis of the great Etruscan center of Marzabotto, starting from the second half of the fourth century BCE, due to widespread Celtic invasions across most of the region. It is no coincidence that the contemporary decline of one settlement, such as that of

La Quercia, probably linked to the agro-pastoral economic organization of the territory, is counterbalanced by the flourishing of settlements with a clear and marked strategic and itinerant nature, like that of Confienti or the last phase of the Monteacuto site. It is a sign of change in a territory that seems to be reorganizing itself and does not completely renounce its role in favor of the more popular eastern routes, such as the one extended along the Idice Valley and connected to the Etruscan-Celtic settlements of Monterenzio and Monte Bibele.

THE SETTLEMENT OF "LA QUERCIA"
Paola Desantis

An exceptional discovery in the locality of La Quercia (Marzabotto, Bologna) was made during work on the Apennine crossing section of the A1 motorway between Sasso Marconi and Barberino del Mugello, the "Variante di Valico," and due to the care taken during the archaeological rescue operation, its findings can be considered exemplary.[27]

The area, at the confluence of the Rio Quercia and the Setta River, has a morphology particularly suited to human settlement, since it is a vast river terrace, about 10 meters above the plain of the flow of the Setta (fig. 6.3). The plateau, which occupies a slope from the mountain to the valley of about 12 meters, is set on the alluvial deposits of the stream below. The excavation made it possible to bring to light the organization and structure of an Etruscan settlement, located on the flatter part of the slope, which constitutes the left bank, facing east, of the Setta River on the southern slopes of Monte Sole.

The settlement is made up of a considerable number of large structures, built with a technique that involved wall footings in rough sandstone topped by elevations and roofs in perishable materials (*opus craticium*). The buildings, which have variable orientations linked to the conformation of the slope, had to be built on sloping levels, all facing east-southeast.

The almost total absence of clay roofing elements[28] suggests a prevalence of wooden and thatched roofs. All the walls, about 0.50 m wide, consist of two flanked rows of stones, only sometimes slightly regularized, in the same drystone technique, with the use of clay as a binder.

The buildings, of which the excavation revealed there to be five (*see plate 17*), occupy the slope, artificially leveled in some points, and follow an arrangement that leaves unoccupied spaces between one area and another, even of considerable size.

Protection of the town from the erosive effects of water coming from the hills behind had to be ensured by what is probably the most characterizing element of the site: a sophisticated water management system, created by combining elements of a different nature and consistency. In fact, water containment must have been one of the main concerns of the inhabitants, as shown by the large channel and the other installations, such as numerous smaller channels as well as two cobblestone basins found in different positions on the site. The persistence of this geomorphological terrain in this same locality seems significant, if one considers that it is still today included in the groundwater protection area.

The existence of productive activities of a certain importance in the settlement is indicated by the discovery of at least five kilns, variously located and surely used for domestic or artisanal purposes.

The considerable amount of materials found allows us to identify the greatest expansion of the site to precisely the fifth century BCE, while traces of the original phase of the urban plan date to the end of the sixth and those of a subsequent temporary and itinerant occupation date to about the middle of the fourth century BCE.

The five large structures found have medium–large rooms, arranged in a row. In at least two cases, the longitudinal development of the building overlooks a large adjoining courtyard space, bordered to the south by a long stone wall.

STRUCTURE 1

Structure 1, located in the easternmost sector of the plateau, is certainly the most interesting among those investigated. In fact, it offers the opportunity to observe a complete plan, which also allows us to reconstruct the internal passages between one room and another. In

FIGURE 6.3. La Quercia, the plateau from the north during the excavations; to the east, the River Setta. Photo: SABAP Bologna Archive.

addition, the water drainage system, which runs along the whole upstream side of the building and then conveys the water downstream, appears to be accurate.

Its rectangular shape (18 × 8.50 m) is the result of the juxtaposition of several rooms of different size. The southernmost room (room A) is of considerable importance, possibly the one built first, to which others were added side by side. In this room, covered by at least four colluvial layers, traces of the collapse of the perimeter wall and of the wooden roof with interlocking beams have emerged, burnt in a fire. Near the middle of the room, a lightweight clay partition has been identified, with traces of at least one hole for a wooden post with a quadrangular section still *in situ*, in a lateral load-bearing position, together with a covering made with the wattle and daub method. Under the collapsed roof and above the reddened ground level, a lower section appears, paved with a wooden plank, as well as the remains of a collapsed and burnt wooden door and a sandstone slab, which must be interpreted as an access step. As for the door, consisting of four longitudinal boards connected with traverse wooden dowels, the hinging system at the west end of the partition, formed by a small upright, was also found.

Along the upstream side of the building, there is a well-structured and deep channel for rainwater drainage. It is laid in counter-slope toward the mountain and, with a bold and massively reinforced elbow bend, conveys the water downstream toward a narrow conduit and then toward a settling tank.

The final phase of use of this structure is particularly evident, in which its functions have changed and, in all probability, been impoverished and deconstructed. The channel, deliberately filled with the *concotto* (baked-clay floor) of the previous elevations, now appears completely abandoned.

STRUCTURE 2

To the west of this, there is a second building, which measures 25 × 10 meters overall. It consists of four flanking rooms overlooking an elongated room, clearly with the function of corridor-portico. The latter faces a large courtyard area, of about 650 square meters, located at a lower level and open downstream toward the Setta River. In the portion of this complex further downstream, a series of rooms have been discovered that delimit the large open area to the south and offer new interpretative possibilities to the proposed housing model.

The discovery in this sector of a row of circular weights, with two spools placed at one end, buried by a large number of fragments of *concotto*, allows us to hypothesize the onetime presence of a vertical wooden loom.[29]

STRUCTURES 4 AND 5

Structures 4 and 5, at the western end of the settlement, have a similar plan. They consist of two or three rooms side by side, of different lengths, but with the same depth, which overlook a single elongated space, possibly interpreted as a corridor-portico, similar to that of the structure 2.

These two structures are separated by a longitudinal channel for water containment, created in the last phase of use of the building. The need to contain the runoff from the slope clearly was present even at the time of the settlement, as evidenced by the cistern found downstream of the structures, datable to that first phase.

STRUCTURE 3

Structure 3, in the central part of the site, close to the slope, appears to be characterized by spaces with a strongly incomplete plan, whose destruction is certainly due to a more direct washout. Only a large rectangular room, which has yielded fragments of wooden furniture, remains in its entirety and, a little further to the south, there is a much smaller room with the remains of a hearth.

Its particular position close to the great channel, the presence of a channel parallel to the upstream wall structures, and the existence of an additional channel crossing the porch of the building confirm the commitment of the local community to the management of water.

The mastery of water control is revealed especially by the presence of the great system of channels. This is absolutely the most characterizing element of the site: it crosses the settlement longitudinally and had to ensure its protection from the erosive effects of the colluvial waters coming from the hills behind. There is a large channel, completely covered with flat river cobblestones, toward which converge small drainage channels of modest flow, also roofed in cobblestones, indicating a sophisticated water management system consisting of well-structured elements of a different nature and consistency.

The investigation revealed the characteristics and different phases of construction of this large channel, over 20 meters long, which crosses the site. It was possible to detect the natural origin of the channel, which, even before the human modification of the area, was aligned with a recess in the slope upstream of the town and directed the rainwater naturally into its bed. The natural channel, probably in a phase contemporary to the great expansion of the site, was then regulated, covering its bottom and banks with river stones. The importance of keeping the duct fully functioning is also revealed by the presence of clear re-excavations and rearrangements of its bed. A series of small channels dug into the ground, coated with cobblestones and with a lithic covering, can be connected to this impressive hydraulic work.

As a further demonstration of the hydraulic mastery of the Etruscans, it should be emphasized that, after this discovery, the Autostrade Company had to move the position of a large sewer used to manage the disposal of the water downstream, as it was in the same position chosen by the Etruscans for this important channeling system.

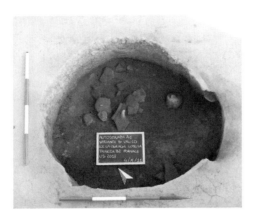

FIGURE 6.4. La Quercia, kiln by the north side of structure 1. fifth century BCE. Photo: SABAP Bologna Archive.

PRODUCTIVE FACILITIES

Five kilns were found in the settlement in various locations, three in the northern sector of Structure 1 (fig. 6.4), one north of Structure 2, and one south of Structure 3. All of the furnaces have a similar structure, characterized by a stoking channel (*praefurnium*), a combustion chamber, and a firing chamber with a perforated floor. In the two best-preserved kilns, the supporting pillar of the perforated floor was also found, in one case still *in situ* and in the other dismantled and abandoned in the *praefurnium*. The furnaces were found completely filled with large number of fragments of *concotto* and ceramics resulting from work carried out near the kilns themselves. In addition, the considerable amount of processing residues around, such as coal, fragments of *concotto* and ceramics, and several portions of the dismantled vault, provide clear evidence of the repeated use of the structures.

CONCLUDING REMARKS

The data obtained from the study of the materials and from the stratigraphic analysis make it clear that the main development of the settlement at La Quercia dates to the fifth century BCE. This is the reference date *ante* and *post quem* respectively, for its initial phase of life, as well as for its subsequent occasional occupation, particularly evident in Structure 1. A further phase must be added to this last stage of inhabitancy, which coincides with a moment of evident implosion of the settlement, dated to the fourth century BCE. In fact, the latter phase corresponds to the definitive abandonment of the site, to which the various collapse events and *colluvium* deposits that covered the archaeological evidence can be traced.

The dynamics of the building and the expansion of each structure are evident in the stratigraphy. In fact, during their maximum expansion, they propose a pattern that recalls the model of the dwelling with a long sidewall overlooking open spaces and divided into a series of rooms in a line. This plan, which refers to a type of "longhouse" common from the sixth century BCE onward, appears characteristic of areas with a low population density. It is basically the same pattern that we find, albeit in less developed forms, in the plain at the mouth of the Reno River[30] and in the *chora* of Adria.[31] Moreover, other examples exist in northern Etruria[32] and refer, in the context of rural building typology, to type B,[33] with lateral development and an open entrance on the long side of the structure.

In La Quercia there is also a clear reference to building typologies with two or more adjacent rooms opening onto a narrow courtyard and provided with a *portico*, such as those found in southern Italy from the sixth century BCE.

The elongated structures of La Quercia, which we could compare to the type of Greek *pastas*,[34] as already proposed for numerous similar cases, represent a clear example of the affirmation, also in the north, of the development along the latitudinal axis of the structures: the new house no longer presents a façade on the short side but on the long one, with the main entrance in the center of this side.

The discovery of the new settlement of La Quercia, located exactly south of Marzabotto, at the junction of the route that probably connected the ancient city and therefore the Reno Valley to the banks of the Setta, sheds new light on the Etruscans of the area. In fact, it offers objective data of extraordinary importance for reconstructing the territorial occupation strategies implemented by the Etruscans of Kainua.

The elements of material culture found on the site[35]

present a village characterized by a subsistence economy, basically an agricultural and pastoral model. If the rarity of imported products, such as precious Attic and Etruscans ceramics, leads to the exclusion of a commercial vocation, it is still certain that this small settlement, originating and developing thanks to its optimal position along one of the principal connecting routes between Etruria Padana and Tyrrhenian Etruria, has a function strictly linked to that of the main attraction of the area, even as regards its own end. In fact, the fall of the Etruscan center of Kainua, due to Celtic invasions and the consequent collapse of the trading system connected to it, significantly coincides with the end of the village of La Quercia, where the archaeological evidence does not indicate destruction, but rather a slow abandonment. In this last phase, the houses were also used as shelters for animals, while the forest gradually reclaimed the entire area.[36]

NOTES

1. For an overview of the topic and references, see Govi 2019b.
2. For an overview of the topic and references, see Guidi and Marchesi 2019.
3. On the occupation of the Samoggia Valley during the Iron Age, see Trocchi 2002; Burgio 2009.
4. For a summary of the population of the Panaro Valley in the early Iron Age, see Locatelli 2009.
5. Sassatelli 2009b:28.
6. For a summary of the archaeological evidence of Casalecchio di Reno, see Ortalli 2002.
7. Scarani 1963:441–445.
8. Kruta Poppi 2009.
9. Von Eles 1987.
10. Vitali 1982.
11. Sani 2009b.
12. Sassatelli 2005; Sassatelli 2008a; Sassatelli 2017b.
13. For these findings and those below, see Scarani 1963.
14. For an overall view, see Trocchi 1999.
15. For bibliographic and archival sources (Archive of the Archaeological Civic Museum of Bologna, hereinafter A.M.C.B.) and for the Confienti website: Trocchi 1999.
16. The A.M.C.B. document dated 1879 refers to bronze "idols" found in a renovation of the church in 1650.
17. Colonna 1970.
18. See Tirtei in chapter 18 of this volume.
19. See below in this chapter P. Desantis, "The Settlement of 'La Quercia.'"
20. Gozzadini 1881:600.
21. For a complete catalog of materials, see Peyre 1965.
22. For a complete review of the bibliographic and archival sources relating to the development and results of excavation campaigns starting from 1882 and for a report of the most recent archaeological investigations, see Lippolis, Pini, and Sani 1998.
23. Sassatelli 1984.
24. Cristofani 1985b.
25. See chapter 10.
26. Lippolis, Pini, and Sani 1998:84–86.
27. I would like once again to express my heartfelt thanks to Luigi Malnati, Superintendent Archaeologist of Emilia-Romagna at the time, who guided me in the direction of this complex excavation with his perceptive observations. I again thank the Autostrade Company that financed it and Kora s.r.l., which executed it with great scientific, technical, and management commitment and, in particular, I would like to thank Alessandro Albertini, Laura Casadei, and Paola Poli. For references, see Desantis 2016; Desantis, Manzoli, and Poli 2022; Degli Esposti, Desantis, and Poli forthcoming.
28. For a single fragment of a clay slab found in Structure 2, decorated with a stamp and possibly of architectural character, see Desantis, Manzoli, and Poli 2022.
29. For the analysis of spinning and weaving materials, see Desantis, Manzoli, and Poli 2022.
30. For a comparison with the settlement in Casalecchio, zone A, but also with the building in via A. Costa in Bologna, see Ortalli 2010.
31. For a comparison with the so-called *Edificio della cortina* in San Cassiano, see Harari and Paltineri 2010.
32. These examples refer in particular to the Acquarossa complex (Building C, zone F) and the farm of Podere Tartuchino, recently discussed in Ciampoltrini 2010:138–139.
33. On rural housing typologies, see Donati and Cappuccini 2010, on type B: 169–170.
34. This reference, also valid with regard to the Ghiaccio Forte residential building (Rendini and Firmati 2010:189, 192n58) is particularly prevalent in the structures of southern Italy (Russo 2010 passim with the previous bibliography).
35. See Desantis, Manzoli, and Poli 2022.
36. As can be seen from palaeobotanical investigations that have reconstructed the entire history of the site, conducted by Giorgio Nicoli s.r.l. Agriculture Environment Center.

CHAPTER 7

ENVIRONMENT, LANDSCAPE, AND ECONOMY

ANTONIO CURCI AND MARIALETIZIA CARRA

Bioarchaeology has the specific aim of reconstructing economic and cultural aspects of the ancient environment and landscape. This discipline comprises specific branches, according to the different biological remains that are found in archaeological contexts: human, faunal, and botanical. Bioarchaeological studies have been part of Kainua's research activities for the last twenty years, adding specific information to the traditional study of architectural structures and material culture. This chapter presents the results of archaeozoological and archaeobotanical investigations, which have converged in their results, allowing us to reconstruct significant aspects of this important Etruscan center, with respect to both its daily life and the ritual sphere, where animals and plants were often the traditional protagonists of meaningful symbolic gestures.

ARCHAEOZOOLOGICAL DATA
Antonio Curci

Over the last few decades, various archaeozoological studies have been conducted on materials originating from the excavations by the Chair of Etruscology at the University of Bologna in the Etruscan city of Marzabotto. An attempt at a general synthesis of the exploitation of animal resources in such a large and complex site is challenging. However, the comprehensive evaluation of quantitative data can provide valuable information, while detailed descriptions are more effectively presented in specific studies.[1]

The overall data obtained from the archaeozoological studies indicate that, taking into account both the evaluation of the number of remains and the computation of the minimum number of individuals, the animal economy of Kainua was almost exclusively based on the breeding of the main domestic mammals: pigs, sheep and goats, and cattle (fig. 7.1).

As a whole, domestic mammals represent well over 90 percent of the *taxa* attested in all the examined contexts, and almost the entirety of the species from contexts of the city linked to production activities. Among domestic mammals, the predominant species are pigs (*Sus domesticus*), which represent about 50 percent of the total, or possibly more, according to different quantification methods, followed by sheep/goats (*Ovis vel capra*), and cattle (*Bos taurus*).

In Marzabotto, 4,091 animal remains come from pigs (*Sus domesticus*), a total of at least 307 individuals (56.6 percent NR, 47.8 percent MNI; see fig. 7.1). Age-at-death estimates indicate that most of the individuals were butchered upon reaching their early adulthood, which would have maximized the amount of meat produced. All elements of both the cranial and postcranial skeleton are well documented. The presence of all the anatomical elements, either rich or poor in meat, suggests that the butchering and consumption of the animals did not occur far from the waste discharge area, or that all animal waste was collected into the same place. A higher occurrence of fragments of the front limbs, compared to the rear, has been documented for House 1 in *Regio* IV, 2 (a similar but less evident pattern was noticed for the Water Shrine, where limb extremities outnumbered other skeletal el-

KAINUA	House 1				Fountain Sanctuary				Total			
	NR	%	MNI	%	NR	%	MNI	%	NR	%	MNI	%
Dog (Canis familiaris)	36	0.7	18	4.0	44	1.9	7	3.7	80	1.1	25	3.9
Pig (Sus domesticus)	2830	57.8	201	44.4	1261	54.0	106	56.1	4091	56.6	307	47.8
Sheep/Goat (Ovis vel Capra)	1013	20.7	123	27.2	686	29.4	45	23.8	1699	23.5	168	26.2
Cattle (Bos taurus)	940	19.2	83	18.3	223	9.6	15	7.9	1163	16.1	98	15.3
Horse (Equus caballus)	1	0.0	1	0.2	6	0.3	1	0.5	7	0.1	2	0.3
Donkey (Equus asinus)	2	0.0	2	0.4					2	0.03	2	0.3
Domestic mammals	**4822**	**98.5**	**428**	**94.5**	**2220**	**95.1**	**174**	**92.1**	**7042**	**97.4**	**602**	**93.8**
Hare (Lepus europaeus)	3	0.1	3	0.7					3	0.04	3	0.5
Brown bear (Ursus arctos)					1	0.04	1	0.5	1	0.01	1	0.2
Badger (Meles meles)					1	0.04	1	0.5	1	0.01	1	0.2
Wild boar (Sus scrofa)	1	0.0	1	0.2	4	0.2	1	0.5	5	0.07	2	0.3
Roe deer (Capreolus capreolus)	3	0.1	2	0.4	1	0.04	1	0.5	4	0.06	3	0.5
Red deer (Cervus elaphus)	36	0.7	6	1.3	106	4.5	9	4.8	142	2.0	15	2.3
Wild mammals	**43**	**0.9**	**12**	**2.6**	**113**	**4.8**	**13**	**6.9**	**156**	**2.2**	**25**	**3.9**
Anurans					1	0.04	1	0.5	1	0.01	1	0.2
Birds	31	0.6	13	2.9	1	0.04	1	0.5	32	0.4	14	2.2
Total	**4896**	**100**	**453**	**100**	**2335**	**100**	**189**	**100**	**7231**	**100**	**642**	**100**

FIGURE 7.1. Total number (NR) and minimum number of individuals (MNI) in the animal remains from House 1, *Regio* IV, 2 (after Curci 2010), and from the Water Shrine (after Sertori 2014–2015).

ements), suggesting a greater consumption of shoulder portions compared to thighs, the latter probably used for hams.

As for sex distinction, the morphology of the canine teeth has allowed recognition of at least 48 males and 34 females, highlighting a slight prevalence of the former, while for the latter it is necessary to consider their role in reproduction. Traces of butchering left by the use of heavy metal blades are particularly numerous. Nine fragments of sawn bones (two distal tibias, three medial femurs, four humeri, of which one is medial and three distal), the diaphyses of which have been used in craft activities, are the exceptions.

Tools, in fact, were usually made from the bones of larger animals. Traces of modifications and smoothing are also documented on some knucklebones, mostly from the Water Shrine (fig. 7.2). Knucklebones are usually interpreted as related to the sphere of gaming and gambling.[2] In some cases, however, they had religious value instead, while a monetary function of symbolic nature has also been proposed.[3] The use of knucklebones as dice or gaming pieces is testified throughout the eastern Mediterranean in various chronological contexts from quite early periods.[4] The Greek tradition usually attributed to Palamedes the invention of the

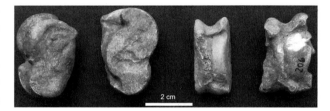

FIGURE 7.2. Pig knucklebones with traces of modification (center) compared with unmodified knucklebones (side). Photo A. Curci.

game of dice (Pausanias, *Description of Greece* 10.31.1), while Herodotus believed it was of Lydian origin (Herodotus, *Histories* 1.94). In particular, the use of knucklebones in divination was associated with Hermes, to whom they were sometimes dedicated.[5] Their use in gaming is the most probable hypothesis for the finds in Kainua, although it must not be forgotten that, as a consequence of its divinatory use, a propitiatory significance with beneficial and auspicious effects was given to the shape of knucklebones.[6]

From a comparative point of view, the pigs of Marzabotto were not particularly large and robust. This evidence also confirms that all the remains, including those from young individuals, belong to domestic pigs.

Sheep and goats (*Ovis vel Capra*) together are attested by 1,699 remains (23.5 percent NR; see fig. 7.1), pertaining to at least 168 different individuals (26.2 percent MNI). Age-at-death estimates indicate that more than 30 percent of the sheep/goats were killed in the first twelve months of life, and another 40 percent did not live for more than three years. It is, therefore, evident that the main economic interest was in the exploitation of these animals for the production of meat. More than two-thirds of the animals were, in fact, culled within the third year of life, when the greatest amount of meat is yielded with the lowest production cost. The rest of the flock (less than 30 percent) was kept alive for other purposes, certainly for reproduction, while interest in milk or wool is less documented. As for the anatomical parts found, there is a high number of horncores, and the forelimb elements are particularly abundant, compared to the rear legs. Based on the elements that allow for identification (in particular horncores, teeth, knuckles, metapodials, and phalanges), at least 43 sheep (*Ovis aries*) and 37 goats (*Capra hircus*) have been positively identified from House 1 in *Regio* IV, 2, while at least 33 sheep, but no goats, have been found in the Water Shrine. This suggests that the composition of the flocks was fairly balanced between the two *genera*, with a slight prevalence of sheep over goats. The presence in the Urban Sanctuary of sheep only might derive, instead, from the needs of specific ritual practices.

Interesting data can be inferred from the numerous traces left by the use of metal saws on horncores (twenty-two elements of both sheep and goats). Most horncores were sawn at the base, some have saw marks visible on the upper part only, and others both at the base and near the tip. These cuts may have been performed to remove the keratin sheath and were, therefore, related to the production of objects made from this raw material.

Bovines (*Bos taurus*) are witnessed by 1,163 remains, testifying to at least 98 individuals (16.1 percent NR, 15.3 percent MNI; see fig. 7.1). The age-at-death of cattle, among which young individuals and sub-adults predominate and there are no older individuals, shows that their exploitation was mainly aimed at meat production. All the anatomical parts of the skeleton are present, with some even overrepresented. The number of horncore remains is, in fact, extremely high, mainly because of their fragmentation. This poor state of conservation prevents the identification of sex, for which some information was inferred from the osteometric data. The number of metapodials is also particularly high (43 metacarpal fragments and 33 metatarsal fragments), largely sawn to allow the use of the medial part of the diaphyseal body (fig. 7.3).

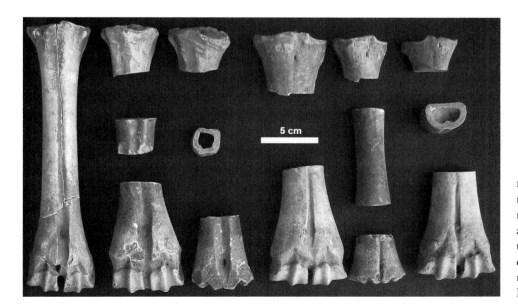

FIGURE 7.3. Cattle metacarpals and metatarsals cut with a metal saw to use the medial part of the diaphyseal body to manufacture tools. Photo A. Curci.

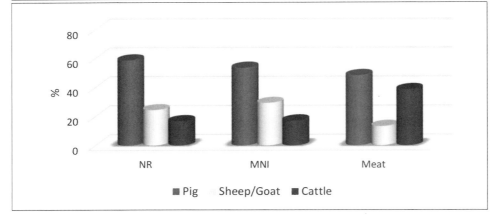

FIGURE 7.4. Comparison of number of identified specimens (NR), minimum number of individuals (MNI), and meat yield of the main domestic species (considering an average of 30 kg for a sheep/goat, 60 kg for a pig, and 150 kg for cattle).

This portion, being particularly robust and having a regular cylindrical shape, was often used in the manufacture of tools. Proximal and distal metapodials cut with a metal saw, most likely waste from the manufacturing process, have been found in the area of the channel outside House 1 in *Regio* IV, 2. Overall, elements of the forelimbs are more represented than those of the rear, testifying to higher consumption of this part of the animal. Numerous traces of variable depth, left by large knives used in the process of disarticulation and butchering, have also been found. The lack of measurable elements did not allow us to deepen our archaeozoological analysis of the size of the cattle.

From a purely economic perspective, Kainua reflects the trend of the main centers of eastern Emilia in the fifth century BCE toward an increase in animal exploitation, based on specialized pig breeding.[7] Even ranking the domestic species based on meat yield only, the predominance of pigs, albeit reduced, is largely confirmed (fig. 7.4).

This evidence suggests an economic model based on the importation of pigs from the surrounding territory to supply the meat requirements of the urban community.[8] Although it is not possible to find confirmation for this hypothesis because the surrounding environment was undoubtedly favorable to breeding a large number of pigs, and also because other, smaller settlements, such as Monte Bibele, show the same trend, the evidence for an increase in the reliance on pigs for meat production remains unquestionable. A previous study of pre-Roman archaeozoology in northern Italy (fig. 7.5) highlighted the fact that most Etruscan sites (including Marzabotto, Forcello, and the Etruscan-Celtic settlement of Monte Bibele) show a high percentage of pigs within the general exploitation pattern of the main domestic species.[9]

This evidence reversed the trend of the Late Bronze Age in the area of the Terramare culture, where sheep/goat breeding was the main practice.[10] Even in Etruria, from the eighth century BCE onward, the demographic change caused pigs to become an important component in the human diet. Pigs, therefore, became the predominant species in large urban centers such as Tarquinia, Roselle, and Populonia.[11] A strong local environmental conditioning is evident in the strategy of animal resource use, but, at the same time, a common trend emerged that linked sites with a shared cultural background.

In addition to the main species of domestic mammals exploited for economic and alimentary purposes, some remains also testify to the presence of other domestic animals, including dogs, horses, and donkeys. Dog remains (*Canis familiaris*) are attested by 80 finds (1.1 percent NR; see fig. 7.1) from at least 25 different individuals (3.9 percent MNI), all adults except for two subadults. All the anatomical portions of the skeleton are attested, including both the skull (jaws, mandibles, and teeth) with the first cervical vertebrae and the limbs (humerus, radius, ulna, tibia, calcaneus, knucklebones, metapodials, and phalanges). In the Sanctuary area, however, mandibles and jaws, and the extremities of limbs were found in a higher number, making it plausible to consider a conscious selection of these parts. The identification of cut marks on fragments of the jaws and mandibles, a radius, and a phalanx attests that both skinning and butchering took place at the site.

Cases of cynophagy are rarely attested and, although reports of such alimentary usage have increased over the past few years, it did not constitute an activity customarily practiced in Italy during this period. Dog bones with butchering marks were found not only at Marzabotto, but also in the settlements of Spina,[12] Forcello di Bagnolo di San Vito,[13] Casale di Rivalta, and Fiorano Modenese.[14] Other cases refer to the sixth and fifth centuries BCE, including Vadena in Trentino,[15] as well as the Etruscan territory at Montecatino in Val Freddana[16] and Veii.[17]

Based on the type and location of the cut marks, such dog butchering activities were apparently related to meat consumption. However, the possibility that they testify to the ritual sacrifice of this animal, which is well attested in the textual sources,[18] cannot be completely excluded.[19] As regards the traces of skinning, it is interesting to recall the connection that some divinities often had with their sacred animals. For example, Aita, the main Etruscan underworld deity, wore a dog- or wolf-skin headdress, the so-called *kuneé*.[20]

Equids complete the picture of domestic animals found in the Etruscan city of Marzabotto. Two remains (0.03 percent NR), identifying two different individuals (0.3 percent MNI), were attributed to the donkey (*Equus asinus*): a lower third molar and an upper molar were identified with this species by their

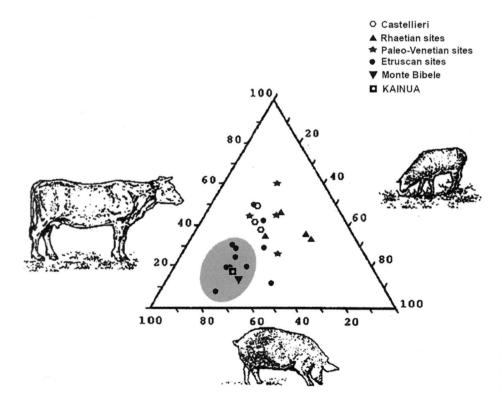

FIGURE 7.5. The main livestock in Iron Age sites in northern Italy. After Curci 2010.

small size and some specific morphological features of the occlusal surface. Seven remains were attributed to horses (0.1 percent NR; see fig. 7.1), indicating at least two different adult individuals (0.3 percent MNI).

Horse and donkey, ever since their first appearance in archaeological contexts in Italy, the first in the Eneolithic and the second in the Late Bronze Age, are always scantily attested from a quantitative point of view, as they were usually bred for riding and transportation rather than food consumption. Their rarity also suggests that they were probably an economically valuable asset, only owned by a small part of the community.

Wild mammals and, as a consequence, the evidence of hunting are mainly represented by red deer (*Cervus elaphus*). Recovered deer remains, however, are largely related to the exploitation of antlers for manufacturing purposes. To be used for making tools, antlers might just have been collected in the woodlands, rather than detached from hunted animals. The other wild species found in Kainua can be regarded as occasional prey, including bear (*Ursus arctos*), badger (*Meles meles*), wild boar (*Sus scrofa*), roe deer (*Capreolus capreolus*), and hare (*Lepus europaeus*). Altogether, they do not even reach 3 percent of the faunal assemblage (3.9 percent considering the MNI).

Hunting in the pre-Roman communities of northern Italy has always been quite a marginal activity. According to the available data from Iron Age sites in the north of the peninsula, for the period between the seventh and the second centuries BCE,[21] although variable in structural complexity, functional typology, and environmental contexts, the remains of wild animals are always quite scanty. Exceptions are Monte Bibele[22] and the Etruscan site of Spina,[23] among the largest centers, and Colognola and Miseria Vecchia,[24] among the smaller ones. In Etruria, evidence of hunting is also attested, mainly on small sites like San Giovenale and Gran Carro, while it seems to have only been an occasional activity at larger centers, such as Cerveteri, Roselle, or Populonia.[25] Deer and wild boar were here the most frequent prey although in this period there is also occasional evidence for the hunting of hare and birds. The limited economic significance of hunting suggests that it was exclusively performed for protection, the supply of skins and furs, and to obtain materials for specific craftwork. On the other hand, archaeozoological data offers little support to the traditional interpretation of hunting as a physical exercise for the elite, a privilege reserved to an aristocratic class with adequate means to draw pleasure from the practice itself, without any actual need for food procurement. This kind of activity finds greater testimony in funerary contexts, where there are numerous representations of heroic hunting scenes, celebrating the ideal of the Etruscan lord.

As far as avifauna is concerned, in addition to a few remains of imperial crow (*Corvus corax*), which are probably intrusive, there is evidence of the breeding of domestic chicken. Remains positively ascribed to *Gallus gallus* are not numerous, but it must be considered that determination was possible only for a few bird fragments. Although it may be assumed that poultry was mainly exploited for eggs, the archaeozoological data set does not support evidence for intensive chicken breeding at Marzabotto. Based on the scant evidence available, chicken was probably introduced in Italy at the beginning of the Iron Age. Until the fifth–fourth centuries BCE, it is mainly attested in funerary contexts rather than settlements. In the Po Valley, remains of *Gallus* are documented from the sixth–fifth centuries BCE at Kainua, San Claudio, and Casale di Rivalta.[26] Even in southern Etruria, the main settlements yielded no poultry remains, neither in the Orientalizing nor the Archaic period. Up to the fifth century BCE, these animals were probably present but still not very widespread and, given their value, they were probably used almost exclusively in cultic and funerary practices.[27]

ARCHAEOBOTANICAL DATA
Marialetizia Carra

The systematic archaeobotanical study of Kainua started in 2009. Sediment samples were taken in each excavation campaign to search for plant remains. The presence of numerous alterations of the deposit by crops made it difficult to find suitable areas for sampling. In fact, for archaeobotanical research it is necessary to sample in areas not affected by agricultural work or other tampering with the original stratigraphy. Another problem concerns the suitability of the sediment with respect to the conservation of the biological remains; the soil does not seem particularly suitable for the conservation of plant residues. For these reasons, large quantities of plant macroremains were never found in the various samples examined.

The archaeobotanical study addressed both the carpological remains (seeds and fruits) and the anthracological remains. Although the analyses are still in progress, it is possible to present the data obtained so far from the two different analyses. The reconstruction of food (human and animal), the study of the state of agriculture, the identification of different agricultural practices and paleoenvironmental reconstruction are the main purposes of the carpological analysis. The reconstruction of the vegetation cover, the uses of different types of wood, and the analysis of the hearths with the various *taxa* that compose them are the aims of the anthracological studies. All these aspects are useful for a contextualization of the archaeological site in its environment.

MATERIALS AND METHODS

The samples taken in the various excavation campaigns were subjected to manual flotation in water with sieve meshes of 300–500 μm; the flotation residue was in turn sieved. Both residues were laid out to dry and then placed in plastic bags, ready for stereomicroscope screening work.[28] The screening work consists of dividing the different types of finds: archaeological remains (ceramic fragments and tiles), bones (macro and micro fauna), malacofauna, and plant macroremains. Subsequently, the carpological and anthracological findings were separated, counted, and identified.

The carpological remains are determined by morphometric analysis, by comparing them with a collection of seeds and fruits (modern and fossils) preserved at the ArcheoLaBio Research Center (University of Bologna) and by means of specific reference atlases.[29] The stereomicroscope is the instrument used for these analyses. The anthracological findings are determined according to the rules codified by Schweingruber (1990) and Vernet (2001), which provide for the cutting of each fragment with a size greater than 2–3 mm, according to the three different fracture planes (transversal, radial, tangential), useful for the identification of different distinctive elements of wood. The metallographic microscope with episcopic light (with light range and dark range) is the most suitable instrument for these investigations. For the botanical identification of anthracological and carpological remains, the nomenclature is based on the text of Pignatti (2017).

RESULTS OF THE ARCHAEOBOTANICAL STUDY

Most of the samples examined so far come from the service rooms of the Temple of Tinia identified in *Insula* 5 of *Regio* 1. These analyses allow us to reconstruct aspects of everyday life in relation to food and the main agricultural activities, which can be inferred from the relationship between the various types of carpological remains.

Cereals and cereal farming appear as the main food source of the city, similarly to what happens for Italy in almost all contemporary settlements (fig. 7.6).[30] Barley (*Hordeum vulgare* L.) and wheat (*Triticum* sp. L.) are the main cereals identified, together with some grains of millet (*Panicum miliaceum* L.), a cereal introduced in the Bronze Age in crop rotation practices. Many fragments of cereals are indeterminable due to the conservation problems already noted, and

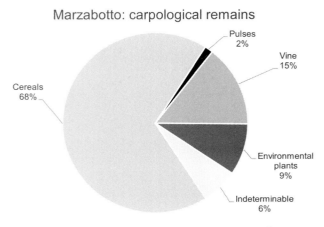

FIGURE 7.6. Subsistence economy attested by the study of carpological samples.

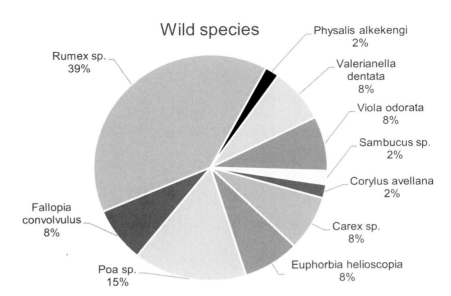

FIGURE 7.7. Carpological study of wild plant species.

even the identification of the different wheat species was not possible.

The vine is the other important plant found in Kainua. Numerous grape pips and fragments have been found in many samples. A detailed examination of whole pips certainly revealed a type of cultivated vine (*Vitis vinifera* L. subsp. *vinifera*). According to old theories, the cultivation of vines in Italy derives from the introduction of domesticated forms in the areas between the Caucasus and Mesopotamia.[31] But it is more likely that viticulture in Italy derives both from contact with the Eastern world and from an indigenous evolution, which progressively developed toward the end of the Bronze Age, also linked to the production of fermented drinks.[32] The presence of the vine in Kainua confirms the importance of this plant in the Etruscan world, in daily life and in ritual practices, as evidenced by both literary sources and the numerous objects found in archaeological excavations. The widespread and homogeneous discovery of grape pips seems to prove that, in Kainua, the vine was grown locally, with a long tradition that has reached the present day. In fact, until the discovery of the archaeological site, the entire Kainua plateau was occupied by the cultivation of vines.

Pulses occupy a marginal place in Kainua. Some fragments of vetch (*Vicia* sp. L.) are the only remains found in the contexts examined so far.[33] Vetch, now used as a forage legume, was used in human nutrition until the Middle Ages. While pulses were scarce in the settlements of northern Italy up until the Bronze Age, starting from the Iron Age pulses were frequently used, especially in crop rotation practices.[34] Both edible pulses and forage legumes are often present in the carpological complexes of Italian sites.[35]

Kainua seems to deviate from this trend; perhaps conservation issues have skewed the data. In addition, the lack of specific contexts related to the processing of foodstuffs can explain this possibility, similarly to what is highlighted by the examination of cereals. In fact, the relationship between the waste elements (spikelets and glume bases) and the food remains (grains and fragments) is clearly in favor of the latter, proving the lack of discovery of food processing areas. At the current state of research, no places suitable for the storage of food have been encountered.

Wild species account for 9 percent of the findings and are detailed in figure 7.7. Their analysis informs us about the paleoenvironment of the settlement area. Hazel (*Corylus avellana* L.) and elder (*Sambucus* sp. L.) represent a small part of the environmental finds and are the only two types of woody plants (which produce edible fruits). The other remains refer solely to herbaceous species. These data are to be expected in an urban settlement area. In fact, the herbaceous plants found are typical of anthropized places, being plants that grow along roads and paths and in urban areas (i.e., *Poa, Fallopia, Rumex, Euphorbia*). In addition, sedge (*Carex* sp. L.), a typical plant of wetlands and the edges of canals and ditches, could indicate areas of stagnant water within the urban context.

Winter cherry (*Physalis alkekengi* L.) differs from other weeds in that it grows preferably on rocky slopes or in the undergrowth. It is possible that this fruit was deliberately brought to the settlement, due to its food and medicinal properties. The fruits are rich in vitamin C and ancient authors, such as Dioscorides and Galen, recommended the use of winter cherry as a diuretic and purifying agent.[36]

The anthracological study, still in its initial phase, is examining the fragments recovered in the floated samples, already examined from the carpological point of view. These are generally small remains (3–6 mm), not always in good conservation conditions, which allow specific determination only in some cases. Structured hearths have not been found; the remains come from charcoal waste, scattered in the sediments. The fragments mainly concern deciduous oak (*Quercus* sp. L.), in association with ash (*Fraxinus* sp. L.), maple (*Acer* sp. L.), elm (*Ulmus* sp. L.), and some types of *Rosaceae* (*Rosaceae* ind.). Conifers have not yet been identified.

This group of species is too small to allow us to reconstruct the reference phytocenosis in detail, but the analyses confirm the presence of mesophilic woods,[37] probably interspersed with open spaces created by humans as cropfields and pastures, distributed in the areas around the ancient city of Kainua. The anthropization of the area is confirmed by the abundant vegetable remains of cultivated plants and the large number of bone remains of farmed animals.

THE RITUAL CONTEXTS

In 2016 the archaeobotanical study dealt with two important ritual contexts that came to light in association with the Etrusco-Italic temple identified in the *insulae* 4a–4b, a monument that can be dated in the period from the end of the sixth to the beginning of the fifth century BCE. In a corner of the temple, three pots were found, deliberately fractured, positioned, and buried, according to a ritual aimed at sacralizing the modification of the wall structure (*see fig. 9.2*).[38]

The contents of the pots were analyzed, looking for plant remains that could accompany the animal bones found in the immediate vicinity. The overall analysis[39] did not reveal large quantities of carpological remains, excluding the presence of offerings of seeds or fruit inside the containers. The in-depth examination of the contents would seem to recall the remains of food preparation (involving cereals, pulses, and fruits), highlighted by the differences that characterize the three samples.

Sample 1 (SU 1178): Statistically insignificant, almost exclusively characterized by indeterminable cereal fragments.

Sample 2 (SU 1179): Cereals (indeterminable fragments), pulses (broad bean and lentil), and fruits (hazel and grape) were found, along with some fragments of eggshells. The sample was interpreted as food preparation with vegetables and eggs.

Sample 3 (SU 1180): Prevalence of grapeseed and fragments, characterized by a kind of "patina," perhaps due to steeping in a liquid. A drink is the possible content.

The second ritual context associated with the Etrusco-Italic temple is the infant burial linked to the structural reconstruction of the northwestern corner of the sacred area. The conclusion of the carpological study made it possible to confirm what was communicated verbally following the preliminary analysis (fig. 7.8).[40] Six soil samples were examined, three taken during the excavation phase and another three derived from the micro-excavation operations of the burial in the laboratory. The screening of the samples confirmed the absence of the grave goods of the individual and allowed the discovery of a tooth and a phalanx, which were later delivered to the anthropologists.

The carpological study did not reveal a great variety of plant species but highlighted the presence of a species not yet found in Kainua in previous analyses: the olive (*Olea europaea* L.; fig. 7.8). The olive tree is not

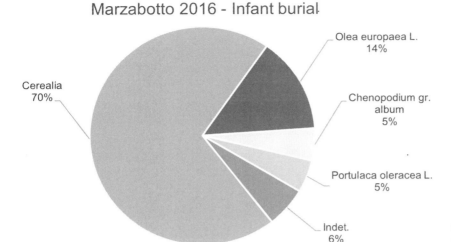

FIGURE 7.8. Carpological remains accompanying the infant burial.

a plant grown in Marzabotto for climatic reasons; the twelve stone fragments probably derive from an import from insular Italy or from contacts with the Balkan world, probably through the great port of Spina, which, from the seventh century BCE conducted a thriving oil trade.[41]

Perhaps the oil was used as a valuable offering, together with a large animal jaw, in infant burial rituals. On the other hand, the other carpological remains are of well documented plants in Kainua and would recall the normal vegetable waste present in anthropized sediments.

CONCLUSIONS
Antonio Curci and Marialetizia Carra

Although the archaeobotanical and archaeozoological analyses are still in progress, it is interesting to underline the amount of information already obtained from the plant and animal worlds, particularly about how the inhabitants of Kainua made use of such resources in both their daily life activities and to perform cults and rituals.

Food resources, as in the whole protohistory, were based on the cultivation of cereals and vines, and the breeding of the main domestic species, especially pigs, to obtain meat and secondary products. Bioarchaeological data also illustrate the role that natural resources had in the sacred sphere of rituals and, more in general, disclose their powerful symbolic meanings. Indeed, all these data enhance our understanding of the complex cultural and economic reality of the Etruscan city of Kainua.

NOTES

1. After the first preliminary analysis (Giusberti 1990), new archaeozoological studies have been conducted on animal remains from both productive and residential areas, including House 1, *Regio* IV, *insula* 2 (Curci, Bigoni, and Ferrari 2006; Curci 2010), as well as from ritual contexts like the Water Shrine (Sertori 2014–2015).
2. De Grossi Mazzorin and Minniti 2012.
3. Holmgren 2004.
4. Gilmour 1997.
5. Bar Oz 2001.
6. For the use of knucklebones in divination at Kainua, see the discussion of the finds at the Water Shrine, in chapter 8.
7. Farello 1995.
8. Farello 2006.
9. Curci and Cattabriga 2005.
10. De Grossi Mazzorin and Riedel 1997.
11. De Grossi Mazzorin 2006.
12. Briccola, Bertolini, and Thun Hohenstein 2013.
13. Trentacoste 2014.
14. Farello 1989; Farello 1990.
15. Riedel 2002: fig. 7.
16. Ciampoltrini, Rendini, and Wilkens 1991.
17. De Grossi Mazzorin and Cucinotta 2009.
18. See, for example, *Tabulae Iguvinae*, Devoto 1948.

19. De Grossi Mazzorin 2008; Curci and Sertori 2019.
20. De Grummond and Simon 2006:57.
21. Cattabriga and Curci 2007.
22. Curci and Cattabriga 2005; Curci, Penzo, and Cattabriga 2006.
23. Riedel 1978; Briccola, Bertolini, and Thun Hohenstein 2013.
24. Farello 1995.
25. De Grossi Mazzorin 2006.
26. Farello 1995; Farello 2006; De Grossi Mazzorin 2005.
27. De Grossi Mazzorin 2006.
28. Pearsall 2015.
29. Mainly Cappers, Bekker, and Jans 2012.
30. Forni and Marcone 2002.
31. Zohari and Hopf 1993.
32. Marvelli et al. 2013.
33. Lentils and broad bean were found in modest quantities in a ritual context (*see p. 69, sample 2*).
34. Pulses are nitrogen-fixing and help maintain soil fertility.
35. Forni and Marcone 2002.
36. Lanzara 1997.
37. Bagnaresi and Ferrari 1987.
38. Govi 2018a.
39. Carra 2018.
40. Govi 2018a; see chapter 8.
41. Sciortino 2012; Gaucci 2013.

PART III

LIVING IN THE CITY

Part III of the volume is dedicated to the city and the citizens. The chapters deal with sacred and domestic architecture, handicraft production, and economic and commercial activities. The study approach is characterized by the social analysis of phenomena as well as artistic and cultural data, in an integrated perspective that highlights the role of the city in the most lively cultural circuits of Etruria.

CHAPTER 8

SACRED ARCHITECTURE AND LANDSCAPE

ELISABETTA GOVI

The foundation of Marzabotto was the result of an act that ritually defined the space of the city. In this way, it was possible to distinguish the civic space from the external one and ensure divine protection of it.[1]

In Etruscan cities, temples were placed in strategic positions for city life, that is, near the gates (both inside and outside the walls) for the cults that protected the city, the status changes of citizens, and commercial activities. They might stand in the civic and commercial core of the city in the center or on the acropolis.[2] But the Etruscan "geography of the sacred" as a field of study awaits systematic analysis and, often, scarce information is available that would allow researchers to properly understand the logic of temple location within the cities. Indeed, little is known about collective ceremonies, the calendar of civic festivals, or the itinerary of processions both inside and outside the city, despite the importance of these elements in the localization and orientation of temples.[3]

Marzabotto is an exceptional case: after the recent discovery of the Urban Sanctuary in *Regio* I, it is possible to investigate this matter from a more complete perspective, despite the absence of documentation for the Acropolis excavations conducted in the nineteenth century. However, this city appears to be an anomaly with no comparisons in Etruria. When considering the sacred buildings in Marzabotto, we should ask ourselves where and why these temples were founded, and what cults were practiced there. The most recent excavations also allow us to make inquiry about their founders.

At Marzabotto, all the sacred buildings are located in the northern sector of the city, creating an ideological and visual axis, *plateia* B, that connects the Acropolis to the Urban Sanctuary, forming something similar to a sacred way. People coming from Tyrrhenian Etruria certainly saw the temples of the city on the raised Acropolis from afar, as well as the imposing ones built in the city and facing south. The sacred buildings controlled both the city and the Reno Valley from above. Five monumental temples, two altars, and a spring water shrine constituted the city's sacred landscape, which certainly defined the city and its citizens in ancient times and influenced its urban layout.

THE ACROPOLIS

Misanello hill was investigated several times in the nineteenth century.[4] During renovations of the park adjacent to Count Aria's Villa, temples and altars were uncovered; however, the excavation was not systematic or properly documented. In the last century, these structures were repeatedly restored. The Superintendence conducted some surveys to clarify structural aspects, and new structures behind the temples were discovered. In recent years, the excavations of the University of Bologna in the Urban Sanctuary and the development of the "Kainua Project" to enable the virtual reconstruction of the city have made it possible to reevaluate the reconstruction of the entire Acropolis and its structures (*see plate 10*).

Natural erosion and anthropic modifications have effaced the original shape of the hill. A structure (Y), built with cobblestone foundations and stone blocks, was placed on the peak, of which only one wall remains visible. It is part of a rectangular podium with internal walls (14 × 3.20 m); a quadrangular structure, perhaps a fence (see map 10), was positioned against one side. E. Lippolis suggested that this podium supported a portico facing southeast.[5] This construction has been interpreted as the *auguraculum*, the starting point for the foundation rite, a hypothesis suggested also by the visual connection with the center of the city, where a *cippus* bearing a *crux* was unearthed.

On the lower terrace, three temples (A, C, E) and two *podium*-altars (B, D) are arranged in an oblique alignment, each maintaining a rigid north–south orientation. The narrow space on top of the hill did not allow a completely straight alignment in the east–west direction. Only Temple E is oriented northeast–southwest, pointing directly toward the urban temples and visually connecting the two sacred areas.

Although attempts have been made to date the Acropolis structures and recognize different building phases,[6] the absence of data and dating materials makes this almost impossible. Certainly, the first and oldest structure was *Podium*-altar B, which is differently oriented and was later hidden from view by the construction of the great Temple C. *Podium*-altar B consisted of a rectangular structure of cobblestones that incorporated a cylindrical well,[7] with a diameter of 0.44 m and depth of 6.55 m. Its construction required the excavation of a large and deep pit. Next to the five-step staircase, a tank made of tiles was built to contain the water used during rites: this structure is no longer preserved (see plate 12). Altar D was a *podium* with frontal steps, built with cobblestone foundations and molded stone blocks (see plate 11). At the time of discovery, some stone *cippi* and *ex-voto* bases were probably located on the altar.[8]

The typology of the *podium*-altar defines a consecrated space representing, in fact, the *templum* on earth.[9] As is well know, the *podium* structure makes the altar suitable for worshiping celestial gods, while Altar B is destined for chthonian cults. The moldings of Altar D mirror iconographic representations of altars, as documented on the figurative *stele* of Marzabotto from the Eastern Necropolis (see fig. 14.3a and b), indicating that the moldings of Altar D are identical to those of stone *cippi* used to support *ex-voto* items and thereby confirming the ideological connection between the altar-*templum*/space and consecrated offerings to gods (see fig. 14.2).[10]

Among the three temples, Temple C is the best-preserved: at the time of discovery, its walls were 1.83 m high, but they were then reduced.[11] Temple C is a "Tuscan" or Etrusco-Italic temple (18.20 × 21.40? m), built with a grid structure divided internally into three *cellae*, with the central one larger than the others. According to G. Colonna, this type of temple originated in the period from the end of the sixth to the beginning of the fifth century BCE. The closest counterparts are Temple A of Pyrgi, the Temple of S. Antonio in Cerveteri, and the Temple of Castor and Pollux in Rome.[12] Building E, previously recognized as a temple,[13] has now been reconstructed as an Etrusco-Italic type thanks to comparison with the urban temple.[14] The width is known, while the length can only be assumed (16.60 × 26.90? m). Temple A is even less well preserved. In fact, only one corner remains (5.86 × 5.28 m). It was probably a small peripteral temple with a center *cella* surrounded by 7 × 4 columns (10.40 × 17.95 m).[15]

During the excavations in the nineteenth century, many tiles decorated with geometric and floral motifs and painted palmette antefixes were discovered on the Acropolis, some of which are now displayed in the museum.[16] Nevertheless, the temple decoration is still mostly undefined. Similarly, no iconographic or epigraphic evidence of the gods worshipped was recovered. As has been shown (p. 31), the *mundus* is, however, related to *Dis Pater*, the god to whom the foundations of the cities in the Po Valley were dedicated, according to ancient sources. This god was connected to the chthonic sphere and thus belonged to the northwestern sector of the *templum*.

On the southern side, at the base of the Acropolis, a system to collect spring water, referred to as an aqueduct, was built near the western sector of *plateia* B. A cult site probably existed close to the structure. This complex system was composed of a bipartite decanting tank (2 × 1.25 m) that was partially covered, two water conduits made of cobblestones, built to collect water, and two stone distribution pipes or aqueducts, one of which was brought to light for a length of 55 meters (*see fig. 14.5*).¹⁷ In this way, the structure ensured the distribution of clean spring water to different points of the city. The water collector was discovered in 1870–1872 but was dismantled and rebuilt on the surface a short distance from where it was found, where modern construction, made in the "Etruscan" style, was placed. Fragments of painted tiles, molded stone blocks similar to the ones of Altar D, and three bronze statuettes were recovered near this building. Five meters from the aqueduct, an imposing "wall" (1.50 m high; 2.80 × 3.40 m) was unearthed together with burnt traces, fragments of tile and pottery, and many animal bones. The function of this structure remains obscure, probably being more similar to a *podium*. However, what is certain is that a place for worship was established near this building, probably a cult connected to spring water.

In the same way, two groups of male and female bronze statuettes were found in 1839 and 1841, on the eastern side at the base of the Acropolis (the "votive deposits of the Acropolis") close to a cobblestone wall near a spring and well. About forty statuettes were recovered as part of such votive deposits. This was a sacred area located not far from the Northern Necropolis, of which unfortunately little is known.¹⁸

THE URBAN SANCTUARY

In *Regio* I, a large sacred area was built at the intersection of *plateiai* A and B. Since 2000, the excavations conducted by the University of Bologna have unearthed two sanctuaries with temples enclosed by a *temenos*. In the larger sacred area, the perimeter wall coincides exactly with the limits of the regular block (*Regio* I, 5). The two temples were placed about 25 meters apart, separated by a *stenopos* wider than the others.

The oldest building is an Etrusco-Italic temple with a deep *pronaos* (19.14 × 25.70 m; fig. 8.1, below). It was built at the end of the sixth century BCE, facing south and oriented north–south. The building is located in the middle of a large area corresponding to *Regio* I, 4a–4b, a fact that probably influenced the division of the blocks in the eastern part of the city (*see map 5*). The temple was not built directly on *plateia* B, but rather it was in a position drawn back from the street: in fact, about 50 meters separated the building from the street, an area that is yet to be investigated. Future excavations will clarify how the sanctuary topography developed and whether there was a public space in this area.¹⁹

Two inscriptions on bucchero vases (fig 8.2) prove the cult to be that of Uni, widespread in Etruria, where the goddess always held a prominent position in the civic structures, either on the acropolis (as Vitruvius prescribed and as documented in Volterra) or in the lower city (as in the sanctuary of Vigna Parrocchiale in Cerveteri, in Perugia, and now in Marzabotto).²⁰ The inscriptions are incomplete and can be dated to the end of the sixth century BCE. The name of the goddess is declined in the locative case, meaning "(in the sanctuary) of Uni" (*see appendix A, no. 5; fig. 10.4: no. 5*; fig. 8.2, right): therefore, the inscription referred to an action that took place inside the sanctuary dedicated to the goddess Uni. One inscription also mentions the goddess Vei, who was probably "housed" in the same sanctuary (*see appendix A, no. 7; fig. 10.4: no. 7*). The name of this goddess also appears on another inscription recovered in an exceptional context,²¹ which will be treated below in this chapter. Thus, the two goddesses Uni and Vei were worshiped in the Etrusco-Italic temple as two distinct but complementary divinities: both protected fertility, symbolizing the birth, development, and prosperity of the civic community. In Etruria, the two goddesses are also worshiped together in the suburban sanctuary of Fontanile di Legnisina at Vulci, placed near a spring.²² This parallel is significant because, in both cases, the same Etrusco-Italic temple model was selected. This association of goddesses recurs frequently, although it is not documented by inscriptions, and can be found in several Etruscan sanctuaries.²³

A few decades later, in the first half of the fifth century BCE, a monumental and larger peripteral temple (21.92 × 35.50 m; fig. 8.1, above) was built in a nearby block (*Regio* I, 5). This was probably a rebuilding of an earlier structure, if the walls found below its foundations are to be interpreted as traces of a preexisting sacred structure.²⁴ The inscriptions recovered in the sacred area and in the furnace on the other

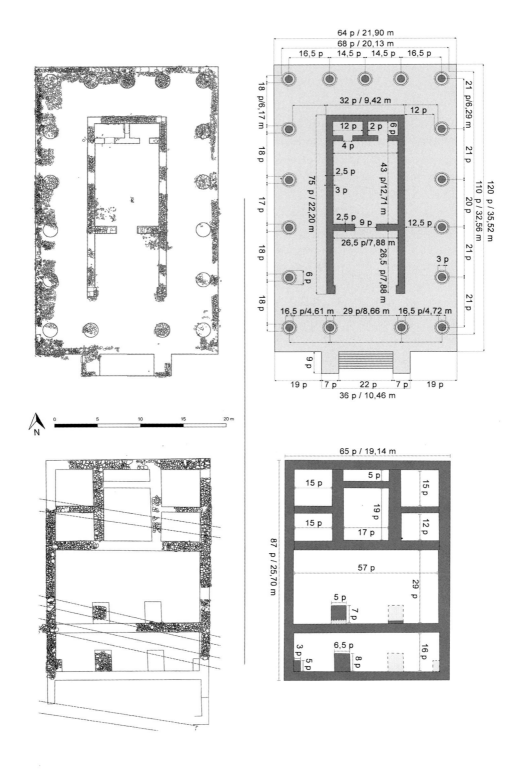

FIGURE 8.1. Schematic plan of the temples of the Urban Sanctuary with measurements expressed in meters and in Attic feet.

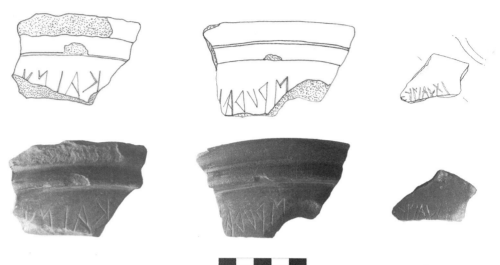

FIGURE 8.2. Inscribed sherds from the Etrusco-Italic temple of Uni, end of sixth century BCE.

side of *plateia* A, which fulfilled the temple's needs, attest that the sanctuary was dedicated to the high god Tinia, consort of Uni (*see appendix A, nos. 11–13; fig. 10.4: nos. 11–13*). Three inscriptions with theonyms were engraved on vases, small *ollae* and *olpai*, shapes widespread in sacred areas (e.g., in Pyrgi and Veii-Portonaccio), where they were used for specific purposes in cult practice, probably libations.[25]

Both sanctuaries also have additional buildings and a well, which is larger in the precinct of the peripteral temple. Unfortunately, the excavation did not collect sufficient documentation to define the precise functions of these buildings and the areas attached to the temples. Thus also there is no information on the furnishings of the temple, although it can be assumed that in the area in front there were altars, *ex-votos*, and statues. Here was probably the marble statue of which the head remains (*kouros*), found not far from the entrance of the Temple of Tinia (fig. 8.3).

To the north of the peripteral temple, a large area was separated by a wide channel/*ambitus*. Although the study of this sector has not been concluded, traces of rituals, votive deposits, and artifacts (e.g., fragments of votive bronze statuettes) suggest a religious purpose for this area, consisting of both open and enclosed spaces.

The two temples, one Etrusco-Italic and the other peripteral, were built side by side, as were the two

FIGURE 8.3. Head of a marble statue (*kouros*) found near the urban temples, 500 BCE.

temples in the sanctuary of Pyrgi and, perhaps, in the sanctuary of S. Antonio at Cerveteri, and are dedicated to the celestial couple Tinia-Uni. In Pyrgi, the couple is mentioned in a prayer bronze plaque, which allowed G. Colonna to identify the cult of Tinia in area C near Temple B.[26]

The large Urban Sanctuary is perfectly inserted into the urban layout, which probably originated in relation to the sacred areas, since the temples influenced and modeled civic spaces. The Urban Sanctuary is placed at the heart of the city, close to residential areas, because this place of worship was of fundamental importance in city life. From a religious point of view, its position is very consistent, since the two temples monumentally translate the different components of society, both male and female, clarifying the founding values of the community.²⁷ The religious and ceremonial life of the city probably revolved around these temples, defining the transition to adulthood, marriage, and procreation—a guarantee of civic continuity. In the same way, the sanctuary of the goddess Uni also housed the goddess Vei, protector of fertility and births, comparable to the Greek Demeter.

The location of the two temples may also find an explanation in the celestial *templum*, because they were built to reflect the exact position of the two divinities in the northeastern celestial quadrant of the *summa felicitas* (*see fig. 4.5*).²⁸ This hypothesis is based on the principle that the city was planned as a reflection of the divine order, transposing on the ground the cosmogonic vision reflected in the *templum*.²⁹ Unfortunately, the lack of documentation regarding the Acropolis's cults means that we cannot assess how correct this hypothesis is, although the *mundus* chthonic character could be related to the gods of the northwest quadrant, as already mentioned. Besides, the Water Shrine could also find correspondence in the position of Nethuns, the god of water, and the location of the Eastern Necropolis may coincide with the goddess Cath, "the daughter," similar to the Greek Persephone, perhaps depicted on the well-known *stele* with a young woman standing on an altar (*see fig. 14.3*).³⁰ If these correspondences are correct, this reconstruction yields an image of a planned city that objectively finds no comparison with other Etruscan cities, making Marzabotto a unique case. However, few cities founded in the sixth century BCE are extensively documented and little is known of the disposition of sacred areas, even though town planning is well documented in Etruria.

THE WATER SHRINE

This small but important sacred area was discovered in the 1970s and, unfortunately, only a general plan and some preliminary publications are preserved from the original excavation documentation.³¹ The Water Shrine was originally classified as "suburban" because it was assumed that the northern limit of the city was located near the so-called Northern Gate, an interpretation that is no longer accepted.³² The sanctuary was undoubtedly located at the edge of the city in a liminal area, probably close to a city gate (*see map 5*). Despite the loss of its spatial connection to the city layout, the proximity to the main extra-urban route to Bologna and the Northern Necropolis is significant. The sacred area and the burial ground were probably on the same sight line. Suburban sanctuaries connected to water cults find several comparisons in Etruria (e.g., the Fonte Veneziana in Arezzo, the sanctuaries of Portonaccio in Veii, of Fontanile di Legnisina in Vulci, of Manganello di Cerveteri, of Acquasanta in Chianciano Terme, of Celle at Civita Castellana).³³ Among these sites, the Marzabotto shrine is particularly similar to the sanctuary of Fontanile di Legnisina, which was placed on the border of the western necropolis of Vulci and was probably connected to the city by a road, and to the sanctuary of Manganello in Cerveteri, clearly visible from the necropolis of Banditaccia. In the latter, water plays an important role, as is proved by the presence of wells, cisterns, and fragments of *louteria*, vessels associated with ritual washing. Moreover, anatomical *ex-votos* connected with the *sanatium* (healing) were recovered among the sanctuary finds,³⁴ just as in Marzabotto, although this aspect is not predominant.

To construct the building, a pit was excavated in a bank of river gravel, lowering the ground level to collect the spring water. The foundation works intruded on an older context, dating back to the Bronze Age, to which can be assigned some materials found mixed with those of the fifth century BCE. The small building (9 × 7.5 m) was built with square blocks of travertine. It contained a water system consisting of a square decanting well 1.5 meters deep, and a rectangular tank (1.42 × 0.72 m; fig. 8.4), from which the water flowed northward through a channel made with cobblestones of various sizes and fragments of travertine, probably recycled materials dismantled during a restoration of the area. The original flooring, consisting of large stone blocks, is partially preserved and originally must have covered the entire sacred area. The sanctuary was divided into two distinct areas: to the west was the collecting of spring water, and to the east was the area destined for votive offerings, arranged on molded

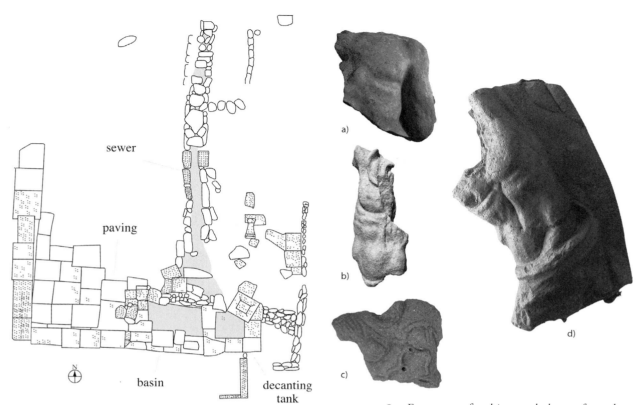

FIGURE 8.4. Plan of the Water Shrine.

FIGURE 8.5. Fragments of architectural plaques from the Urban Sanctuary (a–c) and the Water Shrine (d, not to scale).

bases and *cippi*.[35] Probably only the space with the water structures was sheltered with a cover, while the remaining space was an open-air area. The recovery of numerous fragments of pan-tiles, cover-tiles and one or two pieces of ridge-tiles indicates the existence of a finely decorated roofing system, to which belonged fragments of palmette antefixes and a central *acroterion*, and a main cover tile for a ridge beam (*kalypter hegemon*) with a low relief depiction of a winged man, wrapped in a mantle and raising an arm (fig. 8.5d). The scene has been compared to an episode of the myth of Proitos, Pegasus, and Bellerophon, but G. Sassatelli also recalled the figure of Daedalus arranging his wings on his back, in this way enhancing his influence on water regulation in the Etruscan Po Valley.[36] At the time of discovery, the entire area had been despoiled and was in a state of neglect.

The astronomical orientation of the sanctuary and the construction techniques are quite similar to those documented in the city. The materials testify to the long life of the sanctuary, which extended at least from the last decades of the sixth century BCE up to the Celtic phase, to which belong materials such as the La Tène *fibulae* of the second half of the fourth century BCE and some vessels that were in the past incorrectly dated to the Bronze Age.[37] Twenty bronze statuettes (*kouroi*, schematic male and female figurines of the "Marzabotto Group," and anatomical *ex-votos*) belong to a votive deposit,[38] among which there is a particularly valuable statuette dated to the second half of the sixth century BCE that has been interpreted as a depiction of the god Apollo.[39] Local vases were abundant: many were probably used to collect or contain water (jugs, basins) or to consume food (lidded *ollae*), as well as the metal vases of which only the handles remain (basins, *situlae*). There are also numerous drinking shapes, from bucchero *kantharoi* to cups. The importance of water according to the selection of vessel shapes is also proved by the votive inscription engraved on the rim of a basin, which bears a solemn dedicatory formula addressed to an unknown divinity, composed of the verb *turuke* followed by the devotee's *praenomen* and clan name (*see appendix A, no. 60; fig. 10.7: no. 60*).[40]

Also, the imported ceramics[41] are very significant and consistent and, along with other Etruscan productions, document the oldest phase of the sanctuary, which can be dated to the second half of the sixth century BCE. Therefore, we can confirm that this sacred area was already active in that period, but also played a fundamental part in the development of the town on the plateau. The most refined imports of Greek vases are indeed concentrated here, such as the large and rare Laconian krater and the Siana cup.[42] Moreover, as discussed in chapter 4, the Little Masters cup depicting warriors playing dice had probably been chosen for its iconographic and metaphorical allusion to divination, perhaps referring metaphorically to a foundation act.

In this regard, useful information also comes from the analysis of the zooarchaeological remains found during the excavation.[43] Taxonomic determination has shown that the sample is dominated by domestic species, largely by three *taxa* (*see fig. 7.1*): mainly pig (*Sus domesticus*), sheep/goat (*Ovis vel Capra*), and bovine (*Bos taurus*), inevitably recalling the well-known sacrifice of *suovetaurilia*. There also are the remains of dogs (*Canis familiaris*), belonging to at least seven different individuals, and of horses (*Equus caballus*). Wild species are also attested even though in irrelevant quantity. The remains showed butchering signs. It appears noteworthy that the largest percentage of bones consists of the extremities of limbs, compared to very few long bones corresponding to consumable portions. Moreover, a large number of *astragali* (249) was recovered, whose connection with play, the sacred sphere, and divination is well known. Astragals could, therefore, confirm this type of practice within the sanctuary, without excluding their possible reference to childhood and status transitions (they were offered to a divinity before marriage).

The divinities worshiped in this sanctuary are still unknown. The water and the *sanatium* (as proved by the anatomic bronze *ex-voto* shaped as feet or legs) were strongly connected with the infernal sphere, from which originated the spring water, recalling fertility, regeneration, healing, and purification. The position of the shrine near the gate and the necropolis at the border of the settlement may also indicate purification rituals required to enter the city.[44] The animal remains confirmed these aspects, since the pig is the preferred victim for atonement and the dog is normally connected to the underworld sphere, transitions in status, and also purification in the Greek, Roman, and Italic worlds (see the dog sacrifice described in the Iguvine Tablets).[45] The transition from childhood to adulthood, in the same way, could be a central component of the shrine's rituals, as indicated by astragals. In Etruria, both Heracles and Apollo are closely connected with water,[46] whilst Menerva is the protector of oracular activity.[47] The sanctuary of Portonaccio in Veii, where these deities among others were worshiped, offers an effective parallel to shed light on Marzabotto's Water Shrine cults.

During recent archaeological investigations, the local Archaeological Superintendence has unearthed, 40 meters from the Water Shrine, a large channel oriented southwest–northeast,[48] where molded travertine blocks and *cippi*, along with tiles,[49] votive materials, and bronze statuettes, were recovered. To explain the recovery of these materials dated to the Etruscan period, it was proposed that they had slipped down near the edge of the canal from an original altar located near the Water Shrine. However, these materials could have been thrown into the canal in ancient times or instead they could have been moved in the nineteenth century by the farmers who cultivated the plateau.[50]

Among the finds, a refined bronze figurine, 30 cm high, is worth mentioning: it is in excellent condition and depicts a woman holding a flower bud (fig. 8.6).[51] The considerable quantity and typology of the votive materials could also suggest that these items were originally located near the Urban Sanctuary of *Regio* I, from which they may have been removed. The female statuette, representing a devotee or perhaps a goddess, could indeed relate to the goddess Uni, worshiped in the Etrusco-Italic temple. Moreover, it should be men-

FIGURE 8.6. Votive bronze statuette depicting a woman holding a flower bud (devotee or perhaps a goddess), 500 BCE.

FOUNDATION AND PROPITIATORY RITES

Recent excavations in the Urban Sanctuary allow us to know more about some important rituals, starting from the foundation rite at the Etrusco-Italic temple dedicated to Uni.

In the southwestern corner of the temple, two fragments of an inscribed vase were found among the foundation stones (see fig. 8.2, left and center; *see appendix A, no. 5; fig. 10.4: no. 6*). They belong to a local bucchero amphora, and the inscription was engraved on the neck, under the rim. This type of large amphora is already documented in Marzabotto by two specimens, one of which carried the inscription *mi śatalus̓* and is dated to the second half of the sixth century BCE (*see appendix A, no. 1; fig. 10.4: no. 1*). Perhaps this vase was used for a rite relative to the construction of the *stenopos* adjacent to House 1 in *Regio* IV, 2.[53] These two inscribed fragments from one vessel found in the foundations of the Etrusco-Italic temple carry one word each (*see appendix A, no. 6; fig. 10.4: no. 6*). The first one is the city name, *Kainu*[---], which is also documented in the settlement as *Kainuaθi* (declined in the locative case on two inscriptions, one found nearby in the peripteral temple; *see appendix A, nos. 10 and 44; figs. 10.4: no. 10, 10.6: no. 44*). The second word is the institutional term *śpural*, here in the possessive case, which indicates the political dimension of the city, like *civitas*. As we have seen, **spura* is also documented in the Temple of Tinia (*see appendix A, no. 9; fig. 10.4: no. 9*), being mentioned in the text on the bronze sheet. The two words *kainu(a)* and *spural* on no. 6 were part of a longer votive text and were saved during the deliberate destruction of the vase, due to their ritual importance in the construction of the temple built by the community of Kainua. The written sherds were hidden inside the temple foundations and thus made invisible, inviolable, and sacralized.

Excluding the well-known votive or sacred texts concealed after their display, such as the gold tablets from Pyrgi, this type of rite was quite uncommon and is difficult to classify according to the archaeological and conceptual categories recently delineated by

tioned that G. Gozzadini recovered votive statuettes precisely in the area of the *Terza Stipe* (Third Votive Deposit), northeast of the city, where the Water Shrine was later found.[52] A pivotal sacred area was certainly located in this position, but its actual development still represents an open issue. Therefore, the spring utilized by the Water Shrine and the canal, which perhaps delimited the city, gave primary importance to water in the sanctuary: interestingly, in the layout of the *templum* described in the Liver of Piacenza, the northeastern quadrant is precisely the seat of *Tinsthneth*, meaning "of Neptune (in the house) of Tinia."

M. Bonghi Jovino.[54] In Etruria, the foundation rites of sacred buildings are well documented and involve offerings to divinities, as evidenced by votive deposits below or close to the walls, such as those found in the sacred-institutional complex of the Civita of Tarquinia and in the Etrusco-Italic temple of Vigna Parrocchiale at Cerveteri.[55] Ancient sources describe the foundation rite and *consecratio* of the Temple of Capitoline Jupiter, in which sacrifice played an important role.[56] It is also known that, in Rome, if a civilian made a vow regarding the construction of a temple, it had to be approved by the state, along with the choice of the place and the person who officiated the *dedicatio* of the building. The consecration was preceded by the *inauguratio*, when the area was prepared and the first stone laid. At the end of the construction, on the day of the dedication, the *pontifex* pronounced the solemn formula in the presence of the citizen and the dedication was repeated by placing his hands on the jamb of the temple door.[57]

For the urban Etrusco-Italic temple of Marzabotto, we are not able to specifically reconstruct the rite. It is possible to assume a sacrifice that involved spilling wine, followed by the amphora being ritually broken, and then the pieces being concealed inside the temple foundations. This last step recalls a practice also documented in Etruria, for example at Pontecagnano. This city was refounded in the sixth century BCE, and on this occasion, an *agger* was built where an *oinochoe*, used for the foundation rite, had been buried.[58] On the other hand, the choice of concealing the dedicatory inscription in the foundations of the building is exceptional; besides, the dedication made by the city (the **spura*), rather than by a single individual, stands out strikingly in the Etruscan world. This practice is widely known in Rome, but dedicatory inscriptions for sanctuaries or altars are rarely documented for the Etruscan settlements: the only example is represented by the gold tablets of Pyrgi, which mention the king-tyrant of Caere, Thefarie Velianas, as the author of the dedication of the first monumental complex of Pyrgi. Votive dedication, in which the civic body or a group of citizens took part, can be indirectly recognized through particular *ex-votos*. However, the knowledge gap about temple dedication in Etruria, and the historical circumstances regarding temple construction, remains evident. The documentation from Marzabotto provides useful information to fill this gap, even though a comparison with the text on the Pyrgi tablets is more likely to reveal the ideological differences between the two sanctuaries. The characteristic most specific to Marzabotto is that here the sacred buildings are the emanation and expression of the city itself, revealing a significant overlap, even a coincidence, between the sacred and political spheres.

Thus, at Marzabotto the foundation of the Etrusco-Italic temple is well documented while for the peripteral temple, the rite can only be conjectured, based on a fragmentary inscribed bronze sheet, found in a tile heap next to the temple (*see appendix A, no. 9; figs. 10.1, 10.4: no. 9*).[59] Its palaeography dates the text to the second quarter of the fifth century BCE. The text, expertly engraved, recalls some actions carried out by individuals called by name and clan name (*gentilicium*). The verb *hecce*, meaning "to build," suggests a solemn founding act, probably consisting of several ritual moments, as seen in the tablets from Pyrgi. The text also contains the expression *muntie śpural*, which refers to a place, perhaps a sanctuary. A comparison with the term *munie*, documented on the acropolis of Volterra during the fourth and third centuries BCE and meaning "of the sanctuary," seems relevant here.[60] But also, a possible reference to *munth* and the Latin *mundus* is evocative, since the latter feature is documented on the city Acropolis. Unfortunately the sheet fragment is so small that it is impossible to reconstruct the text, even though it presumably contained the solemn rite relative to the temple building, performed by magistrates or eminent people of the city. If this hypothesis were confirmed, it could lead to an indirect chronological indication for the peripteral temple, which would, therefore, have been built a few decades later than the Etrusco-Italic temple.

The excavations have made it possible to recognize the traces of rites carried out at the Etrusco-Italic temple, despite farming having seriously damaged the ancient stratigraphy. Small votive deposits have been recovered, as proof of rites probably performed during the closure and abandonment of the temple, as suggested by the presence of relevant parts of the roof cover and decoration: e.g., a fragment of a low-relief terracotta slab with a male figure was found in the center of a small pit with pottery fragments (fig. 8.5a).

In contrast, in a long narrow pit parallel to the western *temenos* wall of the Etrusco-Italic temple, an exceptional deposition was found, almost certainly connected to a propitiatory rite. The wall had been restructured, and during these activities several rites were carried out.[61] An infant burial was found inside this pit. It was not a tomb, because the newborn was placed on the earth, near the wall, without any grave goods.[62] The body was supine with the legs curled up, in a natural position. It is still unknown whether the newborn, between 38 and 40 weeks of age and male, was born dead or alive. However, other ritual elements suggest that he was buried as a sacrifice to divinity. Near the body a large animal jawbone was recovered and carpological analysis revealed traces of an oily substance poured near the body (perfume?).[63] The deposition was followed by a rite with offerings of meat and maybe an oil-based liquid.

An exceptional discovery was made 50 cm below this deposition: at the bottom of the pit, the foot of a bucchero vase was found with a *crux* oriented according to the cardinal points, an element that can relate to a founding act, probably concerning the *temenos* and therefore the entire sanctuary. Not far from that vase, the fragment of a plate used during the rite was unearthed. Among the few materials recovered during the pit excavation, a fragment of another plate was engraved with the inscription to Vei (*see appendix A, no. 7; fig. 10.4: no. 7*),[64] a goddess who was worshiped "in (the sanctuary) of Uni," as we have previously seen. The materials and inscription date the filling of the pit and therefore the burial to the sixth–fifth centuries BCE. Thus, a more ancient dating must be excluded, also being a period that is little documented in Marzabotto.

Concerning religious beliefs, the discovery of the newborn in the sanctuary of the goddess Uni, protector of births, and associated with the goddess Vei, goddess of life and death,[65] appears to be very consistent and finds comparison with the burials of newborns in the sacred-institutional complex of the Civita in Tarquinia, where five children were buried in the period from the third quarter of the eighth to the sixth century BCE on bare earth and with no grave goods,[66] just as in Marzabotto. One of the burials in Tarquinia was placed right next to the *peribolos* wall of building *Beta* along with libation remains, suggesting a propitiatory rite. Infant burials inside inhabited areas are widespread and well studied, but the number of case studies greatly decreases when one considers only burials connected to the foundation or de-functionalization rites of sacred buildings. Here, the "sacred huts," burials found below temples, have not been taken into consideration, such as in Satricum and Ardea, where their significance is still an open issue.[67] P. Carafa studied child burials associated with public or private buildings or locations.[68] Recently, the available documentation was enhanced by discoveries in the *Regia* in Gabii, interpreted as the seat of the *rex sacrorum* and the cult of Ops and Mars, where eight perinatal burials in *olla* were placed in the corners or along the walls during construction.[69] Nevertheless, considering the burial methods (presence or absence of body containers and grave goods, and the location with respect to the other structures), the sacred area of the Civita of Tarquinia still remains the closest comparison to the Marzabotto ritual burial.

Many elements lead us to interpret the context as a propitiatory sacrifice made at the time of foundation or reconstruction of the northwestern corner of the sacred area close to the temple: the relationship of the child's deposition to the wall delimiting the sacred area of Marzabotto; its position within the sanctuary; the topographic and conceptual connection between the infant and the *crux*, positioned subjacent at the bottom of the pit;[70] the burial method, with no container or grave goods; and, finally, the association with the goddess Vei, through the inscription on the offering in the filling of the pit. In the Etruscan religion, the *sanctitas* of limits was renowned and its violation, especially in the specific case of a sacred area, must have involved a rite, as proved by the child burial and traces of food offerings. On the other hand, the outlining of sacred areas through the spatial delimitation and their enclosure is part of the city foundation and is, therefore, an action connected to religion and identity.[71]

Looking to cultural anthropology, M. Eliade[72] asserted that the frequent interment of children under buildings or bridges recalls the concept of the archetypal sacrifice, imitating primordial divine creation, because infants represent a universal symbol of life. Thus, construction sacrifices aim to animate the architectural structure, to make it alive, recalling a divine model to achieve eternal durability and protection. Therefore, a construction cannot last unless it is animated through a sacrifice, which can also consist of animals, food, or even precious metal, rich in cosmic energy.

The archaeological perspective, on the other hand, allows us to better understand the context of discovery by looking to the two female deities, Uni and Vei, documented by inscriptions in the sacred area. Uni preserves marriages, births, and status transitions; she is the personification of the woman and the bride, protecting women within civic society, of which she is guarantor along with her consort, the supreme god Tinia.[73] The goddess Uni protects fecundity as the possibility of growth without concern for procreation, which pertains to another goddess, Vei: she is an ancestral deity, equivalent to Demeter and Ceres,[74] goddess of earth and human fecundity, and the deification of generating force. Therefore, she has authority over life regarding birth and growth, and she embodies chthonic forces, an aspect shared with Dionysus, justifying her cult within burial areas, as in Orvieto.[75] Between the end of the sixth and the beginning of the fifth century BCE, her worship acquired a political value in a complex period when transformations of social structures were reflected also in the sacred sphere. Until recently, the goddess cult was documented almost exclusively in southern Etruria, but G. Sassatelli recently collected testimonies in the Po Valley, from Bologna, Mantua, San Polo d'Enza, and now also from Marzabotto, displaying a wide diffusion that seems to indicate stages in the urban reorganization of the entire region.[76] It is therefore not surprising to encounter traces of devotion to the goddess in the Urban Sanctuary of Marzabotto, to which at least five vases with holes at the bottom, *paterae pertusae*,[77] used in ritual practices destined to a chthonic divinity, can be assigned.

The mother-goddess Vei, whom E. Simon suggests could be equivalent to Cel Ati,[78] was perhaps the intended focus of the enclosed area next to the temple, *sub divo*, as is appropriate to the cult of the goddess, as testified in Etruria in the sanctuaries of Cerveteri-Campetti and, above all, on the acropolis of Volterra, where five enclosed areas were reserved for goddess worship. Therefore, in Marzabotto Vei seems to be the protagonist of a rite that involves child sacrifice: it is possible to record the relationship between this specific rite and divinity for the first time, thanks to epigraphy.[79] The extraordinary case of Marzabotto also confirmed Vei's dreadful power, connected to life and death, which, according to V. Bellelli, would justify the linguistic and iconographic prohibition associated with the goddess.[80]

SACRED ARCHITECTURE AND BUILDING TECHNIQUES

Despite the gaps in our knowledge about the Acropolis's monuments, recent discoveries in the Urban Sanctuary provide vital information about the construction techniques used in the sacred structures of the city. The application of ArchaeoBIM has greatly helped the study and reconstruction of the buildings.[81]

Different construction techniques can be recognized in the city, starting from the temple type, Etrusco-Italic or peripteral. The three Etrusco-Italic temples (the urban Temple of Uni, Temples C and E on the Acropolis) are built with a trench foundation, filled with neat linings made of medium–large cobblestones, and sandstone blocks (1 meter long), frequently placed in the corner to strengthen the structure. Peripteral temples (the urban temple of Tinia and Temple A on the Acropolis) have shallower foundations, realized within the perimeter wall and the corners of the *cella*, where squared travertine blocks were set on a cobblestone layer. Therefore, we may ask whether this difference is due to the choice of the architectural type, which perhaps implied different founding techniques, or to the chronology, assuming possibly an evolution over time of the construction system of temple foundations from the exclusive use of river cobblestones, along with sandstone blocks, to exclusively stone blocks. This topic represents an innovation for research on Marzabotto, considering that in the past an analysis of construction techniques for sacred and civil construction has rarely been undertaken, and hardly ever in a diachronic perspective.

Moreover, the selection of different construction methods for the Etrusco-Italic temples is now evident: the Temple of Uni and Temple E had a quite deep *pronaos* (front porch), almost double the normal extension. This type of Etrusco-Italic temple can be compared to some sanctuaries in Etruria and Latium that date to to the early fifth century BCE, including the temples of Fontanile di Legnisina in Vulci and Ardea in Latium. According to G. Colonna, this structure emphasizes the most important part of the *pronaos*, the vestibule, ideologically recalling the aristocratic house and in particular the type with a transverse *atrium*, a space destined to display status and lineage.[82] In Marzabotto, the construction technique with isolated column bases and buttresses against the foundation walls also found a close comparison in the temples of Ardea.

To construct the new Etrusco-Italic temple of Marzabotto a mixed technique was used, a mediation between the separated foundation walls, such as in Temple II in the Ara della Regina, dated to 530 BCE, and the continuous grid foundations, used in the period from the end of the sixth to the beginning of the fifth century BCE. The oldest examples of this latter structure are the Temple of Capitoline Jupiter and the monumental Temple of Castor and Pollux in Rome, followed shortly after by Temple A of Pyrgi and Temple C of the Acropolis in Marzabotto, which is therefore built in a different way than the other Etrusco-Italic city temples. The different construction techniques adopted within the same city probably do not depend on the geomorphology of the area selected for construction, but were influenced by different traditions and architectural styles. The planimetric and dimensional comparisons found for the new temple came from southern Etruria, in particular Cerveteri and Vulci, the same area where on the other hand structural parallels were also found with the peripteral temple, as already stated in past studies. Recently, M. Bonghi Jovino has highlighted the affinities with the Late Archaic temple of Tarquinia, adding further evidence to this hypothesis.[83] The result is a complex scenario of cultural relations between Marzabotto and Tyrrhenian Etruria, affecting the construction and technological skills applied to sacred architecture, a specialized sector for which the circulation of knowledge and workers has now been established.

Furthermore, the discovery of two urban temples has enabled geometric and metrological study, and in figure 8.1 we have compared actual dimensions expressed in meters and those in ancient feet. This analysis allows us to understand the relations with the temples of the Tyrrhenian area, revealing the formation of the architects and the models they followed. The Etrusco-Italic temple has an area of about 492 m², a little larger than Temple C of the Acropolis but less than the peripteral temple of Tinia, which reaches about 780 m². The *stereobate* of the new temple can be compared to Temple B of Sant'Antonio in Cerveteri (500 m²) and the Temple of Vulci in Fontanile di Legnisina (437 m²).[84] The *pars postica* (the back of the temple) has three *cellae*: the two lateral with widths of 4.5 m and the central one wider (5.6 m); the lateral ones are internally divided into two, about halfway along. The central *cella* has a narrow corridor at the back, about 1.5 m wide, leading to lateral rooms, which are the most internal and protected areas, used to store the most precious gifts and the treasure of the sanctuary. The *cellae* division is, therefore, similar to that of Temple C on the Acropolis, but in that case the central room is larger. The ratio between the *cellae* of the new urban temple (3.14:3.71:3.14) corresponds almost exactly to Vitruvius's indication of 3:4:3 (*De arch.* 4.7.2–3). The *pars antica* (the front of the temple) preserves the rectangular bases of columns, aligned with the wall of the central cell and leaning against the two transverse walls of the *pronaos* (the front porch of the temple). The end of the western perimeter wall featured a spur wall, which could indicate a row of four columns at the front and one row of two columns inside.

The peripteral temple has a *cella in antis* (a *cella* preceded by a space delimited by walls) with a bisected *adyton* at the rear (a little room), four columns at the front, five at the back, and six on the long sides, of which the circular bases remain, with a diameter of 1.75 m. The building was built on a consistent module, based on a series of three concentric golden rectangles (plinth, *peristasis*, and *cellae*).[85] The plinth has a ratio of 3:5, bringing the temple of Marzabotto closer to the peripteral temples of the Triangular *Forum* in Pompeii, Satricum, and Pyrgi, even though these buildings are smaller. The ratio of base width to length is 1:6, while the proportion of *cella* width to length is 2:3. The width of the *ambulacrum* around the *cella* is the same on all four sides, exactly corresponding to half of the *cella* width. However, considering the distance from the cell to the perimeter wall, the overall width of the temple is divided by a ratio of 2:3:2.[86]

Both buildings were built using the Attic foot (29.6 cm) as a reference, the same measurement unit as for the urban plan. In the peripteral temple, it was possible to recognize the presence of a module of 3 Attic feet.

At this time, new possibilities can also be proposed for the roof decoration used for the temples of Marzabotto, which previously was considered almost completely absent. Despite the lack of data, due to the systematic spoliation of the buildings, a coherent system has come to light, based on small covering slabs, divided into three and decorated with vegetal motifs (h. 30 cm);[87] low relief-figured slabs; and palmette antefixes.[88] The number of slabs with figured scenes, unfortunately recovered in fragmentary form, has recently increased: before, the specimen with Daedalus from the Water Shrine (fig. 8.5d) and a male torso from the peripteral temple (fig. 8.5a) were the only ones preserved. In the Etrusco-Italic temple a fragment with a depiction of Menerva was recovered, standing with transverse *aegis* (fig. 8.5c): according to a well-known scheme, one arm was probably raised, holding a spear, and the other lowered. However, this iconographic format, assimilating the great Athenian sculpture of the Classical period, is here revisited, mixed with the animal skin worn by the maenads, frequently depicted on red-figured pottery at the beginning of the fifth century BCE. In Marzabotto, this design was used to represent the goddess Menerva on the roof of the Temple of Uni, probably added during a renovation of the decoration dating to the end of the fifth century BCE. This choice reveals the level of acculturation of the artisans, aware of models of Greek provenance that were undoubtedly rare in the Etruscan and Italic area. Another fragment displays a male bust (fig. 8.5b), naked and with a cape around the neck, fastened under the chin with a circular button, according to a common iconographic pattern. The figure probably represents a fighting warrior, or maybe a standing soldier, similar to the well-known high-relief figures from the temple of the Belvedere of Orvieto.

A few figured fragments suggest the existence of slabs covering the *mutuli* of the roofs in the urban temples. The three torsos, two masculine (fig. 8.5a, b) and one belonging to Menerva (fig. 8.5c), have the same dimensional module, which could translate to a height of about 50–55 cm for the figures, compatible with the covering of the *mutuli*. As for the subjects on the slabs, they represent the widespread heroic and divine themes documented in Etruscan sacred architecture of the fifth century BCE, such as the gigantomachy that also involves Menerva. Finally, palmette antefixes can be divided into four distinct types, based on size and decorative pattern. Some fragments from the peripteral temple could come from a *nimbus* antefix with a female head, a type documented in Marzabotto during the nineteenth-century excavations.

These elements of temple architectural decoration preserved traces of color. In fact, archaeometric analysis has demonstrated the presence of white, red, black, and even blue. Moreover, during the excavations of a layer near the western wall of the Temple of Uni, Egyptian blue was found,[89] a pigment also used on the eave tiles on the Acropolis, which were decorated with a checkered motif. Until now, Egyptian blue has only been recovered in architectural terracotta at Caere and Gravisca, but the use of this pigment in architecture is also documented in Orvieto and Capua. In Etruria, the arrival of the pigment during the sixth century BCE is related to Greco-Oriental artists, who use it in wall paintings, as in Tarquinia. Then, the color was also applied to temple terracotta decoration. For the first time, its presence can also be confirmed in Marzabotto in relation to the construction workshops of the urban temples.

To conclude, even these few fragments of architectural decoration indicate that the city can be compared to those of Tyrrhenian Etruria for the decorative systems of its sacred buildings, although here impoverished and certainly simplified. Craftsmen specializing in sacred architecture, who were active in several sanctuaries and have also been recognized in north-central Etruria in Orvieto, Arezzo, and Volterra, must have reached Marzabotto, as shown by the techniques, the planimetric forms of the temples, the decoration systems, and the votive epigraphy. Thus, Marzabotto was fully integrated into the widespread phenomenon of monumental temple architecture that includes the entire Tyrrhenian area, as a reflection of the religious, social, political, and economic values of this city.

NOTES

1. See chapter 4.
2. Colonna 1985 for the categories of temples. A useful case study for the topic is Cerveteri (Cristofani 2002; Maggiani 2013; Bellelli, Mallardi, and Tantino 2018:200–203).
3. Guarino 2011; Gottarelli 2013; Potts 2015:88–89; for the Greek world, an interesting perspective on the motivations, agents, and the places involved in sanctuary creations is in Agusta Boularot, Huber, and Van Andriga 2017; for a critical approach to the topic, in a double view on the Etruscan and Greek world, see Smith 2019.
4. See chapter 1.
5. Lippolis 2001:241–255. For the nineteenth-century excavations, Vitali 2001a:57–58.
6. Lippolis 2001:265–267; Colonna 2006:160.
7. Colonna 2006:140–141.
8. Vitali 2001a:50–51.
9. Colonna 2006:141; Potts 2015:67–74.
10. See chapter 14.
11. Vitali 2001a:38–39.
12. Colonna 2006:156–160.
13. Lippolis 2001:231–241; Colonna 2006:160.
14. Govi 2017b.
15. Lippolis 2001:257–263.
16. Vitali 2001a:59–63; Natalucci 2021.
17. Sassatelli 1991a; Vitali 2001a:71–78. See chapter 14.
18. Miari 2000:216–230; Vitali 2001a:67–70; Brizzolara 2001.
19. See chapter 4.
20. Govi 2017b:164; E. Govi, in *REE* 79 (2017): no. 64 and in *REE* 82 (2020): no. 5.
21. E. Govi, in *REE* 80 (2018): nos. 2–3.
22. Ricciardi 2003.
23. Govi 2018a:631–632.
24. See chapter 4.
25. E. Govi, in *REE* 79 (2018): nos. 60–62 with bibliography. See chapter 10.
26. Colonna 2016:162–165.
27. Torelli forthcoming.
28. Gottarelli 2013:132–134; Govi 2017b:164–165.
29. Govi 2017c for the anthropological perspective developed by studies on urban layouts.
30. Govi 2009b:460–461; Gottarelli 2013:135–137. See chapter 16.
31. Gualandi 1970; Gualandi 1973; Gualandi 1974; Gualandi 1983.
32. Malnati and Sassatelli 2008; see chapter 4.
33. Maggiani 1999; Giontella 2006: in particular, for the sanctuary of Marzabotto, see 56–61.
34. Bellelli, Mallardi, and Tantillo 2018.
35. See chapter 14.
36. Sassatelli 1991a; Sassatelli 1998.
37. See chapter 19.
38. Miari 2000:233–235.
39. Simon 1998:123; Giontella 2006:176–177.
40. See chapter 10.
41. See chapter 15.
42. Baldoni 2015; Baldoni 2017.
43. See chapter 7. The analysis was conducted by S. Sertori in her final dissertation for the Specialization School in Cultural Heritage (Sertori 2014–2015).
44. Giontella 2006:58.
45. Curci and Sertori 2019.
46. Giontella 2006:172–177.
47. Maggiani 1998b:49.
48. Malnati et al. 2005; Desantis and Malnati 2009; Desantis and Malnati 2012.
49. See chapter 14.
50. Sassatelli 2009a:332–333.
51. Desantis and Malnati 2012; see chapter 12.
52. Gozzadini 1865:21, 42; Gualandi 1974:184, 189; Brizzolara 2001.
53. See chapter 10.
54. Bonghi Jovino 2005.
55. Bellelli 2012 with bibliography.
56. Lambrinoudakis 2002; Lambrinoudakis 2005.
57. Colonna 2016.
58. Cerchiai 2008b:405.
59. Govi 2015b.
60. M. Bonamici in *REE* 55 (1987–1988 [1989]): 278–279, no. 3, and in *REE* 73 (2007 [2009]): 276–279, no. 6.
61. See chapter 9.
62. Govi 2018a:624–632; Govi 2021.
63. See chapters 7 and 9.
64. E. Govi, in *REE* 80 (2018): nos. 2–3.

65. Bellelli 2012.
66. Bonghi Jovino 2007–2008.
67. Carafa 2007–2008.
68. Carafa 2007–2008; Baglione and De Lucia Brolli 2007–2008: for child graves found in Falerii in the Scasato locality, see 887–888 for the tomb encountered but reserved during the construction of the temple.
69. Fabbri 2017.
70. For this type of symbol, the *forma quadrans*, and the ritual communication with *sigla*, references in Bagnasco Gianni and De Grummond 2020.
71. Michetti 2013; interesting observations on the Greek perspective in Malkin 1987.
72. Eliade 1990, mentioned in Di Fazio 2001:482.
73. On the Greek perspective of the cult of Hera see de La Genière 1997.
74. Bellelli 2012.
75. See de Grummond 2016 for the Venere della Cannicella, the statue of goddess from the sanctuary in the Cannicella cemetery.
76. Sassatelli 2017b.
77. Bellelli 2010:6.
78. Simon 2006:47–48.
79. In the sacred-monumental complex of Tarquinia. The importance of child depositions as part of the cult of the goddess Uni Chia could be inferred through the inscriptions (Bagnasco Gianni 2014), which were never found in direct connection with the burials.
80. Bellelli 2012.
81. See chapter 3.
82. Govi 2017c:153.
83. Bonghi Jovino 2012:47–50.
84. See Govi 2017c:151–152 also for comparisons with the temples in Etruria and Latium.
85. Baronio 2012.
86. E. Govi, in Sassatelli and Govi 2005b:13–34.
87. Small slabs are documented at Pyrgi, in Orvieto, and at other temples (Govi 2019a:542).
88. Govi 2019a.
89. Natalucci 2021.

CHAPTER 9

CULTS, RITUALS, AND THE OFFERING SYSTEM

RICCARDO VANZINI

Thanks to new campaigns and the reinterpretation of earlier, unpublished excavations, it is now possible to highlight the presence of numerous ritual contexts of high importance, but not of great visual impact. In fact, archaeologists have found evidence of a series of rituals, characterized by the deposition of votive offerings, which took place at significant moments of construction or reconstruction of public and private structures; these are often difficult to identify during excavation and even more difficult to interpret.

This evidence is usually concentrated near sacred buildings or important public structures such as streets and can help us to understand more clearly the forms of devotion of the people of Kainua. The offerings found in these contexts can be of different types, but they are all connected to moments of rupture of the preexisting order, such as the foundation, renovation, or demolition of structures and spaces.[1]

Traces of rituals in the private sphere have rarely emerged in Marzabotto. Recent excavations in residential contexts have not brought to light elements of this type, but some data can be recovered by revisiting the records of previous excavations. In the residential area in general, archaeologists found a small number of tiny bronze statuettes (*bronzetti*) and many miniature vases that could have been elements of small-scale domestic ritual.[2] Only one ritual context is clearly evident in the domestic sphere. In House 5 of *Regio* IV, 1, during a renovation of a perimeter wall, some objects with a ritual value were deposited. They consist of a presenter vase (the *presentatoio*, a vase composed of three small, joined cups, probably used for ritual offerings), a miniature cup, a *kylix* with a Dionysian scene, and a *kioniskos* (support for large vases). After their deposition, these objects were sealed with a layer of cobblestones[3]. The few examples of private rituals that have been found in Kainua have the same characteristics as the rituals found in public places, such as temples and streets.

During the excavation of the peripteral temple of Tinia, several traces of offerings with these characteristics were found, and these have had a notable impact on our understanding of the history of the city. This is the case, for example, for the underside of a bowl bearing the inscription *Tins*, that is, the name of the deity venerated in the sanctuary in the possessive case. It was found at the southwest corner of the temple, under a layer of tiles (fig. 9.1 at *1*; *see fig. 10.4: no. 12; see also appendix A, no. 12*).[4]

A second votive offering was found near the perimeter wall of a service building of the temple. It is the base of a bucchero cup, with the inscription . . .] *ni kainuaθi* ×[. . . (fig. 9.1 at *2*; *see fig. 10.4: no. 10; appendix A, no. 10*). Next to this cup, a hole was found in which a jar and another cup had been placed. The cup probably held liquid or some solid offerings for the divinity. In this case it is difficult to say whether the offering is to be connected to the foundation of a small building annexed to the Temple of Tinia, but it is clear from the presence of the name of the city that this deposition took place during a ritual in which the whole community took part.[5]

During the excavation of the southwest corner of the Temple of Uni, two fragments of a local bucchero

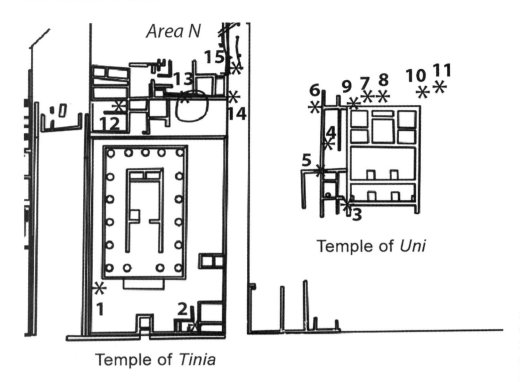

FIGURE 9.1. Location of the rituals at the Urban Sanctuary described in the text. Plan by R. Vanzini.

amphora were found (fig. 9.1 at *3*; *see figs. 8.3, 10.4: no. 6; see also appendix A, no. 6*). They bear the inscription *śpural kainu*[. .], which must have been part of a longer text describing the dedication of the temple by the civic community in its juridical sense (*śpura*).[6] The two sherds were deliberately inserted in the walls of the temple at the time of its construction, probably following a libation ritual that took place with the liquid contained in the amphora itself. In this case it is also clear that in the main usage of these sacred areas, the entire community took part in a series of rituals aimed at obtaining the favor of the gods through the offering of solid food or drinks. Subsequently, the objects used in the ritual were buried near or inside the wall structures, to symbolize their removal from the earthly world and their becoming part of the sacred sphere.

Inside the sacred complex of the Temple of Uni numerous traces of ritual activities have been found, which seem to be common over the entire area. In many cases, the rites are concentrated near the walls of its western *temenos*, an extremely important point of the sacred area, as demonstrated by the pit with the deposition of an infant (fig. 9.1 at *4*).[7] For example, af-

FIGURE 9.2. Ritual offering of two vases discovered in the Temple of Uni.

ter the demolition of the corner between the *temenos* wall and another mighty wall that connects it with the west side of the temple, two jars were set in place (fig. 9.1 at *5*).[8] The two vases were placed together at the same level, at a very short distance from each other (fig. 9.2). Both were ritually broken below the rim, which was then inserted into the vase itself. Finally, they were sealed with fragments of tiles, one also with a flat cobblestone, and the other with a rectangular fragment of unbaked brick. Evidently these elements refer to the building materials used for the construction of these structures and their presence, although in small samples, is meant to represent the whole wall, in a sort of *pars pro toto*. Fragments of cups and jugs were also found near the vases, which could attest a libation carried out during the ritual.

In the inner part of this corner a third jar was found, placed at a lower level than the first two. This vase reflects a different ritual, because it was filled and covered with a thick layer with traces of combustion, a sign of a ritual centered on the use of fire. Carpological analyzes carried out on the contents of the jars revealed the presence of cereals, lentils, broad beans, hazelnuts, grapes, and eggshells inside the vase placed in the center of the wall.[9] The outer vessel contained cereals and grapes (perhaps wine), while the one inside the wall contained only cereals. In addition to these foods, there were also a few animal remains, especially phalanges, ribs, and teeth, related to the triad of the pig, sheep, and bull (*suovetaurilia*).

The importance of this boundary wall is confirmed by the discovery of traces of another ritual that took place further north, again at the intersection with a connecting wall with the temple (fig. 9.1 at *6*). Here was found a shallow pit with the neck of an amphora stuck vertically into the ground, in order to let liquids flow toward the soil, with a small cup on its side. Near these vases was found an overturned plate that covered an animal bone, probably a food offering to the divinity.[10]

The findings described here are almost certainly part of a defunctionalization ritual, carried out when this part of the sanctuary was subjected to a substantial modification of its structures, in order to compensate the divinity in some way for changes made. The materials found here allow us to date this event to a period from the fourth to third century BCE, and therefore to a terminal moment in the life of the city. It is significant that these findings can be compared with other cases known from the Etruscan world, for example, from the sacred areas of Vigna Parrocchiale in Cerveteri,[11] the Civita of Tarquinia,[12] Campetti of Veii,[13] and Monte li Santi–le Rote of Narce.[14]

During excavation of the sector to the north of this temple, numerous other attestations of votive offerings were found, highlighting the presence of a complex system of offerings, connected to the construction and/or demolition of other structures linked to the sphere of the sacred. On the occasion of the defunctionalization of a narrow ditch located behind the temple, some rituals were performed, one at its west end and another in its the central part. In the first case, a large pit was dug and filled with numerous ceramic and tile fragments, among which a fragment of architectural decoration stands out, probably part of the decoration of the temple[15] (fig. 9.1 at *7*). In the other case, in the center of the ditch a large *dolium* was placed upside down (fig. 9.1 at *8*). Between the ditch and the temple there was another pit containing the remains of a *lekythos*, perhaps linked to an offering ritual (fig. 9.1 at *9*).

At the western end of the sacred area, other traces of these rituals emerged. A hole was found containing the upside-down neck of an East Greek amphora (fig. 9.1 at *10*). A few meters east of this was found a reddened soil and a concentration of carpal and tarsal animal bones with evident cutmarks, all fairly close together (fig. 9.1 at *11*).

The numerical difference between the ritual actions that emerged in the last few years of excavation and what was known until then is significant. Apart from the sparse extant evidence from the Acropolis—a basin of tiles and burnt animal remains from Altar B[16]—we have very little data from the rest of the Etruscan city. Probably the absence is not due to a real lacuna, but to difficulties for the excavators of the last centuries in recognizing these elements in the absence of a reliable stratigraphic method. This habitual action probably explains why all the evidence is concentrated in recently excavated areas. This is the case, for example, of the area north (Area N) of the Temple of Tinia, currently under study by our team. This sector is located behind the peripteral temple, overlooking the *stenopos* that separates this *insula* from the neighboring one of the sanctuary of Uni. The area seems to have had a prolonged life span, from the end of the sixth to the fourth century BCE, and is distinguished by several construction phases. Because of the abundance of ritual evidence, this area could be an extraordinary resource for our emerging understanding of the Etruscan system of offerings.

The presence of ritual activities is evident in this area from its earliest phases. During the reconstruction of a wall in the western sector, a jar was placed near the structure (fig. 9.1 at *12*), inside of which was a layer of ash and animal bones. When this area was abandoned more than a century later, another ritual was carried out 10 cm above the first one. Here was deposited an overturned basin, covering a layer of carbon and animal bones. At the same time, a second overturned basin was placed in the same area, along with numerous other vases (cups, plates, and jars). Under the basin were found two *scapulae*, one of a horse and one of a bovine.

During the advanced stage of life of Area N, probably around the beginning of the fourth century BCE, a series of rearrangements was carried out in the entire complex and in the neighboring *stenopos*. This was completely destroyed, with the removal of almost all the gravel paving (*glareatio*) of which it was made. An older stone channel, connecting the street to a rectangular basin, was also destroyed, and a jar was placed inside to seal and sacralize the context (fig. 9.1 at *13*).[17]

A single, limited portion of *glareatio* was deliberately left in the corner of the most ancient wall of Area N, sealed by an expanse of large pebbles and covered by a thin layer of soil. Inside this soil, an elliptical pit was dug near the wall that borders the *insula* to the west. A large young pig was placed inside this hole, cut into different parts that were carefully arranged inside the pit (figs. 9.1 at *14*, 9.3).[18] Later, the animal's body was covered with a layer of soil and sealed by an expanse of tightly set cobblestones. The methods of deposition and the context of discovery are significant because of their unusual nature.

Zooarchaeological analyzes carried out on the animal remains made it possible to determine that the individual must have been a large domestic pig, with a height at the withers of about 85 cm.[19] If we compare these data with those of other pigs found in Kainua, we can observe that it is undoubtedly considerably larger than the local average (around 71.2 cm).[20] It is therefore clear that the animal was chosen for its phys-

FIGURE 9.3. The skeleton of a pig at the time of its discovery. On the right, the stones of the wall; all around, the expanse of cobblestones that covered the remains.

ical characteristics. It was between 12 and 18 months old, so it could have grown further. Through the weight of the skeletal remains (4,355 g), it was possible to calculate its total weight,[21] which turned out to be about 54.5 kg, meaning at least 35.4 kg of meat could have been obtained from the animal.[22]

Finally, it was possible to find traces of postmortem cuts on the vertebrae. In numerous cases many cutmarks in the vertebral body have been highlighted, along the anterior–posterior plane, a sign of an unconventional division of the carcass. Furthermore, the pig was beheaded and cut at the pelvis, to separate the hind legs from the body.

The circumstances of the deposition therefore show the unusual nature of the rite to which the pig was subjected. In fact, the carcass was not laid out in its entirety. At a slightly higher level, the remains of the pectoral girdle and the right forelimb initially emerged,

1. Jewelry from Marzabotto, now lost. After Gozzadini 1865: pl. 17.

2. Panoramic view of Kainua in 2014.

3. View of the Eastern Necropolis of Kainua.

4. Votive bronze statuette (Aplu/Apollo?) from the Water Shrine. Around 470 BCE.

5. The departure of the warrior: statuettes crowning a *candelabrum* from the private collection of the Counts Aria. 425–400 BCE. SABAP Bologna Archive.

6. Terracotta *puteal* (well curb) from House 2, *Regio* IV, 1 (left); terracotta *puteal* from the southern area of the city (right). After Bentz and Reusser 2008; Govi 2007.

7. Examples of local pottery (jugs). After Mattioli 2017.

8. Marble *cippus* from the Eastern Necropolis. After Govi 2007:62.

9. Janiform Attic red-figure *kantharos* in the form of satyr's and woman's heads. On the *calyx*: (a) Menelaos pursuing Helen and (b) a *colloquium* scene. From the tomb of a female in the Northern Necropolis. After Bentz and Reusser 2008: fig. 79:a–c.

10. Virtual reconstruction of the temples of the Acropolis. From the left: Temples E, C, and A. Reconstruction by S. Garagnani.

11. *Podium*-altar D on the Acropolis. After Govi 2007:19.

12. Virtual reconstruction of *Podium*-altar B on the Acropolis, including the water tank next to it. Reconstruction by G. Mancuso.

13. Virtual reconstruction of the Urban Sanctuary. Reconstruction by S. Garagnani; drawing by G. Mancuso.

14. Virtual reconstruction of House 5, *Regio* IV, 1. Reconstruction by G. Mancuso.

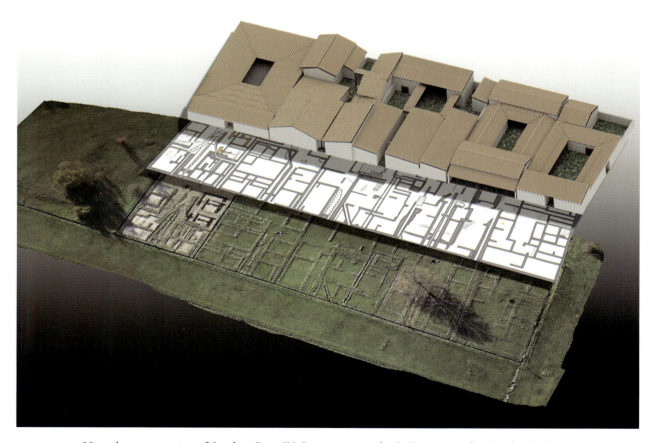

15. Virtual reconstruction of *Insula* 1, *Regio* IV. Reconstruction by S. Garagnani; drawing by G. Mancuso.

16. Digital models of the main buildings overlaid on a panoramic view of the plateau. Reconstruction by S. Garagnani, Studio Kulla, G. Mancuso; image by G. Mancuso.

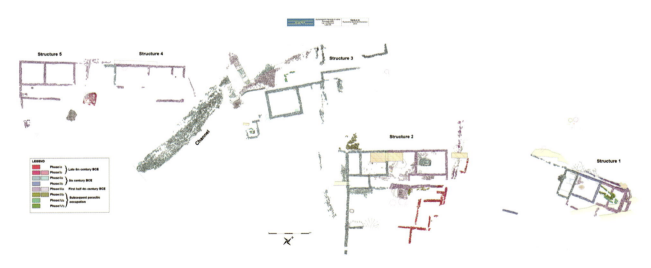

17. La Quercia, plan of the settlement with indication of the chronological phases. SABAP Bologna Archive.

still in anatomical connection (scapula, humerus, ulna, and radius). They covered the second level, consisting of a series of bones of the hind limbs, both right and left, in anatomical connection.

This was followed by the remains of the axial skeleton (vertebrae and ribs), arranged at the edge of the pit, near its eastern and southern sides. These parts appeared to be in partial connection, as the vertebral column was divided in half, both in the anterior–posterior and in the longitudinal direction. After removal of the axial skeleton, the left forelimb also emerged, once again in anatomical connection. Finally, when this level had been removed, the animal's skull was brought to light, placed on the bottom of the hole and oriented east–west. The type of deposition of the pig remains absolutely unique, in the overlapping of the different parts and the method of sectioning the body.

On the basis of the stratigraphy, we can reconstruct the order of dismemberment:

1. After the pig was killed, the skull was detached by beheading.
2. The body was divided by cutting the vertebrae.[23]
3. The pelvis was separated from the spine, with the hind limbs still attached to it. The part of the spine joined to the pelvis was also removed and deposited together with it.
4. The forelimbs were removed perhaps by disarticulation. They were probably still joined to the scapular girdles.
5. Given the dispersion of the vertebrae, we suppose further subdivisions were made at the level of the spine.

It was also possible to outline the sequence of actions relating to the deposition (fig. 9.4):

1. First of all, the skull was placed at the bottom of the hole.
2. A portion of the rib cage was placed in the southern side of the hole, with the vertebrae facing south and the ribs facing north.
3. On the eastern side a second portion of the rib cage was placed, with the vertebrae facing east and the ribs facing west.

FIG. 9.4. The sequence of the ritual deposition: the skull (on the bottom of the hole), the rib cage (above the skull), and finally the forelimbs.

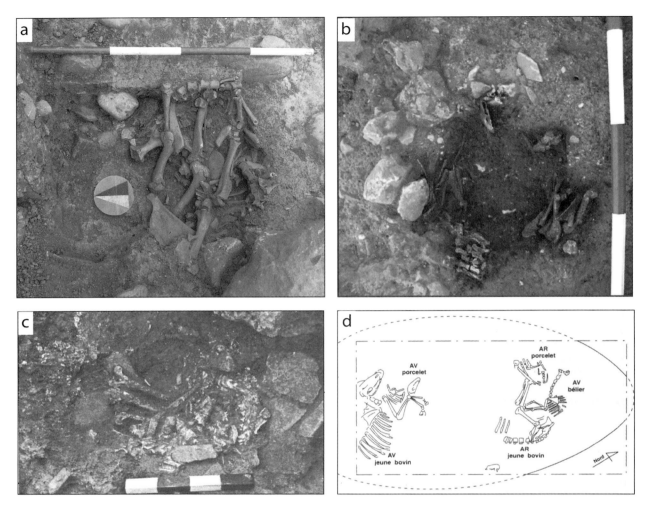

FIG. 9.5. Comparison of the ritual found at Kainua to others in the Mediterranean: (a) the skeleton of the pig of Kainua; (b) Muro Leccese (after De Grossi Mazzorin and Perrone 2013); (c) Pyrgi (after Baglione and Belelli Marchesini 2015); (d) Thasos (after Bondé et al. 2003).

4. Both hind limbs were positioned in the center of the pit, the right one to the north and the left one to the south.
5. The left forelimb was placed next to the portion of the side on the north side.
6. Finally, the right forelimb was placed on its southern side.

From an autopsy analysis on the remains it was possible to verify the absence of traces of combustion, leading to the exclusion of a cooking treatment of the meat. Therefore, after the killing, the animal was intentionally buried without its flesh having been consumed, which is of particular importance when analyzing this unusual rite.

Given these particular characteristics, we tried to estimate the value of this offering and the reasons behind such a detailed and complex ritual. From the historical-anthropological point of view, the purifying or expiatory value of a pig sacrifice is well known, as also attested by numerous Greek, Roman, and Etruscan-Italic sources.[24] Furthermore, we have some archaeological finds showing the purification value represented by the sacrifice of dismembered animals. For example, in Thasos, under the base of the monument of Glaucos, the bones of three animals deposited in an unusual way were found.²⁵ The remains of a pig, an ox, and a ram were deposed inside an elliptical pit (fig. 9.5d). On the southern side of the pit, the front half of the ox and the pig and the rear half of the ram were placed. On the northern side were the rear halves of the first two animals and the front half of a sheep. The bodies of the victims show no other signs, neither of cooking, nor skinning, nor consumption of the meat. This context dates to the first quarter of the fifth century BCE.

Another find of the same chronology comes from the Messapian settlement of Muro Leccese, where two holes with disjointed animal remains were found, which were elements of a ritual for the disposal of a structure.²⁶ In the first case, the animals, all sheep and goats, were removed and laid in a particular way around the perimeter of the pit, while, in the second case, the victims showed signs of subdivision of the parts, probably carried out by disarticulation rather than by cutting (fig. 9.5b). Another example could be the deposition of a dog, cut into various parts and covered with tiles and stones (fig. 9.5c), during the foundation rite of a tower-house in the Ceremonial Quarter of Pyrgi.²⁷

On the basis of the stratigraphic data and the comparisons identified in the ancient sources and archaeological finds, it seems clear that a ritual of expiation and purification was involved here. Probably following the obliteration of the structural elements that formed the *stenopos* and the channel, the community had to atone for guilt derived from the breaking of the preestablished order. In fact, it was an important road, also from the sacred point of view, as it divided the Temple of Tinia from that of Uni, and its construction dates to the foundation of the city.

The type of ritual adopted here presents all the typical elements of atonement rites that we have found in the sources: the choice of a victim that is associated with purification (pig), the separation of the body, its new assembly that aims to recreate the original unity, the nonconsumption of the meat that has absorbed the guilt, and the dedication to the chthonic divinities through entombment.

This hypothesis is confirmed by another ritual found 7.0 m north, during the excavations of 1968, and recently reassessed by our team.²⁸ Here, a jar containing charcoals and pig bones was buried under a layer of soil that obliterated the same *stenopos* (fig. 9.1 at *15*).

In conclusion, from the point of view of rituals, the private and the public spheres share the same ritual formats and a completely matching offering system. In addition, this system and the language of the sacred discovered in this city are the same as those that characterize the entire Etruscan-Italic world of that period, showing us how much this city was linked to the rest of this world, even from a religious point of view.

NOTES

1. See chapters 4, 8.
2. Miari 2000:204–216.
3. Mancuso 2019–2020.
4. Sassatelli and Govi 2005b:38–47.
5. Sassatelli and Govi 2005b:47–55; see chapter 10.
6. Govi 2016; Govi 2017b:158–162; Govi 2018a:615–616; see chapter 8.
7. See the full discussion in chapter 8.
8. Govi 2018a:620–621.
9. See M. Carra, chapter 7 of this volume.
10. Govi 2018a:621–622.
11. Bellelli 2012:457.
12. Chiesa 2005; Chiaramonte Trerè 2016.
13. Carosi 2002:368.
14. De Lucia Brolli 2016.
15. Govi 2019a.
16. Miari 2000:201–202.
17. This channel might have been used for draining liquids or beverage from the street to the basin, perhaps for ritual purposes. Thanks to the stratigraphical data, we could understand that its disposal is clearly linked to the destruction of the street.
18. Govi 2016:204; Govi 2018a; Govi 2017b:167; Vanzini 2015–2016.
19. The calculation of the height at the withers of the individual was estimated on the basis of the coefficients of M. Teichert (Teichert 1969). The measurements were made considering the method and nomenclature of A. Von den Driesch (Von den Driesch 1976).
20. Curci 2010.
21. Reed 1969.

22. Susenbeth and Keitel 1988.

23. These traces were found both on some thoracic vertebrae and on lumbar vertebrae. It is a sign of a slaughtering action that most likely affected the entire spine.

24. Paoletti 2004:24 (Greek); Saladino 2004:78 (Roman); Camporeale 2004:57 (Etruscan).

25. Bondé et al. 2003.

26. De Grossi Mazzorin and Perrone 2013.

27. Baglione and Belelli Marchesini 2015:139–140.

28. Tirtei 2016–2017.

CHAPTER 10

WRITING PRACTICE AND SOCIETY

ANDREA GAUCCI

Besides revealing hundreds of alphabetical and non-alphabetical *sigla*,[1] excavations in Kainua-Marzabotto have brought to light a significant number of inscriptions (sixty) dating to the second half of the sixth and the fifth century BCE. From the mid-fifth century BCE the practice of writing became increasingly rare, and although the city was active at least during the first half of the fourth century BCE and probably later, it has not yielded inscriptions definitely dated to this century. The exceptional importance of this body of inscriptions from Kainua has suggested to us the need to include a complete listing of the corpus (appendix A), along with a full set of illustrations (figs. 10.4–10.7) and a map showing the findspots of the individual specimens (*see map 6; cf. map 5 for labels of each area*). I will refer to these frequently in the following discussion.

Epigraphical evidence comes from sacred, residential, and craft contexts, but not funerary ones. This lack is certainly not attributable to the loss of grave goods during World War II, as it is likely that inscriptions would already have been recovered in the nineteenth-century excavation campaigns. Rather, this seems to depend on funerary practice, more or less matching that of other cities in Etruria Padana.[2] Nor is there evidence of texts carved on stone monuments, as in Felsina (Bologna) from the first half of the fifth century BCE.[3]

Looking at evidence from residential and sacred areas, a lack of knowledge about the ancient settlement of Felsina strongly limits any comparison with nearby Kainua, since only a few inscribed scraps exist from the sacred acropolis at Villa Cassarini and from the residential area.[4] Therefore, among the main cities of Etruria Padana, Kainua features an exceptional *corpus*, surpassed only by Spina during the late sixth–fifth centuries BCE (seventy-three, a number that combines funerary and residential contexts and that will certainly increase given the still unpublished material).[5] The totals from the nucleus of Adria, amounting to twenty-five inscriptions, and that of Forcello di Bagnolo San Vito, with sixteen, all from residential contexts, are considerable but smaller.[6]

In the same period, only one inscription (dating around 475 BCE) is known from the Apennine valleys around the city, that of the sacred shrine at Monteacuto Ragazza.[7] It is a unique monument for Etruria Padana: the text is incised on the surface of a stone base for a bronze *ex-voto*. The inscription was probably written by the very same man mentioned on the text: [*Ar*]*nθ Veianeś*, son of *Laris* and *Aulnei*, who was *furθ* (an official?) and did something (the past tense *puzuke*), probably the votive act. The layout was influenced by models from southern Etruria and the practice of writing on votive bases derived from the Late Archaic Orvieto sanctuaries, while the palaeography is the contemporary one elaborated in Kainua.[8]

EPIGRAPHY IN CONTEXT

The exceptional epigraphical situation of Kainua has made it possible to investigate a great variety of contexts, although with a very different level of quality of the information for individual items. The most recent novelties certainly come from the Urban Sanctuary of *Regio* I.

Important texts, mostly incomplete, have been brought to light from the Temple of Uni and its *temenos*. Bucchero vessels are most common, such as the two fragments of an amphora (no. 6; fig. 10.4; *see fig. 8.2, left and center*), dated around 500 BCE, found inside the foundation walls of the temple and thus indicating an intentional deposition at the time of its construction.

In addition to the bucchero, inscribed fragments of a gray-ware plate and of a coarse-ware jar (*olla*) were found, also part of a ritual act involving the reconstruction of the northwestern perimeter corner of the *temenos*. The fragment of a plate (no. 7; fig. 10.4) comes from a trench parallel to the *temenos* wall, inside of which were found other traces of a rite, including infant sacrifice; the fragment of *olla* (no. 8; fig. 10.4) was recovered in the filling of the trench.[9] This case shows how the epigraphical evidence is given further significance by the context of the discovery itself. Indeed, a cross mark incised on a disk-shaped foot of a bucchero cup found at the bottom of the same trench was placed directly under the burial of the infant and with the mark in the external base oriented according to the cardinal points. In fact, the close relationship between mark, position, and context led E. Govi to recognize it as an element to be linked to a founding rite performed at the time of reconstruction of the wall.[10]

Four inscriptions come from the Temple of Tinia (*Regio* I, 5), all written on bucchero vases, with the exception of the bronze sheet (no. 9; figs. 10.1, 10.4). The latter, found on the western side of the sacred fence is an exceptional document, and, although highly incomplete, it remains the longest text of the city and the second of all the Etruscan sites of Etruria Padana, after the Melenzani small amphora from Felsina (end of the seventh century BCE).[11] With the aid of skilled scribes, the practice of writing on metal sheets started in the second half of the sixth century BCE along with the development of sanctuaries. Metal sheets are purposefully chosen for ritual texts, testifying to the participation of the city in a lively cultural network.[12]

The discovery of an inscribed bucchero cup foot (no. 10; see figs. 10.3, 10.4), which provides the name of the city in the locative case (*kainuaθi* < *kainua+θi*)—and was recovered near a pit containing an *olla* with a cup inside it—is also significant, and probably signals a ritual act.[13] The poleonym, perhaps at the end of a formula that has a polyadic dimension, and the context, probably a ritual act, make it possible to connect this inscribed object to those found in association with the foundations or reconstructions of sacred structures. In the sanctuary of Uni, the systematic selection of fragments with single words has already led E. Govi to suggest the possibility (at least in some cases) that they were *ostraka* or deliberately selected parts of longer fragmented inscriptions. We could suppose that in this case as well, at the end of the ritual and once the vase was broken, only the fragment with the name of the city was deliberately deposited. Moreover, the more ancient bucchero fragment (around 500 BCE) from the "layer of the sixth century BCE" (no. 44; fig. 10.6) supports this hypothesis: here too the same lexeme is the only text preserved. Therefore, in two very distant points of the city two fragments of bucchero with the same inscribed word in the locative case have been found. This coincidence does not seem fortuitous, and it can therefore plausibly be assumed that the vases were probably used in special ceremonies characterized by a similar ritual that was repeated over time.[14]

Unfortunately, no extant evidence has emerged

FIGURE 10.1. Inscribed bronze sheet (appendix A, no. 9) from *Regio* I, 5, around 470 BCE. Copyright R. Macrì.

from the sacred buildings of the Acropolis, amongst the first structures excavated during the nineteenth century.

An overview of the northernmost part of the city is completed by the pottery workshop of *Regio* II, 1, referred to as the Great Furnace. Here, apart from some unpublished inscribed scraps, the most significant inscription is certainly the bucchero cup fragment with the name of the god Tina (no. 13; fig. 10.4), interpreted by G. Sassatelli as a strong testimony of the relationship between the Great Furnace and the sanctuary of Tinia. Other inscriptions are more recent, written mostly before firing on terracotta disks with knobs.[15]

South of *plateia* B, inscriptions are concentrated in *Regiones* IV and V. In *Regio* IV, the extensive excavation of *insula* 1 has uncovered only two inscriptions. This low number is striking, given the elitist character of the houses[16] and also the significant quantitative difference compared to the nearby House 1 on *insula* 2, from which sixteen inscriptions have been brought to light. This difference could perhaps relate to the fact that the excavations of *insula* 1, mainly conducted during the late 1950s and early 1960s, almost never reached the deeper levels of these structures,[17] unlike the systematic excavation of House 1 in *insula* 2. Here, the concentration and variety of epigraphical evidence is remarkable. As for sacred contexts, the preference for bucchero vessels (eight out of sixteen) and the similar gray ware (two) is clearly confirmed, although the fine ware is not uncommon (four). In the latter class the only inscription written before firing is recorded (no. 31; fig. 10.6), whose nature as a numeral expressed as a word (θun = one), clarifies its function within the production process. Overall, House 1 shows two prevalent categories of inscriptions, those of possession and alphabets.[18] Regarding the latter category, a deer horn handle with an abbreviated form of the alphabet (no. 25) is an exceptional object, with the most direct comparisons with those of the Veneto and eastern Alpine territory, where the choice of this type of writing medium is almost the norm.[19]

In the westernmost *insula* (4) Gozzadini recorded the discovery of a terracotta disk (no. 38*; fig. 10.6), found in a well adjacent to a kiln and a room with five other small kilns.

FIGURE 10.2. Inscribed cobblestone (appendix A, no. 39*), from *Regio* V, 2, around 500 BCE, as shown in the nineteenth-century permanent exposition in Villa Aria.

Regio V has been investigated over centuries, starting with G. Gozzadini and continuing up to the present. This situation has led to a varied quality in the collected documentation. During the nineteenth century an inscribed cobblestone, unfortunately lost (no. 39*; figs. 10.2, 10.6), was found in the southern house of *insula* 2, excavated by Edoardo Brizio. With its inscription *mi lavtunieś*, "I [belong to] *Lavtunie*," this is the only "talking" stone among a numbers of lithic objects bearing marks that are understood as numerals and therefore having the function of weights.[20] This object also has marks: three strokes on the side of the text, as well as two strokes and an asterisk (= 100?) in the center on the opposite side, probably all numerals, allowing its interpretation as a weight guaranteed by its owner.[21]

More recently, the houses of the northernmost part of *insula* 3 have been systematically investigated by the École Française. From here a limited number of digraphs (two-letter inscriptions) have been found, all except one on bucchero vessels, probably abbreviations of names (nos. 41–42; fig. 10.6), as well as an incomplete inscription (no. 40; fig. 10.6). Moving west, *insula* 4 yielded two inscriptions on bucchero (nos. 44–45; fig. 10.6), from Archaic levels identified and excavated in the 1950s. Finally, another fragment of terracotta disk was found during nineteenth-century excavations of the westernmost *insula* 5 (no. 52; fig. 10.7).

The most recent excavations of the building complex defined as a "foundry" have brought to light only the exceptional serpentinite calibrator (or, less likely, a wire-drawing tool) on which an ownership text and other letters are traced (no. 51; fig. 10.7). If it had been a tool for quality control of metallurgical production standards, as it seems, it would have been an object of considerable importance and certainly of prolonged use over time.

A couple of inscriptions come from the northernmost house of the *insula*, more precisely from the foundation or sealed Archaic levels. Nearby, a terracotta disk (no. 49; fig. 10.7) was found in the public sewer of *plateia* C. The text is identical to that found by Gozzadini (no. 38*), and so it should be related to the craft complex of *insula* 4.

An inscription written on the rim of a basin (no. 60; fig. 10.7) was found in the Water Shrine, a suburban place of worship. This is an exceptional text, as it is the only one that clearly shows a votive formula from a worshiper.

This overview clearly indicates the particular nature of the epigraphical evidence from sacred contexts, also limited in comparison to that coming from residential and craft areas. Despite this rarity, the quality of the inscriptions clarifies the role of the writing within preeminent ritual practices.

As for the residential areas, the concentration of documents in House 1 of *Regio* IV, 2 is striking. It is certainly an elitist and complex context in its more ancient phase, presenting a widespread use of inscriptions, in contrast with the other contexts systematically excavated in *Regio* V (*insulae* 3 and 5).

THE VALUE OF THE CHOSEN OBJECTS

Kainua preserves forty-seven inscriptions on fragments of vases and thirteen on objects of another nature. In the same chronological period, this variety is completely unique in the sites of Etruria Padana. The Felsina evidence is mostly on *stelae*, and if we look at Spina and Adria, the two other cities most relevant for writing documentation, at the first there are only a few non-ceramic inscribed objects, while there are none at all from Adria.

Examining the pottery, it is possible to identify the most prevalent shape as cups, numbering twenty-five out of forty-seven vessels. The most common fabric is without any doubt bucchero (fifteen), but there are also fine-ware cups (ten). This small quantitative difference between the two fabrics is not found in the rest of the selected pottery shapes. Indeed, the fine ware is represented only by two mortar basins, but this choice is obviously constrained by the fact that this shape is not produced in bucchero.[22] Bucchero is, instead, represented by other shapes (amphora, lid perhaps for this type of vase, chalice/*kantharos*, small *olla*, *olpe*), mainly concentrated in the sanctuaries.[23] Gray ware is rarely chosen: we note some unusual shapes, such as a jug (no. 29), a plate (no. 7), and a single-handled small cup or *tazza* (no. 27).[24] Coarse ware is also under-represented: there are two lid-cups, an *olla*, and three *dolii* (storage jars). Among these, *olla* no. 8 comes from a sacred context, and it is likely that its selection depended on a particular cult practice, also because it would normally be used as a writing surface for non-alphabetical marks with numeral value.[25]

As already remarked by G. Sassatelli, the practice of writing, especially in its most ancient phase, shows the ideological and sacral choices of an elite that closely binds its prestige pottery (i.e., bucchero) to specific uses, highlighted by texts written directly on the ceramic surface. In particular, bucchero and gray-ware jugs and amphoras must have had a selective and significant role in practices related to wine consumption, considering that Attic examples are very rare.[26] Moreover, no inscriptions have been found on Attic pottery so far. This absence of evidence is certainly significant, because in other cities of Etruria Padana, such as Adria, Felsina, and Spina, there are inscriptions on such imported pottery from sacred and funerary contexts. This is to be interpreted clearly as a cultural choice, certainly in contrast to Adria, where the bucchero as a bearer of inscriptions is almost absent and Attic pottery plays a leading role,[27] but also to Felsina, where two of the three inscriptions from the sanctuary of Villa Cassarini are on Attic pottery.[28]

WRITING TRADITIONS

All the inscriptions are in the writing system rooted in Etruria Padana and northern Etruria, except for *akius* (no. 57*, dated around 400 BCE; fig. 10.7), which has mixed features[29] and an exact parallel in Campiglia Marittima (Livorno, Tuscany).[30] Kainua seems to have no relation with the inscriptions in the writing system of southern Etruria found along the Adriatic coast, from Verucchio and Rimini to Adria, referring to people moving along the route between inner southern Etruria and the Po Delta.[31] Nevertheless, influences of this writing practice have been strong in sanctuaries of the Apennine city[32] and also of its territory (see above Monteacuto Ragazza's inscription). In Kainua, we first see it in verbal punctuation using dots, as in nos. 10–11 from the Temple of Tinia.[33] This was part of graphic reform developed in Caere, which arrived in northern Etruria at the end of the century, and perhaps crossed the Apennines from here. Another piece of evidence pointing to southern Etruria is the word *śpural*, for which see the considerations below.

The direction of writing is generally from right to left (sinistroverse), although left-to-right (dextroverse) cases also occur. Generally speaking, the latter is mostly documented in the Archaic period or in a situation of contact with non-Etruscan writing systems. Kainua stands out because, in the rest of Etruria Padana, the dextroverse direction is decidedly rare during this period.[34] Among dextroverse inscriptions, the two mentioning the sanctuary of Uni (nos. 4–5) and the ones mentioning the god Tinia (nos. 11–13) are surely worth mentioning. This consistency and content are striking, and E. Govi has hypothesized that this may depend on forms of editing influenced by a model developed within the sanctuaries. If so, the choice of writing a text following this model is probably due to the consecration of the vase.[35] Not surprisingly, inscription no. 7 mentioning the goddess Vei is sinistroverse. Indeed, this one-word inscription was part of a rite within the *temenos* of Uni probably involving the practice of selecting vessel fragments with single significant words, as for the aforementioned poleonyms. We find the dextroverse direction in other inscriptions.[36] These all belong to the most ancient phase of Kainua's writing practice, confirming an Archaic quality that also clearly emerges from palaeography.

Archaic palaeographic traits are consistently visible in the texts coming from foundation levels and therefore belonging to an older phase than that of the founded city.[37]

The spread of a primary Archaic tradition is confirmed by other inscriptions.[38] Among them, nos. 4, 5 (*see fig. 8.2, right*), and 23 are closely related to each other.[39] As has been widely noted by the critics, the palaeographic characteristics, mainly the cross mark for *theta*, should relate directly to the Chiusi epigraphic tradition of the Archaic period.[40]

A few other inscriptions recall an Archaic tradition.[41] Among them, the fragments of bucchero amphora from Temple of Uni (no. 6), dated around 500 BCE, have the peculiarity of a *pi* with three strokes, a striking element of archaicity, documented in Etruria during the sixth century BCE,[42] and of an angled *alpha* rather typical of the southern Etruscan palaeographic tradition.[43] Also the word *śpural*, among the most ancient attestations together with that of the bronze sheet (no. 9), in its graphemic aspect (i.e., the use of *sade*), refers to southern Etruria, confirming how the institutional meaning of the word lands in Kainua together and closely linked to its graphemic aspect.[44]

Broadly speaking, E. Govi has pointed out the heterogeneous graphic features of the main writing tradition in use in the city during the Late Archaic period. They betray a connection with the northern Etruscan district that may have mediated southern influences. Particular attention has to be paid to Chiusi, which spread its writing style toward the north, and perhaps to Fiesole, which received it and acted as an intermediary.[45]

Nos. 11 and 12 (i.e., the votive inscriptions to the god Tinia) could be strong evidence of a transition phase from the Archaic to a later writing style, characterized by letters with a less elongated and more rounded form, chronologically to be placed in the first half of the fifth century BCE.[46] Other inscriptions could show the ending phase of the Archaic tradition, clearly marked by the abandonment of angled *alpha*.[47]

Regarding nearby Felsina, the Archaic tradition documented in Kainua emerges around 500 BCE, where it is evident in the inscription on the fine-ware cup from tomb 405 of the Certosa necropolis.[48] The rarity of epigraphical evidence in funerary contexts and the lack of knowledge of residential contexts unfortunately prevent us from building on this clue. What is certain is that, from the second quarter of the fifth century BCE, monumental inscriptions on *stelae* show a very different palaeographic tradition,[49] not unlike what was happening during the same period in Kainua. Indeed, here inscriptions (nos. 9, 10, 14, 20, 29) are consistent with a change. Although they still show some aspects related to older documents,[50] new aspects emerge (such as curved *alpha*, circular *theta* with a central dot, hooked *pi*, and *rho* with a curved or triangular eyelet and with no under-advancing stroke).

It is worth noting that in the bronze sheet no. 9, dated around 470 BCE,[51] the first line shows *alpha* and *tau* with bars ascending in the script direction that perhaps betray their scribe's training in sanctuaries in southern Etruria, while in the remaining lines the bars of the same letters are descending.[52] Surely these differences do not depend on carelessness. Indeed, the rendering of the curved lines with small strokes using the burin confirms a wish to faithfully follow a specific writing style. Therefore, the tendencies of a very different writing tradition are confirmed. It seems to be close to that of the stonemasons of Felsina, from which it is distinguished above all by the shape of the hooked *pi* (letter shaped by two strokes in Felsina). The inscription on the aforementioned votive base from Monteacuto Ragazza also references this new writing tradition.[53] It would therefore not be surprising that the individual mentioned, probably the creator of the monument, took part in the tradition of Kainua and therefore belonged to the city community or its territory.

Finally, the inscription on the serpentinite calibrator (no. 51) could represent the emergence of the *corsivizzante* type (from *corsivo* = italics), as already suggested by A. Maggiani.[54] This is a graphic type elaborated in the Chiusi territory at the beginning of the fifth century BCE and then spread to the north. Among its characteristics can be recalled the shape of the *my* composed by five similar strokes and the peculiar rounded aspects of *epsilon* and *digamma*.[55] The rarity of the evidence for this phase, concentrated in the texts of terracotta disks, makes it difficult to determine the incidence of this graphic style, whose consolidated use in nearby Felsina could be dated from the second half of the third quarter of the fifth century BCE.[56] It is not surprising to find this reform, elaborated in Chiusi and seemingly implemented in Etruria Padana precisely during the mid-fifth century BCE, as demonstrated by the territory of Mantua[57] and Polesine,[58] while Spina's documentation about this reform so far starts from the end of the century, without substantial changes.[59]

ONOMASTICS AND SOCIETY

Most of the inscriptions express ownership, providing evidence for onomastics, that is, the names of individual persons. However, their fragmentary state, deriving from the nature of the contexts of discovery, poses serious issues in tracing the lineages of the onomastics.

We can divide the onomastic inscriptions into three main categories:[60]

1. "speaking inscriptions": the object declares its ownership or its destination for a certain person, e.g., *mi larθial pumpunaś*, no. 47: "I [belong to] *Larθ Pumpuna*."[61] A similar format appears in *θina rakaluś* (no. 23), where the pronoun *mi* (i.e., "I") is replaced by the name of the vase *θina* (i.e., "amphora").[62]

2. genitive of the owner, e.g., *larisal kraikaluś* (no. 15): "of *Laris Kraikalu*."[63]

3. absolutive case: identity between the object and the owner, e.g., *lave* (no. 20): "*Lave*."[64]

Onomastics are documented in other kinds of inscriptions, namely the complex text of the bronze sheet from the Temple of *Tinia* (no. 9) and the votive formula from the Water Shrine (no. 60).

First, we can state that only one text shows a possibly female name (no. 30); otherwise all are male. Among them, we can list five cases of *praenomen* (first name) + *gentilicium* (family name) formulas: *Arnθ*

Kapruś, Laris Kraikalu, Larθ Lentiu, Lareke Niritalu, Laris Pumpuna. These suggest a small pool of male first names *Arnθ, Laris, Larθ, Lareke*, to which we can add *Vel, Venel, Larθur*, and probably *Lave*.⁶⁵ There is not complete overlap with the first names most often found in nearby Felsina between 475 and the beginning of the fourth century BCE (*Arnθ[u]r, Vel, Venel, Vetu, Laris, Leve,*⁶⁶ *Pesna*). Among the first names, *Lareke* certainly stands out. It is documented during the Archaic period, especially in Orvieto and Vulci.⁶⁷ It is striking to find this name associated with a *gentilicium* with the genuine Po valley suffix *-alu* and a root probably deriving from a Greek name.⁶⁸

Regarding the male *gentilicia*, first we have to highlight the use of the *-alu* suffix. We find it in two-member formulas, but more frequently isolated.⁶⁹ We recognize different categories of roots: *Kraikalu*, and more doubtfully *Niritalu* and *Śualu* show a Greek origin;⁷⁰ *Rakalu* is formed from the name *Rake/Raku*, already known in the Po Valley;⁷¹ the roots of *Aχalu* and *Śatalu* are documented in Etruria; and *Vetalu* came from the first name *Vete/Vetu*.⁷²

The *-iu* ending is documented in a proper *gentilicium, Lentiu* (no. 9). Other cases are the isolated names *Akiu* (no. 57*) and *Śakiu* (no. 26).⁷³ All of them are probably formed from onomastic roots from southern Etruria: the first occurs in the Archaic period in Orvieto (*Lentena*);⁷⁴ *Śakiu* should be derived from the Archaic *Saχe* of Caere.⁷⁵ It is not surprising that, as *Lentiu* in the bronze sheet, the *gentilicium* also documented in the Via Saffi *stele* of Felsina (*Atiniu* or *Latiniu*) highlights the status of the family that has the suffix *-iu*.

Amongst the *gentilicia, Kapruś* remains isolated, known only more recently in Chiusi and Orvieto.⁷⁶ This family name originated from an individual name (i.e., *Individualnamengentile*) and was composed with an "afunctional genitive," the oldest case of Etruria Padana. The meaning of the genitive suffix (-*ś*) without its proper function is debated by scholars.⁷⁷ The nature of the later *Śinu* (no. 56*) is more uncertain, although it could be a *gentilicium* formed on a Greek or Etruscan root with a *-u* ending.⁷⁸

Finally, there are only two *gentilicia* with the well-known and pan-Etruscan derivative suffix *-na* (*Pumpuna* and *Pereken[a]*) and one in composite form *-nie* (*Lavtunie*, formed from the word *lavtun*, i.e., "family"). The family name *Pumpuna* is one of the most ancient documented within the city. *Perken[a* is originally from inner northern Etruria (Valdelsa). This important family, known up to the Roman age in inner Etruria and identified as the base of some toponyms, shows that it had also directed its interests north of the Apennines in Kainua as early as the fifth century BCE, in Spina, where it is documented in the fourth–third centuries BCE, and perhaps as far as the Rhaetian territory (the Ciaslir at Monte Ozol).⁷⁹

Onomastics leads us to reflect on society. The text of the bronze sheet is divided into two sections in its preserved part, a first (first and second line) in which an action performed by two people (*Larθ Lentiu* and another whose first name is *Vel*) was indicated, with a second (third and fourth line with the mention of *Arnθ Kapruś*) relating to a construction (the verb *hecce* = "build" makes the purpose clear). Govi hypothesizes in this a reference to a sacred monument, if not to the temple itself.⁸⁰ The inscription thus could record a public or private deed on display in the sanctuary, and *Larθ Lentiu* and *Arnθ Kapruś* are probably to be considered part of a civic body, structured at a political and perhaps a priestly level.⁸¹

Regarding private contexts, the recent proposal by Govi of distinguishing two housing units in the oldest phase of House 1 of *Regio* IV, 2, led her to deepen the distribution analysis of the inscriptions within. Excluding the one taken from a surface layer and those incomplete (e.g., no. 30, probably feminine), we can narrow down two *gentilicia* from the northern unit and one from the southern unit.⁸² Among these, the bucchero amphora handle with the inscription *θina rakaluś* (no. 23; figs. 10.3, 10.5) was found in a pit within the courtyard of the house, together with other material that suggests a closing date within the second half of the fifth century BCE. An intact tile was placed in the center of the pit, and then it was sealed by a wall structure.⁸³ The long life of the vase and the deposition circumstances could evoke the inscriptions on other amphora fragments (nos. 1 and 6), both placed in foundation structures. Regarding these cases, Govi has highlighted that the writing practice was likely in

FIGURE 10.3. Fragments of amphoras (appendix A, nos. 1 and 23); pit of the courtyard of House 1, *Regio* IV, 2, where no. 23 was found. After Govi and Sassatelli 2010.

relation to a solemn ceremony that involved the consumption of wine in considerable quantities. Following her argument, the fragment from the *stenopos* near House 1 of *Regio* IV, 2, could indicate a private ritual act in relation to the construction of the road axis.[84] In both cases, after the intentional breaking of the amphora, significant parts were kept, that is, the entire text in number 1 and two words in number 6 (*śpural*

and *kainu*[ ). The handle of the amphora (name *θina*; no. 23) could represent the final act of a private rite, marked by the text itself, which shows the family name (*rakaluś*). Therefore, *Rakalu* of no. 23 and *Śatalu* of no. 1 (fig. 10.3) could perhaps be the family names of two *gentes* that owned the most ancient complexes in the northernmost part of the *insula*.

Other information on society comes from the terracotta disks.[85] Even if their function is not very clear,[86] we can argue that most of the examples come from the vicinity of craft areas (*Regiones* II and IV). The two disks of *Regiones* IV and V, one found intact inside a well and the other in a sewer, show the same name in the absolutive case (*Aχalu*), most probably a *gentilicium*, an Archaic practice that expresses possession. On the other hand, those from the Great Furnace of *Regio* II, 1, present two names of individuals in the genitive case and a gift (*al* in Etruscan). Therefore, those from southern *Regiones* could belong to private contexts with a productive function,[87] while within the Great Furnace freeborn men could have worked or controlled the workshop for the sanctuary. This hypothesis obviously does not solve the problem of their function, and it is certainly important to discover why, in other production contexts, such as House 1 of *Regio* IV, 2, these disks are absent. Regardless of these considerations, in the context of mid-fifth century BCE and later, the use of writing was concentrated solely on these objects, and no longer on vessels.

Akiu (no. 57*), probably an individual name rather than a *gentilicium* (see above), is documented also in the mining lamp found near Campiglia Marittima in the Mining district, suggesting the mobility of people working in the field of mining and metalworking.[88]

GIFTS AS A SOCIAL AND SACRED PRACTICE

The inscription on the fine-ware basin from the suburban Water Shrine (no. 60) is the only votive inscription that clearly shows a gift formula. The sequence *turuke* (= "donated") + *Lareke Niritalu* (name) was probably preceded by the accusative demonstrative *itan* / *itun* (= "this").[89] In inscription no. 11, the space between]*ke* and *tinias* and the greater proximity of

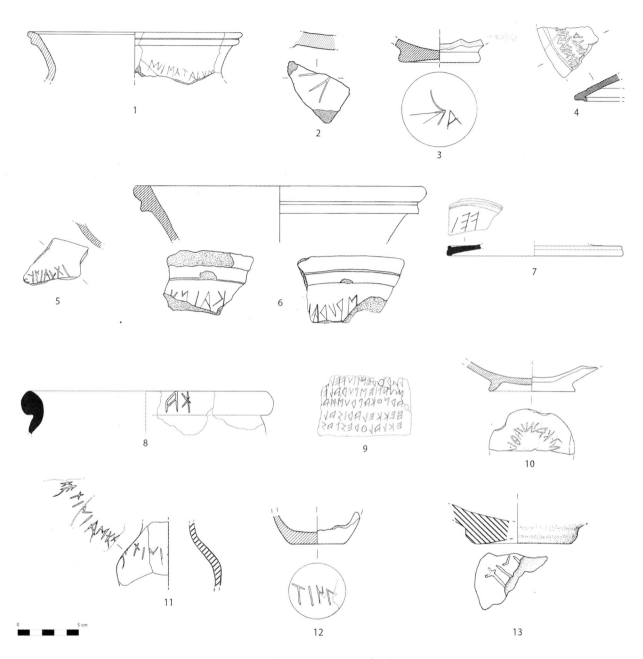

FIGURE 10.4. Inscriptions, appendix A, nos. 1–13.

kappa and *epsilon* could indicate the end of the text and therefore a formula that began with *tinias̀* and ended with the verb, suggesting a formula dedicated to the god, here in the anthropomorphized form: *tinias̀ . ka[--- turu]ke*.[90] These are isolated cases in Etruria Padana of the sixth–fourth centuries BCE, apart from a fragment of an inscription on an Attic cup from the acropolis of Bologna, one curious inscription from the inhabited area of Spina, and also the Greek votive inscriptions from Adria.[91]

Other gift types are documented by the word *al* (i.e. "gift"), incised on two vases, a cup coming from the

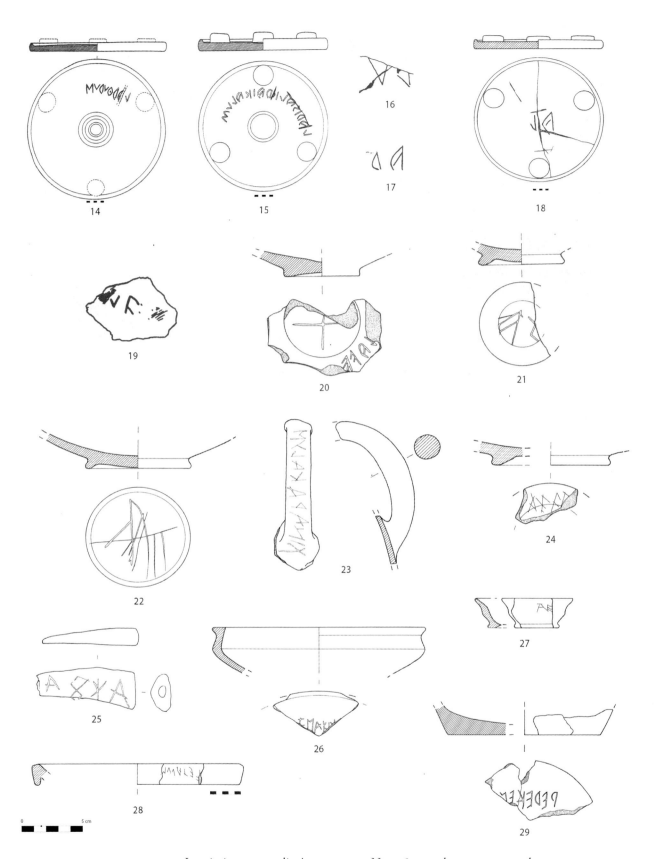

FIGURE 10.5. Inscriptions, appendix A, nos. 14–29. Nos. 16–17 and 19 are not to scale.

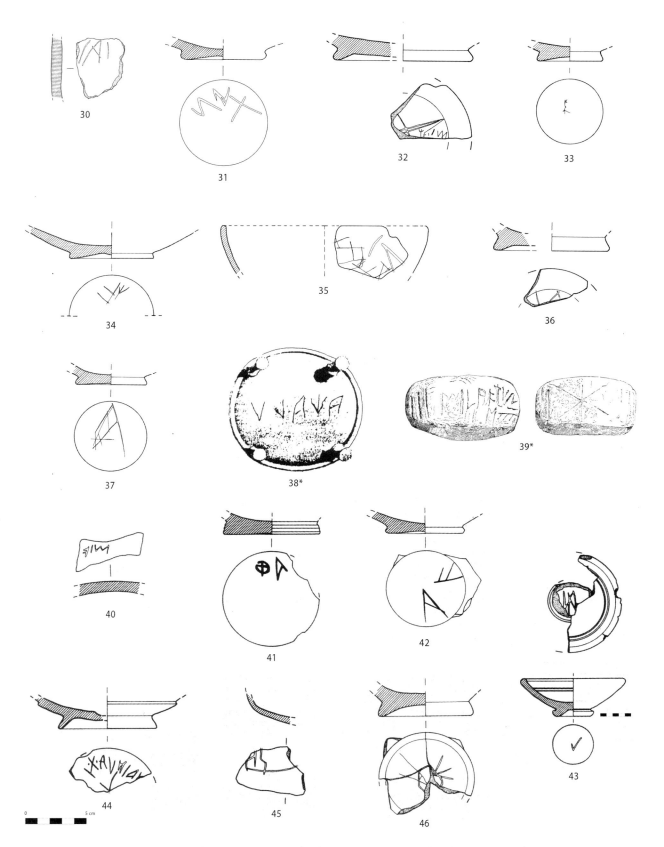

FIGURE 10.6. Inscriptions, appendix A, nos. 30–46. Nos. 38*–39* are not to scale.

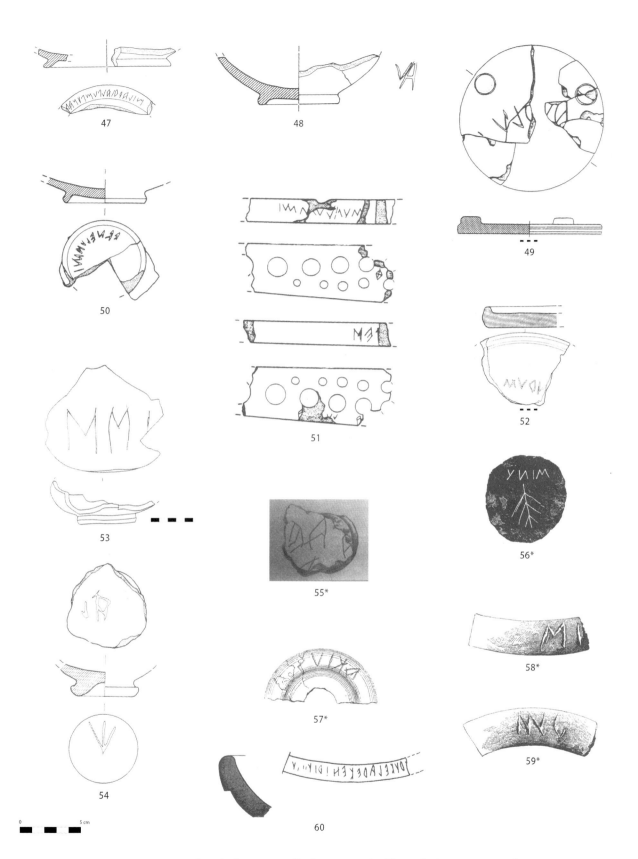

FIGURE 10.7. Inscriptions, appendix A, nos. 47–60. Nos. 55*–60 are not to scale.

foundation levels of House 1 of *Regio* V, 5 (no. 48), and a lid-cup with no definite origin from the excavations of the nineteenth century (no. 54), and on a terracotta disk from the Great Furnace of *Regio* II, 1 (no. 18). The lid-cup is a support that in other cases also seems destined for this particular practice, as shown, for example, by a similar vase from Adria dated to the Late Archaic period.[92] There, it was assumed that the object of the gift was the contents of the *olla*, probably covered by the lid-cup, rather than the vase itself.

The terracotta disk, which suggests a practice of gift-giving regarding this particular category of objects, is far more interesting. The word *al* was incised before firing on a surface bearing knobs, similarly to the other inscriptions on similar disks. The above considerations about the names on the disks prompt us to consider these particular objects as belonging to individuals or as family property, which could occasionally become the object of a gift.

ALPHABETS, SYMBOLS OF SOCIAL STATUS

The quantity of incised alphabets, in more or less abbreviated forms, is significant: nine out of sixty inscriptions. In pre-Roman Italy, this category of epigraphical document is mostly an expression of a degree of Etruscan civilization.[93] Regarding alphabetical sequences, the only certain evidence from residential areas comes from Etruscan contexts of the sixth to third centuries BCE, and a few in northern Italy.[94] Otherwise, the phenomenon of the first and last letter of the sequence is not currently analyzed as a whole, because an adequate statistical basis is lacking. In Etruria Padana, we already find this kind of document in the San Francesco deposit of Bologna, dating to the Orientalizing period, and then in Spina from the late period.[95]

Of the thirty-two alphabets recovered from Etruscan residential areas, most come from Etruria Padana.[96] Their presence in residential contexts characterizes the Etruscan Po Valley in a distinct way compared to the entire Etruscan civilization. These almost always occur on cups produced locally: bucchero and fine ware for the earlier phase and fine ware and black-gloss pottery for the later one. Of the nine alphabets in Etruria Padana dated to the sixth and fifth centuries BCE, five are from Kainua, thus demonstrating the prevalence of this particular kind of writing evidence. They did not necessarily have a direct relationship with learning how to write, as shown by the often abbreviated character of the sequence. This is most likely a socially elevated activity, practiced in the house, where these vases were clearly visible when stored on the walls, and sometimes there is also a clear decorative intent. Alongside this important message, the magical-religious value that the alphabet held in Etruscan civilization, as an extreme synthesis of writing, should not be overlooked.

It is striking that the greatest concentration of these documents is in House 1 of *Regio* IV, 2, concentrated in the first phase of the house's life,[97] although they generally come from surface layers or pits formed later. Here, both categories occur: the beginning of the alphabet, including the first two/four letters;[98] and the first and last letter, in this phase still traditionally indicated with the *chi*, although the 8 sign had already been introduced.[99] In the case of bone handle no. 25, Sassatelli thinks of an abbreviated form made up of the first and last two letters (χf) followed by an *alpha*, perhaps the beginning of a sequence interrupted by the gap.

Although the prestige value of these particular documents is clear, the concentration in House 1 certainly poses a significant question. We can assume that, compared with the residential areas investigated in other sectors,[100] the concentration in House 1, particularly in the area which in the most ancient period was the principal house of the block overlooking *plateia* B, may emphasize the high social status that these documents had.

NOTES

1. See Sassatelli 1994a; Sassatelli and Gaucci 2010.
2. Gaucci, Morpurgo, and Pizzirani 2018:672–673.
3. The most ancient *stelae* are Ducati 137 (Sassatelli 1988: 237, no. 10; Meiser 2014: Fe 1.2; on the funerary context Morpurgo 2018:395–402) and the one from Via Saffi (Maras 2014).

4. Malnati 2010; Romagnoli 2014:202–211.

5. Gaucci, Morpurgo, and Pizzirani 2018:673.

6. Gaucci 2021a.

7. Maras 2009:292–293, with previous references; Meiser 2014: Fe 3.3; on the site, Lippolis, Pini, and Sani 1998: in particular 78 and 85.

8. A. Gaucci, in *REE* 84:252–256, no. 30; Gaucci 2021b.

9. E. Govi, in *REE* 80:236.

10. See chapter 8 of this volume. Govi 2018a:625–629, figs. 11–12; Gaucci 2020:415.

11. For the text of the Melenzani small amphora, see Meiser 2014: Fe 2.1 + 3.1 + 6.1.

12. Govi 2014b:139–140.

13. E. Govi, in *REE* 79:295, no. 59.

14. Gaucci, Govi, and Sassatelli 2022.

15. Nos. 14, 15, 18, and perhaps 17*; an exception is no. 16*, still missing. Disks nos. 14 and 15 were found near the basin made with tiles (Arias 1954:214).

16. Govi 2016:200–203; Gaucci 2016:271–276.

17. Gaucci 2016: passim.

18. Possession: nos. 23, 26, 28, 29, 30?; alphabets: nos. 22, 24, 25, 27, 32, 33, 37.

19. Sassatelli and Gaucci 2010:341.

20. Sassatelli 1994a:16, 18. On the weights, see Cattani 1995. A synthesis in Maggiani 2012a, with previous references.

21. See for the possible parallel of the inscribed serpentinite stone in Genoa, Sassatelli 2008b:338 and *contra* Colonna 2004:303–304, no. 8.

22. Mattioli 2013:61.

23. E. Govi, *REE* 79:302, no. 60; 304, no. 61.

24. The plate had been used for a votive inscription, a very rare purpose for this shape (Maras 2009:166–167).

25. Sassatelli and Gaucci 2010:371.

26. Sassatelli and Gaucci 2010:338.

27. Gaucci 2012a:152–153; Gaucci 2021a:31-32.

28. Romagnoli 2014:204–205, nos. 80–81, fig. 161.

29. The use of *kappa* for /k/ is from the northern writing system, and of *sigma* for the genitive I suffix is from the southern one.

30. Maggiani 1992:184.

31. Gaucci 2012a:154–156, 164, n. 1.

32. E. Govi, in *REE* 79:298–299, no. 59. See nos. 10 and 44, probably no. 11 as well.

33. This feature occasionally occurs in Etruria in the most ancient epigraphy, including for Etruria Padana the Melenzani small amphora from Felsina (see note 11) and *cippus* I from Rubiera of around 600 BCE (Meiser 2014: Pa 1.1). However, it had been established in southern Etruria during the last quarter of the sixth century BCE and it was an innovation together with word wrapping with respect to the *scriptio continua*, due to a graphic reform developed in Caere.

34. E. Govi, in *REE* 79:302, no. 60.

35. E. Govi, in *REE* 79:302, no. 60.

36. Possession: nos. 1, 26, 28, 30, 39*; abbreviations of names: nos. 42, 43; alphabets: nos. 24, 25, 27; also no. 59*, which is probably dextroverse.

37. Nos. 1, 3, 48. These inscriptions are characterized by angled *alpha* with a medial bar descending in the direction of writing, *my* with an elongated vertical stroke, *sade* with two long and parallel vertical strokes, *tau* with a bar tangent to the vertical stroke and descending in the writing direction, *ypsilon* probably with an under-advancing stroke. Still from sealed Archaic levels, inscription no. 47 seems unique, given the manifestation of a different palaeographic tradition (i.e., quadrangular *alpha*, rhomboid *theta* without a central dot).

38. Nos. 4–5, 23, 24, 25, 41.

39. The most relevant aspect is the cross mark for *theta*, which is associated with *epsilon* with no under-advancing stroke, *rho* with a triangular eyelet and under-advancing stroke, *ypsilon* and *digamma* with under-advancing stroke. The form of *epsilon* is similar to *aie* of the San Francesco deposit in Felsina (end of the eighth century BCE), later in the Melenzani small amphora, and finally in the Imola alphabet (around 500 BCE: Govi 1994:70).

40. Sassatelli 1994a:199; Benelli 2000:212–213; Sassatelli and Gaucci 2010:316, 337–338; E. Govi, in *REE* 79:311 (no. 64).

41. Nos. 5, 6, 31, and 44 (distinguished by *ypsilon* without under-advancing stroke).

42. E. Govi, in *REE* 79:307, no. 63.

43. It is an angled *alpha* with a medial bar ascending in the script direction, which unites it to inscription no. 26 (cf. A. Gaucci in *REE* 79:292–293, no. 57 on an inscription probably of the writing tradition of Veii from San Basilio).

44. Govi 2014b:139.

45. E. Govi, in *REE* 79:307–308, no. 63.

46. This is corroborated by the lack of the posttonic vowel in *tinaś* > *tinś*, a phenomenon to be placed after the first decades of the century: E. Govi, in *REE* 79:303, no. 60.

47. Nos. 8, 18, 21, 28, 39*. If we look at no. 60 from the Water Shrine, the appearance of the letters finds particular affinity with those of the inscription on the Via Saffi *stele* from Felsina, dated to the mid-fifth century BCE (Maras 2014).

48. A. Gaucci, in *REE* 82:279–282, no. 33.

49. Gaucci, Govi, and Sassatelli 2021.

50. E.g., epsilon without an under-advancing stroke, as in no. 29, whose text, *pereken*[, does not show the phenomenon of syncope, which emerges right at the turn of the first and second quarters of this century.

51. The proposed dating is confirmed by the presence of syncope (Govi 2014b:114–115).

52. Govi 2014b:113.

53. Govi 2014b and A. Gaucci, in *REE* 84:252–256, no. 30: we record *epsilon* and *digamma* with under-advancing stroke, *rho* with triangular eyelet but without under-advancing

stroke, slightly curved *alpha*, hooked *pi*, *ny* with strokes of similar length.

54. Maggiani 1998a:229.

55. For this graphic type, see principally Maggiani 1990:182–183; Benelli 2000:213–214.

56. The Tombarelle *stele* (Sassatelli 1988: 237, no. 12, note 105; Meiser 2014: Fe 1.12) and the Ducati 25 *stele* (H. Rix, in *REE* 1982:308–311, no. 61c; Sassatelli 1988:236, no. 5, n. 98; Meiser 2014: Fe 1.11) are still linked to the previous tradition, whilst the Ducati 42 *stele* (Meiser 2014: Fe 1.7 + 7.2; Sassatelli 1988: 237, no. 6, n. 99) perhaps is already receptive to innovation.

57. Maggiani 1998a:228, n. 17; Menotti and Maras 2012.

58. *CIE* 21040 and 21060; Gaucci 2021a:53.

59. Maggiani 1998a:229–230.

60. Regarding the inscription *pereken*[(no. 29), the lack of the last part of the text does not allow us to include it in any of the above categories.

61. Nos. 1, 39*, 47, 50, 51, and perhaps the incomplete no. 40.

62. Bellelli and Benelli 2009:142–144, with previous references.

63. Nos. 14, 15, 28 (?), 57*, and perhaps the incomplete no. 52.

64. Nos. 20, 26, 38*, 49, 56*, and perhaps the incomplete nos. 2, 16*, 30.

65. Respectively, nos. 9, 50, 14, 20. For *Larθur*: Sassatelli 1994a:62 (no. 70) sees *larθuruś* as a *gentilicium* rather than a first name.

66. Perhaps we can compare *Leve* of the Ducati 25 *stele* with *Lave*. *Leve* would derive from an Italic form documented in the Faliscan and Latin languages (H. Rix, in *REE* 50:308–311, no. 61c).

67. Sassatelli 1994a:54 (no. 66).

68. Marchesini 1994 and Maras 2009:322–323, Pa do.2, n. 1.

69. Respectively, nos. 15, 60, and nos. 1, 23, 28, 38*, 49, 51.

70. About *Niritalu*, see above; about *Śualu*, see Sassatelli 1994a:181 (no. 293), with previous references.

71. Its presence within the Po Valley is exemplified by the Venetic *Rakos* of the Camin *stele* in Padua (around 520 BCE) and the most recent *Rakvi* of Ducati 12 *stele* in Felsina (cf. Sassatelli and Gaucci 2010:317–318 [no. 434]).

72. Sassatelli and Gaucci 2010: passim.

73. Although *Śakiu* of the Late Archaic period could be a *gentilicium* with an *-iu* suffix, it is not so clear for the more recent *Akiu*, probably an individual name (*gentilicium* in Sassatelli 1994a:19 [no. 3] and 203). If so, the latter testifies that the *-iu* ending does not systematically refer to *gentilicia* with the suffix *-iu*.

74. Govi 2014b:132–133.

75. The *zeta* after the fracture could be the first letter, easily interpreting it as a false starting for the following *sade*.

76. Govi 2014b:133.

77. Cf. Belfiore 2014:95–96, with previous references.

78. G. Colonna, in Brizzolara et al. 1980:114 for the Greek root; Belfiore 2010:122–123 for the Etruscan one.

79. Sassatelli and Gaucci 2010:340–341. More considerations, on the base of the later *sinu* from Adria (*CIE* 20828), are in Gaucci 2021a:101–102.

80. Govi 2014b:136–137, 139.

81. Govi 2014b:132.

82. Respectively nos. 23, 26, and no. 29. See Govi 2016:192.

83. Govi 2010a:78–79.

84. E. Govi, in *REE* 79:306–307, no. 63. This is not surprising, considering that the houses of *insula* 1 of *Regio* IV show differences in the construction of the perimeter walls of the sewer on the side of *plateia* A (Gaucci 2016:273).

85. Fig. 10.5: nos. 14, 15, and 18; fig. 10.6: no. 38; and fig. 10.7: nos. 49 and 52. Five present names declined in the genitive case (nos. 14, 15, 52) or in the absolutive case (nos. 38*, 49).

86. We can list some hypotheses proposed by scholars: small tables equipped with feet; objects related to the potter's wheel if not part of the wheel itself or inserted in a generic way in the tools of the craftsmen; *dolium* or well lids (Sassatelli 1994a:20 [no. 4]; see also Bellelli 2000:23–25).

87. Morpurgo 2017:354–356.

88. Maggiani 1992:184.

89. Maras 2009:456.

90. E. Govi, in *REE* 79:304–305, no. 61.

91. Bologna, Villa Cassarini: Romagnoli 2014:204–205, no. 80 (see also Meiser 2014: Fe 0.1); Spina: Maras 2009:372, Sp do.1 (see also Meiser 2014: Sp 0.4). Adria: Baldassarra 2013:121–127. Two other votive inscriptions, of the third century BCE, are worthy of mention: Maras 2009:373, Sp do.2, from a grave of Spina (see also Meiser 2014: Sp 3.1); *CIE* 21027, probably from a grave in the territory of Adria.

92. Gaucci 2012a:154, 159 (*CIE* 20265).

93. Gaucci 2012b:59–60.

94. Gaucci 2012b:73 with references.

95. Govi 1994:73.

96. Gaucci 2012b:73–74.

97. Sassatelli and Gaucci 2010:339.

98. Nos. 22, 24, 27; in one case intertwined (no. 37).

99. Indeed, we have a *chi* in no. 33, and perhaps exceptionally with a pronoun in no. 32, if the formula *mi a χ* is to be considered complete.

100. The remaining attestations to note come from the preparation layer of *plateia* A (no. 3) and from old nineteenth-century excavations in the southernmost sector of the city (nos. 46 and 55*).

CHAPTER 11

HOUSEHOLD ARCHAEOLOGY AND SOCIETY

GIACOMO MANCUSO, CHIARA PIZZIRANI, AND BOJANA GRUŠKA

OVERVIEW
Giacomo Mancuso

The relationship between house structure and the sociocultural milieu that designs, builds, and inhabits it is well established in the history of archeological studies. The idea that the analysis of dwelling areas and their evolution over time can reveal important clues to the ancient social structure and the behavior of its inhabitants is also well accepted.[1] From this perspective, the ancient city of Kainua-Marzabotto constitutes an incredible setting for the analysis of Etruscan domestic architecture as an expression of the society that produced it. At present it is possible to identify traces of twenty different houses, excavated from the second half of the nineteenth to the end of the twentieth century in various areas of the city.[2] The importance of this evidence does not lie simply in the extraordinarily high number of housing areas per se, but in the opportunity to evaluate these individual structures as part of a complex urban environment. Alternatively, borrowing Rapoport's theory, it provides an opportunity to assess the cultural significance of these individual dwellings as the product of a complex system of settings and activities.[3]

Unfortunately, together with all these possibilities a few limitations must also be mentioned.[4] First and foremost, there is the difficulty of perceiving the diachronic evolution of single domestic units in areas explored via old excavation procedures, where a lack of attention to multiple structural phases has inevitably damaged these pieces of evidence. Also, the agricultural usage of the plateau over the centuries has often irreparably damaged the ancient levels of use, producing an information gap that is often impossible to fill when attempting a functional analysis of the ancient spaces. All these considerations highlight the limits of an analysis conducted exclusively on the remaining groundwork of individual houses and underline the need for a wider approach, extended to the remaining material culture[5] and open to the possibilities offered by new technologies.

All this considered, the main purpose of this chapter will be to provide a survey of the multiple and different housing solutions in the city, trying to read them as an expression of the society that produced them. After this, we will present the interpretational possibilities offered by a new multidisciplinary approach to the problems of Etruscan domestic architecture.

THE PRE-URBAN PHASE
Giacomo Mancuso

Among the few pieces of structural evidence of the phase called Marzabotto II, in the second half of the sixth century BCE, not much can be assigned to dwelling contexts with any certainty.[6] An important exception is the tripartite building found beneath the levels of House 6 (*Regio* IV, 1; fig. 11.1). According to the reports of its excavators, the structure can be dated between the second half of the sixth and the beginning of the fifth century BCE.[7] The building is preserved only at the foundation level and the groundwork consists of small pebbles, partially removed during sub-

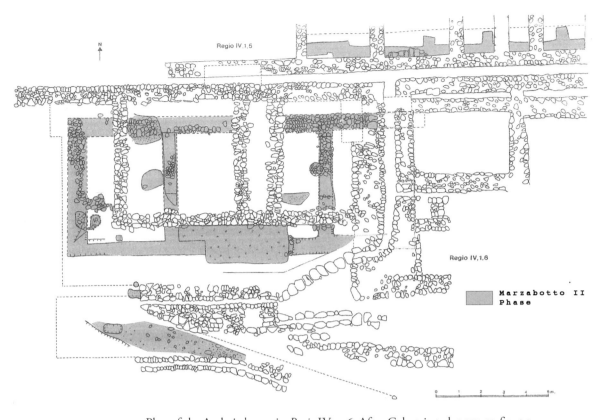

FIGURE 11.1. Plan of the Archaic house in *Regio* IV, 1, 6. After Calastri et al. 2010:45, fig. 2.1.

sequent phases, as attested by the spoliation trenches identified on the ground.

These traces have revealed the layout of a rectangular building, divided into three separate rooms, with the central one open on the south and double-sized.[8] The presence of a post pit in the front of the building indicates the presence of an external porch, while traces of cobblestone in front of it seem to suggest the projection of the house toward a frontal courtyard. The plan of the building shows numerous similarities with houses of the Late Orientalizing and Archaic period, especially the well-known examples of Acquarossa and Accesa and, more generally, laterally developed houses with an external corridor.[9] From a structural point of view, all the foundations seem to be suitable for load-bearing walls, and gaps were found at the joints between the cross-sections for the insertion of support poles. The absence of covering tiles leads us to imagine this building as covered by a thatched roof.

Although the plan and structure are recognizable, this building poses some interpretation problems, due to the preliminary status of the excavation report and the absence of clear data about the material culture, which is necessary for assessment of its function and the social status of its occupants. At our current state of research, a comparison with Etruscan and Greek architecture seems to highlight its domestic nature. Still, the scarcity of other coeval houses imposes some caution when trying to assess the role of this early house within the urban context. This documentation gap invites the risk of overrating the "monumentality" of this particular house, due to a lack of relevant comparisons.[10]

The identification of this building as a dwelling also opens up the possibility of considering the spoliation trenches found a few meters north, beneath House 5 (*Regio* IV, 1), as part of a residential building as well. According to the excavators, this structure seems to share the same chronological framework as the previous one, in this case, attested by the presence of a fragment of early black-figure Attic pottery.[11] Even if not conclusively arguable with the current data, the presence of multiple dwelling structures so close to each other might suggest the presence of a housing solution similar to the urban experiences of Accesa and Acquarossa, where multiple domestic units, close to each other, share common infrastructures.[12]

DOMESTIC ARCHITECTURE FROM THE FIFTH CENTURY BCE
Giacomo Mancuso

Not much can be added for the houses of Marzabotto II. On the other hand, documentation of the later phase, Marzabotto III, is much more abundant (*see map 5*). The refounding of the city, in the period from the end of the sixth to the beginning of the fifth century BCE, surely imposed a new definition of the dwelling space, now necessarily framed within regular square urban blocks. Traces of this rearrangement can be identified at different levels of detail. Although the urban layout of the previous phase is still elusive, it is possible to argue that the new regular plan of the city forced the builders to regularize the spaces between the domestic units, while the geometrical shape of the block imposed a rigid arrangement on the buildings' inside. From analysis of their plans, and considering all the limits set out above, the differences between all the housing solutions seem to highlight the absence of a fixed scheme, apart from the constant presence of open spaces within individual houses (*see map 7*). The courtyard can therefore be considered to be the constitutive element of the house, with the progressive aggregation of individual buildings around it.[13] This can be recognized as the only constant element in such a variety of planimetric solutions, similarly to cases found in the Archaic settlements of Tyrrhenian Etruria or the complex of Fratte in Etruscan Campania.[14] The refounding of the city seems to constitute a catalyst in the definition of house structure, providing new urban facilities such as streets and public water draining channels and imposing an impression of consistency within the domestic context.

The presence of these large courtyards can also be directly connected to the widespread presence of manufacturing activities within the houses. A significant example of this phenomenon is provided by House 1 (*Regio* IV, 2; *see fig. 13.2*), which shows from the second half of the fifth century onward a dramatic increase in the number of craft settings, which progressively transforms the initial home into a large workshop, mainly devoted to ceramic production on a city-wide scale.[15] The clearly evident combination of manufacturing and dwelling aspects within the same household enables these contexts to be defined as "workshop-houses."[16]

Similar arrangements on a smaller scale are visible also in the houses of *Regio* V, 3, and a workshop-house could also be recognized in the great house of *Regio* V, 2, facing *plateia* D, characterized by the presence of a large courtyard probably related to public trading activities. Also, the six small kilns in the northern house in *Regio* IV, 4, facing *plateia* C, could suggest the presence of a workshop-house.[17] The distribution of such houses within the city highlights the close relationship between these ateliers and the urban layout, especially the *plateiai* (*see map 8*). The mixing of production and residential aspects within the same house and their relationship to the chronological and topographical framework constitute one of the most influential factors in the development of such houses. The analysis of the material culture of workshop-houses, especially House 1 of *Regio* IV, 2, seems to suggest that the social description of those inhabitants can fit the profile of families of specialized artisans-entrepreneurs producing goods for a wide, profitable, and not necessarily local market.[18]

The workshop-house is not the only typology attested in the city; the presence of dwelling contexts with a purely residential function is also documented, for instance in House 1 of *Regio* V, 5, and in House 2 of *Regio* IV, 1. At the same time, some houses show traces of small craft settings for domestic usage, as some contexts from *Regio* IV, 1, seem to show.[19]

The houses on *Regio* IV, 1, present some peculiar characteristics that must be considered separately, starting from their room-by-room evolution that progressively led to the occupation of the entire length of the block. The layout of these dwelling contexts eludes

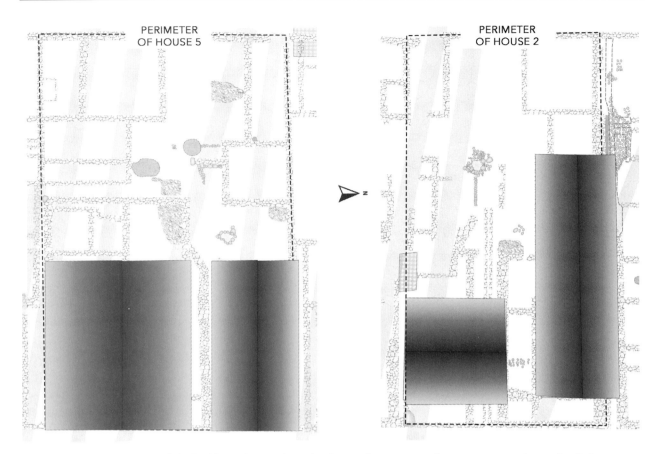

FIGURE 11.2. Disposition of the buildings during the early phases of Houses 2 and 5 in *Regio* IV, 1. Drawn by G. Mancuso.

simple explanation, thus reflecting a complex variety of architectural solutions over time. Built as independent constructions, most of these houses, especially in their initial stages, seem to be characterized by the presence of a long courtyard, located in the central-west portion of the area.

Houses 2 and 5 (*Regio* IV, 1; fig. 11.2) can perhaps be taken as an example of similar processes having considerably different outcomes. During the second half of the fifth century BCE, the first lot is characterized by the presence of two separate buildings, orthogonally arranged to occupy the entire north–south development of the lot.[20] The south one was square, while the other was rectangular and particularly extended toward the west.[21] The space between these buildings created a corridor going toward a vast open space that seems free of other structures. A similar solution seems to be found in the eastern portion of House 5 (*Regio* IV, 1), in a period that seems to be contemporary with, or shortly after, the redefinition of the urban layout. Here again it is possible to identify the presence of two separate buildings, structurally independent but close to each other.[22] The space between them can be interpreted as a long hallway, leading to an open courtyard, paved with cobblestones. The use of travertine blocks in corner positions in the foundations is a feature of this building phase, and a solution that can be interpreted as a structural reinforcement for the overall house, or as a form of monumentalization of the external façade. Similar planimetric solutions during this early phase can also be traced in House 1 of *Regio* IV, 2 (fig. 11.3), and House 2 of *Regio* V, 5,[23] thus suggesting a pattern that needs further investigations.

As previously stated, these two houses present very different outcomes in their second phase, starting from around the mid-fifth century BCE. House 5 seems to show a progressive extension of its previous buildings, supplemented by the construction of new ones, placed logically at the two sides of the courtyard (fig. 11.3). House 2, on the other hand, seems to evolve in the well-known form of an *atrium/cavaedium* house with a cross-shaped central courtyard.[24] In the light of the presence of a previous phase, it seems possible to argue that this plan constitutes the result of a progressive restructuring of the preceding ground plan that seems to favor the overall symmetry of the house, therefore showing another architectural solution also based on the arrangement of multiple structures around a central open space.

This consideration seems to close the gap between this house and the rest of the dwelling types documented in the city, highlighting its construction as a process of the juxtaposition of buildings progressively connected and probably sharing a common covering solution. Still, the construction process must not undermine the overall significance of this kind of house. Scholars widely agree that the architectural solution of the *atrium/cavaedium* house was first conceived in the Etruscan-Latin world as a response to the self-representation needs of the aristocratic class on a city-wide scale.[25] The first pieces of evidence date to the second half of the sixth century BCE, and the development of the Marzabotto houses seems to follow shortly afterward, representing an adaptation of the original model to a new spatial and ideological context.[26] From this perspective, the adoption of this housing solution seems to suggest the high social status of the inhabitants of this house, who, starting from the second half of the fifth century BCE, transformed their home by reworking an aristocratic dwelling model. The important social role that this kind of house represents is confirmed by its scarcity within the city (currently only two),[27] its wide extension, and

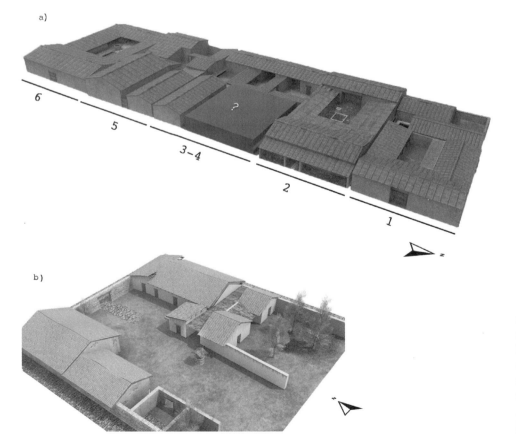

FIGURE 11.3. (a) Virtual reconstructions of the houses in *Regio* IV, 1, created by G. Mancuso. (b) Virtual reconstruction of House 1 in *Regio* IV, 2, created by S. Garagnani.

the important position the houses occupy within the urban layout, along *plateia* A.[28] The recent identification of specifically sized modules (*see map 7*), recurring inside the city and based on the common unit of the Attic foot, allows us to make sense of an apparently chaotic arrangement through a non-uniform parceling scheme, characterized by differently sized units distributed across the city for specific reasons.[29] Even if the dwelling areas seem to be subdivided according to rigid geometrical principles, their occupation responds to a specific need for self-representation. The assignment of these lots seems to be connected to the refounding process, thus attesting the presence of some social stratification from the very first phase of the city.

This process could also be inferred from the persistence in the same zone of dwellings as well as sacred and artisanal areas, a topographical combination that can be interpreted as a sign of continuity. It is thus interesting to observe that the dismantling of the Archaic house in *Regio* IV, 1, seems to be followed by the creation of one of the biggest lots, which was then probably assigned to an eminent family that from the second half of the fifth century restructured its household in the prominent shape of an *atrium/cavaedium* house.[30]

Observing the overall organization of these areas, it also seems clear that the biggest lots tend to look toward *plateia* A, interpreted as the main street of the city and home to its most distinguished citizens.[31] It is possible to argue that the definition of the domestic spaces within the urban block completely redefined the general perception of the household from the outside. The absence of an impressive view of the overall building, juxtaposed between others and perceived only from the fixed point of view of the street, probably led to the development of the façade as an element of self-representation in the city. This principle perhaps also explains why the first phases of some of these houses seem to concentrate on the eastern side of the lot. In this regard the impression of width and probably of decoration surely played a fundamental role as a component of the self-representing strategy of these elites, showing the ability of some eminent citizens to live in a house almost as big as the nearby urban temple of Tinia.[32]

In conclusion, even considering the limits imposed by an uneven documentation, it seems clear that an analysis of the typological and topographical aspects of the housing solutions in Marzabotto reveals the presence of a structured and articulated social body that expressed its own status by means of different and coherent domestic solutions. This promising research field could certainly benefit from further investigation and a deeper and wider contribution from the evidence of the material culture, such as through the analysis of building materials and construction techniques.

BUILDING MATERIALS AND TECHNIQUES IN HOUSEHOLD ARCHITECTURE
Chiara Pizzirani

Investigating the archaeological evidence concerning households in ancient Kainua considerably extends our knowledge of Etruscan construction techniques during Classical times. Indeed, excavations carried out in the nineteenth century as well as more recent investigations have offered many samples of tiles made of fired clay, well known in several ancient cities,[33] and an impressive quantity of mud bricks that, in contrast, are rarely preserved in Etruria.

Although building materials have been brought to light across the whole of ancient Kainua, the archaeological investigations of House 1 of *Regio* IV, 2 (fig. 11.3; *see also fig. 13.2*) have allowed us to analyze in-depth the features of Etruscan building techniques in Marzabotto. More particularly, the considerable importance of House 1 depends on recent excavations, which were followed by an immediate analysis of the archaeological evidence, along with painstaking observations of all the signs and features that could be used for the architectural reconstruction of the ancient walls, roof, indoor areas, and courtyards, as well as the building materials used.[34] This attention to detail is fundamental for the reconstruction of the features of structures such as the walls, since only the stone foundations are normally found in Marzabotto.[35]

In House 1, during the dismantling of the various out-buildings over the years due to the progressive improvement of the building as a handicraft workshop,[36] many building materials were thrown into pits that had been dug into the ground to find clay and then abandoned. Hence, mud bricks, a class of material usually lost because of its perishability, were saved, becoming a critical element of analysis in our investigation of construction techniques. Besides the bricks, which we now know belonged to the walls of the building of this house and more generally to the architectural structure of the whole town of Marzabotto, many fragments of tiles have been discovered. As a result, it is possible to state that the bricks and tiles from House 1, together with clay mixed with twigs (*opus craticulum*) for lighter household structures such as house partitions, have finally given a definitive answer to the long-standing debate about the architectural materials and features of the Etruscan city of Marzabotto.[37] Thus, the evidence for ancient building techniques found in Kainua offers an important contribution to our knowledge of Etruscan architecture in the fifth century BCE.

The measurements of the bricks of House 1 (about 30 × 20 cm) are essentially standard and fit perfectly with the most common width of the building foundations in Marzabotto. According to Vitruvius (Vitr., *De arch.* 2.8.17–18), foundations as large as those built in Marzabotto, with walls made of mud bricks, would have been able to support a two-story building. Among the multiple brick types documented in Marzabotto, the most common in the housing areas seems to consist of a small rectangular brick, probably based on the Attic foot.[38] The dimensions of the stone foundations for the mudbrick walls were 60 cm, so they could be constructed either with three bricks fixed closely together lengthways, or two aligned bricks placed sideways (fig. 11.4).[39] It may be presumed that the two building techniques were associated and alternated within the wall in order to improve the strength of the structures. The difference between the foundation width and the wall thickness was necessary not only for stability but also to allow the application of a protective plaster layer.[40]

The tiles from House 1 are helpful as well. The roofs were made of a mix of Laconian-Corinthian elements, semi-cylindrical cover-tiles, as in the Laconian roofing style, and flat tiles, as in the Corinthian one (see fig. 11.5).[41] The study of finds from the archaeological layers of this house-workshop has led to the recognition of a precise size of tile (about 62–65 × 45–50 cm),

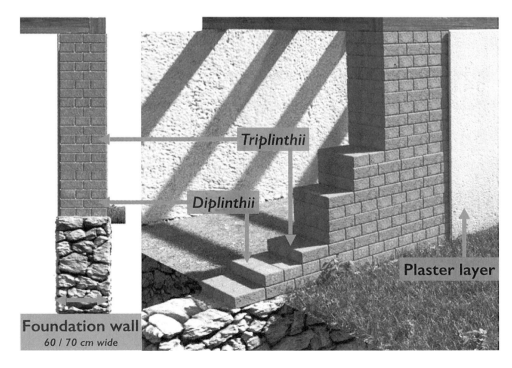

FIGURE 11.4. Diagram of mudbrick walls on stone foundations and surface plaster layer. After Gruška, Mancuso, and Zampieri 2017: 168, fig. 2.

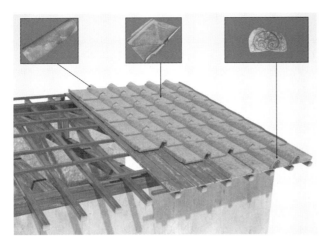

FIGURE 11.5. Reconstruction of a truss-like structure with semi-cylindrical and flat tiles. Created by G. Mancuso.

probably used across the whole city and occasionally in the graves as well.[42] This tile format was certainly used for the construction of the house roofs and for the roof of the Temple of Uni, only recently discovered.[43] Finds in the cistern near the more recent temple of Tinia belong to a larger size class (about 68 × 56 cm), which can be assumed to represent an improvement in building techniques, intended to highlight a temple dominating the entire city (fig. 11.5).

Furthermore, the discovery of a few clay fragments with impressions of twigs attests the usage of wattle and daub or *pisé* technique,[44] probably intended to divide inner rooms, whereas mud bricks were probably meant to form the external and load-bearing walls of the buildings.

It can be said, in conclusion, that the archaeological records of Marzabotto, and especially of House 1, offer the most complete documentation on building materials used in Etruria in the fifth century BCE.

AN INTEGRATED APPROACH TO HOUSEHOLD ARCHAEOLOGY AND VIRTUAL MODELS
Bojana Gruška

During the "Kainua Project,"[45] a substantial part of the research has been directed toward the reconstruction of housing areas that constituted the largest portion of the ancient town.[46] In a site like Marzabotto, hard to envision because of a lack of monumental evidence, virtual reconstructions not only represent an effective and immediate communication tool, but also have the advantage of being able to visualize the "lived space"[47] of the city and contribute to the solution of some scientific problems. The virtual model allows us to appreciate that the arrangement of the sacred buildings on the Acropolis respects both the open view of the *auguraculum* and the need for a spectacular panorama visible from the bottom of the plateau. Moreover, the possibility of experiencing the ancient view of the two urban temples and their connection with the city and with *plateia* B, the sacred road with strong political and social significance, exists for the first time. Equally important are the revelations regarding the dimensions, internal organization, and location of residential and production spaces.[48]

This analysis of household architecture contributes above all to the unveiling of a social structure that would otherwise be difficult to grasp, given the systematic impoverishment of the ancient levels of use and the abandonment of the city.[49] Therefore, a historically reliable virtual reconstruction becomes an efficient investigation tool, based on solid fundamentals derived from archaeological data, ancient sources, building materials, and construction techniques. Elements such as the foundations, the load-bearing structures, and the roofs, but also the materials, their effectiveness and weight, must be the starting point for a reconstructive picture of the elevations of the structures, made by taking advantage of the most innovative digital technologies and through the validation of the ArchaeoBIM method,[50] namely a constant search for a solid architectural and structural foundation for the reconstructive processes.

The first issue that reconstructions of these household contexts raised was the correct identification of the load-bearing walls of the domestic units. The problem itself is directly related to the common usage of continuous foundations across different rooms, the absence of thresholds and ancient pavements due to modern agricultural works,[51] and a situation worsened by the lack of stratigraphic data for most of the excavations conducted before the 1970s.[52] In order to overcome this problem, the structural evidence of House 1, *Regio* IV, 2 (fig. 11.3; *see fig. 13.2*), was used as a guideline for the identification of load-bearing foundations. It is in fact well known that cobblestone foundations differ in depth, width, and construction techniques according to their structural role. The presence of travertine blocks in the perimeter foundations and at the corners of the load-bearing walls of House 5 (*Regio* IV, 1), a structural reinforcement or a form of monumentalization of the façade,[53] can be analyzed in a virtual environment and the reconstructions used as a tool to obtain a 3D image of these houses. Concerning the size of the foundations (the supporting ones had an average width of 60–70 cm),[54] the archaeological evidence points to a wide variation in dimensions, information that obviously has to be compared to the type of elevation, thus revealing the multitude of construction techniques employed.[55] Regarding the techniques of *diplinthii* and *triplinthii* mentioned by Vitruvius (Vitr., *De arch*. 2.8.17; see fig. 11.4), the data provided by BIM simulation of the Temple of Uni confirmed their possible combined use. The maximum height of the dry walls made with these techniques, to avoid stability problems of any kind, has been estimated to be around 2.8 m.

The archaeological aspects of roofing are better known, as both the modular and the typological characteristics have been fully studied.[56] The architectural terracottas from Marzabotto fit perfectly within "Phase 3B," as outlined by Ö. Wikander for the development of Etruscan roof coverage, which begins in the second half of the sixth century BCE and represents the most advanced roofing technique in the Etruscan world.[57]

On the other hand, the reconstruction of the wooden carpentry of the roofs has been challenging, due to the complete absence of any archaeological record concerning the roof entablature.[58] A likely possibility, based on the ancient sources and the BIM simulation of the Temple of Uni, was developed to get around this problem.[59] Among the different archaeological sources, such as funerary architecture and the Vitruvian description of the wooden structural work of the Etrusco-Italic temple,[60] the latter remains the most complete. Even though the author is describing building techniques used in the first century BCE, the Roman tiles he mentions appear to have similar characteristics to the ones used in Marzabotto.[61]

According to Vitruvius (Vitr., *De arch*. 4.2.2), if the span of a roof was large, a ridge beam (*columen*) had to be laid on top of the king post, making a tie beam (*transtrum*) and struts (*capreoli*) necessary as well. If the roof was of a moderate span, only the ridge beam and rafters (*cantherii*) were needed, the latter being of sufficient projection at their ends to drain the water away from the walls. Then, purlins (*templa*) were laid on the rafters, and again, in order to receive the tiles, common rafters (*asseres*) were placed on these. The rafters needed to be of sufficient length to cover the walls and protect them. The choice proposed by Vitruvius is between a self-bearing structure, equipped with a truss-like support, and an externally supported one, integrated with pillars, columns, poles, or walls.[62]

Based on the roof slope, it might seem that the houses in Marzabotto adopted the second solution. However, even if the description could fit, the complete absence of archaeological traces concerning supports inside the individual buildings seems to point to the adoption of a self-bearing solution.[63] This hypothesis is also supported by the architectural decorations visible in Etruscan chamber tombs, particularly the painted tombs in Tarquinia, where the king post is frequently depicted in tombs dating from the last quarter of the sixth to the end of the fifth century BCE. This post is one of the elements that make up the truss, with the important function of supporting the ridge beam,[64] and it is depicted in some tombs at the center of the pediment, mostly in the shape of an altar.[65] According to the latest readings, this element may not be intended as the true representation of an actual architectural feature, but as its funerary interpretation, directly inspired by a real architectural feature.[66] Therefore, a truss-like structure to support the roof was imagined also for the houses of Marzabotto and, in order to support the roofing system, a minimal structure, consisting of *mutuli*, *cantherii*, and *asseres*, has been put in place (see fig. 11.5). The latter were necessary to affix the pan tiles with nails.[67]

With our current state of knowledge, it is impossible to define the measurements of the structural elements or how they were connected to each other. The main theories propose either some kind of embedding or the use of cramps, nails, and ropes. These two kinds of solution are not necessarily to be considered exclusive alternatives.⁶⁸ Reconstruction of roofs has always observed the Vitruvian instructions concerning their extension, specifically the length of the eaves (*stillicidium*, about 1.3 m) for partial coverage and protection of the underlying structure (Vitr., *De arch.* 4.7.5). Each domestic unit has an independent roofing system, formed of a mono-pitched or gable roof, depending on their specific measurements or position, and in order to carry the rainwater inside or outside the house (the possible slope ranged from 10 to 20 degrees). In most cases, the water flows outside, toward the public canalization system or the partition between different domestic units (*ambitus*); or inside, when the archaeological evidence attests angular tiles (inserted into the *compluvia* roofs)⁶⁹ and the presence of water collection systems. Housing units very close to each other for which the use of a common water infrastructure was hypothesized are an exception.⁷⁰

This virtual cityscape allows us for the first time to visualize and re-create the ancient perception and point of view of the streets and buildings of Kainua not through simple virtual reconstructions, but through detailed and historically accurate models that help us to understand Marzabotto's society and living space.

Some of the many problems that can be investigated in a virtual environment are as follows: the absence of a full view of the important houses facing *plateia* A, probably prompting their monumentalization and self-representation through the façade; the installation of gutters rather than large *compluvia* roofs; the use of a common water infrastructure for houses very close together; the presence of travertine blocks in the foundation and in the corners of the walls, probably for structural reasons. An integrated approach to the study of household archaeology through the most advanced digital technologies and the reconstruction of lost reality can provide us with a social framework that would otherwise be difficult to identify.

NOTES

1. This concept is widely discussed throughout the specialist literature. For a critical reexamination of the theoretical work on the subject, with specific attention to Etruscan domestic architecture, see Izzet 2007.

2. For a specific overview of the main domestic contexts of the city see the bibliographic appendix (B) at the end of this volume.

3. Rapoport 1990.

4. On this topic see also the evaluations by E. Govi (Govi 2016:207–211).

5. This task is often complicated by the absence of systematic publication of the excavations, currently just two: Massa Pairault 1997 and Govi and Sassatelli 2010. The necessity for a wider approach on the analysis of domestic contexts is invoked also in Melis and Rathje 1984:382–386.

6. The definition of the three phases of the settlement of Marzabotto is presented in Govi 2014a; Govi 2016; and chapter 4 of this volume. A critical reevaluation of the problem of the Marzabotto I phase, allegedly characterized by the presence of scattered huts, is also discussed in Govi 2016:207–208 with references. A thorough analysis of the archaeological traces of the Archaic phases of the city can be found in Forte 1993b and Govi 2016:203–211, with new finds and references.

7. Forte 1993b:323; Calastri et al. 2010, with references. The chronological framework arises mainly from the orientation of the building, slightly divergent from the one above, and consequentially considered earlier than the refoundation of the city. It has recently been suggested that this difference does not seem to be so evident in the published plans of the context (Govi 2016:209).

8. Its reported measurements are 14.6 × 6.66 m. Use of the Attic foot of 29.6 cm as a measurement unit was argued in Govi 2016:209, as opposed to a foot of 30 cm, argued in Forte 1993b:299.

9. For this kind of house see Colonna 1986:424–425. Wider comparisons for the house in Marzabotto are provided in Forte 1993b:364–366.

10. The monumentality of this complex is openly stated in Malnati 1991–1992:166 and throughout the work of M. Forte (Forte 1993b:361, 368–369).

11. Calastri et al. 2010:43–44 and Forte 1993b:322–326. Specifically, it is a fragment of *kylix* assigned to the Little Master group.

12. On the Accesa and Acquarossa sites see respectively Camporeale 2016 and Östenberg 1975, both with references.

13. Govi and Sassatelli 2010:302; Govi 2016:196.

14. Pontrandolfo 2009.

15. Govi and Sassatelli 2010.

16. Govi and Sassatelli 2010:303–304, with references on the evolution of this definition.

17. On the workshop-houses of *Regio* V, 3, see Massa Pairault 1997. On the house of *Regio* V, 2, see Brizio 1890. The hypothesis that this building could also have served for some kind of public trading comes from its position, close to the city limits, and the retrieval of a river cobblestone engraved with the inscription: *mi lavtunieś* (appendix A, no. 39; Sas-

satelli 1994a:15–18; Govi 2016:200). On *Regio* IV, 4, see Morpurgo 2017 with references.

18. For recent analysis of the traces of workshops in the city see Morpurgo 2017. In House 1 of *Regio* IV, 2, the social profile of its inhabitants is elevated by the continuous presence of imported goods, especially pottery, that seems to suggest the high-level lifestyle of the inhabitants (Govi and Sassatelli 2010:304–306).

19. The houses of this block, extremely well known in the archaeological literature, have recently been subjected to a critical reexamination in the light of the discovery of extensive (and unpublished) documentation assembled during excavation. The preliminary analysis is published in Gaucci 2016. The analytical process continued with a PhD dissertation discussed by the present author in 2020 (Mancuso 2019–2020). The analysis of this "new" data led, among other results, to the recognition of new house plans, acquired through the systematic comparison of all the available sources and a better understanding of the context of the archaeological finds.

20. The confirmation of the presence of different phases in this house is a result of the latest excavations (Bentz and Reusser 2010b). The chronological framework for these structures is provided by a goblet found within the foundations of the southern building.

21. Compared to the reconstruction provided in Bentz and Reusser 2011: fig. 2, the length of this building can be extended toward the west, as suggested by the analysis of a picture taken in 1952 during the excavation works (SAER archive, inv. 14416).

22. The existence of multiple phases in this house is argued in Gaucci 2016:260–265. Comparing these two architectural solutions in Houses 2 and 5 of *Regio* IV, 1 (fig. 11.2), it is interesting to observe that during this phase the northern building (measuring 6.8 × 14.5 m) is dimensionally quite similar to the equivalent on the northern one in House 2 (*Regio* IV, 1), measuring 6.9 × 28.4 m, which seems to be double in length. The metrical comparison seems significant due to the contemporaneity of the buildings and could attest the usage of a common model during this early stage of the city.

23. Respectively: Govi and Sassatelli 2010 and Baratti 2005:239–240.

24. This definition was recently advanced in Jolivet 2011: 12–36 to define the *plan canonique* of the *atrium* house, avoiding obvious anachronisms.

25. On this topic Colonna 1986:444–445; Carandini and Carafa 1995; Cifani 2008:273–278; Govi and Sassatelli 2010: 299–300; Prayon 2009; Zaccaria Ruggiu 2003:393. The latest and most comprehensive work on this topic remains Jolivet 2011.

26. The problem of *atrium* houses in the town was first considered in Mansuelli 1963a, negating the possibility of the construction of a Tuscanic *atrium* inside the houses of *Regio* IV, 1. Colonna (1986:444–445) proposed that some of the dwelling units were organized with a cross-shaped courtyard and *compluvium* roof covering. The accuracy of the reproduction leading to this hypothesis has, however, been questioned, in the light of its difference from the later Roman *domus* and doubts regarding the suggested roofing system that would have been adopted, according to de Albentiis (1990) and Wallace Hadrill (1997:234).

27. Houses 2 and 6 in *Regio* IV, 1.

28. Similar structures can be perceived also from the traces from the geophysical survey conducted on *Regio* III, 5, as interpreted in Govi 2016:198, fig. 9.

29. Govi 2016:195–200, with a wide and in-depth analysis of the presence and the distribution of differently sized parcels across the city.

30. Govi 2016:211.

31. This idea was partially expressed also in Mansuelli 1962a:21–22.

32. Govi 2016:201. G. Sassatelli observed also that the "house" of the god Tinia occupies a regular urban block of the city (Sassatelli and Govi 2005b:47).

33. For instance, obviously, Wikander 1993 and Chiaghi 1999.

34. Govi and Sassatelli 2010 and Govi 2010c.

35. Sacred buildings on the Acropolis seem to have been an exception in this regard.

36. See chapter 13.

37. Govi 2010b; Pizzirani and Pozzi 2010.

38. Pizzirani and Pozzi 2010:305; Pizzirani 2019.

39. Pizzirani and Pozzi 2010:305.

40. Pizzirani and Pozzi 2010.

41. Ciaghi 1999:1–5.

42. Pizzirani and Pozzi 2010. See chapter 17 for tiles as cinerary urns or grave flooring. These tiles were of a standard size (about 64 × 40 cm), except for one, whose dimensions were 90 × 70 cm. A similar one might have been found in *Regio* IV, 1.

43. Govi 2017b; Govi 2018a.

44. Massa Pairault 1997:90–96; Govi 2010c:213–214; Gruška, Mancuso, and Zampieri 2017:167.

45. See chapter 3.

46. Gruška, Mancuso, and Zampieri 2017:165–176.

47. Govi 2017c:88.

48. Govi 2016:187–241.

49. See G. Mancuso in this chapter.

50. Garagnani, Gaucci, and Govi 2016:251–270; Garagnani 2017:141–149; Gruška, Mancuso, and Zampieri 2017; see also chapter 3.

51. Govi 2010c:205–210.

52. A schematic history of the excavations appears in Lippolis 2005:154–157.

53. G. Mancuso in this chapter; the travertine blocks

prove the existence of a unified construction project for the perimeter of the house (Gaucci 2016:261).

54. Govi 2010c:210, fig. 355.

55. These techniques have already been highlighted in this chapter by C. Pizzirani.

56. Pizzirani and Pozzi 2010 and see C. Pizzirani in this chapter.

57. Wikander 1993.

58. For a detailed discussion about the roof structure see G. Mancuso in Gruška, Mancuso, and Zampieri 2017:168–172.

59. Garagnani, Gaucci, and Govi 2016; Garagnani, Gaucci, and Gruška 2016a; Gruška, Mancuso, and Zampieri 2017:168.

60. Chiesa and Binda 2009:66.

61. Adam 1984:229–230; Pizzirani and Pozzi 2010.

62. Giuliani 2006:89–96; see G. Mancuso in Gruška, Mancuso, and Zampieri 2017:168–172.

63. Gruška, Mancuso, and Zampieri 2017:170.

64. Giuliani 2006:92–93.

65. Colonna 1986:445; Roncalli 1990:234.

66. Naso 1996:388.

67. Donati 1994:92; Gruška, Mancuso, and Zampieri 2017:170.

68. Garagnani, Gaucci, and Govi 2016:259.

69. Based on the latest research, it is advisable to think of prolongations, achieved by extending the dripping edges of the pitches of the roofs that overlooked the courtyard, rather than large *compluvia* roofs. Regardless of the characteristics, this type of house in Marzabotto surely underlines the expression of a high social status.

70. See G. Mancuso in this chapter.

CHAPTER 12

ART AND ARTISANS
Metal Production

GIULIA MORPURGO

During the sixth and fifth centuries BCE, the metallurgical sector, which was already active in the Villanovan era, became one of the most significant productive sites of the economy of Etruria Padana.[1] A substantial restructuring process took place in the area at the time and provided a fundamental stimulus to production, giving new life to the trade routes.[2]

In this context, a leading role was played by Kainua, a center in the Reno Valley with a strong handicraft vocation, concerning which research over time has brought to light a well-developed production structure in both ceramics and metallurgy (*see map 8*).[3]

More precisely, metalworking has been repeatedly indicated in the literature as one of the key aspects for the economic and cultural characterization of this settlement, as well as playing a role in the more general context of Etruria Padana. The range of evidence is wide and varied, especially when compared to the lack of evidence we have for other pre-Roman centers, and makes Marzabotto an extraordinary context for study. The available data set allows us to examine the subject in depth, not only from the point of view of the products, but also through the more technological aspects, such as the equipment used, or the production processes implemented. The city also lends itself to general observations about the topographical relationships that could have existed between the urban space and the craft facilities. Finally, the contribution of the most recent surveys is extremely valuable and, together with a revisiting of the old excavation data, currently offers a renewed perspective on the city and its productive activities.

Given the reasons behind the founding of this center, it is not surprising that manufacturing activity in metallurgy can be recorded from the beginning of the settlement; various evidence, unfortunately not specified in terms of structural consistency and production, can already be dated to the second half of the sixth century BCE. This evidence helps us to form a picture of the phase, including economic and commercial aspects, that preceded the urban project, whose characteristics certainly appear to be more complex than was assumed in the past.[4]

As is well known, in the period from the end of the sixth to the beginning of the fifth century BCE, the city underwent radical monumental transformations, through a founding rite that reflects the religious principles of the *Etrusca disciplina*.[5] Although we cannot currently specify the reasons for these great changes, it is reasonable to imagine that the flourishing of artisan activities contributed significantly to the architectural and urban renewal process of the center.

As often happened with sacred and residential structures, most of the workshops active in the Archaic period were also reorganized within the orthogonally planned town with substantial continuity, which could be explained by obvious reasons relating to the productive economy but might also indicate a single family's continuous management of the activities.

The evidence of metallurgical production linked to the new, well-structured city certainly is more conspicuous and better understood. Similarly to what can be observed in the ceramics sphere, a precise plan appears evident in the structuring of urban workshops with different scales. In fact, alongside elements that suggest the presence of processing areas aimed at satisfying the needs of a family or of a small group of people, there are also contexts which, due to their structural complexity, internal layout, and the characteristics of the materials present, could indicate production on a commercial scale, intended for the local community or possibly for export.

Certainly, the dialectic between house and workshop must have been much more complex than was recognized in the past. Emerging data contradicts the idea of a strict separation between simple household production and large public craft workshops, enhancing the important role played by contexts in which residential functions are combined with large-scale production activities,[6] as known from other contexts. This model, in fact, even without detailed comparisons in the Etruscan world, allows us to relate Marzabotto to some important realities at Greek sites and in Magna Graecia, confirming considerable sharing of the urban planning experience in the sixth century BCE among these cultural spheres.[7]

A fundamental leading role in the realm of metalworking was certainly played by the so-called Foundry, identified in *Regio* V, 5, next to *plateia* A, the main road that crossed the city in a north–south direction. The context was brought to light and published in preliminary form in the second half of the 1960s by G. V. Gentili.[8] More recently, a systematic review of the documentation has been carried out, together with some excavations that had the aim of clarifying some crucial aspects to define the production profile of the area more precisely.[9]

The available data have therefore made it possible to verify that the casting, production, and finishing of bronze artifacts took place in the western sector of the workshop. These activities are suggested by a series of facilities, including "hearth-pits," *concotto* fragments, and a system of communicating channels, as well as by the extensive presence of technological indicators such as slag, clay molds, and fireclay.

On the other hand, the hypothesis that the mineral processing or reduction of semi-worked derivatives was carried out within this workshop, which would exceptionally point to a complete metallurgical cycle, is more problematic. In this regard, the discovery of a particular structure, in the eastern side of the building, is central. This find has been interpreted as an oven, from comparison with similar specimens from the area of Campiglia Marittima,[10] which could be linked to the operations of metal extraction.[11] However, the resumption of investigations in this sector, aimed mainly at gaining a better knowledge of this facility, has revealed its great complexity, preventing us from understanding its functions, which even today are not clear.[12]

Regardless of this aspect, which is not easy to resolve, the great productive dynamism that must have distinguished this workshop is indisputable, and the high-quality fusion techniques used and the remarkable stylistic skills of its craftsmen have already been underlined in the past. Traditionally considered a "public" workshop, in the light of the most up-to-date research on the manufacturing organization of the city, it is also possible that this atelier was not only intended for production on at least an urban scale, but that some of its rooms had a residential function. The limits of the building to which the workshop belonged were not revealed during the investigations,[13] and there is also a need to clarify the real purpose of the area bordering the "Foundry" on the north, to which the workshop area could be related, according to some preliminary information.[14]

What the evidence suggests certainly allows us to document a series of massive renovations that seem to have mainly concerned the eastern side of the complex, after the end of the fifth century BCE. These renovations involved a change of function from a working environment to a residential space.[15] This interrelationship between productive and domestic vocation, undoubtedly a characteristic feature of buildings in this settlement, is revealed to be extremely dynamic over time. The most recent findings provide confirmation that these buildings are often subject to substantial changes, mostly due to the needs of craftsmanship.

In this regard, the evidence offered by investigations conducted in *Regio* IV, 1, is emblematic (*see map 8*). The discovery inside some houses in this area of iron slag, lumps of coal, fragments of melting pots, and a pair of blacksmith's tongs (fig. 12.1) led the discoverer,

FIGURE 12.1. Blacksmith tongs from *Regio* IV, 1, 510–350 BCE. After Govi 2007:33.

G. A. Mansuelli, to coin the term "workshop-houses." He assumed a strong contrast between internal rooms intended for private life and the rooms overlooking *plateia* A, used as workshops in which metal was worked and manufactured objects were sold.[16]

In this case too, recent studies of the excavation documentation have brought to light many new elements that have important implications for this production aspect. It has been possible to highlight that this sector was subjected over time to numerous structural changes, contradicting past assumptions and producing a much more complex picture than previously formed. In particular, the data points from "House 5" are of great interest, for in the second half of the fifth century BCE, a series of impressive renovations were carried out, which appear to indicate constant production enhancement. These measures mark the conversion of the complex into a metalworking area, perhaps strictly dependent on the adjacent dwelling unit.[17] Concrete evidence of this includes the recovery of large quantities of iron slag, at least one hearth, and frequent traces of reddening in the ground.

The same mixture of functions also characterizes a large and well-structured housing complex, excavated in *Regio* V, 3, within which some rooms seem to have specific apparatus related to metallurgical activity (*see map 8*).[18] The clearest traces are the concentrations of fragments of matrices in different points of the excavation; the ground shows visible signs of combustion, which could correspond to the open-air areas. However, it is what excavators conventionally call "sector VI" that has provided the most consistent evidence, allowing us to reconstruct all the necessary stages in a metallurgical workshop. Here we find a large oval-shaped deposit of ash, mixed with slag, fragments of matrices, vitrified pebbles, and bronze drops. All these remains are most likely linked to the presence of ovens, built and then destroyed as required. The discovery of tanks used for the cooling of metal and conspicuous fragments of pumice stone, in some cases blackened by contact with metal, which could indicate the practice of cold polishing, is also significant.

Finally, some remains of metallurgical activity were also recovered inside the house located in *Regio* IV, 2, conventionally called "House 1" (*see maps 8 and 12*). This is a recently published context offering a worthwhile contribution to our knowledge of the productive organization of the city.[19] Some evidence has made it possible to document that the house, in addition to its predominant role in producing ceramic artifacts, also acted as a foundry for the creation of bronze objects and as a forge/smithy for the creation and repair of iron tools to be used in craft practices and daily household chores.

If we examine this evidence in relation to the urban plan, an almost systematic concentration emerges, in correspondence with the main communication routes, indicating the road system in the urban plateau and especially near *plateia* A, which crossed it in a north–south direction.

The lack of a topographical area destined for production, often highlighted as a peculiar characteristic of Marzabotto, is actually more comparable with Greek contexts, where the latest research invites us to reconsider the often-abused concepts of "zoning" and "artisan district."[20] Like the ceramic industry, metallurgical workshops are also located in prominent points of the urban space and, above all, near the main road axes. This invites us to reflect on the probable strategic positioning of processing facilities and those intended for the sale of products.

This hypothesis, already advanced by Mansuelli in relation to the "workshop-houses" of *Regio* IV, 1, seems to have found confirmation in the excavations of the "Foundry" of *Regio* V, 5. In fact, in the stretch of road facing the latter atelier, some common technological indicators have been found, as well as several anthropomorphic bronzes, probably goods intended for sale.[21] The large number of fragments of metal ingots found in the area of *plateia* A, probably intended as a means of exchange for economic transactions, is equally significant.[22] After all, the city was undoubtedly capable of "minting" this particular type of pre-coinage unit. This aspect is also indicated by the discovery of a mold with a negative print of the so-called *ramo secco* ("dry branch"), used to make bronze ingots to be exploited in commercial exchanges.[23]

The sacred areas of Kainua must have exercised a strong influence on where these large production plants and their shops could be located within the urban system, according to dynamics increasingly comparable to the contemporary Etruscan or, more generally, Mediterranean context. As noted previously (especially in chapters 8–9), two monumental temples dedicated to the celestial couple Tinia-Uni have recently been found in the northern sector of the urban area. This discovery helps to indicate the productive dynamism of the center, since a significant proportion of the products would certainly have been reserved for the manufacture of votives and functional tools for religious purposes. Sanctuaries were normally full of *ex-votos* dedicated by the devoted to the divinity, and a preference for bronze is well known in internal northern Etruria, from Orvieto, Chiusi, and Volterra to the Po Valley.[24] The great demand for votive images has been recognized as one of the determining factors in the creation of local workshops, within which each center developed its own style and figurative language.[25]

Therefore, if the theme is explored from the perspective of the artifacts, we have a rich corpus of evidence confirming the importance of Marzabotto in this specific craft sector (*see fig. 2.1*). In general, although bronze technology is not the only one documented within the center, it is certainly the predominant one. The discovery of several clay molds in the "Foundry" of *Regio* V, 5, is well known in the literature. In the past, these findings had already made it possible to revisit the question of figured bronze art in Etruria Padana, enhancing the role of Marzabotto as a nonexclusive reception center. In this context, the recovery of a fragment with the impression of a small portion of the head and parts of a body, identifiable as a draped statue almost one meter high, appears to be significant (fig. 12.2). In particular, the head made with this mold shows surprising stylistic and dimen-

FIGURE 12.2. Fragment of clay mold with the print of a *kouros* head from the "Foundry" of *Regio* V, 5, first decades of the fifth century BCE. After Morpurgo 2017:64, fig. 8.

sional similarities with that of a *kouros* in Parian marble, dating from around 500 BCE, found in the urban area and actually connected to the sanctuary of Tinia (*see fig. 8.3*). It is believed that the artisans of Marzabotto were inspired by this model, imported from Greece, to create this bronze sculpture, whose skillful and refined features imply a high level of craft specialization and remarkable stylistic and formal skills.

As further confirmation of what has been outlined above, we may cite the recent discovery of a bronze statuette of striking artistic quality (*see fig. 8.6*),[26] found in the northeastern sector of the city near the edge of the collapsed plateau, not far from the Urban Sanctuary, to which it is probably related. Intact and in excellent condition, the bronze is 30 cm high and represents a female figure, modeled after the Greek *korai*. The woman lifts a corner of the long *chiton* with her left hand, while offering a lotus flower bud with her right. A large mantle, the typical Etruscan *tebenna*, highly decorated, covers her head, except for a high lunate diadem, and her back, down to the top of her calves, with large folds made by incision. While the style and elaborate details of the clothing characterize the woman as high-ranking, her exact identification is more uncertain, oscillating between a divinity, perhaps *Uni* or *Turan*, the Etruscan counterpart of Aphrodite, and a figure in the human sphere.

The truly exceptional quality of this statuette, dated to the beginning of the fifth century BCE and possibly locally made, denotes the great technical-stylistic skill of its craftsman. In fact, direct knowledge of contemporary Hellenic productions is combined here with an expert ability to rework foreign figurative forms to satisfy the taste of Etruscan customers.

If this small bronze statue can currently be considered the most representative result of local bronze craftsmanship, other evidence helps to outline the productive character of this center, operating for a clientele that is certainly heterogeneous in economic and social terms. The votive finds, mostly belonging to deposits excavated during the nineteenth century but also coming from the different urban sectors investigated over time, are noteworthy here (*see fig. 2.1*).

As in the case of the female bronze just described, the almost constant presence of tenons cast beneath the feet of the figurines suggests that these objects would have been placed on simple wooden bases or, in cases of greater formal commitment (like the Kainua Lady), attached to a shaped base of travertine or some other stone that sometimes survived. In most cases, these are schematic figurines, falling within the "Marzabotto Group,"[27] that is, rapidly executed bronzes representing a male or female devotee or offerant. However, there is no lack of finds made in a more naturalistic way that also include works of a certain value. Among these, there is a type of *kore* (maiden), always depicted in the act of lifting a corner of her dress with her hand, while holding out an offering to the divinity (fig. 12.3).[28]

There are also numerous male figures, among which we find the generic *kouros*,[29] which, in one case, was identified with the god Apollo (called Aplu in Etruscan), originally equipped with a bow and arrow.[30] We can distinguish a javelin thrower and the image of a male wearing a *toga*, both coming from the votive deposits of the Acropolis and made by the hand of an up-to-date bronze artist, who may have worked in a local shop.[31] From the area of the "Foundry" of *Regio* V, 5, comes the representation of a devotee holding his beard with his right hand. The small bronze, also of excellent workmanship, dates to the end of the sixth century BCE.[32]

This brief review is completed by some anatomical *ex-votos*, most of which come from the Water Shrine located north of the city and connected to generic cults of healing. Among the bronzes, a male leg is exceptional for its decidedly above average size (fig. 12.4). Due to its good craftsmanship, it was initially considered a Greek product,[33] but doubts as to its origin have been raised.[34]

In the light of the findings outlined, and in accordance with the most recent literature on the topic,[35] there is no doubt that Marzabotto should be recognized as a center of primary importance for bronze production. Proof of this lies in the quantity and complexity of its craft facilities, but also in the excellent quality of its work. The latter, in some cases, was also of considerable size, according to the measurements calculated on the fragment of matrix preserved for the *kouros* in the "Foundry," and to those handed down in relation to the discovery of some bronze sculptures

FIGURE 12.3. Bronze *korai* from the votive deposit of the Acropolis, fifth century BCE. After Gozzadini 1865: pl. 11.

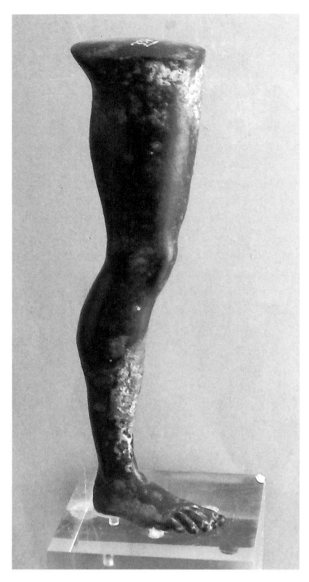

FIGURE 12.4. Anatomical *ex-voto* from the Water Shrine, fifth century BCE. After Govi 2007:58.

in a phase preceding the start of regular investigations in the center.[36]

Kainua is revealed as a center that is perfectly integrated in a network of fashions and models, not only of northern Etruscan origin, but also from Greece, perhaps without mediation. It is precisely the multiple references visible in the various objects that make it possible to recognize Marzabotto as a place of independent innovation, capable of expressing itself independently even at high levels. Therefore, the idea that these workshops were destined to satisfy the requests of customers from the city and the surrounding territory, belonging to a stratified social context, becomes increasingly evident.[37]

While the descriptions above offer substantial arguments about the creation of votive artifacts, it is not easy to define a precise picture in relation to all the other categories of bronze or other metal work, which must also have been produced in local ateliers. In fact, with the exception of some objects, namely *fibulae*, which can reasonably be interpreted as production waste caused by defects or casting residues, it seems more difficult to verify the local origin of universally common objects, which only rarely have decorative motifs indicating style.

However, even recently, there has been no shortage of hypotheses around this question. For example, a series of bronze mirrors, coming from the city necropoleis and characterized both by the absence of decoration and by the presence of a framing border on the reflecting side—a quite unusual practice—were indicated as locally manufactured. These elements appear to be unique to Bolognese documentation and, more generally, to Etruria Padana.[38]

The possible local origin of bronze vessels still has to be investigated: this category is part of the artistic craftsmanship of Etruria, also very well documented in Marzabotto,[39] which is well known and had a strong development in the fifth century.

More generally, the topic has long been at the center of a wide and lively debate: the substantial monopoly of Vulci outlined in the past is, in fact, contradicted by the appearance of several production centers throughout the Etruscan territory. As mentioned above, although their provenance is difficult to establish due to the often ordinary and standardized nature of these objects, it has been suggested that Etruria Padana, and especially Marzabotto, played a leading role in this category.

Certainly, the large-scale smelting activity implied by the archaeological evidence would have required a general availability of raw materials. On this issue, the idea of the exploitation of local mines has long been discarded in favor of the importing of raw metals from the Tuscan mining areas, on which hypotheses have been made in the past.[40]

Finally, a question remains about the main actors in these activities, the metal craftsmen, whose social profile does not appear easy to define in the current state of knowledge. However, integration of the available data allows us potentially to recognize a class of specialized artisan-businessmen, characterized by a high standard of living, guaranteed by the sale of products and by important onomastic elements, such as a *gentilicium* (an example is given below) as well as the ability to write, also for craft purposes.

As regards the metallurgical sphere, the so-called calibrator in serpentinite stone found in the area of the "Foundry" of *Regio* V, 5, and one of the tools used for bronzework, is particularly significant (fig. 12.5). The object is incomplete and has a series of drilled holes arranged in two rows, with a progressively increasing diameter. It is to be interpreted as a die, a tool used to obtain regular threads by forcefully passing coarse ones, made by pouring or hammering through holes, or, more likely, as a calibrator.[41]

Nevertheless, the most interesting find for this question is an inscription bearing the name of the owner of this metalworking tool, which also reflects a wide "instrumental" use of the letters of the alphabet (*see appendix A, no. 51; fig. 10.7: no. 51*). On the sides, in fact, we find a bi-member onomastic formula composed of a largely incomplete *praenomen* and a possessive *gentilicium*, ---]*sualus mi*, only questionably restored and formed with the suffix -*alu*, typical of Etruria Padana. In addition, on the two faces, near some of the holes, we find some isolated engraved letters, possibly marks related to the different diameters of the holes themselves.[42]

There is also a significant clue, once again in the epigraphic field, that perhaps allows us to reconstruct the presence of specialized migrant workers, attracted by the great technological, productive, and commercial potential of this center. These workers would have been the bearers of empirical knowledge which, according to dynamics well known in the Etruscan context, they divulged and passed on. In this regard, the *Akius* inscription, engraved on the foot of a bowl coming from previous excavations in the urban area, turns out to be significant (*appendix A, no. 57; fig. 10.7: no. 57*). Although today it is lost, evidence of it remains in one of the publications about the investigations into the Etruscan center by G. Gozzadini.[43] This *gentilicium* reflects an adaptation to southern Etruscan spelling rules, an absolutely exceptional case for Marzabotto, and finds a precise parallel in an inscription from Campiglia Marittima, coeval to ours, and with the same contradictory elements as regards the spelling rules adopted.

This anomaly, and the fact of its being incised onto a "miner's" lamp, have suggested the hypothesis that this *Akiu* should be identified as an individual who came from southern Etruria to the Campigliese area, with particular skills in the metallurgical field. The same interpretation could therefore also be applied to the character documented in Marzabotto.[44]

FIGURE 12.5. The so-called calibrator from the "Foundry" of *Regio* V, 5. After Govi 2007:43.

The evidence for metallurgy at Kainua-Marzabotto is thus very rich and evocative. At Marzabotto we see unusual patterns in the location of the metalworking shops in the heart of town, along with the remarkable coexistence of residential quarters with workshops. There is abundant evidence for the technology and production of bronzes, as well as many objects probably locally made. Finally, we have the highly suggestive evidence of the social status of the artisans themselves, who must have prospered and enjoyed an elevated position, due to their wealth, skills, and contacts within and outside the city.

NOTES

1. For a review of the evidence relating to metallurgical installations in Etruria Padana, see Moretto 1995. For the latest news on excavations in the center of Bologna see Calastri and Desantis 2010:206.

2. On the changes recorded in Etruria Padana starting from the second half of the sixth century BCE and in particular on the economic-commercial structure, see Sassatelli 1990; Sassatelli 1993a; Sassatelli 2008a.

3. The importance of Marzabotto in the study of these aspects has always been recognized in the history of scholarship. On these issues see, e.g., Curri and Sorbelli 1973; Cuomo di Caprio 1971–1972; Sassatelli 1989a:53–74; Nijboer 1998:119–129, 196–202. The topic was recently discussed by Morpurgo (2017).

4. For the phase that precedes the regular and planned city, evidence of metallurgical activity has been identified in *Regio* III, *insula* 4a (De Maria et al. 1972), and in *Regio* V, *insula* 5, in correspondence with the "Foundry" (see below; Locatelli 2005:216). On the oldest phases of the center, see Govi 2016.

5. On the founding rite see Sassatelli 2017b and Gottarelli 2017, as well as chapters 8 and 9 above.

6. Govi 2016; Morpurgo 2017; Mattioli, Morpurgo, and Pizzirani 2017:113–118.

7. As confirmed by recent research, the case of Olynthus is emblematic. The city is characterized, in fact, by a wide range of productive activities, well distributed in the urban system and located within complexes also intended for residential use (Cahill 2005). This same duality, equally significantly, also exists in Athens, in the houses identified near the Agora (Tsakirgis 2005). On this topic, with an extensive review of contexts, see also Sanidas 2013.

8. Gentili 1968.

9. Locatelli 1997; Locatelli 2005; Malnati and Locatelli 2006.

10. Minto 1954.

11. Hypothesis initially formulated by Sassatelli (1989a: 64–65) and Sassatelli (1990:68–75), and later taken up and enlarged by Locatelli (1997; 2005).

12. In this regard, the significant results of archaeometric analysis on the sampling of technological finds from this workshop seem to exclude the presence of indicators attesting a process of mineral reduction (Chiarantini et al. 2010:452, n. 31).

13. Gentili 1968:116.

14. Baratti 2005.

15. D. Locatelli in Malnati and Locatelli 2006:352.

16. Mansuelli 1963a.

17. For a history of the investigations in this block with an updated interpretation of the excavation data, see Gaucci 2016, with previous references.

18. Massa Pairault 1997: esp. 105–111.

19. Govi and Sassatelli 2010.

20. Esposito and Sanidas 2012.

21. Locatelli 2005:218.

22. Locatelli 2005:218.

23. Sassatelli 1985b:147, no. 6.14.

24. Colonna 1985:24.

25. Cristofani 1985a:32.

26. Desantis and Malnati 2012; see also chapter 8 of this volume.

27. Colonna 1970:62–63. The classification of these specimens in the Umbrian-northern production is now outdated, also in this case in favor of a local production.

28. Brizzolara 2001: esp. 127–143, nos. 19–32.

29. Brizzolara 2001:106–115, nos. 1–8.

30. Brizzolara 2001:114, no. 7.

31. Brizzolara 2001: respectively, 154–155, no. 42, and 164, no. 49.

32. Richardson 1983:214, no. 1.

33. Mansuelli 1971:31, fig. 8.

34. Gualandi 1974:65, n. 98 and Brizzolara 2001:159–160, no. 47.

35. In the past, some scholars, on the basis of the matrix fragments found in Regio V, 5, and connected to a sculpture of striking artistic quality, had already suggested recognizing Marzabotto as a center of bronze production of no small importance (Gualandi 1970:223; Cristofani 1985b:258–259; Sassatelli 1989a:64; Sassatelli 1990:69–74, 87–88). Now, other research conducted on the preserved bronze material has also reached the same conclusions (see in particular Brizzolara 2001, with further references, and Desantis and Malnati 2012).

36. See Brizzolara 2001:97, who recalls the loss of "two bronze idols of several feet in height." They must have measured no less than 80 cm, since the modern Bolognese foot corresponded to 38 cm.

37. The hypothesis that Marzabotto was the center of bronze production in the territory had already been formulated in the past (Galestin 1987:163) and taken up more recently in Desantis and Malnati 2012:173.

38. Govi 2018b:23.

39. Muffatti 1968; Muffatti 1969.

40. For a review, see Locatelli 2005:231.

41. Sassatelli 1985b:146–147, no. 6.13.

42. On the epigraphic issue, see especially Sassatelli 1994a: 180–184, no. 293, and Gaucci in this volume.

43. Gozzadini 1865:30.

44. Sassatelli 1994a:19, no. 2, with further references.

CHAPTER 13

FROM CLAY TO VASES
Operative Workflow

CHIARA MATTIOLI

Because of its great production dynamism and strong manufacturing vocation, the city of Kainua-Marzabotto offers an extraordinary opportunity to analyze ceramic production in all its aspects.[1] The investigations carried out over the years, the most recent discoveries,[2] and the systematic review of the oldest excavations provide an exceptional starting point for investigating this aspect of life in the city (*see map 8*).

Recent excavations have fundamentally changed our concept of the city's appearance, revealing its great political and institutional unity.[3] One of the most meaningful new achievements is the discovery of the Urban Sanctuary,[4] in which a large quantity of ceramic material was recovered, suggesting its probable use in rituality. The complete publication of some sectors[5] and the systematic review of unpublished areas investigated in the past[6] have allowed us to analyze the production system from a new perspective, although sometimes contradicting the interpretative schemes previously applied to the city. It has, therefore, been possible to highlight areas of the city dedicated to pottery production, to categorize and date the kilns, to reconstruct the production cycle, and, lastly, to carry out archaeometric analyses on the ceramic classes that were produced within these structures. This data collection also led to a classification of vessel shapes.[7]

To start with the structures destined for pottery production, both small domestic kilns and dedicated workshops have been documented in the city. The larger productive structures were internally organized to resemble real "factories." Small kilns were probably intended for limited production and the needs of small groups, whereas production in the more organized structures concerned the entire population and perhaps was even exported.

A production complex commonly defined in the literature as the *Grande Fornace* (the Great Kiln)[8] is located in *Regio* II, 1. This workshop is perhaps the most striking example of a large public structure, showing how the recent discoveries in the urban sacred area have introduced new interpretations of production.[9] This structure was excavated in the last century, and unfortunately, only a small portion of the complex was examined. The excavation took place at different times, thus hindering a complete reconstruction of the stratigraphic sequence.[10] In recent times, the recovered material was studied systematically, and the analysis of Attic pottery[11] in particular has allowed us to define different chronological phases. The complex was certainly used in two distinct but consecutive periods: at the end of the sixth–early fifth century BCE and in the fifth century BCE. Among the archaeological finds, material from the Celtic phase was recovered, but this did not indicate continuity into the Gallic period.[12] Although it is not possible to reconstruct a detailed internal plan of the Great Kiln and the actual purpose of its western sector, the complex appears to be divided into three main areas, aligned in a north–south direction and facing onto *plateia* A. The most important finds were discovered in the central space. In the southeast corner, a rectangular basin containing purified clay residues was recovered and interpreted as a tank used to prepare raw material (fig. 13.1, at A). Not far away, water was collected inside a tank, made

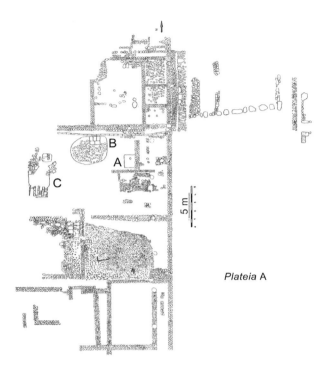

FIGURE 13.1. *Regio* II, 1, Great Kiln, plan of the main structures for the production of ceramics and bricks. After Morpurgo 2017:358, fig. 1.

with cover-tiles juxtaposed and sealed to ensure that it was waterproof (fig. 13.1, at B). This structure covered a previous pit, lined with cobblestones, intended for the same function. The tank was filled via a channel constructed of pantiles, tucked into each other, and fed by a natural spring from the hill where an aqueduct had been built (*see fig. 14.5*).[13]

Slightly to the west, a rectangular kiln (fig. 13:1, at C) covered a smaller one used in the first phase of the production complex.[14] Only part of the combustion chamber of the rectangular kiln is preserved. It was built with a terracotta floor and coarse brick walls. Four air vents of different sizes held the perforated top, used to support the artifacts during firing. The discovery of many fragmented cover-tiles and pantiles, sometimes deformed and vitrified, together with ceramic fragments,[15] suggests that not only pottery but also building materials were produced. This hypothesis is supported by the considerable size of the kiln. No evidence was recovered of either the *praefur-nium* (the heating channel) or the vault, which was normally destroyed at the end of each firing.

In the southern part of the central space, the focal point of the production, a series of north–south postholes were found, which must have supported a large portico, probably used to shelter products during the drying process and to display finished artifacts meant for sale. Before firing, the clay products had to undergo a complete and careful drying process called in Italian *ritiro a crudo*, referring to a process to shrink the raw clay to eliminate excessive moisture trapped inside it. This process prevented the formation of cracks, fissures, and/or deformations during firing, which would have made the products unusable. Finally, to the south of the central area, a cobblestone paving was recovered and interpreted as the support of an original wooden floor, poorly preserved.

After the discovery of the Temple of Tinia, located in the eastern block adjacent to *plateia* A,[16] it now seems that the Great Kiln had a prominent role in the urban plan of the city of Kainua. It has indeed been suggested that the primary purpose of this structure was to fulfill the needs of the sanctuary:[17] namely, its construction and the maintenance of the roof, as well as the constant demand for pottery to be used in daily life and cultural practices. This new interpretation, and consequently the intrinsic value of the Great Kiln in the development of the city of Kainua-Marzabotto, is supported not only by its undeniable topographic proximity, but also by the finds recovered inside the structure, which could be linked to the temple. In particular, there is a pair of molds of votive heads and an inscription incised before firing on the bottom of a coarse-ware pot with the theonym *tin*[- - -], referring unequivocally to the god Tinia worshiped in the temple (*see appendix A, no. 13; fig. 10.4: no. 13*).[18]

Recently, the publication of House 1 in *Regio* IV, 2, excavated by the Chair of Etruscology at the University of Bologna, provided another significant contribution (fig. 13.2).[19] The scrupulous stratigraphic analysis and the systematic study of the finds have illuminated a large building complex that, during its existence, underwent several important structural modifications, changing its function from a simple residential area to an exclusively production role.[20] It was possible to recognize a first phase, dating to the end of the sixth century BCE, with two distinct residential units,[21] and a second phase in the first half of the fifth century BCE, in which the northern sector was completely converted into a ceramic atelier.

Inside House 1, nine kilns were recovered, dating to the different phases of this complex;[22] investigators were able to document their destruction and the construction of new ones. Four kilns were found in the northwestern sector of House 1 (Sector III), three circular or oval and one rectangular. According to the stratigraphy, they were partly built over each other, showing that despite their proximity they functioned in different periods, even though it is not possible to reconstruct a chronological sequence. The three circular or oval kilns (β, γ, δ) were small and had a similar structure: the entrance was made using a *dolium* rim.[23] The fourth kiln (α) was rectangular in shape and larger. Moreover, a sophisticated system conveyed rainwater into a small cistern, supplemented by at least one pair of tanks lined with cover-tiles, which could be used not only as a water reserve but also for clay purification through decanting, a fundamental step in the production process (fig. 13.3).

In the middle of the fifth century BCE, House 1 underwent substantial structural modifications, probably connected to the significant increase in manufacturing as the city reached its maximum expansion. From this period onward, the complex had a unified structure with an overall size of over 1,270 square meters, truly becoming a production complex. The northern sector was completely restructured, eliminating the previous structures. The area was transformed into an open-air space, where the three small circular/oval kilns were built, constructed with a combustion chamber dug out of the earth and a perforated floor.[24]

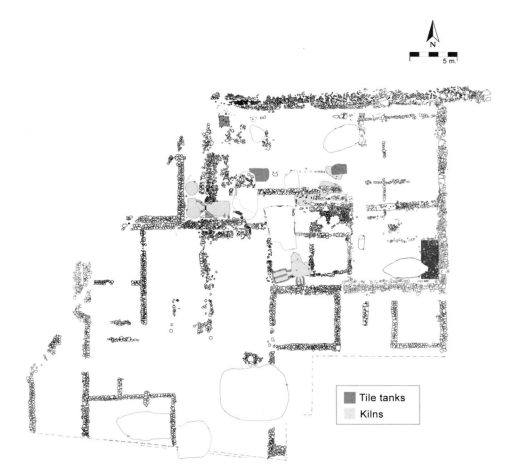

FIGURE 13.2. House 1 in *Regio* IV, 2, the main pottery workshops. After Morpurgo 2017:360, fig. 5.

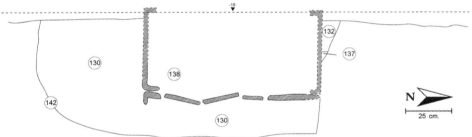

FIGURE 13.3. House 1 in *Regio* IV, 2, photo and cross-section of paving of one of the tiled basins. After Morpurgo 2017:361, fig. 6.

As noted, it is not possible to establish the precise stratigraphic relationship between these structures, nor can we determine their chronological sequence. But it is clear that in the same period, the water tank was enlarged, and a deep pit was dug for the purpose of extraction of clay, as proven by archaeometric analyses.[25] In the vicinity, a cobbled floor and a small porticoed building housed activities necessary for the production cycle, as seen in the Great Kiln. In the southern part of the house, obvious structural transformations were made in the middle of the fifth century BCE, relating both to ceramic production and to metalworking.[26]

In the first half of the fourth century BCE, the structures in the northern sector were abandoned and manufacturing was so reduced that only two rectangular kilns and an axial wall are documented (fig. 13.4). The mouths of both kilns were connected to an irregularly shaped deposit, interpreted as a trench for fuel preparation and combustion because of the presence of a blackish carbon-rich soil.[27] Near the kilns, a tile-paved area was identified, probably a work surface.

Moreover, a general analysis of the structure of House 1 yields a complete overview of the spatial organization within the workshop during the various stages of the production cycle for ceramic manufacturing.[28] The first step was to determine the location of the clay pit[29] to collect the raw material, followed by a series of operations necessary to prepare an optimal clay paste. Clay is a natural sedimentary soil with variable particle size and may contain other elements, commonly referred to as clasts, which decrease its plasticity and shrinkage during drying and firing. It was therefore essential to obtain a clay paste with the best workability, by carefully controlling the relative amounts of plastic and nonplastic components.[30] To achieve that state, after extraction the clay was left to "rest," to allow for the decomposing of any organic elements. Within House 1, this process probably took place in a graveled area discovered near the clay pit.

The second phase of manufacturing was clay purification, or decanting, and was carried out in water tanks usually made of tiles, just like those recovered both inside House 1 and in the Great Kiln.[31] Only after this preparation was the clay ready to be shaped

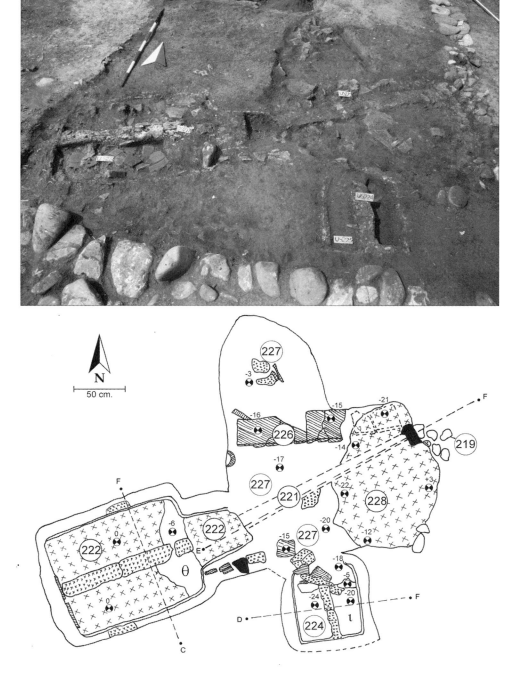

FIGURE 13.4. House 1 in *Regio* IV, 2, photo and plan of the ceramic kilns of the latest phase. After Morpurgo 2017:362, fig. 7.

into vases. Afterward, the vessels had to be laid out to dry, in order to remove excess water accumulated during crafting, which could ruin them irreversibly during firing. Drying was supposed to take place in an open area protected from sun and bad weather. An optimal solution was to store them under a porch like the ones recovered both at the Great Kiln and House 1. The production process ended with the firing, the success of which depended essentially on how the pots were placed and the intensity of the fire. Inside the firing chamber, the pots could either be stacked on top of each other or separated from each other by ceramic fragments[32] or by terracotta distance spacers with vent holes to eliminate water vapor and the gases produced during firing. Moreover, the use of spacers permitted an even distribution of the artifacts. A large number of distance spacers have been found in the Great Kiln and near the production facilities of House 1.

Another manufacturing complex, now no longer available and thus unable to be described precisely, seems to have been recovered in *Regio* IV, 4, a sector of the town that has collapsed over time into the Reno River (*see map 8*). In January 1885, six kilns were found during farming activities, probably related to a large production complex rather than to a family workshop.[33] Five pipe-type kilns with an almost elliptical shape were located in a rather large rectangular room; the sixth kiln, shaped like the others, was placed in an adjoining space along with a well for water. At the time of discovery, E. Brizio reported that these kilns had a short *praefurnium* with a semicircular mouth and part of the brick walls still preserved. The presence of a perforated floor was suggested by the discovery of perforated clay brick.[34] In his study of the city drainage system, G. Sassatelli[35] suggested that this production complex was directly connected to the aqueduct on the slopes of the Acropolis through one conduit (*see fig. 14.5*). To stress the large-scale manufacturing function of the structure, it is worth noting that Brizio mentioned the previous recovery of similar kilns in the same area, about which no other information is known.[36]

In addition to these large complexes, the discovery of smaller pottery kilns scattered through the town has been recorded. Due to their location and characteristics, these structures would have provided a limited production, reserved for residential units. Among the main pieces of evidence in *Regio* III, 4b, a pipe kiln[37] was found, which differed from the other known ones, because it had a longitudinal wall bisecting the combustion chamber and supporting the perforated floor. The presence of charcoal inside only one of the two compartments suggested that the pottery could sometimes also be stacked in the other sector to increase productivity. Another small pipe kiln, built in the second half of the sixth century BCE,[38] was found in the northern sector of the plateau, specifically in *Regio* V, 5, where intensive excavation unearthed the entire plan of a house (*see map 8*).

In the northernmost area of *Regio* I, 5, just north of the urban temple of Tinia (the *Area Nord*: *see map 8*), the floor of another dismantled workshop was found inside a room that could be dated stratigraphically to the late Archaic period.[39] G. A. Mansuelli recovered another small kiln during excavation of House 1 of *Regio* IV, 1,[40] but the structure cannot be classified due to the scarcity of available data.

With the review of the documentation on manufacturing areas complete, it is now necessary to focus our attention on the characteristics of the finished products. The shapes were made in what is commonly referred to as *ceramica etrusco-padana* (Etruscan pottery of the Po Valley) because of its diffusion range. This ware type is indeed documented from the middle of the sixth until the fourth centuries BCE within Etruria Padana, especially in the two cities of Bologna and Marzabotto, as well as in the western territory, in the Etruscan port of Spina, which served the entire Po Valley, around Mantua at the settlements of Forcello and Castellazzo della Garolda, and also in Romagna. Moreover, it was even exported from these production centers to other areas of northern Italy that conducted commercial relations with Etruria Padana, such as the Veneto (Este, Padua, and Altino), Liguria, and Lombardy (Golasecca culture) (*see map 2*).[41]

The main characteristic of this ceramic production is that it can be classified into four distinct classes: fine ware, whether plain or decorated with painted bands, coarse ware, bucchero, and gray ware (*see plate 7*).

Thanks to a profitable collaboration with the Department of Biological, Geological, and Environmental Sciences (BiGeA) of the University of Bologna, the Chair of Etruscology has been able to conduct archaeometric analyses on the pottery of Marzabotto.[42] The mineralogical and chemical analyses and the subsequent statistical processing (cluster analysis) confirmed local production at Kainua-Marzabotto, since all the samples had the same compositional structure. This contribution was also decisive in the morphological study, leading to the creation of a typological atlas of shapes made in *ceramica etrusco-padana*, that is, the pottery of Etruria Padana[43] recovered not only at Marzabotto but throughout the entire region. The possibility of creating a typology became feasible when the Bologna team began to systematically study the large amount of pottery found in House 1 of *Regio* IV, 2, in preparation for publication.[44] The absence of a system of classification dedicated to this body of material, which could detail shapes and other descriptive terminology, was immediately recognized. It was indeed necessary to define a common vocabulary, relating both to the shapes and the vessel parts, which could be applied to the findings scattered throughout Etruria Padana.

Utilizing an online database, the study began with a detailed review of all the published pottery from various sites in the region. Over time, this database has been constantly implemented with new data from the systematic study of various unpublished areas of the city of Marzabotto, from the Bologna necropoleis of Certosa,[45] De Luca, and Battistini,[46] from Villa Cassarini[47] (Acropolis of Bologna), and, last but not least, from the settlement of Spina[48] and its necropolis at Valle Trebba.[49] At present, the *ceramica etrusco-padana* database contains nearly sixty thousand records, the largest nucleus ever assembled for creating a typology. The typological atlas creates a reference point whenever the *ceramica etrusco-padana* is systematically studied. By reconstructing the complete framework of this production, this study allows us to examine the ancient tendency to differentiate artifacts according to their use and functionality, as not all the shapes were made in all four classes. Both the potters and their clients had a precise intent for and idea of the vessels' functional needs, the various production techniques, and their significance to the social group that selected them. Some pottery shapes were indeed produced in all four classes, while the rest were made in the most refined ones, such as bucchero and gray ware. Further, ceramic production can be divided into three main categories: vessels destined for daily food preparation, vessels used for cooking, and others reserved for storage. Thus, the choice of ceramic class depended both on the practical function and its qualitative value.

Further archaeometric analyses were also carried out on samples of black-gloss ceramics, a production that is well documented throughout the city. The aim was to verify the presence in Kainua of local black-gloss pottery, imitating Attic ceramics and/or the production of Tyrrhenian Etruria.[50] The results confirmed that black-gloss ware was indeed produced in Marzabotto in imitation of products from Attica and Tyrrhenian Etruria,[51] adding another important aspect to the manufacturing and cultural context of the city. The integration of archaeometry with archaeology has thus provided scientific certainty about the technical and technological knowledge of the artisans in the city of Kainua, thereby enriching our understanding of the production system.

To conclude, it is extremely interesting to focus on the topographic distribution of these manufacturing complexes, which appear to be widespread throughout the city, an aspect that finds many comparisons in the Greek world, where recent urbanism studies have looked, more prudently, at the idea of spatial marginalization of manufacturing.[52] At Marzabotto, large workshops were purposefully placed on the main roads.[53]

In particular, the area between the intersection of *plateiai* A and B was for a long time considered a peripheral sector,[54] and now, instead, is regarded as the focal point of the urban plan, due to the presence of the large temple of Tinia, which, as previously mentioned, had an active and important role in the creation and progressive enlargement of the production complex. Its proximity to the Urban Sanctuary on *plateia* B, viewed as a true sacred way, could also explain the progressive transformation of House 1 into a workshop.[55]

Therefore, this framework makes it possible to add nuance to the idea of a strict separation between simple domestic structures and public complexes, by enhancing the important role played by a large building in which residential functions were combined with large-scale manufacturing, a context that finds precise evidence once again in the Greek sphere.[56] A residential function cannot indeed be excluded even within the "public" structures, such as the Great Kiln.[57] More specifically, not only is the complete plan unknown but the precise function of a series of rooms in the southern area of the complex is uncertain, because no evidence of crafting was documented there, while systematic study has highlighted the presence of domestic implements.[58] As G. Morpurgo states,[59] another pivotal aspect concerns the diachronic distribution of the collected finds, which shows that productive structures often underwent significant structural modifications over time—proof of great manufacturing flexibility and dynamism. First, the available data proved that production activities had been a fundamental part of the city ever since its foundation, thus enriching our knowledge of the phase that preceded the planned city.[60] In the period from the end of the sixth to the beginning of the fifth century BCE, most of these complexes were inserted within the orthogonal urban plan. In the second half of the fifth century BCE, a substantial strengthening of manufacturing is recorded, for instance, within House 1 of *Regio* IV, 2, which could therefore be related to an increasing need during the maximum economic expansion of the city.

With our present state of knowledge, an attempt to outline the social profile of the craftsmen is much more complicated. Perhaps it is possible to recognize a class of artisans, defined by significant onomastics such as the *gentilicium*, who had a high standard of living guaranteed by the sale of their products. Moreover, they were able to use writing also during manufacturing, as attested by a cup from House 1 of *Regio* IV, 2, on which the potter, evidently literate, engraved the Etruscan word for the number "one," instead of a simple number mark.[61]

Therefore, as already recognized by E. Govi,[62] the layout of Kainua-Marzabotto appears less uniform than was assumed in the past, while the production facilities acquire a greater importance. These structures were managed by specialized craftsmen belonging to one or more families,[63] suggesting a work organization and type of production whose complexity clearly indicates the active presence of an urban authority.[64]

NOTES

1. Morpurgo (2017:353, n. 2), stating the well-known importance of Marzabotto in the study of production, with reference to additional treatment of these issues: Curri and Sorbelli 1973:245–266; Cuomo di Caprio 1971–1972; Sassatelli 1989a:53–74; Nijboer 1998:119–129 and 196–202.

2. For the most recent surveys see Govi 2014a with previous bibliography.

3. Morpurgo 2017:353.

4. Govi 2017b.

5. The investigations by the École Française de Rome in *Regio* V, 3 (Massa Pairault 1997), and excavations by the Department of Archaeology of the University of Bologna in *Regio* IV, 2, House 1 (Govi and Sassatelli 2010).

6. Gaucci 2016.

7. Mattioli 2013.

8. In 2010, the area was reburied due to conservation issues, so the structure is no longer visible.

9. Sassatelli 2011:150–158.

10. At the Pian di Misano, the first discovery took place during farming at the end of the nineteenth century under the supervision of E. Brizio (Brizio 1890:281–283, pl. VIII, nos. 7–7A). In 1954, other limited interventions were carried out under the direction of the superintendent, P. E. Arias. Ten years later an extensive excavation campaign was conducted, but only a preliminary report of that campaign remains (Saronio 1965) and it does not allow a reconstruction of the stratigraphic sequence of the area where the production complex was located.

11. Ossani 2003–2004; Pozzi 2004–2005.

12. On the Celts at Marzabotto see Morpurgo 2016 with previous bibliography.

13. Sassatelli 2011:153. On the aqueduct and its relation to the city's production facilities see Sassatelli 1991a:183–188.

14. Saronio 1965:45, who observed in her stratigraphic analysis how the large furnace of fifth century BCE cut into the eastern part of an earlier quadrangular structure with smooth edges, unfortunately too little documented.

15. Ossani 2003–2004; Pozzi 2004–2005.

16. Govi 2017b.

17. Sassatelli 2011.

18. Sassatelli 2011:153–156.
19. Govi and Sassatelli 2010.
20. For the detailed analysis of the various phases and their reconstruction, see Govi 2010a and Govi 2010b.
21. Govi 2016.
22. Pozzi 2010:257.
23. Precise comparison can be found with kilns found in Trebbio near San Sepolcro (Arezzo): Iaia, Moroni, and Lanfredini 2009. This analogy allows us to hypothesize the absence of the perforated floor with consequently no distinction between the cooking and the combustion chamber: probably vessels were placed directly in contact with the fuel.
24. Pozzi 2010:262.
25. Morandi et al. 1997:40–45. Archaeometric analyses of clay residues present in the trench proved that their chemical and mineralogical composition was quite similar to the local vessels produced in House 1 and recovered in the city of Kainua-Marzabotto.
26. Structures used for metalworking are particularly difficult to identify. Numerous pits connected to crafting have been found, but the demolition and the related filling are documented dating back to the end of the fifth through the first half of the fourth century BCE.
27. Pozzi 2010:266, n. 15. In 2006, an experimental archaeology project at the Forcello Archaeological Park was carried out based on these kilns, consisting in their reconstruction and a test of pottery firing. See Deriu and Zamboni 2008: 178, no. 6.
28. For a detailed analysis of the ceramic production cycle, see Cuomo di Caprio 2007 for a schematic framework.
29. Clay is a fine-grained sedimentary soil consisting mainly of clay minerals but can include also other elements. Moreover, coarser contents can be willingly added, such as rock fragments, sands, ceramic fragments (*chamotte*), etc. Clay is widespread in the territory and, therefore, clays and minerals found near the manufacturing areas would usually be selected for crafting. For further information, see Levi 2010:32.
30. Levi 2010:39.
31. *Regio* II, 1, Saronio 1965:400–401. The tank found near Villa Cassarini (Bo) should also be mentioned (Taglioni 1999: 189 and Romagnoli 2014).
32. Cuomo di Caprio 2007:527–528.
33. Brizio 1890:281–283, pl. VIII, nos. 7–7A. All the information at our disposal was collected by E. Brizio, who was invited to see the structures before their demolition to plant a vineyard.
34. For some hypotheses on this structure's functioning and its precise chronology, see Curri and Sorbelli 1973:250–251, 256–257.
35. Sassatelli 1991a:187.
36. Brizio 1890:282.
37. De Maria, Sassatelli, and Vitali 1978a:70–71, fig. 10.

38. Malnati 1990a:134; Forte 1993b.
39. Govi 2016. The structure was found during the excavations conducted by the Chair of Etruscology of the University of Bologna.
40. In the publication of the excavation of house 1, *Regio* IV, 1, G. A. Mansuelli does not mention the discovery of the structure. A. Gaucci found indications of the kiln in an unpublished manuscript of Mansuelli. See Gaucci 2016.
41. Mattioli 2010:95.
42. Morandi et al. 1996:341–350; Morandi et al. 1997: 40–45.
43. Mattioli 2013.
44. Govi and Sassatelli 2010.
45. Govi forthcoming. I thank Elisabetta Govi for making available the unpublished data on pottery in her study.
46. Morpurgo 2018.
47. Romagnoli 2014.
48. Zamboni 2016.
49. The systematic study of the local ceramics from the necropolis of Valle Trebba, collecting a total of 1,215 tombs, is in press (Mattioli forthcoming). Thanks to A. Gaucci, A. Grandi, M. Natalucci, S. Romagnoli, M. Ruscelli, A. Serra, and C. Trevisanello for having made available unpublished data on the *ceramica etrusco-padana*.
50. Nannetti et al. 2010.
51. Gaucci 2010.
52. Esposito and Sanidas 2012.
53. This aspect had already been suggested through the hypothesis of interpreting the rooms on the *plateia* A as for ceramic production. Specifically, for *Regio* IV, 1, see Mansuelli 1963a:62.
54. Mansuelli 1966; Sassatelli 1989a:67.
55. Govi 2016.
56. For a general analysis on the subject: Sanidas 2013. Recently, in Olynthus, many productive activities have been found to be distributed over the city and are located within residential complexes (Cahill 2005). This aspect is also known in some houses near the Agora in Athens (Tsakirgis 2005).
57. The hypothesis has been already proposed in Nijboer 1998:123–124 in relation to the Great Furnace of *Regio* II, 1. See also Govi and Sassatelli 2010:306.
58. In the master's theses of M. Ossani (Ossani 2003–2004) and A. Pozzi (Pozzi 2004–2005), the database documented for example bronze toiletries, spinning and weaving tools, local vessels, and a wide and heterogeneous repertoire of Attic pottery.
59. Morpurgo 2017:367.
60. Govi 2016 with previous references and bibliography.
61. Appendix A, no. 31; fig. 10.6: no. 31. Sassatelli and Gaucci 2010: 330–331, no. 445.
62. Govi 2016. See Sassatelli and Gaucci 2010: 335–341.
63. Epigraphic testimonies have provided useful support

to this theory. For the documentation belonging to House 1, *Regio* IV, 2, see appendix A, nos. 22–37; figs. 10.5–10.6: nos. 22–37; Govi and Sassatelli 2010:304.

64. G. Morpurgo (Morpurgo 2017: 366, note 2) states that the great political and institutional solidity of Marzabotto is even more relevant in the most recent research, suggesting targeted planning as a result of collective choices similar to the management of the productive aspects that characterize this settlement.

CHAPTER 14

CARVED STONE MONUMENTS

GIACOMO MANCUSO

The information offered by the finds of stone monuments in Marzabotto is surely one of the broadest and most considerable of the whole of Etruria Padana. The large number of monuments discovered within the city confirms a widespread appreciation of carved stone, as well as its usage in many aspects of ancient life. This phenomenon eludes simple numerical quantification, since the basic count could be exponentially increased due to extensive architectural usage, but it could also be undercounted because of the widespread practice of the reuse of stone remains attested from late antiquity to the modern era. Regardless of the exact amount, the presence of specialized local workshops operating within the city is easily inferred but yet to be completely well defined. Therefore, this question will be the main focus of this chapter.[1]

CARVED STONE MONUMENTS IN SACRED CONTEXTS

Stone cutting is well documented within the sacred context of the city in the form of votive bases and architectural features. Surely one of the best-preserved examples of stone architectural monuments is provided by *Podium*-altar D on the Acropolis (*see plate 11*).

The building encompasses an area of almost 80 square meters, accessible by a narrow stairway. Both the exterior of the precinct wall and the stair parapet are enriched with complex moldings (fig. 14.1).[2] Originally interpreted as a grand tomb,[3] the structure is now agreed to be a large open-air *podium*-altar connected with the foundation rite and probably intended as a monumentalizing of the adjacent *auguraculum*.[4]

In this case, though, the high travertine *podium* does not simply respond to a need for monumentality, but seems to embody a deep religious belief. By framing and raising the ground level, the monument becomes a sort of miniature raised *temenos*, which could serve the same formal role as a *templum minus* or *templum in terra*.[5] The construction of large *podia* in Marzabotto and other contexts was indeed common practice in the Etruscan world, widely used to architectonically render the connection between the sacred space and the *templum*. Those structures could assume either the form of self-standing places of worship, such as *podia*-altars B and D, or be arranged as a temple pedestal.[6]

This kind of structure, made of travertine but unfortunately partially spoliated, was found in the temples of Tinia[7] and Uni.[8] An architectural use of travertine is documented also in the Water Shrine, north of the city (*see map 5*), where traces of pavements and walls were found.[9]

Not far from there, at the northeastern edge of the city and very close to its slope, a recent excavation has documented a large deposit of stone materials with numerous votive bases and molded blocks.[10] The area has been interpreted by the excavators as the collapsed remains of a sacred context, referred to as the *Terza Stipe*, but it has also been convincingly suggested that this entire area could be the result of the modern dumping of architectural elements from the nearby Urban Sanctuary of *Regio* I.[11]

Whatever its interpretation, this area has yielded the highest number of votive bases in the city.[12] Similar monuments were found in other sacred areas, such as the Water Shrine[13] and the votive deposit on the

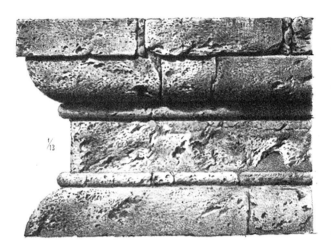

FIGURE 14.1. The moldings of *Podium*-altar D on the Acropolis, second half of the fifth century BCE. After Gozzadini 1865: pl. 6.3.

northern slope of the Acropolis.[14] This type of monument was originally intended to support and exhibit the *ex-votos* dedicated by devotees in sacred contexts. This practice is not exclusive to Marzabotto and can be considered a widespread habit in Etruria Padana, while it seems less common in other Etruscan regions.[15] Most of the supports are made out of travertine, but marble, sandstone, and marl specimens have been documented.[16] These monuments were to be fixed in the ground, as may be deduced from the presence of a plinth at the bottom, generally unworked and only roughly shaped. The upper surfaces of the bases often bear signs of small irregular holes, which were needed to secure the *ex-voto* to its surface.[17] Most of these offerings consisted of small bronze figurines, often with insertion pins on their base.[18]

From a technical standpoint, these bases were ei-

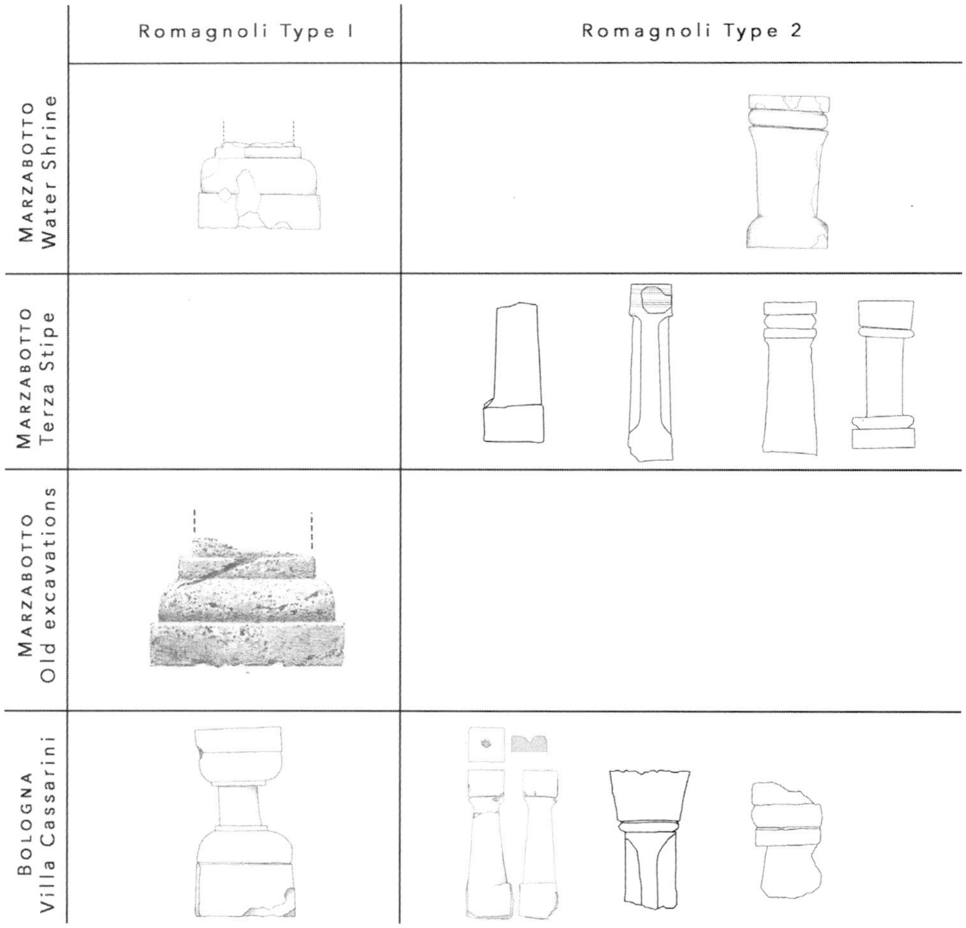

FIGURE 14.2. Typological comparisons of votive bases from Marzabotto and Bologna, based on Romagnoli 2014:270–271, fig. 190. Drawings not to scale.

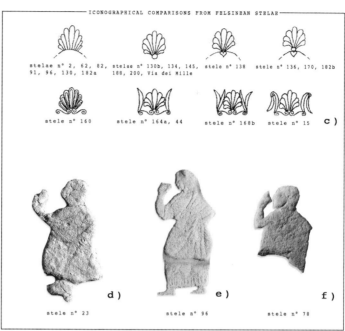

FIGURE 14.3. *Stelae* from the shrine of the Eastern Gate with comparisons among Felsinean *stelae*. After (a) Gozzadini 1870: pl. 2.4; (b) Malnati and Sassatelli 2008: pl. V.b; (c) Govi and Sassatelli 2004: fig. 19; (d–f) Govi 2014c: fig. 10.

ther monolithic or were formed from the superimposition of multiple blocks, progressively wedged in. The shape of these monuments is varied, and sometimes unique, but can be traced back to two main prototypes: one with symmetrical reverse *cymae* and another with a simple pillar shape.[19] The votive bases from Marzabotto show a close relationship with monuments from Villa Cassarini in Bologna and could well have been produced by the same workshops, or at least by linked workshops influencing each other. The morphological correspondence between these monuments is so strong that a common typological solution was recently proposed by Romagnoli (fig. 14.2).[20]

The numerous comparisons highlighted for each specific type[21] suggest the close relationship between these monuments in their molding profiles and architectural elements, especially altars. The typological resemblance seems to be intentional, thus suggesting a similar purpose behind a similar shape. Among the various similarities, the comparison with *Podium-*

altar D on the Acropolis seems to be the most significant, both in shape and as regards religious aspects, suggesting that these votive supports could be intended as small scale *templa*, too. Analogously to the *podia*, the votive base could thus represent an *ager effatus*, a space freed from the spirits, defined by corners (*anguli*) and consequently framed and raised from the ground,[22] and therefore ready to accept and display the votive offerings placed on top.

The connection between the *templum*, the altar, and the votive base is accentuated by the representation of deities standing on similarly shaped monuments. Probably the best example from Marzabotto consists of the *stele* from the Eastern Necropolis, which was recently referred to as a small shrine, outside the eastern gate of the city.[23] The monument, sculpted in low relief from a single block of limestone, portrays a female figure, standing still upon a small altar while raising an object toward her mouth (fig. 14.3a and b).[24] The many iconographic comparisons suggest that the woman can be identified as a deity, and more specifically as Persephone.[25]

The style of the figure and the overall decorative scheme can be compared with a small series of Felsinean *stelae* (fig. 14.3d–f),[26] hence suggesting the possibility that this monument could either be a product of the Felsinean workshops, or made by a Felsinean artisan. The use of sandstone, as well as the rarity of this kind of monument within the city of Marzabotto, seems to support this hypothesis.

CARVED STONE IN FUNERARY CONTEXTS

Worked stone is also widely used in funerary contexts, either as part of a tomb structure[27] or as gravestones. Almost 80 percent of tombstones are simple field stones, rarely even worked,[28] while the remaining are carved in stone, probably marking graves of exceptional individuals.

Among the funerary tombstones it is possible to identify three different kinds of monuments: spherical, bulb-shaped, and pillar-shaped. The examples in the last category are found almost exclusively in the Northern Necropolis and are made of travertine; half of these monuments are shaped like unfluted columns,[29] while the rest resemble squared pillars with moldings on top.[30] Their base was rounded or squared, and leveled in such a way that the tombstone could be placed securely atop a *cassone* (chest) tomb, or on the ground.[31] From a morphological standpoint, these monuments use the same decorative language as the votive bases, consisting of moldings and taking inspiration directly from architectural elements. The similarity—suggesting common manufacturing, perhaps even at the same workshop—is so strong that a clear definition of use can be assigned only according to the find context.

An unusual kind of column-shaped *cippus* also comes from the Eastern Necropolis.[32] It differs from the other specimens of the class in its monolithic form, the presence of a bulb-shaped crowning element, and the use of limestone. The monument seems to be a mixture of two different models, thus combining high visibility and the monumental impact of the column-shaped *cippi* with the weighty significance of the bulb-shaped ones.

Monuments in the shape of a bulb or a pinecone are common in northern Etruria and Etruria Padana, and are almost exclusively made of marble (fig. 14.4).[33] These tomb markers consist of a globular body with a slightly in-curving profile at the bottom. The upper portion tapers progressively upward, finishing in a pointed element. A specimen from Sasso Marconi demonstrates the relationship between these *cippi* and their marble bases, squared and decorated with high-relief rams' heads at the corners (fig. 14.4e).

The origin of this form is rooted in the Pisan district, and it seems to appear in Etruria Padana a little later.[34] In Marzabotto it is possible to identify four *cippi* and one base (fig. 14.4a–d).[35] Additionally, the tomb marker from Sasso Marconi can be added to the count, since it was most likely produced within the city.[36] While the morphological aspects of this kind of *cippus* and bases are very similar to the Tyrrhenian specimens, the presence of elaborate carved decorations, originally enlivened by painting, seems to be a peculiarity of local marble production.[37]

The tomb marker from Sasso Marconi presents a complex decoration on a linear band, representing two people standing and followed by a Dionysiac procession.[38] On the base, between the horns of the rams, is a carved psychopomp Hermes. Likewise, a *cippus* from the Eastern Necropolis bears complex decoration on three different bands. In the lower level it is possible to identify four armed *desultores* involved in jumping on and off horses with a single running warrior among them. The scene probably represented a funerary celebration for the deceased, related to his military and institutional role.[39] On the central band of the *cippus* there is an alternation of pomegranates and lotus flowers,[40] while the upper level shows a decoration, often defined as a star flower, consisting of four slim reversed triangles. The same ornament decorates the top of a bulb *cippus* from the Northern Necropolis.[41] This detail and the overall shape seem to suggest that one of the possible prototypes of the model was a blossoming bulb, intended to be a symbol of afterlife rebirth.[42] Another possible prototype for the shape of this kind of monument can be identified in the pine-

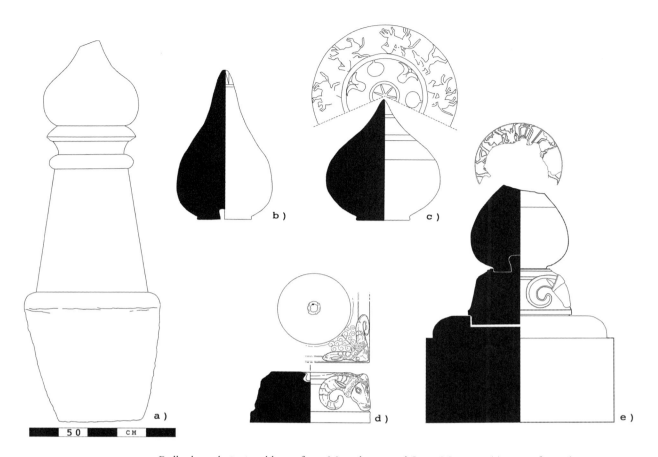

FIGURE 14.4. Bulb-shaped *cippi* and bases from Marzabotto and Sasso Marconi: (a) *cippus* from the Southern Necropolis (drawing by Morrone); (b–c) *cippi* from the Northern and Eastern necropoleis (after Sassatelli 1977: figs. 6–7); (d) base from the Northern Necropolis (drawing by Morrone); (e) *cippus* and base from Tomb 1 in Sasso Marconi (after Sassatelli 1977: figs. 9–10).

cone, as suggested by the decoration of a *cippus* from Casale Marittimo.[43] Just like the bulb, the pinecone constitutes a strong symbol of afterlife rebirth and is often associated with Dionysiac iconography, where it is recalled in the *thyrsus*, the wand held by the followers of Dionysus.[44] The symbolic value of these *cippi* was surely enhanced by their marble bases, whose significance relates both to the field of sacrifice and to otherworldly rebirth in the name of Dionysus.[45]

The last kind of *cippus* documented in Marzabotto is spherical. Only one specimen is preserved from the Northern Necropolis, and it can be compared, because of its shape, to a series of similar grave markers from Bologna.[46]

CARVED STONE IN CIVIC AND DOMESTIC CONTEXTS

Cut stone is recognizable also in public and domestic contexts. The latter mostly include small installations, such as angular travertine blocks within the foundations[47] or collection tanks in the courtyards.[48] The monumental aqueduct from the southern slope of the Acropolis can be identified as the only stone public monument within the city (fig. 14.5).[49] The entire structure was made out of travertine, including the long canalization system, more than 55 meters long. The stoneworking techniques of the monument resemble those used for the *cassone* tombs, therefore

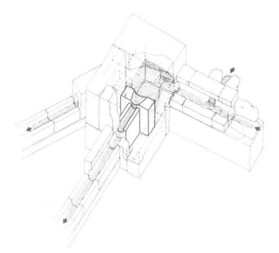 

FIGURE 14.5. The aqueduct on the Acropolis. Drawing by E. Govi (Sassatelli 1991:186); reconstruction by G. Mancuso.

suggesting the involvement of those workshops in its construction.

CONCLUSIONS

From this brief overview of the city's stone monuments it is possible to draw some conclusions concerning the presence of specialized workshops within the city, as well as the extent of their production.

It seems natural to assume that the first necessary component for the presence of a workshop has to be the availability of the raw material. Among all the types of worked stone documented in Marzabotto, travertine is certainly the most used for every class of monument, and almost all of the architectural and funerary structures. The enormous amount of travertine found within the city suggests that the quarry must have been quite close to Marzabotto itself. Particularly for this kind of stone, the proximity of the extraction site to the workshop does not seem to be simply a matter of logistics, since it is well known that travertine was better processed when still humid.[50] At present considerable petrographic research has established that the travertine used in the city can be traced to the quarry of S. Cristoforo di Labante, 15 km from the city (*see map 3*), along the Reno River.[51]

Regardless of class or purpose of use, it is possible to observe that most of the products made out of travertine share the same style, directly inspired by architectural elements. This stylistic analogy can be observed in the quality and extent of the moldings on architectural blocks, votive bases, and some kinds of tomb markers. Even the construction of *cassone* tombs can be added to this cluster, as well as more impressive monuments, such as the aqueduct at the slope of the Acropolis. The wide use of travertine for the construction of tomb structures indicates its local crafting by artisans also able to adapt their technical expertise to the erection of more complex monuments, characterized by the reelaboration of a common architectural language. The absence of data showing the connections between the tomb structures, the gravestones, and the funerary goods prevents an evaluation of the extent of this kind of production over time. However, since this entire production seems strongly dependent on the reelaboration of architectural elements, it is possible to argue that the initial incentive for this process was indeed provided by architectural needs, probably the monumentalizing of the sacred urban areas.[52]

The temples of Uni and Tinia hint at the wide usage of travertine in the construction of their *podia* and for the column bases and capitals.[53] Unfortunately, the practice of spoliation of those structures prevents us from making a specific comparison between the architectural solutions adopted and their possible reelaboration in smaller monuments, such as the votive bases.[54]

It is difficult to evaluate the orbit of exchange of all these products, unlikely to be limited to the city alone, as the presence of travertine work on nearby sites seems to suggest.[55] The strong morphological resemblance between the votive bases of Marzabotto and Bologna opens up the possibility that the Felsinean city was included within the orbit of exchange of these workshops. However, the documented presence in Bologna of ateliers dedicated to and specializing in stone carving means that assumptions cannot yet be made and further research is necessary. Nonetheless, the relationship with Bologna now seems to be supported by the analysis of the *stele* from the Eastern Necropolis, surely inspired by the production of Felsinean artisans, and perhaps even made by one. The monument can be related to a small group of objects made out of sandstone, an infrequent material among those documented in Marzabotto.[56]

Finally, it is necessary to mention the working of white marble, a hard, tough material whose production requires specific technical expertise.[57] Its presence poses some problems regarding its provenance, as this stone cannot be considered local to Marzabotto or any of the adjoining cities. A recent analysis of the entire documentation of white marble monuments from Etruria Padana has revealed two different trade routes: from Greece along the Adriatic Sea, and from the Apuan Alps through the Apennine Mountains.[58] The reason for this dual provenance is yet unclear, but can probably be explained by the exploitation of specific trade routes over time.[59] The manufacture of marble monuments in the city seems to be mostly directed toward the production of tombstones,[60] directly inspired by Tyrrhenian models, yet reworked to meet the specific requirements of the local clients. The carved and painted decorations constitute a peculiarity of local production, seemingly intended to enhance the social status of the owner and the overall significance of the monument itself. These funerary monuments surely constitute the highest artistic and conceptual level reached by the stone workshops of the city, able to satisfy the needs of a rich and cultured clientele.[61]

Even in the light of these considerations, many problems still remain unsolved, such as the evolution of this production over time and the orbit of exchange of its products; these are important issues that will probably be resolved by further studies.

NOTES

1. For this reason, the focus will not be certain well-known monuments, whose nature as imported finished products is well established, such as the marble male head from the Temple of Tinia or the marble basins in various areas of the city. For these monuments see Sassatelli and Mancuso 2017.

2. A detailed description of the monument is in Vitali, Brizzolara, and Lippolis 2001:45–53.

3. Gozzadini 1865:23–25

4. Sassatelli and Govi 2005b:44–45.

5. See Colonna 2006:140. Altars on platforms, sharing similar characteristics, can be found also in Vignanello (Faliscan territory) and at the Patturelli site in Capua.

6. The use of *podia* can be considered a typical aspect of Etrusco-Italic architecture, as underlined by Torelli (1986:187).

7. Sassatelli and Govi 2005b. For the travertine blocks found in the area of the temple, see Sassatelli 2009a.

8. Garagnani, Gaucci, and Govi 2016:257–258; Govi 2017b: 149.

9. Gualandi 1970.

10. Malnati et al. 2005; Desantis and Malnati 2009. Among the votive bases were found a few bronze figurines, one of them very well made.

11. The idea was suggested by Sassatelli (2009:332–333).

12. An exact number was not given but can be deduced from the plan published by Desantis and Malnati (2009:313, fig. 2).

13. Gualandi 1970.

14. The provenance of the travertine monuments published by Gozzadini (1865: plate III) is quite problematic, due to the absence of clear data about their origin, either the slope of the Acropolis or the Northern Necropolis. Out of the thirteen stone finds published only numbers 3 and 10 can be effectively considered tombstones, on the basis of comparanda. The others can be assigned to the votive deposit beneath the Acropolis, as suggested by Vitali (Vitali, Brizzolara, and Lippolis 2001:67–70).

15. MacIntosh Turfa 2006:100–101. Twenty-two votive bases were found in the Sanctuary of Villa Cassarini in Bologna (Romagnoli 2014:260–298). A wider analysis of this cus-

tom would be useful, and could highlight the extent of this practice in Etruscan territories.

16. Votive supports not made out of travertine are documented only from the *Terza Stipe* (Desantis and Malnati 2009:209).

17. Small holes can be found on top of a specimen from the Water Shrine (Gualandi 1974:48–49).

18. Numerous examples can be found among the specimens from the Water Shrine (Gualandi 1970; 1974) and the votive deposits from the slope of the Acropolis (Vitali, Brizzolara, and Lippolis 2001:107–190).

19. These typological distinctions were first highlighted by Gualandi (1974:43–50).

20. Romagnoli 2014:260–298. She emphasizes that the connection between the two cities seems even stronger, considering that most of the small bronzes from Villa Cassarini can be referred to as the "Marzabotto Group."

21. Many examples from the sacred architecture of Etruria Padana and Tyrrhenian Etruria or Latium, as well as representations on Attic pottery and Etruscan mirrors, are presented by Romagnoli (2014:268–288).

22. Torelli 1986:187.

23. See Sassatelli in Malnati and Sassatelli 2008:448–450.

24. The state of preservation of the monument does not allow us to specifically recognize the object, perhaps a flower or a fruit, according to the interpretation offered by Sassatelli (Malnati and Sassatelli 2008:449).

25. Sassatelli in Malnati and Sassatelli 2008:449–450; Govi 2009b:460–461.

26. Specific comparison can be made with type IV women highlighted by Govi (2014c:140–143, fig. 10) on *stelae* 23, 78, and 96 (fig. 14d–f). The palmette above the figure also has close similarities with the same representations on funerary stones of Bologna (Felsinean *stelae*; fig. 14c), significantly placed at the top center of the frame (Govi and Sassatelli 2004:255–259, fig. 19). The main difference between the monuments from Bologna and Marzabotto lies in the representation of the female figures, which are always in motion in the Bologna examples, but standing still in the Marzabotto examples.

27. See Pizzirani, chapter 17 of this volume.

28. Marchesi 2005:203–204.

29. Two of them were published by Gozzadini (1870:14, and pl. II, no. 5); a third one, very fragmentary, is still unpublished but visible inside the necropolis.

30. Two of them are published by Gozzadini (1865: pl. III, nos. 3, 10); a picture of a third was published by Brizio (1928:17, fig. 7).

31. The absence of an unworked plinth on most examples of this kind of *cippus* argues for their positioning on another solid surface such as the lid of the tomb. On the problem of the original location of the travertine tomb structures, above or below ground, see Pizzirani, chapter 17 of this volume.

32. Brizio 1886:27; Brizio 1890:273–407, pl. X, no. 28; Mansuelli 1971:31, fig. 2.

33. In archaeological literature these monuments have received various descriptive names that try to relate their shapes to bulbs, pinecones, pears, or onions. For a recent survey of this kind of marble monument in Etruria see Sassatelli and Mancuso 2017.

34. For the Pisan workshops see Bonamici 1991; Bruni 1998; Maggiani 2004; Maggiani 2017.

35. Sassatelli and Mancuso 2017: nos. 43–45, with references. The presence of a fourth *cippus* is inferred from the finding of a bronze crowning element (Sassatelli 1980a:49). For the base see Sassatelli and Mancuso 2017: no. 46, with references.

36. Sassatelli and Mancuso 2017: no. 36; see also Tirtei, chapter 18 of this volume.

37. Sassatelli and Mancuso 2017:109–110; while the Tyrrhenian specimen seems to show a preference for phytomorphic low-relief ornaments, as noted in the catalog edited by Bruni (2014:27–31).

38. See Sassatelli 1977:133–139; also Tirtei, chapter 18 of this volume.

39. Sassatelli 1993b:66–67.

40. The pomegranate is a meaningful Dionysiac symbol, as underlined by Govi (2009b:459).

41. A similar decoration can also be found on the Pisan specimen from Via della Pera (Sassatelli and Mancuso 2017: no. 157; Bruni 2014:27–31, no. 1).

42. This hypothesis was already suggested by Maggiani (2005:42).

43. Sassatelli 1979:109–110; Sassatelli and Mancuso 2017: no. 245.

44. Govi 2009b:459. For the importance of the *thyrsus* in Dionysiac representations of the afterlife see also Bonamici (2014:48–49).

45. See Govi 2009a:49.

46. Sassatelli 1989b:931–932.

47. See Gaucci 2016:261–265, with references.

48. As noted in *Regio* IV, 1, 2, 3–4 (Gaucci 2016:254, 256, 261), and *Regio* V, 3, 1 (Massa Pairault 1997:13–15).

49. Sassatelli 1991a:185–188; Vitali, Brizzolara, and Lippolis 2001:71–76.

50. Romagnoli 2014:262.

51. Sighinolfi in Desantis and Malnati 2009:305–307. Also, a recent archaeological exploration of the site confirmed an Etruscan presence in the area from the sixth century BCE (Bondini et al. 2018:107–108).

52. Sassatelli and Govi 2005b:21–27; Govi 2017b:148–149.

53. On the use of travertine for the Temple of Uni see Garagnani, Gaucci, and Govi 2016:258. The construction of the travertine bases of the temples seems to be the earliest wide use of this kind of stone in the city.

54. The morphological similarity with the molded blocks from the base of the Temple of Tinia argues for this hypothesis, as well as the blocks from the *Terza Stipe*, if their origin in *Regio* I were to be proven (Sassatelli 2009a:332–333).

55. Such as the travertine base from Sasso Marconi, or the presence of *cassone* tombs in Sibano (Millemaci 1999:136).

56. The provenance of this type of stone in Marzabotto and Bologna is not yet fully understood. The wide use of this stone type in Bologna seems to suggest the utilization of local quarries (Romagnoli 2014:262). On the other hand, the presence of ancient limestone quarries close to Marzabotto, in Montovolo, could suggest another possible provenance. Ancient use of this specific type was proven by the petrographical analysis made by De Vecchi on the *stelae* from Gazzo Veronese (Gamba and Gambacurta 2011).

57. Maggiani 2004:153.

58. The provenance of the raw material was assessed through a series of petrographic analyses conducted by Professor R. Braga of the University of Bologna. Preliminary results of this study are presented in Sassatelli and Mancuso 2017.

59. Sassatelli and Mancuso 2017:110.

60. Traces of other usage of the same materials are documented by the presence of a large marble slab or a portion of an architectonic frame (Sassatelli and Mancuso 2017: nos. 40–41).

61. On the autonomy of the local workshops see also Sassatelli and Mancuso 2017:109–110.

CHAPTER 15

A WORLD OF IMAGES
Attic Pottery

VINCENZO BALDONI

Greek pottery—mainly Attic—can be found in Kainua from the very early phases of the city's development in the first half of the sixth century BCE. In this period, Greek pottery was very rare and belonged to different productions (Corinthian, Ionian, Laconian), while the earliest vases from Athens were imported from the middle of the century.[1] From this period onward Attic imports gradually increased, in tandem with the economic and political restructuring of the Etruscan Po Valley, where Kainua became a key center (see map 2).

Starting with the earliest archaeological excavations in the nineteenth century, pottery imported from Greece was found in Kainua, especially in its necropoleis (see map 5),[2] drawing the attention of many scholars. Among them we recall J. D. Beazley, who had the opportunity to visit the collection at the old museum of Marzabotto before World War II and gave attributions to masters for a great number of Attic red-figured vases (fig. 15.1).[3]

When excavations started again in the second postwar period, the quantity of Attic pottery found in the Etruscan city—in residential as well as sacred and productive areas—increased.[4] In the last few decades, research on these findings has intensified and substantially changed our understanding of the phenomenon of Greek pottery imports to Kainua; in accordance with the most recent lines of research in this field, the focus has shifted from the most traditional aspects (such as the analysis of the painters, shapes, and subjects) to historical and commercial aspects and—especially in recent years—to the examination of usage contexts.[5]

From this point of view, Kainua is a fruitful field of study: thanks to the different known contexts (sacred, residential, productive, and funerary), it is actually possible to investigate how the various shapes and images were used in different social spheres like banquets or in funerary and religious practices. As we can see below, the contextual perspective is essential to properly analyze the quantitative and qualitative data and to understand many phenomena otherwise difficult to explain, such as the substantial absence of Attic pottery in the oldest funerary sets, or the differences between the Kainua and Bologna imports, especially after the second half of the fifth century BCE.[6]

Considering the amount of available data on Attic pottery found in Kainua during almost two centuries of archaeological investigations, we would like to propose an overall synthesis of our knowledge, updated to include the most recent studies and the excavations of recent years, and focusing on some of the most significant vases. In presenting the data, we shall proceed in chronological order, emphasizing the different contexts of pottery usage and future areas of research in this field of study.

State-of-the-art knowledge leads us to affirm that the most ancient Attic pottery arrived in Kainua in the middle of the sixth century BCE and was used both in domestic and—chiefly—in sacred areas.[7] Two Siana cups and one Little Masters band cup came from the excavation of the Water Shrine, located in the suburban area and brought to light during the 1960s (see map 5).[8] In the sanctuary these vases could possibly represent precious dedications (anathemata) and/or were used as instruments for cult rituals (libations).

FIGURE 15.1. The old museum of Marzabotto in 1933: a display in the cases of Room 5, with some of the Attic pottery found in nineteenth-century excavations in Kainua (city and necropoleis). SABAP Bologna Archive, inv. no. 1497.

Among them, particular attention should be paid to a large band cup, attributable to the Group of Rhodes 12264 and datable about 520 BCE (fig. 15.2).[9] On both sides, it shows a scene with two warriors playing with dice or knucklebones (*astragalizontes*), recalling the famous subject of Achilles and Ajax, found on Attic pottery from the third quarter of the sixth century BCE and taken up in a masterly manner by Exekias in about 530 BCE.[10] For this scene different— and even very dissimilar—interpretations have been proposed. Among them, we mention one recently proposed about the Kainua cup and its use in the sanctuary: the action of the two heroes could be a divination practice.[11] Certainly, this could be one of the possible meanings of the image, and relevant to the context of Etruscan Kainua.

Scholars have also hypothesized that the scene was a metaphorical representation of city planning. Even in this meaning, the cup seems particularly useful to express what the Kainua elite were busy doing in the final decades of the sixth century BCE, when the city, just like other Etruscan Po Valley centers, was refounded and reorganized.[12]

This reorganization had a tangible effect also at a commercial level. During the final decades of the century, Kainua already belonged to a well-organized commercial system, and a large amount of Attic pottery as well as other goods circulated in the city. We observe an immediate increase in the diffusion of cultural practices with a Greek origin.[13] One can read the signs of these changes by observing the presence in tombs, for the first time, mostly of black-figured pottery, just as in the inhabited area, where the number of Attic findings significantly increased.[14]

Apart from this pottery, vases crafted with the new red-figure technique arrived early, along with the first black-gloss pottery. Among the red-figure vases, a few prestigious examples stand out: the parade cups, consisting of very large vases that could be used in sacred contexts for specific rituals, as happens in the Greek world with the cult practices of *theoxenia* or *heroxenia*.[15] Belonging to this class is a *kylix* from the recently discovered Tinia sanctuary and a cup attributed to Kachrylion, one of the most important potters from the end of the sixth century BCE.[16] The attribution to this potter was confirmed by his signature, which appeared on the edge of the foot of the cup. Unfortunately, the vase—found during nineteenth-century excavations—is now lost, as it was destroyed during the bombing of the local museum in 1944. Based on the available data, we can conjecture that the vase was found in the same area as the Temple of Tinia or Uni, and possibly the foot belonged to the oversized cup mentioned above.[17]

Late Archaic *kylikes* were also used in houses, as demonstrated by a few fragments of eye-cups, in red-figure or bilingual (combined red-figure and black-figure) technique, coming from the house recently excavated in *Regio* IV, 2.[18]

As for the tombs, only a few black-figure vases from this period were found, but they are very significant. The vase shapes indicate that they were to be used in

FIGURE 15.2. Attic black-figure band cup from the Water Shrine: Achilles and Ajax playing dice. Group of Rhodes 12264, about 520 BCE. Photo V. Baldoni. Drawing E. Govi.

FIGURE 15.3. Attic black-figure *stamnos* from the tomb of a female in the Eastern Necropolis. Left: erotic scene with satyrs and a maenad; right: Dionysiac procession. 510–500 BCE. After Baldoni 2009: fig. 38.

an event involving drinking: vessels such as *kylikes* and *skyphoi*, large containers for wine (amphorae, kraters, *stamnoi*). Since the vases are mostly fragmentary, we can recognize only a few images: among these, we note a departure scene on a column krater and a very rare Dionysiac scene on a black-figured *stamnos*.[19]

This latter vase is of great interest because of its shape—rare in Attic black-figure production[20]—its decoration, and finally its find context. On its main side there is an erotic scene involving two satyrs and a nymph[21] in a setting evoking the symposium (*kline*, table with food, lyre);[22] on the other side there is a Dionysiac procession (*thiasos*) with Dionysus in the center and a nymph and satyr at his side (fig. 15.3). The subject on the main side, for which no specific comparison can be suggested, belongs to an iconographic context illustrating erotic interactions between satyrs and nymphs. As pointed out by C. Berard,[23] the scene, characterized by a sacred atmosphere and *eros*, metaphorically conveys the sense of possession by Dionysus: this relation between *eros* and the sacred sphere is consistent with the Greek mentality.

Adhesion to Dionysism and the expression of the condition of "Dionysian happiness," as defined by C. Isler-Kerenyi, have a specific meaning, even in the funerary sphere.[24] Even the scene of the *thiasos* on the secondary side evokes the religious experience of contacting the god: at a symbolic level, the epiphany of Dionysus represents a guarantee of success in the transition from one state to another.[25]

The *stamnos* was found in a female tomb of the Eastern Necropolis, where the vase was used as a cinerary urn for the deceased, and it was the central element of the funerary assemblage.[26] Notwithstanding its apparent simplicity, the tomb is surely significant: the incineration ritual with the ashes collected inside an Attic vase is common in Etruria, Sicily, and Magna Graecia, being generally reserved for a few high-status deceased. The ritual has very ancient origins in the Greek and the Etruscan cultures and seems to respond to a specific choice and a willingness to express a salvific religious belief.[27]

The Kainua tomb is one of the most ancient ones with this burial ritual in the Etruscan Po Valley and stands apart in the choice of the *stamnos*. This shape, originating in the Etruscan culture as a container for ashes, has the function of containing pure wine, a product of metamorphosis and therefore of Dionysus himself: not only is the choice to use this shape in the tomb designed to express an adhesion to the god, as proof of the social status of the deceased woman; such a shape and its figured decorations are also meant to express an adhesion to Dionysiac religiosity, as a hope or desire for rebirth.

Thanks to the crucial establishment of the Spina emporium and the interest shown by Athens toward trade in the Adriatic area during the first decades of the fifth century BCE, imports of Attic pottery in Kainua and the Etruscan Po Valley increased considerably, mostly from the second quarter of the century. In this period Kainua confirmed its role as a key center for the distribution of Attic pottery within its territory and in northern Etruria (*see map 3*).[28] Figured vases reached Kainua from some of the main workshops of the Athenian potter's quarter (*kerameikos*), for instance, those *calyx* and column kraters with elaborate subjects found mostly in funerary sets.[29] Attic pottery was placed in tombs not only to recall the symposium practice; in some of them, functional shapes were chosen to contain perfumed substances, as witness to the arrival of luxury products in the city. An interesting example is one of the richest tombs in Kainua, containing a black-gloss *askos* of the "deep" type:

in this case a rather modest Attic vase is given the task of communicating the refined habits of a wealthy deceased woman.[30]

The import of Attic pottery to Kainua increases even further from the middle of the fifth century BCE, with a large variety of subjects and vase shapes. Among the subjects there are not only mythological ones, with a prevalence of Dionysiac themes, but also scenes with *colloquia* and courtship, athletes, and those more generically referable to "everyday life."[31] Large symposium vases are still employed in every usage context, especially *calyx* kraters, column kraters, and bell kraters, while volute kraters are absent, the opposite of what happened in Bologna, Spina, and Adria. Among other shapes, drinking vessels, especially figured and black-gloss *kylikes*, *skyphoi*, and *kantharoi*, are very abundant. The black-gloss pottery showed the widest variety of vase shapes in every context: among the rarest, we find vases containing perfumed substances or toiletries, such as *lekythoi*, *pyxides*, *lekanides*, and an *exaleiptron*.[32]

Among the imports from this period, a red-figure molded *kantharos*, found in a high-ranking woman's tomb in the Northern Necropolis, is of particular interest (*see plate 9*).[33] The *kantharos*, a unique piece found in the Etruscan city, has been attributed by J. D. Beazley to his Group R (450–430 BCE).[34] Its janiform body has the shape of a satyr's head and a woman's head. On the obverse of the *calyx* there is a representation of Menelaos pursuing Helen, along with a female figure, possibly a goddess; on the reverse, there is a colloquium scene with two women and a mantled man holding a stick. Head vases are particularly common in the cult and funerary sphere, even in the Etruscan Po Valley. The most frequent ones are the *oinochoai* with female heads, while the rarest are the *kantharoi* and *rhyta*.[35] There is much debate among scholars as to the meaning of these molded representations, especially when female figures are concerned: for some, they represent marginalized identities in society;[36] for others, the female face, combined with other subjects (satyrs, Herakles, Dionysus, African men) would point to the function of women in religious and funerary cults.[37]

The identities to which such female representation can refer should be linked to the Dionysiac cult (nymphs or maenads, or Ariadne) or chthonic religion (Demeter or Kore) and could therefore be interpreted as a reference to salvific beliefs. This is particularly convincing especially if one considers the use of head vases in sacred spheres linked to these cults and more specifically in a restricted number of tombs inside the necropolis. In the case of Kainua, we observe that the *kantharos* strongly evokes a symposium practice, being a typically Dionysiac vase, like the *rhyton*.

However, the shape of the vase, its molded representation, and its decoration, namely, the scene of pursuit, are highly likely to express a further symbolic meaning: the adhesion to Dionysus as an eschatological belief. One should finally point out that this *kantharos* was found in a woman's tomb, as frequently happens for head vases in other tombs in the Etruscan Po Valley.[38]

Among the most important finds emerging from recent studies, there is a remarkable number of Attic imported vases in Kainua in the second half of the fifth and in the fourth centuries BCE. This commercial trend corresponds to what we have learned about other important centers in the Etruscan Po Valley (Spina and Adria), with a clear difference in the data relating to the Attic imports in Bologna. On the one hand, the phenomenon shows a strong connection between Kainua and Spina, the main center of reference for Attic commerce in the Etruscan Po Valley during this period; on the other hand, it allows us to assume that Attic pottery was abundantly available, as shown by the findings in Adria, Spina, and Kainua, while the scarce documentation in Bolognese tombs of the same period could be due to a specific choice, or to the fact that its settlement has been little excavated until today.[39] Among the Athenian workshops belonging to the end of the fifth through the beginning of the fourth century BCE and well represented in Spina and Kainua, there is, for example, the workshop of the Jena Painter, from which comes a *kylix* found in a tomb, with a representation of Herakles and Dionysus on the interior surface (fig. 15.4).[40]

The scene highlights the connection between the hero and the god, both depicted in their youthful forms, as usually happens in this period. The atmo-

FIGURE 15.4. Attic red-figure cup by the Diomedes Painter from an undefined funerary context. Interior: Herakles and Dionysus. About 390 BCE. After Bentz and Reusser 2008: fig. 81a.

sphere is already very different from the typical ones of the previous period, when the hero was engaged in his labors and struggles; in this representation, Herakles is entrusted with supporting the drunken god. They are embracing each other while walking and exchanging glances. On the exterior of the cup are two libation scenes, a ritual sometimes connected with the idea of departing. In their funerary context, both of the scenes could be seen as metaphorical allusions to a long journey and a happy destiny beyond earthly life.

Kainua's role in the commercial trade scenario of the Etruscan Po Valley is still evident in the first decades of the fourth century BCE, since Attic pottery continues to arrive through Spina's intermediation, although the number of vases progressively decreases toward the middle of the century.[41] Only in the second half of the century, concurrent with the changes affecting the entire territory at a historical, political, and economic level, does Kainua cease to provide documentation of pottery produced in Athens.

In conclusion, Attic pottery found in Kainua offers a great deal of useful information concerning the history, commercial exchanges, cultural dynamics, and social and religious practices of the community living in this important center of the Etruscan Po Valley between the sixth and fourth centuries BCE. A contextual analysis of the finds allows us to understand more specifically the reception and usage of Attic vases in different spheres, where these products were effectively and consciously used. From the historical, commercial, and cultural points of view, recent research on these materials highlights the role of Kainua in the Etruscan Po Valley scenario and—beyond a few peculiarities—enables us to perceive many common elements in the documentation relating to other important centers in the region.

NOTES

1. Lippolis 2000; Baldoni 2015 (Laconian krater, Ionian cup). We must point out that our knowledge of pottery imports from Greece of the Archaic period is still only partial, due to the lack of a complete publication of the fragments from twentieth-century excavations in *Regio* V, 4, when a stratum was encountered that may be attributed to the first phase of Etruscan Kainua.

2. No Attic vase can be certainly connected to the Acropolis excavations of the nineteenth century.

3. Baldoni 2009:31–32. The old museum and its collection were severely damaged and partially destroyed by the bombing in 1944. For the scientific debate on Kainua in the nineteenth and twentieth centuries, see G. Sassatelli in chapter 1 of this volume.

4. The Kainua necropoleis were completely excavated during the nineteenth century (for the necropoleis, see C. Pizzirani, chapter 17 in this volume). For Attic pottery from twentieth-century excavations: Govi 1995 (Water Shrine); Massa Pairault 1997 (*Regio* V, 3); Locatelli 2005 ("Foundry," *Regio* V, 5); Lippolis 2000 (Archaic levels of the city); Bentz and Reusser 2004 (House 2, *Regio* IV, 2); Brizzolara and Baldoni 2011 (House 1, *Regio* IV, 2); Baldoni 2015 (sacred areas). For the location of those contexts, see map 5 in this volume.

5. For a general overview on Attic imports in Kainua, see Baldoni 2009:243–256 (necropoleis and settlement); Baldoni 2015 (sacred areas), with previous literature.

6. For the decrease of Attic imports from Bologna necropoleis: Govi 1999:172–173.

7. See Baldoni 2008; Baldoni 2015.

8. For the Water Shrine and the Siana and Little Masters cups: Govi 1995; Baldoni 2015.

9. Marzabotto, National Etruscan Museum, inv. 489, E 28. For the cup and its interpretation, see Baldoni 2017, with previous bibliography.

10. The scene was documented for the first time on a cup of type A1 (550–540 BCE), Vatican, Gregorian Etruscan Museum, inv. A 343: *BAPD* 2508; *LIMC* I, s.v. *Achilleus*, no. 398, pl. 97). Exekias depicted the scene on an amphora, now in fragments (Cambridge UP 114e; Leipzig T 355a–c, T 391; *ABV* 145.15; *Paralipomena* 60.18bis; *Paralipomena* 40; *BAPD* 306982 [Cambridge], 310397 [Leipzig]; Mackay 2010:311–314, no. 30, pl. 73) and on the famous amphora Vatican, Gregorian Etruscan Museum, inv. 16757, ex. 344 (*ABV* 145.13, 672, 686; *Paralipomena* 60; *Addenda*² 40; *BAPD* 310395; Mackay 2010:327–351, no. 32, with previous references).

11. Bundrick 2017. This interpretation fits well with the rituality of the Water Shrine in Kainua: as a matter of fact, excavations revealed the presence of numerous *astragaloi*, which could be used for divination practices (see Baldoni 2017:426, n. 43).

12. See Govi 2014a:107–108; Baldoni 2017:428–429. For the foundation and refoundation of Kainua, see E. Govi in chapter 4 of this volume.

13. Sassatelli 1993a; Lippolis 2000; Sassatelli 2008a.

14. From about 550–520 BCE, Attic imports (cups) were found solely in settlement or sacred areas: see Baldoni 2008; Baldoni 2009:70–76; Baldoni 2015.

15. For distribution and uses of oversized cups and other shapes, with particular regard to Etruscan contexts, see Tsingarida 2020, with previous bibliography.

16. The cup from the sanctuary of Tinia comprises two joining fragments with a very refined subsidiary decoration: the vase must have depicted a very complex scene, which is now very poorly preserved. The Kachrylion cup was found in excavations conducted in the urban area; most probably it belonged to the sacred structures recently identified and explored in this part of the ancient city (the sanctuaries of Tinia and of Uni). For the two vases, see Baldoni 2015, with earlier literature.

17. See note 9 above.

18. Brizzolara and Baldoni 2011. Other Late Archaic red-figure cups were found in nineteenth-century excavations: Baldoni 2009:151–155.

19. Marzabotto, National Etruscan Museum, inv. 355. The shape is attributed to the class of the New York 96.18.51 *stamnos*: Philippaki 1967:9–11, 19–20. For the vase and its find context: Baldoni 2009: cat. 4; Baldoni 2011; Baldoni 2012.

20. The *stamnos* is rare in Attic black-figure production. The Kainua vase is the only one from Etruria Padana. The other *stamnoi* from this territory are all painted in the red-figure technique and are more recent: Baldoni 2011:96–97; see also Morpurgo 2018 for Attic *stamnoi* from necropoleis of Bologna. For bronze *stamnoi* from Etruria Padana, see Morpurgo 2018:423–424.

21. For the distinction between nymphs and maenads: Hedreen 1994; Bonansea 2008, with previous bibliography.

22. For the interpretation of the setting as a symposium: see Bérard 1992:18.

23. Bérard 1992:17.

24. Isler-Kerenyi 2001:171.

25. See Baldoni 2012, with references, for a wider discussion on the subjects depicted on the vase and their interpretation as expression of a religious creed.

26. The funerary assemblage includes a bronze *phiale*, a bronze mirror, and an *alabastron*, all placed between the pit and the *stamnos*. The Attic vase, defunctionalized by the breaking of the handles, was covered by a bowl. On the mouth of the pit there was a stone. For the tomb see Baldoni 2011; Baldoni 2012:84–85. For the funerary rituals in the Kainua necropoleis, see C. Pizzirani, chapter 16 in this volume.

27. In Bologna and Spina, Attic kraters were being used as cinerary urns by the first decades of the fifth century BCE and most often by the second quarter of the century. Earlier other containers were utilized, such as large pots produced locally (*dolia*). On the ritual and its meanings in Etruria Padana: Govi 2009a:34–35; Govi 2009b:462–463; Morpurgo 2018:541–545, with additional literature.

28. This phenomenon is well documented by numerous findings in settlements located along the river valleys of the Apennines as, for instance, La Quercia or Gonfienti: see Baldoni 2022, with literature. For a wider framework on trade in the Po Valley and the trade connections with northern Etruria: Sassatelli 1993a; Sassatelli 2008a; see also S. Santocchini Gerg in chapter 5 of this volume.

29. Such as the Niobid Painter, Villa Giulia Painter, Agrigento Painter, Orchard Painter. For a broader list, see Baldoni 2009:93, fig. 140.

30. Reusser 2009:785; Baldoni 2009:286–287, cat. 1100; Baldoni 2012:86–87, fig. 7.

31. See, e.g., Baldoni 2009:93–94, fig. 141.

32. See Baldoni 2009, for findings from necropoleis and settlement: 92, fig. 139 (red-figure vases), and 193, fig. 557 (black-gloss pottery); see also Brizzolara and Baldoni 2011:11, fig. 2 (House 1, *Regio* IV, 2); Baldoni 2015 (sacred areas). For other contexts, see note 4 above for references.

33. Baldoni 2009:118–120, cat. 156; Baldoni 2012:87–88. Among the funerary goods, a rare writing tool (*stylus*) can be noted.

34. *ARV*², 1547.8; *BAPD* 218642.

35. See Morpurgo 2018:299 for jugs (*oinochoai*) with a woman's head in Etruscan sanctuaries and necropoleis, with references to debates on the meanings of such vase shapes. The three *kantharoi* from the Spina necropoleis dating from the second quarter of the fifth century BCE are: *ARV*², 1533.2; *Addenda*², 386; *ARV*², 266.85 and 1537.5; *Addenda*², 205; *ARV*², 1545.21; *Addenda*², 387.

36. See for example Lissarrague 1995.

37. Lewis 2002:169–170.

38. See Morpurgo 2018:299, for examples from Bologna necropoleis and for updated references on head vases and their meanings.

39. For an overview of the Attic imports in Bologna: Govi 1999; Macellari 2002; Reusser 2002; Morpurgo 2018.

40. Baldoni 2009:146–148, figs. 347–349, with previous literature.

41. Among the latest Athenian vases found in the Kainua excavations are some *skyphoi* of the Fat Boy Group (e.g., Baldoni 2009:130, cat. 181) and a few cups (e.g., a stemless cup by the Group of Vienna 116: Baldoni 2009:143, cat. 233).

PART IV

DYING IN THE CITY

The necropoleis of Marzabotto have received uneven treatment because they were excavated in the nineteenth century and the documentation has not been fully preserved. Part IV undertakes a reconstruction of the funerary landscape of the city and its territory, through the analysis of the structures and grave goods, for the first time interpreted in a social mode.

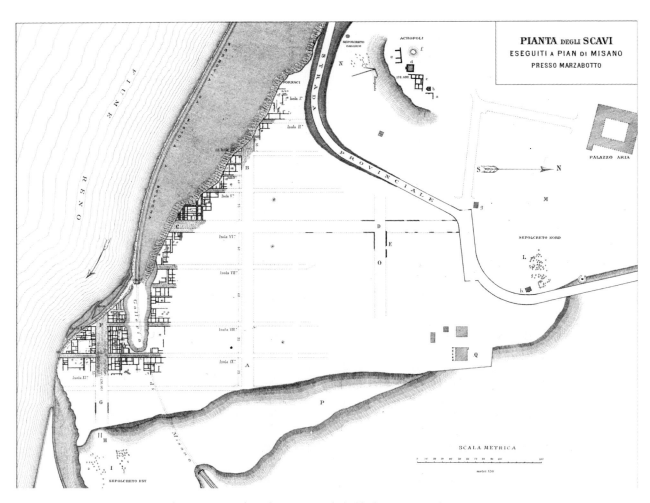

FIGURE 16.1. V. Levi's excavation plan, drawn up on behalf of E. Brizio. After Morpurgo and Pozzi 2009.

CHAPTER 16

FUNERARY PRACTICES

CHIARA PIZZIRANI

Funerary practices in ancient Kainua are only scarcely known, and yet from what survives they seem to represent an extraordinary phenomenon.

The Etruscan tombs of Marzabotto date from the end of the sixth century BCE to the first half of the fourth century BCE. In these two hundred years, almost three hundred Etruscan inhabitants of the city were buried within the two necropoleis set at opposite ends of the Pian di Misano (*see maps 5 and 13*). Funerary practices and the whole "performance" of the funeral[1] aimed to celebrate the dead person's role in the urban community and, at the same time, guarantee him a safe journey to the afterlife.

THE LOSS OF THE BURIAL CONTEXTS

Despite the importance of funerary practices in Etruscan civilization, features of the funeral celebrations in Marzabotto and the actions performed in this context are only partially known. An unfortunate sequence of events caused the loss of many objects, both in ancient times and after the excavations of the necropoleis during the nineteenth century. Moreover, even when objects have been preserved, most often they cannot be connected to the original burial context and to the totality of the grave goods.

Giovanni Gozzadini and his assistant Filippo Sansoni carried out excavations between 1867 and 1870 in the Northern Necropolis, and between 1867 and 1873 in the Eastern Necropolis.[2] The tombs they discovered, and the ones that had accidentally been brought to light before that period,[3] were described in concise reports.[4] Therefore, the graves' measurements, depth in the ground, burial practice (inhumation or cremation), and a general list of the grave goods, sometimes together with a sketch of some objects, are recorded for many tombs.[5] Nevertheless, many difficulties remain, diminishing our understanding of the Marzabotto necropoleis.

Unfortunately, Gozzadini and Sansoni discovered tombs that had already been robbed.[6] Violation of the tombs can probably be attributed to the fourth century BCE Celts, who also destroyed part of the *podium* of the Temple of Tinia in the city.[7] Evidence of Roman presence on the site[8] could be linked to tomb violations as well.

Besides this, returning to the nineteenth-century excavations, the most serious problem is the lack of a general plan of the necropolis areas. Several nineteenth-century plans of the whole city are available.[9] The architect Vittorio Levi's excavation plan, drawn up on behalf of E. Brizio, is surely the most detailed, showing, in the Northern Necropolis, the eastern group of tombs,[10] and, in the Eastern Necropolis, both groups of tombs, set on each side of the suburban road.

However, the plan is extremely small and not sharply drawn enough to permit a reliable understanding of the ancient burial grounds. Moreover, the western group of tombs in the Northern Necropolis is lacking, and handwritten diaries by F. Sansoni[11] are unable to fill the gap. He often specified the distance between two tombs, but the orientation and direction of the measurement within the space remain unknown, so trying to redraw a necropolis plan becomes effectively impossible.

However, the information concerning several graves that had been placed close to one another by the Etruscan inhabitants of the city is important. Even though neither their exact location within the necropolis space nor their identification with the preserved monuments can be precisely stated, an idea of the ancient appearance of the burial ground, partially organized in plots, can be obtained. Often those tombs closest to one another had similar objects placed in the grave for the dead. Therefore, they are likely to be part of the same family or linked by a particular kind of relationship.

Another significant difficulty in understanding the Marzabotto funerary practices derives from the vague descriptions of the objects found in each grave. In Sansoni's notes, as is to be expected, very archaic words are used to define the Etruscan and Greek objects collected in the tomb, but an expertise in interpreting nineteenth-century handwritten texts can help considerably with this issue. Nevertheless, the Athenian black- and red-figured vases cannot often be linked to any particular tomb. Indeed, the vase shape is sometimes clear, but the figurative themes are never recorded. As a consequence, it is generally feasible to presume that in an individual tomb there was, for example, a *kylix* (sometimes a black- or red-figured one), but which particular vase was found in which tomb remains impossible to determine.

Furthermore, this difficulty cannot be solved by an analysis of the grave goods collected during the excavations, as is possible in the case of the Etruscan necropoleis in Bologna.[12] In fact, in the nineteenth century, all the materials were exhibited in the Etruscan Museum in the Villa Aria, and later in the museum newly created close to the city's archaeological area. In the museum, all the funerary assemblages were divided to permit a typological display of the objects found in the Etruscan city, as was the custom during the nineteenth century, and the link between an object and the tomb in which it was originally placed was irreparably lost. Moreover, in 1911 individual items of jewelry and whole sets for adornment found in the graves were robbed and to make matters worse in 1944 a World War II explosion destroyed one wing of the Marzabotto museum, obliterating many ancient Etruscan objects (*see plate 1*).[13]

NOTES ON THE TOPOGRAPHY OF THE NECROPOLEIS

Although a general plan of the burial areas is lacking, a few documents are available that enable us to infer fragmentary information about their original topography. Unfortunately, none of these documents includes all the tombs and, even when a match can be found, they do not provide a general picture of the entirety of the necropoleis areas.

For the Northern Necropolis, in addition to the unknown location of the western group of graves, Levi's plan (fig. 16.1) is barely decipherable. Seventy-four tombs were surveyed, whereas ninety-one were known to exist in this area.[14] Moreover, understanding the tomb type according to this plan—and consequently sometimes the burial custom—is, unfortunately, not possible.

Sansoni's plans of the area are incomplete as well, but clearer. Drawn up at different moments during the excavations, and describing thirty-five (fig. 16.2a) and fifty-eight (fig. 16.2b) tombs respectively, they are quite similar, but do not correspond perfectly, as can be detected by carefully observing the grave dimensions and their respective locations. Therefore, it could be argued that they are the results of two different measurement campaigns in the field.[15] Nevertheless, the discrepancies in Sansoni's plans are in fact minor, and on the whole the plans provide a credible guide to the state of the tombs in the nineteenth century.[16]

Generally, when considering the city plan and the main suburban roads, coming north from Bologna and east from Tyrrhenian Etruria, the graves do not look haphazardly or irregularly located. Instead, they seem to approximately follow east–west parallel lines, the oldest possibly nearer the city and the later tombs farther away.

If the tombs have a rectangular structure, they are often east–west oriented as well. Furthermore, when they are inhumations, they respect the ritual orientation of the dead that was more common in Etruria Padana,[17] with the dead person's head lying to the west. Some graves are differently oriented, as a result

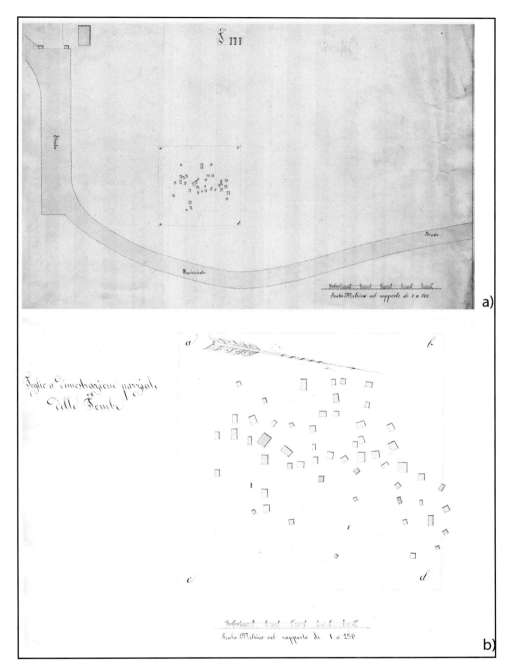

FIGURE 16.2.
Sansoni's plans of the eastern group of tombs in the Northern Necropolis, drawn up in two different periods (a–b) during the excavation in 1867. After Morpurgo and Pozzi 2009.

of the presence of secondary streets among the necropoleis, cult areas, or family plots.[18] Indeed, according to what is known in other necropoleis in Etruria Padana, family plots can be presumed to have been present in Marzabotto.

Cremation tombs used to reflect different orientation practices, following the ritual rules that fixed the location of the dead person's ashes and goods in the grave. A similar situation is well known in the necropoleis in Felsina.

For the Eastern Necropolis, a detailed analysis of the graves' location is not feasible on the whole. Nevertheless, Levi's plan and Brizio's sketch of a small group of twenty-eight graves (fig. 16.3)[19] suggest that there

FIGURE 16.3. Brizio's sketch of a funerary area in the Eastern Necropolis. After Morpurgo and Pozzi 2009.

was originally a similar presence of parallel east–west alignments, following precise ritual rules.

At present, the only preserved tomb, dug into the ground and then internally lined with cobblestones—so probably never moved since ancient times—is east–west oriented (*see fig. 17.5*). Moreover, a comparison between Brizio's sketch and the present archaeological remains in the Eastern Necropolis confirms that the *cassone* tombs now visible in the necropolis are today in the exact location where they were originally discovered.[20]

CEREMONIAL LANDSCAPE, BURIAL CULT PRACTICE, AND GRAVE RITUALS

In ancient times the Marzabotto necropolis areas were simultaneously monumental spaces and a ceremonial landscape. Giuseppe Sassatelli emphasized the monumentality of the Felsinean necropoleis in an important paper on the topic published in 1988.[21] As the funeral monuments suggest, the Marzabotto necropolis areas reflect a similar importance attached to the monumental arrangement of the landscape. Huge stones sometimes similar to eggs, columns, and pinecone *cippi* created a suggestive space for those entering the Etruscan city.[22]

Furthermore, the necropoleis were ceremonial landscapes as well and an excellent location for burial ceremonies to be "performed." This was a space for funerary rites celebrated by the urban community, and for individual actions of devotion intended to honor a deceased relative. For this reason, interesting evidence of rituality has been discovered in the ancient Kainua necropoleis.

In the Eastern Necropolis, a small sanctuary area was probably located near the city gate. Recently, a figured *stele* found there, representing a woman standing on an altar and smelling a flower, has been interpreted as a cult sculpture rather than a burial stone (*see fig. 14.3b*).[23] For a long time, the sculpture was considered to be a unique example of a *stele* decorated with a figure, like the Felsinean *stelae*. However, an explanation of the sculpture as a cult monument is more likely. A similar situation occurs in the Cannicella necropolis in Orvieto, where a statue of a female figure was discovered in a small sanctuary dedicated to funerary cults.[24] Both sculptures undoubtedly depict a goddess, possibly corresponding to the Greek Persephone,[25] the wife of Hades. In the Marzabotto sculpture, the smelling gesture, recalling Persephone's iconography, seems to confirm this explanation.[26] In the Northern Necropolis, no similar small shrine or monument has been found. Nonetheless, this exact situation reflects the "geography of the sacred" in Etruscan Volsinii, due to the presence of the goddess cult in the eastern necropolis (Cannicella), whereas again nothing similar is documented in the northwestern one (Crocifisso del Tufo).[27]

Moreover, several wells[28] discovered in both necropoleis were probably meant for ritual usage. A marble well cover decorated with a chain of pomegranates and lotus flowers has been found in the S. Cerbone necropolis of Populonia and has been interpreted as an element connected to funerary cults celebrated in the necropolis. Another well cover or similar element has been found in Bologna in the Arnoaldi necropolis, although wells do not seem to be documented in the burial grounds.[29] Indeed, several streams passed through the western necropoleis of Felsina and provided the necessary water to the area. A similar situation is known for the Felsina acropolis.[30]

On the other hand, in Kainua, a water supply provided by streams is lacking both on the Acropolis and in the necropoleis. As is well known, waterworks were created on the Acropolis in order to provide a supply to the pottery workshops of the city[31] and perhaps in answer to the requirements of the cult actions celebrated in the Acropolis.[32] The same situation could exist in both necropoleis, as indicated by the excavation of several water wells.

FIGURE 16.4. *Cista cordonata* (chest with pattern of cords around it) from tomb no. 19 in the Northern Necropolis. After Morpurgo and Pozzi 2009.

In addition, there is other evidence of ritual actions performed by the city inhabitants within the ceremonial landscape of the necropolis areas. Although the majority of tombs were robbed in ancient times, a few graves that survived violation contain traces of these rituals. For instance, tomb no. 19 in the Northern Necropolis represents an excellent example of the ritual actions performed during the burial ceremony.[33]

This grave is part of a small burial plot of three, characterized by the same tomb structure (pit), and burial rite (cremation). In the fifth century BCE, the woman buried in it was cremated, and her ashes were placed in a *cista cordonata* (fig. 16.4), together with her own goods, set into the pit one at a time and between layers of soil.[34] A *patera*, which is the main instrument in ritual actions such as libation, was found on the ashes of the dead, as evidence of a last burial libation on the body before grave closure. Around the pit when it had been closed were more grave goods—or ritual gifts: earrings, a nail with a broken tip, and a small spear end.

In the eastern group of graves in the Northern Necropolis, an *alabastron*, that is, a perfume holder sometimes used in burial rituals, was placed on the ashes of the dead in two neighboring tombs.[35] Moreover, a small vase, probably an Athenian one, whose shape has not been specified by Sansoni, was put on the dead person's ashes in tomb no. 74.[36]

The simple arrangement of funerary goods in the grave space allows us to speculate that a precise sequence of ritual actions was performed during the burial ceremony. Indeed, in *cassone* tombs, the corners are meaningful areas in which particular objects were put, as may be observed in some of the few tombs that have been found undisturbed.[37] Although it is often unclear which of these corners should receive specific objects in respect to the astronomical grave orientation—as we know, for instance, in the Felsinean square graves with cremated dead—the habit of laying vessels (*oinochoe, situla*)[38] or a mirror placed face down in these areas was noted in the diaries of Gozzadini and Sansoni diaries.[39]

Moreover, elsewhere in both necropolis areas, grave goods, burial gifts, or ritual instruments were found near a grave or scattered among the tombs. Sometimes they are assumed to be evidence of a violation, but an original significance as ritual objects (gifted or used in rituals) cannot be excluded. This interpretation is supported by an analysis of the ritual practices celebrated in the unviolated tombs (e.g., tomb no. 19 in the Northern Necropolis) and by an evaluation of the types of objects discovered in the necropolis areas. Indeed, in Sansoni's diaries, several *paterae* are mentioned, discovered among the graves—for example, 50 centimeters from a tomb discovered in the Eastern Necropolis,[40] or in pairs, one inside the other, in the Eastern Necropolis[41]—presumably used in celebrating the dead[42] rather than as grave goods put near the dead person's body and then robbed and scattered on the ground.

THE BURIAL CUSTOMS

Burial customs in the Marzabotto necropoleis are particularly unusual within Etruria Padana. However, it is difficult to find any connection to contemporary experience in Tyrrhenian northern Etruria, where Late Archaic and Classical grave contexts are not preserved and are quite unknown, with a few exceptions.[43]

In the necropoleis of Etruria Padana, and particularly in Felsina and Spina, inhumation is the more commonly practiced burial custom, whereas cremation is a more exclusive choice throughout the entire period of use of the necropoleis.[44] Indeed, in some necropoleis of Felsina cremation tombs were at most 31–38 percent,[45] on average 26 percent. In Spina cremation graves were even fewer,[46] as is to be expected for an exclusive burial custom like cremation.

In Marzabotto, the opposite seems to be true. The burial custom is known for 72 percent of the Marzabotto tombs, and it is preeminently cremation. Moreover, the remaining 28 percent of the graves have funerary structures that are usually connected to the cremation ritual custom, such as *cassone* tombs.[47] This information suggests a different calibration of the burial custom in the Marzabotto necropoleis, such as 60 percent cremations versus 40 percent inhumations, and even more in the Northern Necropolis (67 percent vs. 33 percent).[48]

Unfortunately, fifth-century BCE graves in Tyrrhenian northern Etruria are almost completely lacking,[49] so a comparison with this geographical area seems to be difficult to make. Nevertheless, it can be argued that several inland or northern cities in Tyrrhenian Etruria (Chiusi, Volterra) seemed to be partial to the cremation burial custom during their existence. On the other hand, the Populonian *cassone* graves, which are frequently mentioned as a comparison to the Marzabotto grave structures,[50] are substantially reserved for inhumations.

GRAVE GOODS AS ASSEMBLAGES FOR THE DEAD

The violation suffered in ancient times by the majority of tombs in the Marzabotto necropoleis, together with other difficult situations concerning their sets of grave goods, has produced incomplete knowledge of the ancient tombs in Marzabotto. These were conceived as complex contexts, created—or "performed"—by means of a specific tomb structure, the deposing of the dead inside following a precisely elected burial custom, the placing of selected grave goods beside or around them while respecting meticulous ritual rules, and the celebration of rites over the dead body or on the already closed grave.

In almost all the graves few, if any, grave goods have been discovered, and very few funerary contexts have escaped violation and thus preserved their original identity.[51]

According to Gozzadini's excavation reports, only two *cassone* tombs were found unexplored and undisturbed.[52] Moreover, another pit grave is understood to have been found intact, namely the already mentioned tomb no. 19, in the Northern Necropolis. When discovered, the stone cover slab was still in place and the grave goods and funerary gifts were substantially complete.[53] Furthermore, it may be supposed that two more pit tombs in the Eastern Necropolis could have been discovered undisturbed as well, because the cinerary urns were still covered with a tile and a stone slab, respectively.[54] Both of them had a bronze *stamnos* containing the ashes and had been dug in the same area within the necropolis, in the southern group of tombs. A third Athenian black-figured *stamnos* used as a cinerary urn has been found in the same necropolis, within the northern group of tombs (*see fig. 15.3*), in a pit that was probably undisturbed.[55] Another pit tomb in the Eastern Necropolis with a *cista cordonata* as a cinerary urn may also have been spared violation.[56]

Although undoubtedly other graves were probably undisturbed at the moment of discovery in the nineteenth century,[57] the intact condition of only the above-mentioned contexts seems to be attested by excavation reports. As can be observed, the sample does not correspond to ancient reality and does not present a coherent picture of the Marzabotto graves. In fact, it is unbalanced toward pit graves, which were an eminently rare kind of grave structure,[58] but were certainly less likely to be identified and consequently violated.

Although this reality cannot be ignored, an initial investigation of the intact contexts is enough to give the impression of a well-defined funerary ritual standing out as unique. In each of the two preserved *cassone* tombs, the ashes of a cremated woman were accompanied by the same selection of objects: *kados*, that is, a kind of *situla* with a pointed bottom and a chain for hanging it up, mirror, extraordinarily rich amber and glass jewelry sets, cloth with gold decorations, *alabastron*, and a barely varied ritual with the mirror—or the *alabastron*—put on the ashes. A comparable ritual practiced on the remains of the dead is documented in tomb no. 19, thanks to the use of a *patera* instead of the *alabastron*, and in the same grave a necklace has been found formed of amber elements that are very similar to those mentioned above. Therefore, despite the varied grave structures (*cassone* and pit) and overall tomb set-up, a fundamental coherence in the ritual actions seems to be observed.

A similar solidarity in ritual characterizes three outstanding cremation tombs in the Eastern Necropolis, with *stamnoi* used as cinerary urns. They seem to be particularly ancient, dating back to the end of the sixth century BCE,[59] and are highly valued because of their ritual significance.

Although *stamnoi* are documented in Felsina graves, always in extraordinary funerary contexts and with exceptional scenes by the principal Athenian painters,[60] none of them were used as cinerary urns, and the same is known for Spina. However, the use of the *stamnos* in fifth-century BCE Chiusi is impressive, providing a comparison from Tyrrhenian Etruria.[61] It might be argued that in Felsina the more common krater, or possibly the rarer *pelike*, could play the role of the *stamnos* as a cinerary urn documented at Marzabotto. As a matter of fact, in Marzabotto, *pelikai* are almost absent, being documented in one or perhaps two cases, whose provenance is unknown. Thus the two shapes seem to trade places regarding their use and prevalence in the two cities.

At the same time, in Marzabotto there is an extremely rare practice in the sixth–fifth centuries BCE, since the ritual removal of both handles is testified in two of seven graves considered, in the black-figured Athenian *stamnos* and in a different kind of tomb, known as a *cista cordonata* cremation.

Therefore, the autonomy of ancient Kainua in funerary practice can be deduced by considering the few tombs still preserved, despite the huge loss of original funerary contexts, which cannot, therefore, be accurately analyzed.

However, through this fragmentary documentation, many impressive details can be observed:

- the extraordinary presence of an ostrich egg and of a rare Athenian *oon*, that is an egg made of pottery and painted by Athenian vase painters;
- the rare use of a pair of candleholders in two or more tombs, and the interestingly high number of candleholders found in the necropoleis;[62]
- an affection for the bronze shape of the *kados*;
- the probable presence of the *stylus* as a grave object in young adult tombs;
- an extraordinary amount of *aes rude* reserved for only one deceased person in several tombs, perhaps reminding us of the abundance of metals in the Etruscan society of Marzabotto;
- the outstanding and unusual presence of gold and precious objects, decorations, and adornment sets in the graves; and
- the ritual use of *alabastra* and *paterae* in funerary actions within the cults of the deceased in the tombs and throughout the burial ground.

These are only a few characteristics of a complex ritual funerary practice that still needs to be explored in depth.[63]

GRAVES AND ICONOGRAPHY IN ANCIENT KAINUA

Lastly, an evaluation of the iconographic themes documented in funerary contexts is essential to complete an overview of the funerary practices in the city. In the following paragraphs, we address the places where objects were produced and their prevailing themes; some items were created locally and others were imported.

Concerning trade connections,[64] whereas the candleholder statuettes are possibly locally produced,[65] due to their impressive originality and to the selection of themes, the import of Athenian pottery follows the routes through Etruria Padana, as scholars argue[66] and as the study of Athenian painters, whose works are documented in Marzabotto, confirms. Indeed, for example, painters such as the Orchard Painter and the Niobid Painter, whose vases are impressively integrated in the Felsina and Spina funerary practices, are absent in the archeological contexts of Chiusi and Populonia. Therefore, the iconography might be also influenced by the Athenian market addressed to Etruria Padana.

Nevertheless, the iconographic themes attested in Marzabotto seem to be particularly impressive. One extraordinary theme concerns the rare figure of the Ethiopian, here represented in a candleholder statuette from a tomb in the Eastern Necropolis (fig. 16.5).[67] This tomb was a rectangular *cassone* with a houselike hip roof as a cover and a selection of objects as grave goods, highly reminiscent of another amazing tomb in the Northern Necropolis, which contained another famous candleholder statuette from Marzabotto, depicting the departure of the warrior (*plate 5*). An object that seems to be different in the Eastern Necropolis tomb is the necklace, which could be interpreted as an offering to the deceased person, instead of an object belonging to them.[68] Bronze furniture feet are documented in both of these tombs, which might possibly imply that the deceased are men. The iconography of the Ethiopian of the candleholder seems to be quite original. It might be connected with the myth of Herakles but seems to refer to a different perception of reality, which fits well with a funerary context.

The Ethiopian connotation of the figure, and the similar context mentioned for the other candleholder statuette, brings us to another theme, which seems to be highly relevant to Kainua's funerary practices: the departure of the warrior and images of fighting and war, which could have the same meaning of acknowledging death.

Indeed, in another tomb in the Eastern Necropolis[69] a very interesting red-figured column krater has been found, whose decoration refers to the fight between Achilles and the Ethiopian Memnon. This scene is rarely documented in Felsina, always in *calyx* kraters, and in impressively high-ranking funerary contexts. It represents a valuable variation, compared to the departure/death of the warrior, celebrated by a woman with a *patera* and also figured in the well-known candleholder statuette from Marzabotto (*plate 5*). War returns as a figurative theme in a precious two-headed *kantharos* and in a *calyx* krater, decorated with a gigantomachy of Apollo, a deity who is never the protagonist of this fight in Etruria Padana, but whose iconography seems to be well represented in Populonia.

The Gigantomachy, the fight between Achilles and Memnon, and warrior departure are obviously very high-ranking iconographic themes, conceived as me-

FIGURE 16.5. Statuette from a candleholder discovered in a tomb of the Eastern Necropolis, 450–400 BCE. After Gozzadini 1870.

diation messages between high rank in society and honorable death.

Lastly, a very notable importance is reserved for Dionysus in the iconographic themes found in Kainua graves, considering the quantity of images depicted on various classes of materials (Athenian pottery, bronzes, *cippi*). For instance, the presence of a *phiale mesomphalos* depicting the god, in a city where libation seems to be a primary ritual practice, deserves to be mentioned. Moreover, the singular Dionysus candleholder statuette from nearby Pontecchio Marconi is noteworthy.[70] It is a unique work of handicraft, which possibly indicates an urban society, such as that of ancient Kainua, whose preference for this kind of object seems to stand out.

NOTES

1. About the expression used, see Cerchiai and Menichetti 2017.
2. Marchesi 2005:191–194. See also chapter 17.
3. Gozzadini 1865:20.
4. Archiginnasio Library, *Manoscritti Gozzadini*; Gozzadini 1870; Brizio 1890: appendix B, 345–422.
5. Research on the matter has been carried out by Marinella Marchesi. As a PhD candidate, she worked to collect all the information, thanks to Sassatelli's handwritten notes, about each tomb and tried to analyze the Marzabotto necropoleis as a whole (Marchesi 1995–1996).
6. Sansoni's diaries record evidence of ancient violation of the majority of the tombs.
7. See chapter 19.
8. See chapter 20.
9. Morpurgo and Pozzi 2009:105–106. These were commissioned by G. Gozzadini, G. Chierici, and E. Brizio.
10. After the excavations of the graves, the western group of tombs (letter M on Levi's plan) was destroyed in the nineteenth century due to the creation of an artificial lake in the Villa Aria's gardens (Brizio 1890:270–271, pl. I, letter M).
11. See Brizio 1890:352–353, 361–362, 365–366.
12. Govi 1998; Macellari 2002; Morpurgo 2018.
13. At the present it is called MNMEA, Museo Nazionale Etrusco "Pompeo Aria." About the Museum's birth, see A. M. Brizzolara, in Mansuelli et al. 1982, and chapter 2.
14. Marchesi 2005:197.
15. Marchesi 2005:197.
16. M. Marchesi does not believe the plans are correct. Gozzadini asserts that the tombs had been moved after works in the Villa Aria's gardens and near the artificial lake, but unfortunately this is uncertain.
17. Marchesi 2005:205.
18. See Macellari 2002:41, in Bologna, in the Arnoaldi necropolis "*nell'ultimo venticinquennio del VI secolo a.C. è il tracciato della strada ad esercitare una forte attrattiva sulle scelte deposizionali.*" See also Macellari 2002:41–42 about areas devoted to funerary cults and secondary streets among the tombs. Lastly, the occupation of the area was organized from south

to north, with the older tombs next to the street and the later ones farther away (Macellari 2002:42), a situation that could be similar to that in Marzabotto. See also Govi 2009a:27–29.

19. Marchesi 2005:198, fig. 8; Morpurgo and Pozzi 2009: 198, no. 169.

20. Marchesi 2005:199.

21. Sassatelli 1988.

22. See chapters 14 and 16.

23. Malnati and Sassatelli 2008.

24. Another funerary shrine is documented in Populonia as well (Romualdi 2000:353; Romualdi 2004:186–187). In all these sanctuaries settled in necropolis areas, libation seems to be the main ritual action, clearly prescribed in Populonia thanks to an inscription written on an altar that is very similar to the one figured on the Marzabotto *stele* (M. Martelli, in *REE* 1978:325–327, no. 58).

25. Colonna 1987:23. Govi 2009b:461. But see de Grummond 2016:201.

26. Govi 2009b:460–461.

27. Moreover, comparing this evidence to the *deorum sedes* on the Piacenza liver, Catha, the *seχ* (the "daughter"), sometimes linked in sacred perceptions to Persephone, is one of the inhabitants of southeastern places.

28. Marchesi 2005:201.

29. Macellari 2002:41. The object is linked to ritual practices celebrated in the burial ground.

30. Many sanctuaries provided water near their temples (Maggiani 2012b), e.g., the Portonaccio Etrusco-Italic temple (Colonna 2019, and bibliography), Campo della Fiera shrine (Stopponi and Giacobbi 2017:124–129).

31. See chapter 13.

32. Vitali 2001a:78; Marchesi 2005:201. See also chapter 8.

33. Marchesi 2005:208; Morpurgo and Pozzi 2009:179, no. 133.

34. They were all quite tiny, because they were glass and amber jewels, but they were each found separated from the next deposit by 7 centimeters of soil.

35. Marchesi 1995–1996:115–116, 118–119.

36. Govi 2018b:33–34.

37. For example, Gozzadini 1870:20 and 83–84, n. 74; Brizio 1890:415.

38. That is a ritual practice that is known, for example, in Pyrgi, southern shrine, deposit rho (Belelli Marchesini 2013: 19–20; Baglione 2013:78–83; Marziali 2019).

39. Brizio 1890:415.

40. Brizio 1890:355–356.

41. Gozzadini 1870, pl. 14, no. 5.

42. Marchesi 2005:208. In the Populonia necropolis and in Greece, a *patera* was used as a cremation grave cover and has been connected by scholars to the last funerary libation in honor of the dead (Romualdi 2004:182; Romualdi 2010:123). A pair of *paterae* was also placed in tomb no. 103 of the De Luca necropolis in Felsina, a female cremation (Morpurgo 2018:362–378).

43. For example, Romualdi 2000. The same loss of information hinders our knowledge of grave goods.

44. See Morpurgo 2018:477–482.

45. Morpurgo 2018:479, fig. 64.

46. The study of the Spina necropoleis is ongoing thanks to SABAP and the University of Bologna (Desantis 2017; Govi 2017d), but this is understood to be the ancient situation in the fifth century BCE.

47. Only eight inhumations in *cassone* tombs are documented (Marchesi 2005:204).

48. Marchesi 2005:204.

49. The Tomb of the Meidias Hydriai is an outstanding exception together with a few graves in Populonia (Romualdi 2000; Romualdi 2004).

50. See chapter 17.

51. Morpurgo and Pozzi 2009:172–173 for some of them.

52. Gozzadini 1870:19–20 and 83–84, n. 74; Marchesi 2005: 208–209, fig. 12 (tomb no. 80 in the Northern Necropolis).

53. Gozzadini 1870:21 and 25, and pls. 2:1 and 11:2; Brizio 1890:271 and 365; Marchesi 2005:208.

54. Brizio 1890:275, 407, 410.

55. Baldoni 2009:55–57, no. 4; Baldoni 2012.

56. Brizio 1890:417.

57. The above-mentioned tomb with an Athenian black-figured *stamnos* used as a cinerary urn is supposed to have been intact at its discovery (Baldoni 2009:57).

58. See chapter 17.

59. Marchesi 2005:207.

60. For example, in *tomba* De Luca 103 (Morpurgo 2018: 362–378) and Certosa 41 (Zannoni 1876–1884:88–90), and also in Arnoldi tomb 110 in bronze (Macellari 2002:226–233) and in Via Saffi (Desantis 2014). In Felsina, *stamnoi* are preferably present in inhumation graves, with the outstanding exception of *tomba* De Luca 103.

61. The source is the Beazley Archive. The themes documented here are absolutely outstanding.

62. For instance, eight or nine candleholders have been found in the Northern Necropolis, which contains 170 tombs.

63. An initial remark about the topic is in Marchesi 2005. For the mentioned objects, see Gozzadini 1870; Brizio 1890; Morpurgo and Pozzi 2009; and Baldoni 2009 for Attic pottery found in Marzabotto.

64. See chapter 5.

65. See chapter 12.

66. See chapter 15.

67. Gozzadini 1870:38–39; Brizio 1890:274 and 351.

68. The single elements have been found in various places above the body.

69. Possibly the one described in Brizio 1890:405–406, which is understood to have brought to light an Athenian vase with four human figures.

70. Bruni 1996.

CHAPTER 17

THE NECROPOLEIS
Tomb Structures

CHIARA PIZZIRANI

The necropoleis on the Marzabotto plateau are remarkable areas of the city. The same must have been true in ancient times, when Etruscan Kainua rose as a flourishing city in the Apennine Mountains between Felsina and Tyrrhenian northern Etruria. For someone approaching the city from the south or from the north, the necropoleis were the first part of Kainua to be encountered, characterized by their numerous grave markers and stone monuments, traces of the burials of nearly three hundred individuals.

THE CITY AND THE NECROPOLEIS

The discovery of the Acropolis and of the Northern Necropolis in 1839 coincided with the discovery of the Etruscan city itself.[1]

First, Giovanni Gozzadini together with Filippo Sansoni investigated the Northern Necropolis (fig. 17.1) when the Aria family decided to renovate the park near their mansion.

Many years later, when regular scientific excavations had been established and Sansoni was exploring the Northern Necropolis, a worker suggested investigating a different area where similar stone tomb fragments were emerging from the ground.[2] Hence the Eastern Necropolis was discovered in September 1867 and then investigated during the following months, while excavations in the northern one were continued. Thus, the Etruscan city of Marzabotto actually had two suburban areas that were intended to be necropoleis (*see maps 5 and 13*).

An early presence of other necropolis areas elsewhere around the city seems to be unlikely, although the southwestern part of the city is now lost because of the Reno River's erosion of the plateau. Indeed, the plateau facing toward the west and the south possibly did not offer a suitable place for other necropoleis.[3] Moreover, in the sixth century BCE it seems that several major Etruscan cities organized their burial grounds by creating two distinct main areas of occupation. In Volsinii (Orvieto), they were the northwestern necropolis of Crocifisso del Tufo and the southeastern necropolis of Cannicella, whereas in Felsina (Bologna) they were the western necropoleis and a southeastern necropolis at the Giardini Margherita.[4] Consequently, the two necropoleis of Marzabotto are imagined to be the main burial grounds of the ancient city, even though it could be argued that nearly three hundred tombs could be too few, considering that a community lived here for more than two centuries.[5]

The Marzabotto necropoleis are located at opposite ends of the city, toward the north on the way to Felsina and toward the southeast, leading to Tyrrhenian northern Etruria (*see maps 3 and 5*). As scholars often emphasize, the entry roads to the city were used to create a focal area for the necropolis, collecting tombs along their sides. For this reason, in both of the Marzabotto necropoleis, two large groups of tombs were discovered near the sides of the roads. Tombs were aligned along the road, as can be observed in the Eastern Necropolis and probably also the Northern one, sometimes gathered together in small groups of two, three, or more graves.[6] Such an arrangement of burial grounds was intended to offer a monumental appearance to foreign visitors, as is archaeologically documented in the contemporary Felsinean necropoleis.[7]

FIGURE 17.1. The Northern Necropolis during the nineteenth-century excavations. After Morpurgo and Pozzi 2009.

Tombs, grave markers, and sacred areas used to perform funerary cultic acts filled a space in front of the city gate, which was seen by everyone reaching ancient Kainua.

KAINUA TOMB STRUCTURES: THE *CASSONE* TOMBS

In the Marzabotto necropoleis, several types of structures are documented, with an interesting variety scarcely known in nearby cities.

The preeminent tomb structure is the *cassone* tomb. The reference to the term *cassone* ("chest") to define this kind of tomb structure recalls the funerary architecture of Populonia, where beginning from 540–530 BCE *cassone* or sarcophagus tombs were widely present in necropoleis.[8] Although the use of this term is common in both of these geographical areas—and indeed some architectural features are shared in the related necropoleis—the Marzabotto *cassone* tombs have their own specific characteristics.

The Marzabotto *cassone* tombs are absolutely unique in funerary architecture in Etruria. They might be connected to individual features encountered in the Po Valley or in Tyrrhenian Etruria, but a precise overall comparison cannot be found. First, it is important to note that the Marzabotto *cassone* tombs are not the same everywhere in the city's necropoleis. A modest variety of measurements and proportions can be observed among the preserved monuments and the ones known through archive documentation.

There are *cassoni* with a square base and generally a cubic shape, which have the same dimensions on the base sides and often a similar one in height (figs. 17.2–17.3). On the other hand, there are parallelepiped *cassoni*, which are more or less elongated in shape (figs. 17.3–17.4).[9] Indeed, a considerable difference exists between the length and width of some tombs (for example, 220 × 145 cm),[10] but it should be borne in mind that this is the largest discovered tomb, and that the average dimensions are much smaller (for example, 115 × 77 cm).[11] Otherwise, the difference in the proportions is quite minimal in the parallelepiped *cassoni* (for example 163 × 142, 190 × 160, 173 × 160 cm,[12] the measurements of three tombs which are close to each other).[13]

CASSONE TOMBS WITH A SQUARE BASE

Cassoni with a square base or cubic shape are a unique case in Etruscan funerary architecture. They are built with four vertical stone slabs, often cut and set up near each other to create a chest shape, sometimes with the corners open instead of overlapping and closed (figs. 17.2–17.3). Occasionally, this type of stone structure needed to be reinforced or monumentalized with cobblestone heaps, which were piled externally against the tomb walls.[14] Rarely, the vertical stone slabs—which are effectively the tomb walls—are replaced by stone blocks.

The covering is one or more stone slabs—side by side or occasionally overlapped. Often under the stone slab roof, there is a recess in the vertical slabs about three centimeters beneath the top of the walls, where these vertical elements narrow in thickness. Edoardo Brizio suggested this feature might have been used to provide space for a wooden slab intended to better sustain the weight of the stone cover.[15]

Sometimes the stone cover slabs were cut to represent a house with a hipped roof[16] as a symbol of the dead person's high rank. In the Northern Necropolis, a small group of three tombs was characterized by a hipped roof as a cover.[17] Otherwise a flat slab was often put on the grave as a cover.

FIGURE 17.2. *Cassone* tombs with a square base, 550–350 BCE. After Gozzadini 1870.

FIGURE 17.3. *Cassone* tombs with a rectangular base and with a square base, 550–350 BCE. After Brizio 1890.

Exceptionally, in the most monumental tombs, another stone slab is used as a floor.[18] In one grave, where an adult and a child were buried together, an enormous upturned tile (70 × 90 cm) was used to create a flat surface.[19]

The stone chamber thus created would have a grave marker on the top, which was a large stone carved to be long or round or to look like an egg. The marker could also be a small column or some other feature (see fig. 17.1).[20] It was fixed to the stone cover slab, which was sometimes carved to contain it and not always at the center of the surface; at other times, the marker was found on soil about 30–40 centimeters above the burial chamber, as the excavation diaries registered.

Relating to the inner grave space, several nails still hammered into the walls were discovered when the tombs were brought to light.[21] Therefore within the walls the grave space, whose volume was approximately 1 to 4 cubic meters, was set up as a chamber, as might be seen in painted tombs where cups hang on the walls. As in Tyrrhenian Etruria, similarly in Etruria Padana beginning in the Orientalizing period, some tombs are meant to be proper chambers, built with wooden walls.[22]

The most frequent burial custom connected to this tomb structure is definitely cremation. Indeed, square *cassone* measurements are generally unsuitable for inhumation, except for a few cases whose maximum length is about 170 centimeters (and width 160 centimeters), but these are cremation tombs as well.[23] Moreover, in Etruria Padana and particularly in Bologna, the strong connection between cremation and square-shaped graves is well known and follows a long tradition in funerary customs, maintained from the Orientalizing period to the Bologna Certosa phase (about 550–350 BCE).

CASSONE TOMBS WITH A RECTANGULAR BASE

Besides the square-shaped or cubic *cassoni*, there are rectangular ones that are similar in structure. Their process of construction is almost the same, although a particular structure in stone blocks, instead of slabs, seems to be more strictly linked to this kind of tombs.[24]

FIGURE 17.4. *Cassone* tombs with a rectangular base, 550–350 BCE. After Brizio 1890.

The cover system is sometimes different because of the various proportions of these stone monuments.

These graves are in effect rectangular at the base, although their base sides can have very similar measurements, varying about 20–30 centimeters. Otherwise they might have 2:1 proportions. In the first case, the cover system is often exactly the same as that used in square-based tombs. In the latter case, the shorter walls have a triangular shape at the top to accommodate a gabled roof, and the cover is made up of two tilted stone slabs, as documented in the Populonian Archaic *cassone* tombs.

When the grave dimensions are large and the stone cover might have been too heavy, the tomb walls were cut to create recesses, intended to hold wooden beams to support the roof. Here too the inner space of the grave was set up as a chamber, as nails on the walls testify.

Sometimes these structures are low in height. Indeed, in a little plot of tombs in the Northern Necropolis, a few large graves (one of them 2 × 1.5 meters) have walls only about 40 cm high.[25]

Despite the different proportions in comparison to

the square-based *cassoni*, proportions that are nevertheless very often unsuited to inhumation, the rectangular *cassone* graves are primarily cremation tombs, except for a total of eight examples in both necropoleis.[26]

TOMBS MADE OF STONE BLOCKS

Writing in 1988, G. Sassatelli accurately described the building technique of using stone blocks together with the sarcophagus shape of a tomb discovered in Bologna, Giardini Margherita, relating its features and the possible descent from the Populonia sarcophagus tombs.[27] However, the Marzabotto graves, even when they were built in stone blocks, are substantially different in dimensions and monumentality from this evidence, as Sassatelli himself argued.[28] The Giardini Margherita sarcophagus is 380 centimeters long, 240 wide, and 250 high, whereas the only tomb with rectangular stone blocks in Marzabotto whose measurements are known was a rectangle of 118 × 82 centimeters. Hence, they differed in dimension from the Bologna example and in dimension and proportions from the funerary graves in Populonia, which are generally about 2:1 in proportion.[29]

Therefore, despite the building technique, tombs with stone blocks are probably meant to be quite similar to square and rectangular *cassoni*, built of stone slabs on each side of the burial chamber, or sometimes with two stone slabs for each side, or with stone blocks.

According to the ritual link between the practiced burial custom and the *cassone* tombs, in tombs with stone blocks the dead were cremated, whereas the Populonian sarcophagus graves were inhumation burials,[30] as was the one in the Giardini Margherita.

A TOMB WITH A SQUARE BASE MADE OF COBBLESTONES

Besides the square-based *cassoni*, a rare example of a square tomb with cobblestone walls has been documented. This building technique is well known in Marzabotto and nearby but is generally reserved for rectangular graves and linked to the inhumation burial custom.

Moreover, a large stone slab served as a cover.[31]

TILE BOX TOMBS

Another kind of structure is found in tombs made of ordinary tiles. Only three burials of this type have been discovered.[32] Moreover, these tombs are concentrated exclusively in a limited space in the Northern Necropolis, and two of them were quite close to each other in the same area.

A particular feature of this kind of tomb is that the burial chamber is completely made of tiles. The measurements depend on the tiles' dimensions, an ordinary tile being normally about 64 centimeters long and 40 centimeters wide. Where the tiles have not been found in fragments,[33] it has been observed that the box consisted of four tiles vertically embedded in the ground, with one more tile used as a cover, and in one case one more tile upside down on the box floor. All three tile boxes were found empty except for ashes from the dead in two of the three cases. However, no grave goods were in the boxes, perhaps due to the very particular burial and, secondly, because of its extremely limited dimensions. Indeed, *cassone* tombs characterized by similar dimensions are documented in the Marzabotto necropoleis. They have been discovered empty of grave goods, but this lack may be due to violations of the tombs, since *cassoni* are usually supplied with a selection of objects given to the dead.

On the contrary, the tile box seems to work as a cinerary urn, intended to contain exclusively the dead person's ashes. Furthermore, while two of the three tile boxes were buried in the ground, and for this reason probably would not have been discovered by raiders, the third one was discovered within a *cassone* tomb, being a meaningful part of this chamber grave. Although the ritual seems to be very simple, it was probably perceived as quite exclusive. The proximity of the tile box tombs suggests a precise choice in burying the deceased. Moreover, in the neighborhood of the two tile tombs, which were close to each other, one of the marble tomb markers was found, together with a base decorated with rams' heads on its corners (*see fig. 14.4d*).[34]

Sansoni interpreted these tombs as Roman, because of the use of tiles as building materials, but in 1897 Isidoro Falchi discovered some graves built of tiles with a stone cover in Populonia, and Antonella Romualdi suggested that the exceptional Tomb of the Hydriai of Meidias could have been one of them,[35] although a more recent paper by Andrea Camilli does not seem to agree with this interpretation.[36]

As for the burial practice, in Marzabotto tiled box tombs are meant to be reserved for cremation, being essentially a kind of cinerary urn.

FUNERARY PITS

Among the grave structures preferably linked to cremation, simple circular pits, buried about 60 centimeters deep in the ground, are occasionally documented in the Marzabotto necropoleis. There are hardly more than a dozen among the nearly three hundred tombs discovered in both necropoleis.

Often these kinds of graves have been found close to each other, in little groups of two or three.[37] Sometimes, the inner wall of the pit has been covered in cobblestones[38] as a symbol of particular relevance, following a well-known tradition in Etruria Padana and elsewhere from the Villanovan period.

Different kinds of cinerary urns have been put into pits: local vases, such as *dolia*, or often more precious vessels like bronze *cistae* or *stamnoi*, or an Attic black-figured *stamnos* (*see fig. 15.3*), ritually deprived of both handles.[39]

SIMPLE RECTANGULAR TOMBS AND RECTANGULAR TOMBS WITH COBBLESTONE WALLS

Whereas several kinds of tomb structures are documented relating to the cremation burial custom, only a few types were designed to contain the inhumed bodies of the dead.[40] They are essentially simple graves dug into the burial ground. Sometimes the grave walls were covered in cobblestones (fig. 17.5), like some pits. Furthermore, according to Sansoni's diaries these structures were probably covered by a cobblestone tumulus.

It seems possible to argue that this kind of tomb structure is rarely documented in Tyrrhenian Etruria. In contrast, it is quite well known in Etruria Padana. Moreover, just as pits and graves internally lined or cov-

FIGURE 17.5. Rectangular tomb with cobblestone walls, 550–350 BCE. After Mansuelli 1971.

ered on top with cobblestones were discovered in Villanovan remains and in the fifth-century necropoleis of Bologna, an inhumation rectangle grave, monumentalized by cobblestone walls, has recently been brought to light in Crespellano near Bologna by the Superintendence for Archaeology, Fine Arts, and Landscape.[41]

A VARIETY OF TOMB STRUCTURES AND SEVERAL ISSUES

The features of tomb structures in the ancient city of Kainua are generally well documented. Nevertheless, some unanswered questions still remain.

Although many *cassone* tombs are still preserved or were rebuilt in the nineteenth century to be visible to visitors, so that they are quite a well-known class of monuments, important information about this kind of structure was unfortunately lost during the excavations and is now difficult to trace. It is uncertain if such an impressive kind of tomb structure, built of monolithic slabs, was visible in ancient times or instead perhaps was covered by earth, letting only the tomb marker emerge from the ground, as has always been maintained in the literature.[42] In the Brizio excavations report, this type of burial structure was understood to be underground, not visible on the surface, except for the marker.[43] In Sansoni's diaries "a ground level corresponding to that of the tombs" is mentioned, suggesting that the original ground level had been identified and kept in mind, and it was, in that area, about 250 centimeters deep.⁴⁴ The idea that *cassone* tombs were underground perfectly agrees with perceptions of the *cassone* as the stone version of the more often documented wooden tomb chest,⁴⁵ for example in the Felsinean graves. Indeed, several arguments endorse this theory, although it needs a more accurate demonstration. Answering this question might decidedly define the original appearance of the Kainua necropolis landscape.

Another issue concerns the place of the Marzabotto tomb structures between the two poles of Felsina and the cities of Tyrrhenian northern Etruria. This question is interconnected with the issue of the appearance of the tombs and is actually more urgent, inasmuch as it relates to an overall definition of Kainua as an Etruscan city. Traditionally, the Marzabotto tombs and *cassoni* graves have been traced to Populonia.⁴⁶ Nevertheless, an overall review of the tomb structures in the city leads us to suggest that funerary architecture in ancient Kainua was a more original hybrid.

On the one hand, the Marzabotto and Populonia graves share the principal use of stone slabs as building materials, respectively travertine and *panchina*. Moreover, they are approximately contemporary and sufficiently close to one another geographically. Other elements, such as the tomb markers and possibly the use of tiles in funerary architecture, confirm this cultural relationship, which is historically well documented.⁴⁷

On the other hand, many characteristic features distinguish the tombs of the two cities. Although the building technique is similar, the probable—or possible—emergence of the tombs from the burial ground seems to be different, as is consequently the burial landscape. The tombs of Kainua were most likely covered with earth and those of Populonia were meant to be visible above ground. Furthermore, the tomb shape is quite dissimilar, and while proper sarcophagus graves with Populonian proportions and features of the tombs are not or are only rarely documented in Marzabotto,⁴⁸ a square tomb shape represents a traditional and long-lasting feature in the Felsinean funerary ritual. Moreover, this shape is impressively reflected in one of the structures on the Acropolis, the chthonic altar B, which is a perfect square with sides that are 14.5 Attic feet long. In this perspective, shape was possibly meant to have a stronger significance than the building materials, such as in the square tombs documented with cobblestones. Lastly, tomb structures built with cobblestones pertain to the funerary tradition of Etruria Padana, during a period of time that essentially corresponds to the Etruscan presence in this area and along a route that could be followed from Felsina to Kainua, through the minor Etruscan centers in the hills.

In conclusion, the funerary architecture of Kainua is an impressive hybrid manifestation of ritual beliefs, wealth-associated monumentality, and technical skill. Although Mansuelli suggests that the city is lacking in its own traditions,⁴⁹ the Kainua necropoleis seem to demonstrate the contrary.

NOTES

1. Ancient structures emerging from the ground in Misano have been attested since 1551 (Sassatelli 1989a:7–19; Vitali 2001a). See chapter 1 for more detailed information about the discovery of the city and the consequent scientific debate. Tombs in Marzabotto were found in 1839–1841, before 1862, and then after 1867, when the lake near the mansion of Villa Aria was dug (Marchesi 2005:191–194).

2. Sansoni's diaries, attachment no. 3 (Brizio 1890:348–349).

3. *Contra* Bentz and Reusser 2008:70. Brizio agreed with G. Chierici's suggestion regarding the previous existence of four necropoleis, at the end of two main urban roads, two of them destroyed by the River Reno erosion (Brizio 1890:267).

4. Only a few tombs are elsewhere around the city, for example, the Via del Cestello tomb (Govi 1999:46 no. 16) and the little Tamburini necropolis (Govi 2011:195–196).

5. Also in Felsina *princeps Etruriae* (Colonna 1999) nearly one thousand tombs have been discovered from the same chronological period.

6. See chapter 16 and related maps.

7. Sassatelli 1988.

8. Biagi et al. 2015:42 and note 11.

9. The difference between these kinds of tombs can be observed in figures 16.2 and 16.3.

10. Brizio 1890:349.

11. Brizio 1890:367.

12. Brizio 1890:410.

13. As will be noted below, Populonian *cassone* tombs are different in shape and proportions.

14. See for example Brizio 1890:359 and 370.
15. Brizio 1890:269.
16. Brizio 1890:269 and 373.
17. Brizio 1890:373–374. Moreover, see Brizio 1890:274 and 351 as an example in the Eastern Necropolis.
18. Brizio 1890:268.
19. Brizio 1890:371.
20. See chapter 14.
21. Brizio 1890:272, 354.
22. For some recently discovered examples, see von Eles, Mazzoli, and Negrini 2018; von Eles 2019; Bentini et al. 2019; Esposito 2018; Esposito 2019.
23. Brizio 1890:355–356. Many other tombs have a maximum length of 150 cm.
24. See Brizio 1890:366 (tomb measurements 114 × 82 cm) and a Giardini Margherita tomb (Sassatelli 1988:229–231). Another tomb of stone blocks is mentioned, the first one discovered in Marzabotto in 1841 (Gozzadini 1865:20; Marchesi 1995–1996). However, the dimensions are unknown.
25. Brizio 1890:358–359, 362. Among them there is a square-based tomb, whose measurements are 80 × 80 × 25 cm (Brizio 1890:359).
26. Marchesi 2005:204. It must be argued anyway that in several cases burial custom was not documented during excavations or was not clear.
27. Sassatelli 1988:230–231.
28. Sassatelli 1988:231.
29. Some measurements in Biagi et al. 2015.
30. Biagi et al. 2015.
31. Brizio 1890:366.
32. Brizio 1890:373, 375–377.
33. As was the case for the first tile box tomb discovered by Sansoni; see Brizio 1890:373.
34. Chapter 14. See Brizio 1890:376–377 about the discovery.
35. Romualdi 2000:353 and Brizio 1890:269.
36. Camilli and Meli 2015 and Camilli 2018: the Tomb of the Hydriai of Meidias is no. 204. However, tiles were possibly used in Populonian tomb structures (Camilli 2018).
37. See for instance Brizio 1890:365–366, for the description of three pits in the Northern Necropolis: one of them is tomb no. 19 (Marchesi 2005:208; Morpurgo and Pozzi 2009: 179, no. 133).
38. For instance, Brizio 1890:271.
39. Chapters 15 and 16.
40. M. Marchesi argued that eight *cassoni* were inhumation tombs (Marchesi 2005:204).
41. Soprintendenza Archeologia, Belle Arti e Paesaggio per Bologna e le province di Modena, Reggio Emilia e Ferrara (= SABAP). The tomb, discovered in 2016–2017 in Via Cassola, is unpublished.
42. But see Sassatelli 1989a:48.
43. Brizio 1890:270 and 272.
44. Brizio 1890:351. Nevertheless, the heavily disturbed ground in the necropoleis due to violation of the tombs is a factor that calls for caution in judging the original ground level.
45. Sassatelli 1988:230–231 relating the Marzabotto tombs.
46. For instance Bentz and Reusser 2008:71, but see Sassatelli 1988:230–231, where a clear distinction was made among the building models.
47. Martelli 1984:416–417; Sassatelli 1989a:75.
48. Further research will be carried out on the matter.
49. Sassatelli 1989a:76.

CHAPTER 18

THE TOMBS OF SASSO MARCONI

MATTEO TIRTEI

GEOGRAPHICAL CONTEXT AND THE DISCOVERY OF THE TOMBS

Sasso Marconi is a city located about 10 kilometers north of Marzabotto (*see map 3*). This location is relevant because of its strategic geographical position, at the confluence of the Reno River and the Setta River. In the period from the sixth to the fourth century BCE, this was the main trade route between the Po Valley and Tuscany. This position, then, must have been very attractive, especially because it guaranteed considerable control of traffic. The site also stands at the foot of a majestic cliff that further constrained the road system, making the surveillance of the location even more crucial.

Here in October 1969, following work for the construction of a building, a couple of fifth-century BCE Etruscan tombs were unearthed. The first burial, the larger one, was unfortunately excavated by the property owner, who recovered the grave goods but scrambled the context.[1] Therefore, we can say nothing about the original position of the finds within the burial.

The intervention of Superintendent of Antiquities of Emilia-Romagna G. V. Gentili, on the other hand, took control of the area, allowing the second burial to be discovered and carefully excavated. He found the grave goods and the skeleton of the deceased. Gentili's short contribution remains to date the only study relating to this small but relevant group of tombs.[2]

THE TOMBS

The two graves were located a few meters west of Via Porrettana, at street number 252/3. The tombs were parallel to each other, spaced approximately 1 meter apart, and both oriented east–west (fig. 18.1). This feature is consistent with what we already know about the urban necropolis in Felsina/Bologna. Even the position of the skeleton of tomb 2 followed the Bologna custom, with the head on the west.[3]

The proximity and regular orientation of the tombs suggests that they belong to a small family burial ground, perhaps aligned along a road.

TOMB 1

Tomb 1, as stated, was improperly excavated, resulting in the loss of information about the original context. Therefore, the following considerations will necessarily be hypothetical and limited to its dimensions and grave goods.

The tomb consisted of a rectangular pit, oriented east–west, 4.30 × 3 m, and about 3 meters deep. On the ground, a pinecone-like marble stone, decorated in a bas relief, marked the burial.

The rectangular pit structure is the most common type of tomb in the Bolognese necropoleis.[4] In the city burial grounds, the dimensions of these pits are usually around 1.5–2 × 2.50 m.[5] The prominence of this type of burial emerges in comparison with the customs of the Bolognese upper class and gains even

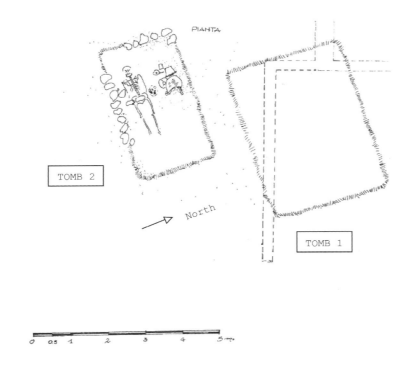

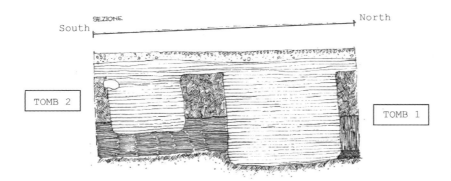

FIGURE 18.1. Plan and section of the two burials of Sasso Marconi. After Gentili 1970:243; map by M. Tirtei.

more importance if compared with the largest burials of Felsina. If we consider the Arnoaldi, Giardini Margherita, De Luca, and Battistini burial grounds, we can see that many of the wealthiest graves have smaller dimensions than Sasso Marconi tomb 1. Note the rich tombs Arnoaldi 96, 110, and 120, whose dimensions are respectively 3 × 2 m; 3 × 2.50 m; and 3.80 × 2.50 m;[6] or Battistini, 4.3 × 2 m.[7]

Only tomb Arnoaldi 104 and the *Tomba Grande* seem to be comparable to tomb 1, with a dimension of 4.50 × 3.00 m[8] and 3.50 × 2.50 m.[9] Perhaps we can also include the De Luca tombs 101, 103, and 109, for which we can assume a length of more than 3 meters.[10] Finally, it seems that tomb 1 is comparable in size only to a few prominent urban burials.

We can establish a comparison with the wealthiest tombs of Bologna even through the amount of grave goods recovered (fig. 18.2). These include forty-two objects, a number that—within the Bolognese necropoleis—is equal to or bettered only by two of the most sumptuous burials: the *Tomba Grande*[11] and De Luca 103.[12]

Grave goods include Etruscan bronzes, Attic red-figure vases, local pottery, jewelry (a gold ring and a silver Certosa brooch),[13] thirteen game pieces in glass paste, fragments of an *alabastron*, and fragments of metal objects. The bronze assemblage consists of a *stamnos*,[14] a *situla*, a beaked jug, an *oinochoe*, a tall *kyathos*, three small *kyathoi*, a pan, a *patera*, two ladles, a strainer,[15] a *kreagra* (torch holder),[16] four furniture leg caps,[17] a small handle, and a candleholder.[18] The set of Attic red-figure vases is made up of a volute krater,[19] an *oinochoe*,[20] two cups,[21] a "Saint Valentine" *kantharos*,[22] and two stemmed plates.[23]

FIGURE 18.2. Some of the grave goods from tomb 1 at Sasso Marconi. Marzabotto, Museo Nazionale Etrusco "P. Aria." Elements a, b, c, f, and g after Gentili 1970; d and h, photo by M. Tirtei.

Finally, the local pottery includes a gray-ware small amphora, three gray-ware plates, and three fine-ware cups.[24]

The quality of the grave goods confirms the extraordinary wealth of the burial. At first glance, it seems possible to observe an exaggerated desire to display one's economic power and one's social status. All the vases, except for the local pottery ones—intended for food offerings—relate with a certain redundancy to the sphere of the symposium. There are three large containers (*stamnos*, *situla*, Attic krater), three pouring vases (two bronze jugs, an Attic *oinochoe*), three drinking vases (two cups, one *kantharos*), and, above all, an unusual association between ladles and small *kyathoi*,[25] objects that perform the same function, that is, measuring out wine and water with accuracy.

Some of these vessels may have originated in a diversified function, such as for funeral rites. Despite the strong impression that a display of prosperity guided the family in the composition of the grave goods of the deceased, we lack many elements to reconstruct the gender and age. However, we can make some assumptions.

The structure of the burial itself may help us in our task. In the Bolognese necropoleis, especially in the Certosa burial ground, E. Govi pointed out how in large cremation pits, "the trend to emphasize the heroic values of the military *areté* and athletics" emerges and suggested that these secondary cremation burials are typical of the male components of the society.[26] Tomb 1 lacks any trace of a corpse. Superintendent Gentili carefully examined the terrain dug up by the landowner; he found a lot of pottery fragments but no anthropological remains. It is therefore not too risky to suppose that this burial was a cremation.

If so, we could assume that at least some of the numerous vessels had a connection with this specific ritual context.

A reference to military virtue seems to be present on the volute krater, where we see a scene of weapons being delivered to a young man, solemnly seated on a throne-like chair. Thanks to S. Matheson,[27] we know that this representation refers to a specific event in the life of young Athenians. At the end of the first period of their two-year service, ephebes were invested with shield and spear by the state. Besides, the "throne" on which the young man is seated gives an aura of heroism to the scene, further emphasized by the laurel crown put on his head by a young female.[28]

Athletics appear on the exterior of a cup,[29] with a scene of young athletes in the presence of Herakles; the demigod, with whom they identified,[30] may represent a further reference to the heroic nature of the deceased. Furthermore, athletics is also featured on the edge of the candleholder, where we can see a young naked *discobolus* holding two discs in his hands.

In the tondo of the cited cup, two draped youths are holding two roosters ready to fight. In Athens, there was a close connection between cockfighting, the celebration of virility, and the critical transition between adolescence and adulthood.[31]

So, it seems that the iconographic program of this tomb refers to the same values that we have identified for the wealthiest male burials in Bologna: heroic values, military virtue, athletics.

The thirteen game pieces in glass paste may confirm this theory. In fact, according to recent readings,[32] table games and athletic practice, preparatory and complementary to military practice, are all necessary for the education of a young upper-class man.[33]

To sum up, even if we cannot be sure that the Etruscans attributed the same meanings to painted scenes as Athenians did,[34] nevertheless, it does not seem possible to ignore the internal coherence of the whole assemblage. We can spot many aspects concerning the male universe, while nothing seems to refer to the female world. So, considering all the evidence, we can tentatively suggest that the deceased of tomb 1 was a male, perhaps of a young age and that he or his family chose the military, athletic, and heroic values to highlight his belonging to the upper class.

There is one more thing to mention before we move on to the next burial: the Dionysian sphere. If we observe the funerary monument, we can see that everything in it refers to Dionysus. It consists of three parts: a travertine base; a small marble one above it; on the top, a marble pinecone-like stone.[35] The marble base is decorated at the corners with four ram heads: this animal is the utmost sacrificial victim to Dionysus and had a prominent role in his cult. The shape of the stone itself gives a further reference to the god. It recalls a pinecone, a fruit with a Dionysian value, the emblem of rebirth that contains a regenerating power.[36]

Finally, even the bas-relief decoration of the monument refers to the Dionysian sphere. It shows a farewell scene between a man and a woman. The woman greets the man, who holds a stick, ready to leave for his final journey. A procession of satyrs, maenads, and dancers with a clear connection to Dionysus surrounds these figures.

Perhaps we can recognize a similar reference within the grave goods. Maybe the *kantharos*, the drinking vessel of Dionysus par excellence, represents a link to the god, since the presence of two cups makes it reasonable to think that this vessel was not strictly necessary for drinking purposes. Besides, on the exterior of the second Athenian cup, a detailed scene of *komos* is taking place, just like on the pinecone-like monument.

Finally, even the *kreagra* may have a Dionysian meaning, according to the theory that sees in it a torch-holder, and not a sort of fork to grasp the meat.[37] In fact, due to its particular shape, this tool would not be suitable for grasping solid objects: the tips are curved and too thin to be strong enough to stick into flesh; its hollow part also reduces its ability to retain food. Moreover, it has an attachment in the middle, which creates a considerable obstacle to the collection of food, reducing its capacity and ability to grasp. For these reasons, we believe that the torch-holder function better fits its shape.

A ritual or Dionysian value would also explain its extreme rarity: only eighty-two specimens have been found in thousands of Classical era tombs.[38] Such a rare object seems more suited to a particular, elite function, rather than to meat consumption, which was widespread among the upper classes. Besides, Dionysus is a deity linked to light, especially in the epiclesis *Iacchos* with whom initiates worshiped him in Eleusis. And in the Eleusinian Mysteries he was a torchbearer.[39]

For these reasons, we cautiously suggest that the Etruscans associated this tool with the cult of the god and with its initiates. The use of it by a small group of privileged men should explain quite well its rarity in the fifth-century BCE Etruscan world.

TOMB 2

Tomb 2 luckily provides an intact context. It is an inhumation in a rectangular pit, and anthropological remains made it possible to identify an adult male.[40]

The burial conforms entirely to the Bolognese ritual practice: rectangular pit oriented east–west (2 × 3.50 m, 2.20–2.30 m deep); inhumation rite, prevailing in the urban necropoleis; deceased lying supine along the south side of the pit; head placed west; grave goods arranged along the north side of the tomb; less wealth interred than for cremations,[41] with only eleven objects, in line with the average of the Bolognese burial grounds.

From figure 18.3, we can see that the grave goods were next to the bust of the deceased. From top to bottom (fig. 18.4)), there are a tall *kyathos*, a strainer, two ladles,[42] a *kalathos*-like *situla*,[43] the red-figure cup, and a column krater, a pan, and, near the pelvis, a jug.[44] On the ribs, due to the collapse of the chest, was a bronze brooch of Certosa type.[45] Near the right hand, finally, was a small hollow bronze cylinder with traces of wood inside, perhaps what remains of an implement of power.

Grave goods show us the complete symposium set, with a single vase for each function. Even the Calliope Painter cup[46] alludes to the symposium through a set-up scene in the banqueting hall. The column krater of the Orestes Painter, on the other hand, seems to recall the essential values of the *polis*.[47] On one side, we see a Centauromachy at Peirithous's wedding. In the myth, Theseus intervenes to protect his friend Peirithous and to restore the social norms of the *polis* disrespected by the Centaurs.[48] In addition to this reading, closely related to Athenian culture, the struggle between heroes and monsters probably also refers to the military valor of the deceased, perhaps as a metaphor of the threats that his soul will have to face to reach the afterlife.

The small hollow bronze cylinder is also important. As we have stated above, it was near the right hand of the deceased, and it contains wooden traces. We can suppose that it was the base of a small stick-like item, maybe a sign of political/religious power or authority (perhaps a *lituus* or a sort of scepter?). If so, we should

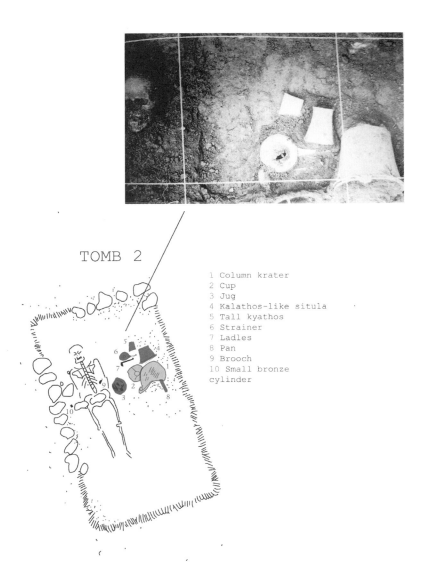

FIGURE 18.3. Drawing of tomb 2 at Sasso Marconi and a picture taken during excavations. After Gentili 1970:243. SABAP Bologna Archive, drawn by M. Tirtei.

not overestimate the differences in wealth and importance between the deceased of the two burials.

Finally, thanks to the anthropological examinations performed by Prof. G. Gruppioni, we can state that the deceased suffered from diffuse idiopathic skeletal hyperostosis (DISH), a disabling disease that causes the fusion of some vertebrae, especially the thoracic and lumbar ones. This pathology occurs mainly in men of advanced age,[49] thus confirming the gender of the deceased and his maturity.

CHRONOLOGY OF THE BURIALS

The two contexts date to the end of the fifth century BCE. In fact, for both burials, the *terminus post quem* is fixed around 430–425 BCE. The two most significant objects for dating are the *oinochoe* of the Shuvalov Painter (tomb 1) and the cup of the Calliope Painter (tomb 2). A. Lezzi Hafter, a scholar who studied these painters, proposes about 425 BCE for the first and approximately 430 BCE for the second.[50] The presence

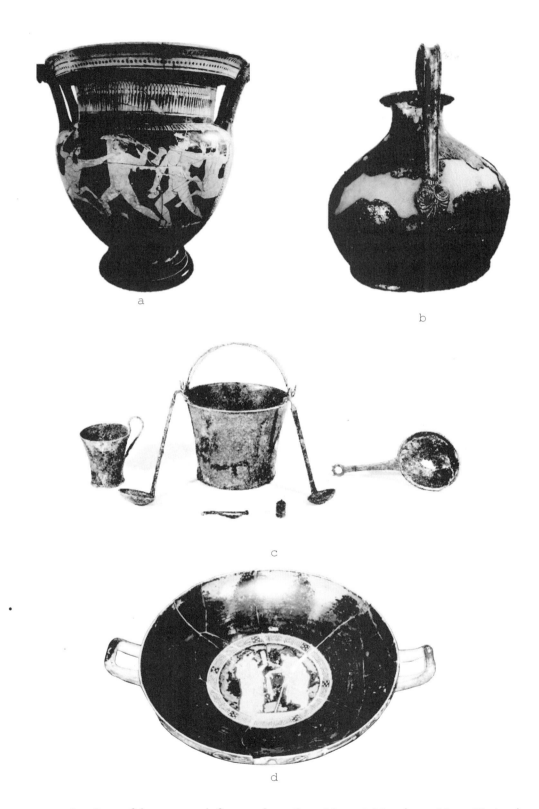

FIGURE 18.4. Some of the grave goods from tomb 2 at Sasso Marconi. Marzabotto, Museo Nazionale Etrusco P. Aria. Elements a, b, c, and d after Gentili 1970; b, photo by M. Tirtei.

of two stemmed plates in tomb 1 provides further confirmation, given that this specific form spread from around the last thirty years of the fifth century BCE.

CONCLUSIONS

To summarize the data that emerged from this study, one can state that tomb 1, perhaps a cremation, is comparable in size, consistency, and quality of grave goods only to the wealthiest burials in Bologna; the iconographic program seems to focus on the athletic, military, and heroic values of a young aristocratic male. Finally, the *cippus*, *kreagra*, a cup, and *kantharos* make it likely that the deceased was an initiate to mystery (Dionysian?) cults.

On the other hand, the size and contents of tomb 2 are within the average of the Bolognese burials, reflecting isonomic ideals; it is the inhumation of an adult male with spinal disease and, perhaps, a position of power or authority in the community; the iconographic program seems once again to evoke the military virtue of the deceased and his adherence to the ideals of the *polis*.

The research has therefore highlighted the considerable wealth of this pair of tombs, maybe belonging to the same family group. This prosperity is probably due to the control exerted over a commercial hotspot of primary importance for the region's economy.

Finally, the quality of the grave goods and their agreement with expressive models similar to the most prestigious Bolognese findings make it difficult to think of this small community as peripheral. Indeed, it seems to belong to a network of the most sophisticated Etruscan elites in the Po Valley.

NOTES

1. "*Il Resto del Carlino*," Friday 10/24/1969.
2. Gentili 1970:241–249. I am publishing the burials.
3. Govi 2005:273–274.
4. Morpurgo 2018:482–488.
5. Morpurgo 2018:482–488.
6. Macellari 2002:199, 226, 268.
7. Morpurgo 2018:420–428.
8. Macellari 2002:218.
9. Guidi 2004.
10. Morpurgo 2018:483.
11. Guidi 2004.
12. Morpurgo 2018:362–378.
13. Teržan 1977:332.
14. Shefton 1988:136–145.
15. Bini, Caramella, and Buccioli 1995:13–15, 27–30, 79–81, 88–91, 104–107, 121–122, 143–162, 164–166.
16. Hostetter 2001:138.
17. Bini, Caramella, and Buccioli 1995:586–589.
18. Testa 1989:134.
19. Manner of Niobid Painter (Gentili 1970:241–249).
20. Shuvalov Painter (Lezzi Hafter 1976:105).
21. The first attributed to the Louvre G 456 Painter (M. Tirtei); the second to the Workshop of the Penthesilea Painter (Gentili 1970:244), and to the Veii Painter (M. Tirtei).
22. Cf. Howard and Johnson 1954.
23. Cf. Beazley's Various Group.
24. Cf. Mattioli 2013:97–134, 208–220, 262–266.
25. Known only from a fourth-century BCE tomb of Tuscania (Bini, Caramella and Buccioli 1995:91).
26. Govi 2009a:35.
27. Matheson 2009:374–413.
28. In this vase, she is presumably a relative, but deities like Nike and Athena often perform the same task.
29. Red-figure cup by Louvre G 456 Painter.
30. Lunt 2009.
31. Csapo 2006.
32. Benassai 2004:220–221.
33. L. Cerchiai, instead, thinks of aged men with real political/military experience (Cerchiai 2008a).
34. Some scholars believe that the Etruscans bought the vases without understanding the painted scenes, others that they were fully aware; and some thought they repurposed the vases for their own rituals and beliefs.
35. Apuan marble (Sassatelli and Mancuso 2017:103–130).
36. Bonamici 1985:123–137; Govi 2009a:21–36.
37. Mascelli 2013:167–234.
38. Mascelli 2013:185–222.
39. Paleothodoros 2010.
40. Thanks to Prof. G. Gruppioni for the useful recommendations.
41. Govi 2009a:21–36.
42. Bini, Caramella, and Buccioli 1995:13–15, 27–30, 79–81, 88–91, 104–107, 121–122, 143–162, 164–166.
43. Giuliani Pomes 1957:54–59.
44. Bini, Caramella, and Buccioli 1995:13–15, 27–30, 79–81, 88–91, 104–107, 121–122, 143–162, 164–166.
45. Teržan 1977:332.
46. Lezzi Hafter 1988:48–57.
47. Mannack 2001:31–33, 85, 113.
48. Servadei 2005:145–149.
49. Colina 2006:104–111.
50. Lezzi Hafter 1976; Lezzi Hafter 1988.

PART V

THE END OF
THE ETRUSCAN CITY

The end of the city and the phases following the Etruscan one are dealt with in Part V, the last section of the volume. This is a short story, but one that is clearer today and less simplistically attributable to traumatic events that in the past were summoned to explain the end of the city. The Celtic phase appears more complex, and the Roman one will probably be better understood with future investigations.

CHAPTER 19

THE CELTIC PERIOD

GIULIA MORPURGO

After the remarkable Etruscan period, there was a phase of occupation of the site by people of trans-Alpine origin, long identified with the Boii.

It is well known that from the first half of the fourth century BCE, the Etruscan economic, political, and territorial network in the Po Valley was gradually disrupted by the invasions of Celtic tribes. These populations, who had already settled north of the Po, invaded northern and central Italy, going as far as Rome. The sack of Rome, an event that according to sources took place in 387–386 BCE, led to the disruptive entry of these people into the history of the Mediterranean world. From then on, and for over two centuries, they became an integral part of those populations from Italy fighting for hegemony or their own survival against the nascent Roman power.

Evidence from Marzabotto in relation to this period derives from excavations carried out mostly in the second half of the nineteenth century, which played a leading role in the history of the discipline, marking one of the starting points of Celtic archaeology in Italy. In fact, at the Fifth International Congress of Anthropology and Prehistoric Archaeology held in Bologna in 1871, scholars such as the French Gabriel de Mortillet and the Swiss Édouard Desor, thanks to their experience in contexts beyond the Alps, recognized evident links with the trans-Alpine world in some of the grave goods from the tombs that were being brought to light at the time in the Etruscan city.[1] Over time, some considerable new discoveries were added to the nineteenth-century findings, the result of both new ground investigations and useful reviews of material coming from old excavations.

This evidence has always made Marzabotto one of the most cited contexts within a now vast scientific production dedicated to the characteristics of the Boii in the Cispadana in the period from the fourth to the second century BCE. It is important to emphasize that this topic, especially in the Bolognese area, has benefited from a significant increase in the evidence from the Celtic La Tène period: isolated tombs, small or large necropoleis, and remains of inhabited areas brought to light on the high plain and in the middle of the Apennines.[2]

The first records that can be traced in the literature mentioning the presence of Celts on the site of ancient Kainua relate to the discovery of eight burials. These tombs were in the southern sector of *Regio* III, 4 (*see map 9*), in the center of the urban area, and were excavated between 1867 and 1871 by Giovanni Gozzadini and Filippo Sansoni, his field assistant.[3] Furthermore, between February 20, 1870, and October 17, 1871, Sansoni discovered seventeen other tombs at the foot of the Misanello hill, the site of the ancient Etruscan Acropolis[4] (*see maps 9 and 10*).

The corpus of nineteenth-century finds belonging to this phase also includes several abandoned wells, reused for burials,[5] and a fair number of isolated materials, recovered more or less fortuitously in different areas of the city, but no longer connected to a specific context (*see map 9*).[6]

Knowledge of this evidence is unfortunately compromised by a series of issues, starting with the excavation procedures. The latter, in fact, according to the traditions of the time, not only did not consider the original composition of the grave goods, but also lacked any general recording of findspots. Furthermore, the tomb materials, initially exhibited inside Villa Aria, were organized according to exclusively typological criteria, and then were mixed and confused over time with other Celtic objects from different areas of the city.[7] A single exception is represented by two of the tombs discovered at the foot of the Acropolis: they were literally torn from the ground, with a technique developed during those years by Antonio Zannoni while excavating at the Certosa of Bologna, and thus displayed. In this way, their original composition was effectively preserved.

In the end, many of the objects collected up to that time were lost or damaged in the fire that in 1944, during the Second World War, destroyed the Etruscan museum of Marzabotto, already in its new location (*see fig. 2.3*). Especially in the light of this last event, the 1887 publication on the Gallic tombs and necropoleis of the province of Bologna is central to our knowledge of this late phase of the site. In this volume, Edoardo Brizio published among other things a summary of the finds made in Marzabotto at that time, still substantially unpublished, accompanied by precious illustrated plates in which the memory of the objects no longer traceable is preserved.[8]

More recently, the nineteenth-century finds have been the subject of some useful revisions: mainly chrono-typological studies,[9] integrated by equally important attempts at a philological reconstruction of the contexts, starting from the original excavation documentation,[10] which, despite the limitations mentioned above, allows us today to recall some general aspects.

As noted, these are almost exclusively funerary records. Therefore, it is from the analysis of the burials and related grave goods, further disadvantaged by the lack of anthropological data, that useful elements must be recovered for the reconstruction of aspects of Gallic life in the ancient Etruscan city.

Inhumation was practiced almost exclusively: the deceased were laid, when known, in a supine position and with a rather variable orientation, inside a rectangular pit. The pit may have simply been excavated from the bare earth, although there is evidence of more complex tomb structures. It is possible to document the presence of either pits covered internally, and in some cases even at the top, by a layer of large river cobblestones, or pits covered only with tiles or tiles and travertine slabs, all reused materials from the Etruscan city.

A single tomb, belonging to the burial ground on the slopes of Misanello hill, was distinguished by the presence of a *cappuccina* structure, with a floor of tiles and a roof formed of three pairs of double sloping tiles.

As regards the grave goods, present in twenty-one of the twenty-five tombs discovered, there is a general sobriety and uniformity, traditionally justified by the strong attachment to the funerary rites and uses typical of the land of origin.

Tombs of females were characterized by modest items of adornment limited mostly to *fibulae* of the Celtic La Tène type in bronze or iron, as well as some rings and bracelets often worn asymmetrically on both arms.[11] Among these, there is evidence, for example, of one of the simple iron ring type, and one of silver serpentine type,[12] a model that has been attested in several Celtic necropoleis in northern Italy from the end of the fourth to the beginning of the third century BCE.[13]

Around the middle of the third century BCE, there are several examples, unfortunately all with no context, of *ovoli*-type bronze bracelets (fig. 19.1), a variant that reflects strong links with the central trans-Alpine Celtic world, Moravia, and above all Bohemia.[14] To explain this presence in the center of the Reno Valley, a second migratory wave from those regions was therefore hypothesized. The arrival of these people expanded the Celtic community that had already settled in Marzabotto.[15]

In the tombs of males, when the dead was buried as a warrior, there were some ornaments, mostly *fibulae*, and typically Celtic-style panoplies consisting of a sword, its hanger chain, and iron spear points. Despite the poor state of conservation of the weapons, making it difficult to identify a precise classification, the analysis of some aspects, such as the length and width of the blades, has made it possible to compare the known specimens with forms widespread from the end of the fourth to the first half of the third century BCE (fig. 19.2).[16]

A few more elements can be recovered from the

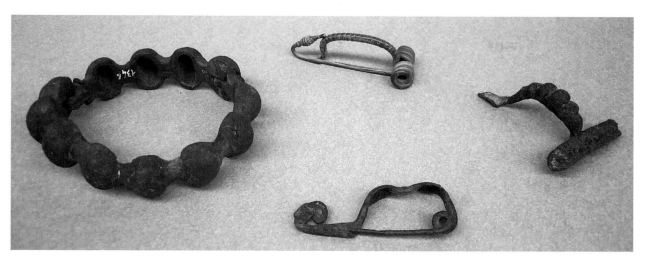

FIGURE 19.1. Metallic items of adornment (*ovoli*-type bracelet and La Tène type *fibulae*) from the Celtic tombs of Marzabotto, end of the fourth–3rd centuries BCE. After Govi 2007:74.

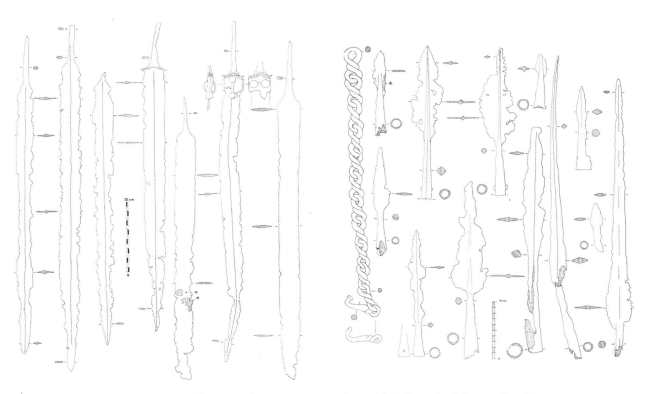

FIGURE 19.2. Iron swords, spear points, and metal belt from the Celtic tombs of Marzabotto, end of the fourth–third century BCE. After Morpurgo 2016: fig. 3.

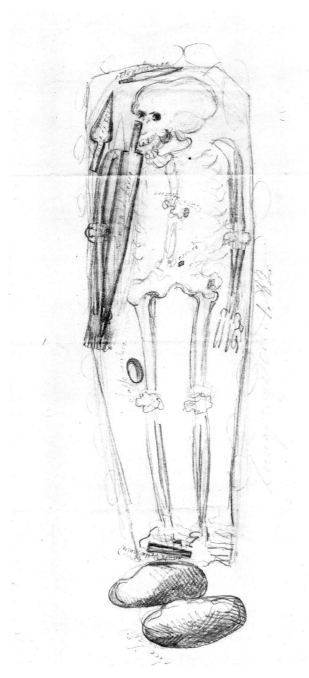

FIGURE 19.3. Sketch of a Celtic tomb from the necropolis discovered at the foot of the Acropolis, first decades of the third century BCE. Copyright Archiginnasio Public Library. After Brizzolara, Lippolis, and Vitali 2001:81.

study of belts. In fact, three tubular rings in bronze sheeting, published by Brizio and unfortunately no longer preserved, attest to a suspension system with straps made of leather or another organic material. It is a peculiar typology from a period that does not go beyond the recent Dùchcov-Münsingen Celtic phase, dating from the final decades of the fourth and the beginning of the third century BCE. This belt precedes the introduction of the metal chain, a typology also documented in at least two cases in Marzabotto (fig. 19.2) and that—from the beginning of the third century BCE—must have been widespread.[17]

The scarce representation of the Celtic warrior figure, recognizable only in four of the twenty-five tombs discovered, is apparently anomalous. This aspect, which is not easy to explain,[18] is not however isolated. In fact, it brings Marzabotto closer to what has been learned from Bologna and especially the necropolis excavated in the 1990s in Casalecchio di Reno (*see map 3*),[19] a context with which close ties have been highlighted several times.[20]

As observed in the tombs of Casalecchio, and differently from what is documented in Bologna or in the sites of the Idice Valley, also in Marzabotto, for example, the presence of pottery within the grave goods is completely sporadic.

On the other hand, at least four burials attest the practice of placing a small piece of metal in the hands of the deceased, or in proximity to them, which can be interpreted as "Charon's obol." This custom is the result of a purely local tradition and finds precise comparisons in the Etruscan-Celtic grave goods of Monte Bibele (*see map 3*).

As already mentioned, during the nineteenth-century investigations no cartographic documentation was made, only a series of isolated sketches, unfortunately not correlated with each other (fig. 19.3). A few years later, the generic presence of tombs with small *cippi* arranged randomly in the area of the Misanello hill was reported.

The architect V. Levi, who created a map of the visible urban structures on behalf of E. Brizio, recorded the position occupied by these grave markers, which unfortunately had nothing to do with the actual ancient distribution of the Gallic tombs.[21]

Only in recent years has an extensive review of the nineteenth-century documentation allowed us to put forward some hypotheses about the original layout of this small funerary nucleus.[22] It was in fact possible to recognize three groups of tombs distinct from both a spatial and partly a typological point of view. Among these, a group of three individuals emerges, possibly identified as a family unit: next to a warrior's tomb unique in this burial ground, there were two tombs of females that could belong to an adult and an adolescent. Finally, as already mentioned, several burials with *fibulae*, some bracelets, and in an exceptional case a bronze necklace type referred to as a *torque*,[23] an ornament traditionally unrelated to the Boic custom, suggest the reuse of wells inside Etruscan houses as burial places.[24]

The panorama thus outlined has been integrated with a series of discoveries made during the most recent investigations. The latest discoveries at the site, responsible for having significantly changed the perception of the Etruscan city of Kainua, have also concerned the later phases of the center.[25] Research conducted in the sanctuary of Tinia has revealed four other inhumations in the southwestern corner of the sacred building, one of a newborn of about five to eight months old, that seem to belong to the Celtic settlement[26] (*see map 9*). The tombs, although mostly already disturbed, were furnished with grave goods and above all had structural aspects found in the Gallic necropoleis investigated during the nineteenth century.

As already observed in the burial ground on the Acropolis, for example, it is interesting to highlight the documented reuse in one of these burials of a large quantity of travertine that had been part of the temple *podium*. This practice suggests that at the time of the burials the sacred building was not only no longer used, but had already been quite substantially despoiled.

While this evidence enriches the panorama of funerary discoveries, some recent reflections shed new light on this phase of the settlement also from other points of view. Some new information has emerged about the relationship between the end of the Etruscan city and the beginning of the Celtic occupation. Marzabotto has always been considered the paradigmatic context of the process of urban deconstruction that must have happened in Etruria Padana during this period. It is common knowledge that following the Celtic invasion the city was quickly divested of all its urban functions, thus becoming an austere military outpost of the Reno Valley. This trade route was part of a significant reorganization in favor of the easternmost trans-Apennine routes, where settlements such as Monte Bibele in the Idice Valley (*see map 3*) have played an important mediating role since then.[27]

Some scholars have consequently suggested that Marzabotto could represent the site *Melpum* mentioned by literary sources. The latter is a city in Etruria Padana still unidentified by archaeologists and of disputed geographical location, which was reputedly destroyed by a coalition of the tribes of Insubres, Boii, and Senones in 386 BCE on the same day on which Furius Camillus conquered Veii (Pliny, *N.H.* 3.125).[28]

Nevertheless, if we remain firmly anchored to the data currently available, on the one hand, a gap emerges between the end of the Etruscan presence, datable from the archaeological point of view to around the middle of the fourth century BCE, and the beginning of the period of permanent settlement of the plateau by groups of trans-Alpine origin, dated from the end of the fourth century BCE; on the other hand, there is also a substantial absence of evidence regarding the destruction of the center by "invading" Gauls.

Starting from these elements, some research has begun to propose the hypothesis that the changes recorded in the Etruscan settlement are not necessarily linked to dramatic and sudden events, but rather represent an indirect consequence of wider changes that the Celtic invasion caused to the trading system of Etruria Padana.[29] Therefore, exactly around the middle of the fourth century BCE, some clues allow us to highlight a sharp decline in contacts with the Tyrrhenian Etruscan manufacturing centers. This could not fail to harm Marzabotto, a city with a strong handicraft vocation that fulfilled the role of intermediary with the Tyrrhenian sector.[30]

The most interesting new evidence, however, more specifically concerns the features of the community that settled in the ancient Etruscan center from the end of the fourth century BCE, which are more complex than previously recognized.

A review of the materials from the old excavations, supplemented by some new lucky finds, has made it possible to collect a small, but very significant, corpus of Etruscan production materials from outside of Marzabotto. These finds date to a period from the end of the fourth into the third century BCE, allowing us to relate them to the phase of the Gallic occupation of the plateau.[31] These objects enrich the already quite substantial panorama of Tyrrhenian Etruscan imports north of the Apennines, but above all they prompt us to review the characteristics of closure and isolation traditionally attributed to this phase in Marzabotto.[32]

For example, a small fragment of an Etruscan red-figure *kylix*, dated to the end of the fourth century BCE, has been traced to a northern Tyrrhenian production, possibly from Chiusi. Moreover, due to the presence of a characteristic braid decoration, it can be related to the group of over-painted *kylikes* of the "Sienese Workshop."[33]

Within the already well-known landscape of imports in the Po Valley, thanks to the finds in Bologna and the Etruscan-Celtic centers of the Idice Valley, there is a fragment of a bronze mirror with a depiction of Lasa (fig. 19.4), probably produced during the first half of the third century BCE by a workshop in northern Etruria, perhaps Volterra.[34] The well-known commercial contacts of Volterra with the Po Valley during the fourth and the third centuries BCE are even more evident thanks to a series of fragments of the most common black-gloss productions, including some *ky-*

FIGURE 19.5. Fragment of *skyphos* belonging to the Group of Ferrara T. 585 from the old excavations in the urban area, end of the fourth–first decades of the third century BCE. After Morpurgo 2016: fig. 9c.

likes and a bell krater, which is a shape that is not so common in this territory.[35]

A fragment of a large *skyphos* is also of Volterran production. Due to its shape, the clay mixture, and the presence of a peculiar over-painted spiral motif (fig. 19.5), it easily fits into the "Group of Ferrara T. 585," dated to the moment of transition from the fourth to the third century BCE.[36]

Some old and new findings enrich this overview of possible contributions from Tyrrhenian Etruria, allowing Marzabotto to be situated precisely among other well-known entities in the area.

Among the materials found in the nineteenth century there is a black-gloss *kantharos* with knotted handles. If in some aspects its shape seems to distinguish itself from the typically Volterran production prototypes well documented in Etruria Padana,[37] it compares quite precisely with a specimen of possible production from Arezzo (*see map 1*), dated to the end of the fourth century BCE.[38]

From the area of the sanctuary of Tinia come three fragments of an over-painted red-figure *kylix*, probably connected to the "*Sokra* Group." This find is quite significant, as it extends the panorama of possible origins also to the Tiber River district.[39]

Finally, there is a mirror in the Marzabotto museum whose precise context of discovery is not known, which due to the characteristic of the pear-shaped disc looks like a product of Praeneste from the first half of the third century BCE.[40]

The arrival of artifacts of such different origins therefore reveals how even in the fourth and third centuries BCE, Marzabotto maintained its role within the Apennine road network that continued to ensure robust exchanges between the Tyrrhenian and the Po

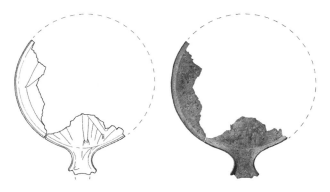

FIGURE 19.4. Fragments of a bronze mirror with a depiction of Lasa from the western *stenopos* near House 1, *Regio* IV, 2, end of the fourth–first decades of the third century BCE. After Govi 2018b: figs. 3a–b, d.

Valley areas, in a renewed political, economic, and cultural context.

Moreover, the fact that these objects circulated in the settlement testifies not only that the city was not excluded from the most up-to-date commercial circuits, but also that the choice of including them or not in the grave goods probably depended on ideological factors and on the different degree of cultural contact with the Etruscan element, rather than for economic reasons. The same situation is also recorded for the nearby Celtic community of Casalecchio di Reno,[41] a site with which close links have already been highlighted (see map 3).

To the small groups already installed in Casalecchio di Reno can be attributed the initial settlement in the Kainua plateau in the last decades of the fourth century BCE.[42] However, the most recent finds make it possible to revise our assessment, also from this point of view, enhancing the probable mixed nature of the community that settled here. According to the information that is emerging about the population of the area during this phase, several clues point to the fact that even in Marzabotto, groups of trans-Alpine origin, possibly stratified over time, may have been integrated with individuals of different origin.

One potential source of information derives from the observation of a particular class of material, well documented within the center and the object in recent times of a completely renewed attention, because of the interesting implications it offers on a cultural level: this is pottery for domestic use, handmade and often with coarse inclusions and irregular surfaces, and whose frequent chromatic variations appear to depend on firing processes carried out in structures with low technological quality. These aspects, the morphological characteristics of the vases and at times the decorative schemes adopted, make these finds essentially unrelatable to the typical repertoire of the Etruscan Po Valley production, allowing them instead to be placed within the sphere of well-known Ligurian traditional craftsmanship.

Furthermore, these finds do not appear to be isolated, but are part of an increasingly rich body of evidence that even in these more eastern areas of the Bolognese Apennines[43] may allow us to recognize the as yet unspecified role of this ethnic component.[44] Moreover, the cooperation and alliances between Celts and Ligurians are documented in numerous circumstances by literary sources,[45] and frequently consistent clues, especially in the Emilian area, allow us to document this integration also on an archaeological level.[46]

A recent investigation with petrographic analyses has ascertained the production of these ceramics in Marzabotto, and highlighted a particular concentration in contexts of the Etruscan city linked to the presence of water, for which a sacred purpose, although uncertain, seems at least conceivable.[47]

Among these, the Water Shrine, a small sacred area linked to the cults of healing and built on the northern edge of the city at a natural spring (see map 5), is particularly noteworthy.

The recovery of this type of ceramic, notable both for its quantity and for its variety of forms, contributes to our understanding of a phase of frequentation of the sanctuary following the fall of the Etruscan city, that other materials, including an ancient bronze La Tène–type *fibula*, had already indicated.

The evidence reviewed, therefore, allows us to reconstruct an overview that, although partial and sometimes elusive, provides a new and decidedly more complex image of the city during this later phase. A picture emerges of a place that, although undoubtedly modified and resized in its urban structure, nevertheless maintained an active role in the commercial and cultural dynamics of the territory, remaining less extraneous to the influences of the Greek-Etruscan world than previously thought.

An impression that actually adheres to what has been handed down from the literary sources seems to be gradually reconstructed. The sources refer to an organization of the Celtic population without cities and urban centers, but structured in villages on the plain (*vici*), places of exchange and trade (*fora*), and hillside settlements in a strategic position (*castella*). Within such a wide and diversified framework, the available data allow us to recognize Marzabotto as a village not only linked to the rural exploitation of the territory in this later period. Perhaps by virtue of its sanctuaries, whose value was at least partially recognized, it became a meeting place for a population that evidence of material culture invites us to imagine as ethnically heterogeneous.

NOTES

1. On this issue, see Sassatelli 1983 and Vitali 1984, with further references.
2. For recent papers and previous references on this topic, see Malnati and Violante 1995; Sassatelli 2003; Ortalli 2004; Vitali 2004; Vitali 2007; Kysela 2010.
3. Gozzadini 1865: pl. I, P; Gozzadini 1870:3, pl. II, figs. 1–3.
4. Brizio 1887a:508–515; Brizio 1890:150–161.
5. Gozzadini 1870:5–6; Brizio 1887a:515–526; Brizio 1890: 87–100.
6. For a recent review, see Morpurgo 2016: fig. 2.
7. Brizio 1887b:48–49.
8. Brizio 1887a: esp. 502–532.
9. Kruta Poppi 1975.
10. Vitali 1985a:58–68; Vitali 2001a.
11. Combinatorial analysis starting from Marzabotto's grave goods led researchers to consider the placement of the bracelets in an asymmetric way, with a very clear preference for the left arm in terms of number and quality, one of the distinctive elements of Boic women compared to those of the other Celtic Cisalpine groups (Kruta 1980:30). On this issue, see the doubts expressed in Vitali 2008:15.
12. Brizio 1887a: VII, 21.
13. Kruta Poppi 1975:356; Vitali 2001a:84.
14. For a recent summary of the Italian evidence with relative distribution chart, see Fábry 2008:128, figs. 2–3.
15. Fábry 2011:296.
16. For swords, see Kruta Poppi 1975:358, nos. 27–33, fig. 7; for spear points, see Kruta Poppi 1975:360–363, nos. 34–45, fig. 8.
17. Kruta Poppi 1975:359–360. For nonpreserved specimens, see Brizio 1890:397–398.
18. The anthropological determinations carried out on the unarmed male burials of the necropolis of Monte Tamburino revealed that they were elderly individuals (Vitali 2005:378). It seems risky, however, to automatically extend the data to other contexts.
19. Ortalli 1995a; Ortalli 2008.
20. Vitali 2005:370.
21. Brizio 1890: pl. I.
22. Vitali 2001a.
23. Vitali 2008.
24. To explain the existence of this practice of burial in wells, initially interpreted as a particular form of funeral ritual (Gozzadini 1865:14; Gozzadini 1870:10; Brizio 1890: 87–90), more recently these have come to be regarded as reflecting an accidental recourse to such structures in emergency conditions (Malnati and Violante 1995:106, with further references). For a recent discussion of the topic, see Zanoni 2011.
25. For an updated summary on the Celtic phase of Marzabotto, see Morpurgo 2016.
26. Sassatelli 2009a:330.
27. See for instance Malnati and Violante 1995:103; Sassatelli 2003:237; Vitali 2005:368–371.
28. De Marinis 1977:29; Baldacci 1983:153. This theory was later refuted; see Colonna 1989:22, n. 25.
29. Kruta 1987:313 and, more recently, Kruta 2008:226.
30. Noteworthy, for instance, is the case of bronze vases in the grave goods from Spina highlighted in Govi 2006:113–114.
31. Morpurgo 2016:147–151.
32. Cf. chapter 5 of this volume.
33. Gaucci 2010:67, no. 131, figs. 63, 72, with references.
34. Govi 2018b:27–28; *CSE* Italia, 8, no. 3.
35. Morpurgo 2016:148–151; Gaucci 2010; Gaucci 2022.
36. Morpurgo 2016:151.
37. For an overview of the evidence, see Morpurgo 2016: 151.
38. For some vases found in the necropolis of Monte Tamburino near Monte Bibele, the possible albeit rare provenance of the black-gloss pottery from the area of Arezzo has already been hypothesized, as it is difficult to distinguish this production from the Volterran one due to its good technical qualities (Parrini 2008:110–111).
39. Gaucci 2022.
40. Govi 2018b:32, *CSE* Italia 8, no. 12. The possible involvement of the Praenestine workshops in the commercial dynamics of this phase had already been highlighted in relation to the discovery of strigils in the Celtic contexts of Bologna and surrounding area (Vitali 2006:2, with references).
41. Also in this case in relation to a strictly Celtic funerary documentation, the presence of imported Etruscan materials in contexts attributable to the Celtic-phase settlement is attested (Ferrari and Mengoli 2005:19–25; Ortalli 2008:317).
42. Vitali 2008:14.
43. If the contacts with the Ligurian *ethnos* are well known from the archaeological point of view in the Western Emilia sector, especially in the territory between the provinces of Piacenza, Parma, and Reggio Emilia, some clues partly already exploited in the past show that the Bolognese territory too has not remained isolated from these influences (for the testimonies from Monte Bibele, see most recently Penzo 2016; for some preliminary reflections on Ligurian material culture in Marzabotto, see Vitali 2006; for the documentation from Casalecchio di Reno, see Ferrari and Mengoli 2005:37–45 and 114–133. In general, on the topic, see also Vitali 2014).
44. On the issue and with further references, see Morpurgo 2016.
45. Peyre 1987:103–104; Salomone Gaggero 2003:127–133.
46. On the relations between Ligurians and Etruscans, see the rich summary with an extensive bibliography in Macellari 2008. For the most recent period, when as is well known the collapse of Etruscan dominance following the Celtic invasion led to a consistent control of the Emilian Apennines by the Ligurian populations, see instead Kruta Poppi 1981; Malnati 2004: esp. 161–163; Vitali 2009, all with further references.
47. Braga, Tirtei, and Trevisanello 2022.

CHAPTER 20

THE ROMAN PERIOD

ALESSANDRO CAMPEDELLI

In the middle of the third century BCE the Italian peninsula was unified under Roman rule from the Straits of Messina to the city of Rimini and the Magra River line. The territory located to the north of this geographic limit, known by the name of Gallia Cispadana (that is, present-day Emilia-Romagna)—called *Regio VIII* in the Augustan age and subsequently Aemilia—was populated by various Gallic tribes (Polybius, *Histories* 2.17.4–8). Among these the Boii, who occupied the central-eastern Apennine area south of the fertile Po Valley, were certainly the most numerous, proud, and organized.[1]

The Romanization of their territory and more generally the grafting of Roman culture onto the Po area found its significant *terminus post quem* in the foundation of the Latin colony of Ariminum (Rimini; see *map 1 and map 2*) in 268 BCE (Livy, *Periochae* 15.5), but only the defeat of the Gallic coalition in the Battle of Talamone in 225 BCE (Pol. 2.22–25; Livy, *Periochae* 20) proved a milestone in the subsequent colonizing expansion of Rome in this area. It is no coincidence that, subjected to the insurgents, in 218 BCE the Roman government decided to found the Latin colony of Placentia (Piacenza)[2] on their territory, thus creating the northernmost Roman outpost of the Po Valley (Pol. 3.40.3–4; Livy, *Periochae* 20.18). At the same time, Rome promoted the spontaneous settlement of Italic peoples in the Etruscan-Celtic centers of Mutina (Modena) and Bononia (Bologna) at the foot of the Apennine ridge, in order to enhance the Roman presence along important military itineraries and commercial routes.[3]

The Second Punic War (218–202 BCE) and the descent of Hannibal into Italy arrested and froze Roman expansion in the Cispadana. The Gallic peoples of the region not only participated as protagonists in the Hannibal campaigns, but they continued to fight fiercely against the Romans even when Hannibal had left the peninsula.[4] In 200 BCE, the Boii, together with other Gallic and Ligurian tribes, even conquered the colony of Placentia. In addition to this episode, the Romans continued to suffer other failures, but finally managed to take their revenge against the Boii, who were definitively subdued. In fact, from 191 BCE the Gauls of the Cispadana no longer constituted a real threat to Rome (Livy, *History of Rome* 36.40.5).[5]

The Roman conquest of the Po Valley resulted in the general abandonment of the Gallic settlements, located on the lower hillslopes at the mouth of the Apennine rivers in the plain or, as in the case of Marzabotto, with a strategic function for control of the river valleys, whose crossings connected with Etruria, to the advantage of settlements corresponding to urban standards, in less steep and flatter areas.

However, physical geography and historical events also contributed to different modes of occupation and distribution of the Roman population between the plains and the Apennines. Romanization, carried out in the years between 190 and 183 BCE, was a process that derived from the need to cover, with the five colonies (Placentia, Parma, Mutina, Bononia, and Ariminum) located at the foot of the Apennines, a line of vital importance, namely, the northern border of the Italic federation that had been repeatedly violated by the Gauls and by Hannibal about thirty years earlier.[6]

The strategic significance of the operation was reaffirmed by the creation of the Via Aemilia by Aemilius Lepidus in the year of his consulate (187 BCE). This was an axis intended to connect the various colonies to each other, enhancing their resistance.

The process of metamorphosis that the Romans created in the Apennine and foothills area of the Reno Valley therefore began with the foundation of the Latin colony of Bononia in 189 BCE (Livy, *History of Rome* 37.57.7–8), around which the organization of the surrounding area and its population was to gravitate.[7] For the most part covered with forests and dotted with marshes, the *ager bononiensis* was now divided by the orthogonal lines of centuriation.[8] Deforested and gradually rehabilitated, the vast strip of plain downstream of the Via Aemilia was ready to welcome the fruit of the land tradition of colonial origin, that is, an organizational model characterized by a stable order, based on an agricultural population distributed in a rather structured way, almost according to modular schemes, and widespread in the countryside of the plain.[9]

The situation was different in the Apennine areas, where, in the initial phase of Romanization, more archaic organizational structures survived, characterized by scattered housing units and inserted within a pastoral world, whose main resources consisted in farming, in milk and other dairy products, and in skins and meat from their flocks. The forest characterized the landscape, and no intervention to adapt to human needs intended as a real reclamation was carried out during this period. Added to this, the Via Flaminia minor was officially established in 187 BCE, which led to a temporary downgrading of the trans-Apennine routes in the Reno Valley, and the shift of the main road network to the Idice Valley, further east.[10]

This situation began to change at the beginning of the first century BCE, when the space occupied by *saltus* and *silvae* (groves and forests) characterizing the foothills of the Reno Valley was reduced, thanks to the development of some population concentrations (in the forms of *pagus* or *vicus*), such as those documented in Casalecchio di Reno and Sasso Marconi (*see map 4*).[11]

In Casalecchio di Reno, in addition to the remains of the ancient centuriation, with fields divided by gravel roads and lateral drainage ditches, archaeological research has made it possible to identify important evidence of a complex urban-rustic villa (first century BCE to first century CE), located in the center of a productive and commercial space extending over an area of over 10,000 square meters, including a rustic part (with vases, *dolii*, tools for agricultural production) and a residential part, more elegant, with antefixes on the roofs and worked downspouts.[12] The presence in the vicinity of other traces of permanent occupation and above all of two vast necropoleis, with a total of three hundred tombs, datable to a period from the first to fifth century CE, certainly refer to a rural territorial district, presumably a *pagus*, which arose in the immediate hilly hinterland of the funerary finds.[13]

Important signs of the Roman presence are also found in the center of Sasso Marconi, whose territory occupies the first hilly zone of the Apennines. The area is in fact inserted within an anthropic landscape that was heavily populated in Roman times (settlement structures, places of worship, necropoleis) and where it is likely that a significant aggregate of houses and land (*vicus*) developed after the end of the Republican age.[14]

From the middle of the first century BCE, several individual Roman farms brought a new population to the innermost area of the valley; these were connected to each other by a network of minor roads that crisscrossed the hills between the Reno and its main tributary, the Setta stream.[15] The presence of a significant number of these productive systems (*domus rusticae*) has made it possible to determine the guidelines for the *positio loci*, for which ridges seem to be preferred, on slopes that were open to the south or southeast, whose exposure enabled the cultivation of vegetables and fruit trees, as in the case of the contexts identified in the locality of Sibano, Cantaiola, Fontana, and Pian di Venola, in the middle section of the Reno Valley, and in the locality of Osteria Leona and Canova di Ignano, along the Setta Valley (*see map 4*).[16]

The best-known cases show a general tendency to use modest architecture, with minimal differentiation of interior spaces, barely perceptible thanks to the rare presence of mosaic floors, as opposed to an abundance of terracotta floors (*opus spicatum*), suitable for work activities and therefore related to craftsmanship and the processing and conservation of products, or to agricultural practices. The foundations were mostly made with local, easily available materials, and few traces of the elevations, probably built in perishable material (clay and wood), are preserved. These farms, although small properties, testify to the spread of the Roman productive and organizational model even in these peripheral areas, although limited to forms of material self-subsistence and economic self-sufficiency.

There are, however, more complex situations attributable to rustic buildings (*villae rusticae*), always directly managed and probably associated with more numerous family communities, but functional for the management of a more extensive and exploited landed property with mixed cultivation. The internal economy of these more complex realities is based on the processing and conservation of agricultural products, or products derived from livestock. Although the exploitation is mainly aimed at the subsistence of the inhabitants of the farm, it is possible that in some cases it included the production of a surplus, probably destined for the rural market. The proximity of these installations to main roads or river traffic routes supports this hypothesis, as does their organization in correspondence with the wider terraces of the left bank of the Reno River, as happens for the best documented cases in the Pian di Misano (*see map 4*), in the area pertaining to Marzabotto. Moreover, the agricultural toponym "Misano," with which the hypothesized name of the Etruscan city of Marzabotto (*Misa*) has long been incorrectly associated, refers to a Latin land name.

The Roman settlement of the Misano plateau dates to the middle of the first century BCE, when a rustic building was installed there for the agricultural and pastoral exploitation of the area (fig. 20.1). The remains of the villa, identified during the excavations of 1966 and 1974–1976, are located at the extreme northeastern edge of the fluvial terrace (*see map 5*). While some installations (kilns) are inserted within the limits of the Etruscan block, what remains of the the villa structure (rooms A, B) is built on the roadway of the *plateia* B of the Etruscan city, between *Regiones* I and III (*see map 5*). These circumstances confirm that the remains of the ancient city had for the most part already disappeared, obliterated by levels of land and vegetation that left the plateau free and available for agricultural exploitation.[17]

The rooms of the farm, of which only traces remain of the foundations made of dry stones, were built right on *plateia* B. They incorporated the wall of the northern limit of the *plateia* into the new structures. These are probably service areas, rectangular in shape, side by side, with the larger (room B) characterized by the presence of an interior well for water, lined inside with a jacket made of small and medium-sized river stones. From the compartment on the side (room A) a drainage channel begins with an oblique northwest–southeast course, flowing further south into a second, larger water pipe. The latter connects to the complex water drainage system that all the rustic buildings had and which allowed the rainwater to drain to the east, toward the river. It is very likely that the system developed in correspondence with the southeastern sectors of the *Regio* I, judging from the plan of what has been recognized, but the structure was never completely excavated.

What remains of the villa is characterized by very modest building techniques and materials. Notices of the discovery in this sector of the plateau of some fragments of mosaic pavements and of clay column bases and the recovery during excavation of some fragments of monochromatic painted plaster suggest a structure with simple decorative forms, but nevertheless equipped with a residential sector (*pars urbana*). It probably had a colonnade and a productive part, devoted to the processing and conservation of agricultural products (*pars fructuaria*).

Next to this organization of spaces, there was also a sector located a little further south that was used for the production of clay materials (mainly building bricks, but the production of domestic pottery, *opus doliare* and *instrumentum* are not excluded). Here were the remains of two kilns, located about 1.5 m from each other, which testify to the level of self-sufficiency of the rustic complex.[18] The western one still retains the structure of refractory clay walls that must have supported a perforated cooking floor, also made of refrac-

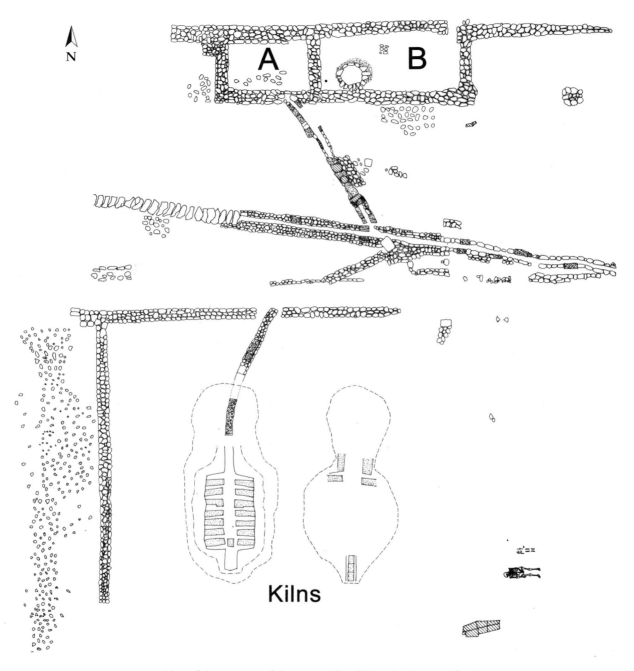

FIGURE 20.1. Plan of the remains of the rustic villa of Pian di Misano. After Govi 2007:76.

tory material, on which the material to be fired was placed. The remains of the kiln on the east are less consistent, despite having dimensions and a shape quite similar to the previous one. No elements pertaining to the covering of the kiln structures have been documented, an indication of a probable construction in nondurable materials, which were changed at each firing cycle.[19]

Recently, Roman materials and remains of production/craft installations have also been identified northeast of the rustic villa. The proximity of these installations to the site occupied by the peripteral temple of

Tinia, in addition to partially modifying the Etruscan structures, indicates that in this phase a significant activity of spoliation and recovery of building material was carried out for the construction needs of the new Roman building.

As documented by the *FORTIS*-type stamps on the lamps, the Arezzo *sigillata* pottery, and other objects of material culture, the rustic productive plant of Pian di Misano is located within a chronological period from the first century BCE to the first century CE, and conforms well to the population picture that characterized the middle Reno Valley in this period. The commercial relations of this hilly area are also clear, attesting the arrival of *sigillata* from Arezzo in the early imperial age, as part of the normal commercial circuits that led from the Tuscan city to the Po Valley, perhaps also on a renewed route along the road that reached Bononia from the Apennine ridge.

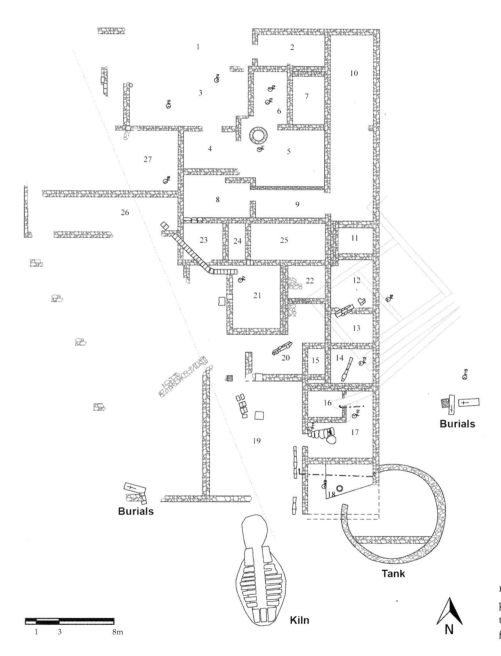

FIGURE 20.2. Sassatello, plan of the Roman structures. After Roversi 2013:131, fig. 7.

Moreover, in the same period, other artifacts such as oil lamps indicate commercial exchanges, mainly with the Bononia territory, as well as with the Po Valley in general.

Similar chronological developments, almost identical structural components (there was a kiln in this case, too), and production purposes characterized the layout of the rustic villa identified in Sassatello (fig. 20.2),[20] a little further downstream from Marzabotto. In this case the number of excavated rooms is greater and therefore the organization of the spaces is more perceptible, with a distinction between production rooms, characterized by simple rammed earth floors, and residential ones with hexagonal flooring, in *opus spicatum*, in *cocciopesto* and in mosaic with black and white tiles.[21]

This type of agricultural exploitation, centered on the *fundi* of rustic villas settled along the valley floor, lasted for almost two centuries, until starting from the second century CE, the effects of a more general economic crisis began to affect the settlement and the productive organization of the Apennine area, with results that are often clearly perceptible in the archaeological record, as in the case of the production plants of Marzabotto[22] and Sassatello.[23] During the second and third centuries CE, unlike what happened in the Po Valley, where the phenomenon did not lead to a complete depopulation of the fields, the signs of deterioration and the demise of many residential areas testify to a real diminishing of the ancient population.[24] The human presence seems to be reduced to itinerant and perhaps occasional uses of preexisting structures, as in the case of the rustic villa of Sassatello after the fourth century CE,[25] until it reaches a low point and in many cases a definitive collapse during the profound crisis of the sixth century CE.

In the area of the Marzabotto site, structural remains of the period of Late Antiquity are almost completely missing, with the exception of three late burials identified to the west of the kilns.[26] Only sporadic material evidence is reported, consisting of a few coins[27] and some ceramic vases recovered inside an Etruscan well.[28] This archaeological documentation leads to a hypothesis of occasional or passing frequentation of the plateau, linked to the transit and temporary shelter of those who were still plowing the now unpaved track of the ancient *Via del Reno*.

NOTES

1. Vitali 2001b:227–239. In particular on the Boii, see sources, discussion, and bibliography in Bandelli 2009:192–193.

2. The Placentia deduction aimed to cover the western side of the Stradella Pass and the road that connected northern Etruria to the Cisalpina, and at the same time to guard the ford further downstream along the Po River.

3. Vitali 2004:283–284; Ortalli 2005:479–482.

4. Brizzi 2015:112–113.

5. Cicala, Donati, and Susini 2006:23–24.

6. For a general overview of the historical assumptions and characters of the colonization of this area, consult the references offered in Marini Calvani 2000; Sassatelli and Donati 2005.

7. Curina 2015:164.

8. For the specific case of the *ager centuriatus* of Bononia: Bottazzi 1991:43; Giorgetti 2000:65–66.

9. On the settlement structure of the suburban area of Bononia see Scagliarini 2005. On the rustic settlement typologies of the region, as well as of the specific Bolognese area, see Ortalli 1994.

10. On the situation of the local road network, in relation to the regional framework, and for other bibliographical references, see Quilici 2000:75–77. For specific studies on the route of the Via Flaminia minor see Foschi 2003:19–36.

11. The first center, Casalecchio di Reno, is located about 4 km west-southwest of Bologna, at the foot of the hills, exactly at the outlet in the plain of the Reno River valley and, consequently, at the intersection of important traffic routes in use since ancient times. Conversely, Sasso Marconi occupies the first hilly area of the Apennines between the lower valley of the Reno River and the lower portion of the valley of the Setta stream to the southeast (*see map 4*).

12. The various excavation campaigns made it possible to identify a dense infrastructural network set on the axis of the centuriation, characterized by regular road axes and effective water control (Ortalli 1995b:81–82).

13. Ortalli 1997:602

14. The *vicus*, probably built around a large urban-rustic villa, developed in the area occupied today by the church of San Lorenzo. Here on several occasions since the end of the nineteenth century in the surroundings of the ecclesiastical building, the fields have revealed that they conceal hexagonal flooring, fragments of precious marble, and mosaics. Among these, fragments of a large mosaic decorated with a colonnade adorned with leaves, which extended from the old cemetery (closer to the church than the current one) to the road (re-

mains of this flooring were long preserved in the rectory). A bas-relief with a child's head also seems to come from the same area (where there was a cemetery from the imperial age with *cappuccina* tombs and grave goods consisting of clay oil lamps and bronze coins) (Michelini 2004:141–144). The *vicus* area seems to be able to extend also to the whole area between the Podere Chiusura (Palazzo Vescovile, now called Villa Marini) and the railway station, where numerous ceramic fragments were found (Penzo 2007:19–21).

15. For a study of the Reno Valley see Scagliarini Corlaita 1989; De Maria 1992.

16. For the individual contexts see Scarani 1963; Venturi and Foschi 1980; De Maria 1992.

17. Govi 2007:76–77.

18. The kilns are of type IIb (Cuomo di Caprio 1971–1972:429–434; Cuomo di Caprio 2007:522–524, fig. 169), well documented in Emilia Romagna.

19. De Maria, Sassatelli, and Vitali 1978a:82–91.

20. The Sassatello site is located at km 70 of the SS 64 Porrettana, within an area bounded to the west by the State Road and to the east by the Bologna-Pistoia-Florence railway section (*see map 4*).

21. The archaeological excavations of this context took place in 1972 during excavation works for the construction of industrial warehouses. The structures were only partially excavated and then reinterred (Scagliarini Corlaita 1978:20, 30–31; Mansuelli 1982:80–81).

22. De Maria 1992:226–227.

23. Roversi 2013:127–129.

24. Ortalli 1996:12–16.

25. This settlement phase is evidenced by a series of channels that cut the walls of the previous structure, made up of brick material probably reused. The area is also affected by the presence of three simple interment burials. The ceramic data seems to frame this phase chronologically in the period fifth–seventh centuries CE (Roversi 2015:131–138).

26. These are two simple graves in the earth (one of which is for a child) and a *cappuccina* burial built with clay tiles. The chronology remains uncertain due to the almost total absence of accompanying elements (Govi 2007:77).

27. The Roman coin finds consist of a specimen from the Tiberian period, a Trajanic *denarius*, an *antoninianus* of Diocletian, and a *follis* of Licinius.

28. The four jugs, two of which have been completely reconstructed, have shapes that can be traced back to late Roman or Byzantine specimens. These were recovered within the "layer II" of the well of House 2, "Mansuelli Block" of *Regio* IV, 1 (Durante and Gervasini 1987:317).

APPENDIX A

INSCRIPTIONS FROM KAINUA-MARZABOTTO

ANDREA GAUCCI

Inscriptions are listed in order according to location. An asterisk (*) after the inscription number indicates that the document is lost.

ROADBEDS

1 (figs. 10.3, 10.4). Bucchero amphora.
 mi śataluś
 From the roadbed of the *stenopos* west of House 1, *Regio* IV, 2. Sassatelli and Gaucci 2010: no. 435.

2 (fig. 10.4). Bucchero open shape.
 ]*iu*
From the roadbed of the *stenopos* west of House 1, *Regio* IV, 2. Sassatelli and Gaucci 2010: no. 438.

3 (fig. 10.4). Bucchero closed shape (?).
 a χ
From the roadbed of *plateia* A near the head house of *Regio* V, 5. Sassatelli 1994a: no. 279.

REGIO I, 4A–4B: TEMPLE OF UNI AND ITS TEMENOS (PRECINCT)

4 (fig. 10.4). Bucchero lid.
 ]*alθi veia*[/] *urur*
From a circular altar. *REE* 82: no. 5.

5 (fig. 10.4; *see also fig. 8.2, right*). Bucchero open shape.
 ]× *unialθi*
From a layer north of the temple. *REE* 79: no. 64.

6 (fig. 10.4; *see also fig. 8.2, left and center*). Bucchero amphora (two fragments).
 kainu[*śpural*[
Within a foundation wall of the temple. *REE* 79: no. 63.

7 (fig. 10.4). Gray-ware plate
 vei
From the trench parallel to the reconstruction of the northwestern perimeter corner of the *temenos*. *REE* 80: no. 2.

8 (fig. 10.4). Coarse-ware jar (*olla*).
 ka
From the layer within the trench, parallel to the reconstruction of the northwestern perimeter corner of the *temenos*. *REE* 80: no. 4.

REGIO I, 5: TEMPLE OF TINIA AND ITS TEMENOS (PRECINCT)

9 (figs. 10.1, 10.4). Bronze sheet.
 larθ lentiu vel[× ---]
 muntie śpural v[× ---]
 arnθ kapruś śa[× ---]
 hecce larisal [× ---]
 eklalθrestas[× ---]
From the western side of the *temenos*. Govi 2014b.

10 (fig. 10.4). Bucchero cup.
 ]*ni kainuaθi* ×[
From the *temenos*. *REE* 79: no. 59; also Meiser 2014, Fe 3.4, with wrong chronology.

11 (fig. 10.4). Bucchero jug (*olpe*).
 tiniaś . ka[*---turu*]*ke*
From the *temenos*. *REE* 79: no. 61.

12 (fig. 10.4). Bucchero jug (*olpe*) or jar (*olla*).
 tins
Layer from the western side of the *temenos*. *REE* 79: no. 60; also Meiser 2014: Fe 4.1.

REGIO II, 1: POTTERY WORKSHOP ("GREAT FURNACE")

13 (fig. 10.4). Bucchero cup.
tin[
From the northern sector. *REE* 79: no. 62.

14 (fig. 10.5). Terracotta disk.
   larθuruś
Sassatelli 1994a: no. 70; Meiser 2014: Fe 2.8.

15 (fig. 10.5). Terracotta disk.
larisal kraikaluś
Sassatelli 1994a: no. 69; Meiser 2014: Fe 2.7.

16* (fig. 10.5). Terracotta disk.
  ]*lu*
Sassatelli 1994a: no. 71.

17* (fig. 10.5). Terracotta disk.
  ]*ar*[
Sassatelli 1994a: no. 72.

18 (fig. 10.5). Terracotta disk.
  al
Sassatelli 1994a: no. 74.

19 (fig. 10.5). Undefined shape (coarse ware?).
  ]×*v* : [
Sassatelli 1994a: no. 73.

REGIO IV, 1: HOUSES OF THE BLOCK

20 (fig. 10.5). Fine-ware cup.
  lave
Unknown context. Sassatelli 1994a: no. 90; Meiser 2014: Fe 2.27, ?]*lave*[?].

21 (fig. 10.5). Bucchero cup.
  ]*sa* but better *sa*
From House 1. Sassatelli 1994a: no. 91.

REGIO IV, 2: HOUSE 1

22 (fig. 10.5). Bucchero cup.
  a e v
From a surface layer. Sassatelli and Gaucci 2010: no. 439; Meiser 2014: Fe 9.1.

23 (figs. 10.3, 10.5). Bucchero amphora (handle).
  θina rakaluś
From a pit before the construction of the courtyard walls. Sassatelli and Gaucci 2010: no. 434; Meiser 2014: Fe 2.23.

24 (fig. 10.5). Bucchero cup.
  ] × *a e v z*
From the sewer along *plateia* B. Sassatelli and Gaucci 2010: no. 436; Meiser 2014: Fe 9.2.

25 (fig. 10.5). Deer horn (probably a handle).
  a χ f a ×
From a pit, probably a dismantled kiln. Sassatelli and Gaucci 2010: no. 440; Meiser 2014: Fe 0.7,]*a χ × a* —[.

26 (fig. 10.5). Bucchero cup.
  ]*z śakiu* [but probably better <*z*>*śakiu*[
From a pit, probably a dismantled kiln. Sassatelli and Gaucci 2010: no. 437; Meiser 2014: Fe 2.22; see also Maggiani 2009: 227,]*z śakn*[.

27 (fig. 10.5). Gray-ware one-handled cup (*tazza*).
  a e
From the sewer along *plateia* B. Sassatelli and Gaucci 2010: no. 441; Meiser 2014: Fe 9.3.

28 (fig. 10.5). Fine-ware mortar basin.
  ] *vetaluś* [
From a surface layer. Sassatelli and Gaucci 2010: no. 443; Meiser 2014: Fe 2.29.

29 (fig. 10.5). Gray-ware jug.
  pereken[
From a pit within the courtyard area. Sassatelli and Gaucci 2010: no. 442.

30 (fig. 10.6). Dolium.
  ] ×*iai*
From a pit, probably a dismantled kiln. Sassatelli and Gaucci 2010: no. 444; Meiser 2014: Fe 0.4.

31 (fig. 10.6). Fine-ware cup.
  θun
From a surface layer near a dismantled kiln. Sassatelli and Gaucci 2010: no. 445.

32 (fig. 10.6). Fine-ware cup.
  mi a χ[-?-]
From a surface layer. Sassatelli and Gaucci 2010: no. 446; Meiser 2014: Fe 2.28.

33 (fig. 10.6). Fine-ware cup.
   a χ
From a surface layer. Sassatelli and Gaucci 2010: no. 447.

34 (fig. 10.6). Bucchero cup.
   χui
From a pit, probably a dismantled kiln. Sassatelli and Gaucci 2010: no. 448; Meiser 2014: Fe 0.3.

35 (fig. 10.6). Bucchero cup.
   Probably a writing exercise (unreadable text)
From the sewer along *plateia* B. Sassatelli and Gaucci 2010: no. 449.

36 (fig. 10.6). Bucchero cup.
   ]iu[or *]ui[*
From a surface layer. Sassatelli and Gaucci 2010: no. 450.

37 (fig. 10.6). Bucchero cup.
   a e (?)
From the remains of a floor within room II of D compartment. Sassatelli and Gaucci 2010: no. 451.

REGIO IV, 4: CRAFT AREA

38* (fig. 10.6). Terracotta disk.
   aχalu
Inside a well near a kiln. Sassatelli 1994a: no. 4; Meiser 2014: Fe 2.12.

REGIO V, 2: SOUTHERNMOST HOUSE (*DOMUS LAUTUNI*)

39* (figs. 10.2, 10.6). Cobblestone.
   ||| *mi lavtunieś* (an asterisk and two strokes on the other side)
From the well within the central courtyard. Sassatelli 1994a: no. 1.

REGIO V, 3: NORTHERNMOST HOUSES

40 (fig. 10.6). Bucchero cup.
   mi v[
From the courtyard of zone VI. Sassatelli 1994a: no. 207.

41 (fig. 10.6). Bucchero cup.
   aθ
From the courtyard of zone VI. Sassatelli 1994a: no. 208.

42 (fig. 10.6). Bucchero cup.
   av
From a shovel test inside zone III D. Sassatelli 1994a: no. 209.

43 (fig. 10.6). Coarse-ware lid-cup.
   la
Origin uncertain. Sassatelli 1994a: no. 210.

REGIO V, 4: LAYER OF THE SIXTH CENTURY BCE (*STRATO DEL VI SEC.*).

44 (fig. 10.6). Bucchero chalice or *kantharos*.
   ] ×*ainuaθi*
Sassatelli 1994a: no. 261; Meiser 2014: Fe 0.2,]*ainuaθi* [.

45 (fig. 10.6). Bucchero cup.
   sa[
Sassatelli 1994a: no. 262.

REGIO V, 3–4: SHOVEL TESTS IN THE AREA OF NINETEENTH-CENTURY EXCAVATIONS

46 (fig. 10.6). Bucchero open shape.
   a χ
Sassatelli 1994a: no. 254

REGIO V, 5: NORTHERNMOST HOUSE

47 (fig. 10.7). Bucchero cup or chalice.
   mi larθial pumpunaś
Layer sealing the Archaic phase. Sassatelli 1994a: no. 277; Meiser 2014: Fe 2.24.

48 (fig. 10.7). Fine-ware cup.
   au but better *al*
From foundation layers. Sassatelli 1994a: no. 280.

49 (fig. 10.7). Terracotta disk.
   aχalu
From the sewer along *plateia* C. Sassatelli 1994a: no. 278; Meiser 2014: Fe 6.2.

REGIO V, 5: "FOUNDRY"

50 (fig. 10.7). Bucchero open shape.
   venelus̀ mi
Sassatelli 1994a: no. 292; Meiser 2014: Fe 2.2.

51 (fig. 10.7). Serpentinite calibrator.
]śualuś mi / θ /]teś /]a, lu]a
Sassatelli 1994a: no. 293; Meiser 2014: Fe 2.4+0.6.

REGIO V, 5

52 (fig. 10.7). Terracotta disk.
]miruś or]niruś
Inside a well of a house then ruined in the Reno River. Sassatelli 1994a: no. 9; Meiser 2014, repeated twice: Fe 2.11,]m̥ruś; Fe 2.26,]n̥ruś.

GENERICALLY WITHIN THE URBAN GRID, FROM NINETEENTH-CENTURY EXCAVATIONS

53 (fig. 10.7). Fine-ware cup.
śśi[
Sassatelli 1994a: no. 11; Meiser 2014: Fe 0.5.

54 (fig. 10.7). Coarse-ware lid-cup.
al
Sassatelli 1994a: no. 10.

55* (fig. 10.7). Cup (class not defined).
a / a e / v (?)
Sassatelli 1994a: no. 8.

56* (fig. 10.7). Lead ingot.
śinu
Sassatelli 1994a: no. 2; Meiser 2014: Fe 2.21.

57* (fig. 10.7). Fine-ware cup.
akius
Sassatelli 1994a: no. 3; Meiser 2014: Fe 2.9.

58* (fig. 10.7). Small *dolium*.
]iś
Sassatelli 1994a: no. 5.

59* (fig. 10.7). Small *dolium*.
mi[
Sassatelli 1994a: no. 6.

WATER SHRINE

60 (fig. 10.7). Fine-ware basin.
[-?-t]uruke lareke niritalu
Inside the sewer of the sanctuary. Sassatelli 1994a: no. 66; Maras 2009:322–323, Pa do.2; Meiser 2014: Fe 3.2, t]uruke lareke nirit̥—u̥.

APPENDIX B

LIST OF PUBLICATIONS AND EXCAVATIONS

GIULIA MORPURGO

Since the first investigations in the nineteenth century, the Etruscan city of Marzabotto has been at the center of a broad-ranging debate that has produced, over time, a copious bibliography.

Although it is as comprehensive as possible, the following overview of all the contributions pertaining to the different sectors of the city brought to light over time is undoubtedly far from complete. The bibliographic entries are organized according to topographical criteria, primarily based on the urban grid.

The assembly of this information, updated with the most recent contributions, benefited from previous bibliographic reviews dedicated to the site. First of all, this appendix includes all the enties listed under the heading "Marzabotto" in the *Bibliografia topografica della Colonizzazione greca in Italia*, edited by G. Sassatelli and A. M. Brizzolara and published in 1991, where almost all the relevant research published up to 1989 was collected (Sassatelli and Brizzolara 1991). Equally valuable are the register of excavations edited by E. Lippolis (Lippolis 2005) and that of the streets and canals by S. Romagnoli (Romagnoli 2010). A thorough bibliographic study, organized both topographically and thematically, was undertaken by Dr. Tobia Moroder as part of his undergraduate dissertation in Etruscology and Italic archeology, presented at the University of Bologna in 2005.

REGIO I

Insulae 2–3, Etruscan and Late Republican and Proto-Imperial Roman Structures:
   Gozzadini 1865: pl. I, Q, T; Muffatti 1967; Sassatelli 1991a: 191, 193, no. 4–5.

Insulae 4a–b, Sanctuary of Uni:
   Garagnani, Gaucci, and Govi 2016; Garagnani, Gaucci, and Gruška 2016a; Garagnani, Gaucci, and Gruška 2016b; Garagnani 2017; Gaucci 2017; Govi 2017b; Govi 2017c; Govi 2017e; Santocchini Gerg et al. 2017; Gruška, Mancuso, and Zampieri 2017:168–172; Sassatelli et al. 2017a; Sassatelli et al. 2017b; Govi 2018a; Govi 2018c; Govi 2019a; Govi 2020; Govi 2021.

Insulae 4b–5, Northern Gate:
   Mansuelli 1969a; Campagnano et al. 1970:59–60; Poppi 1971; Brizzolara et al. 1980:117; Mansuelli et al. 1982:82; Malnati and Sassatelli 2008:450–452.

Insula 5, Sanctuary of Tinia:
   Chierici 1883:147, n. 7; Brizio 1885:222; Brizio 1890:253, 280–281; Mansuelli 1962a: n. 9; Verger and Kermovant 1994; Lippolis 1997:53; Govi 2001–2002; Sassatelli 2004; Ranieri 2005; Sacchetti 2005; Sassatelli and Govi 2005b; Govi 2007:23–25; Sassatelli 2007; Bentz and Reusser 2008:54–56; Sassatelli 2009a; Sassatelli and Govi 2010; Baronio 2012; Vitali 2013; Govi 2014a; Govi 2014b; Sassatelli, Govi and Baronio 2014; Govi 2016; Garagnani 2017; Gaucci 2017; Govi 2017b; Govi 2017c; Govi 2017e; Sassatelli et al. 2017a; Sassatelli et al. 2017b; Govi 2018a; Govi 2018c; Govi 2019a; Govi 2020.

Insula 5, northern sector of sanctuary of Tinia, *"Area Nord"*:
   Govi 2016:203–206; Govi 2017b:167.

REGIO II

Insula 1, "Great Furnace":
   Arias 1954; Arias 1955; Pellegrini and Fogolari 1958:114–115; Saronio 1965; Mansuelli 1970; Campagnano et al. 1970:60–61; Cuomo di Caprio 1971–1972:448, nn. 10–17; Curri and Sorbelli 1973:249; Brizzolara et al. 1980:110–111; Mansuelli et al. 1982:82–83; Sassatelli 1985a; Malnati 1987; Sassatelli 1989a:70–81; Sassatelli 1990:68; Sassatelli 1991a; Sassatelli 1994a:57–64; Nijboer 1998:120–123; Govi 2007:39–41; Bentz and Reusser 2008:96–98; Sassatelli 2011; Mattioli, Morpurgo, and Pizzirani 2017:117–118; Morpurgo 2017; Zeidler 2017.

REGIO III

Insulae 2–5, surveys in the central area of the city:

Arias 1950; Arias 1951–1953; Arias 1953; Mansuelli 1969a; Campagnano et al. 1970; Campagnano et al. 1970:62–65; De Maria et al. 1972; Mansuelli 1972; De Maria, Sassatelli, and Vitali 1976; De Maria, Sassatelli, and Vitali 1978a:57–96; De Maria, Sassatelli, and Vitali 1978b; Brizzolara et al. 1980:115; Mangani, Rebecchi, and Strazzulla 1981:96–97; Mansuelli et al. 1982:120–122; Sassatelli 1991a:190–197, 204, no. 18, 21, 204, no. 42–44; Sassatelli 1994a:65–70; Nijboer 1998:123, 199; Morpurgo 2009; Govi 2014a; Boschi 2016; Govi 2016:198; Gruška, Mancuso, and Zampieri 2017:172–175.

Insulae 2–5, Celtic tombs:

Gozzadini 1865: pl. I, P; Gozzadini 1870:3, pl. II, 1–3; Brizio 1887a:505–508; Bertrand 1889:240, 348–355; Kruta Poppi 1975; Brizzolara et al. 1980:118; Vitali 1985a; Vitali 2005; Govi 2007: 74–75; Bentz and Reusser 2008:104–109; Morpurgo 2016.

Insulae 2–5, Late Republican and Proto-Imperial Roman Structures:

Muffatti 1967; De Maria, Sassatelli, and Vitali 1976; De Maria, Sassatelli, and Vitali 1978a:57–96; De Maria, Sassatelli, and Vitali 1978b; Cuomo di Caprio 1981:91, n. 11; Mansuelli et al. 1982:122–125; De Maria 1985; Govi 2007:76–77.

REGIO IV

Insula 1, *Isolato* Mansuelli

Arias 1950; Arias 1951–1953; Malavolti and Mansuelli 1951–1952:221, 234; Arias 1952; Arias 1953; Arias 1954; Magagnini 1953–1955; Arias 1958; Mansuelli 1958; Mansuelli 1959b; Mansuelli 1960; Mansuelli 1961; Mansuelli 1962a:21; Mansuelli 1962b; Mansuelli 1963a; Staccioli 1967:114–115; Campagnano et al. 1970:65–66; Staccioli 1970; Prayon 1975:141–143; Bouloumié 1976; Brizzolara et al. 1980:112–114; Rebecchi, Strazzulla, and Mangani 1981:96–97; Mansuelli et al. 1982:86–94; Colonna 1986:463–467; Durante and Gervasini 1987; Sassatelli 1991a:198, no. 22, 204–205, no. 45–49; Sassatelli 1994a:71–89; Carandini and Carafa 1995:270; Izzet 1997:41–49; Nijboer 1998:199–200; Gros 2001:34; Bentz and Reusser 2004; Govi 2007:31–33; Bentz and Reusser 2008:81–89, 101; Morpurgo 2009; Bentz and Reusser 2010b; Calastri et al. 2010; Govi 2014a; Gaucci 2016; Govi 2016:197–198; Gaucci 2017; Govi 2017c; Mattioli, Morpurgo, and Pizzirani 2017:116; Sassatelli et al. 2017a; Mancuso 2022.

Insula 2, "House 1" excavated by the University of Bologna:

Sassatelli and Brizzolara 1990; Sassatelli and Brizzolara 1991a; Sassatelli and Brizzolara 1991b; Sassatelli 1991a; Sassatelli 1991b; Sassatelli 1991c; Sassatelli and Taglioni 1991–1992; Sassatelli 1994a:91–126; Sassatelli 1994b; Sassatelli and Brizzolara 1995; Marchesi 1997; Mattioli 1997; Sassatelli et al. 1997; Nijboer 1998:124–125; Govi 2001–2002; Sassatelli 2004; Govi 2007:34–36; Govi and Sassatelli 2010; Govi 2016:189–196; Mattioli, Morpurgo, and Pizzirani 2017:118–122.

Insulae 3–4, Southern front, near the modern escarpment of the plateau (discovery of a well and some kilns):

Brizio 1885:214; Brizio 1886:24; Brizio 1890:184, 281–282, 284, 335–336, 359, pl. VIII, 7, 7a, 8; Sassatelli 1991a:198, no. 23–24; Nijboer 1998:119; Morpurgo 2009; Morpurgo 2017.

REGIO V

Insula 2, southern front, building known as *Domus Lautuni*:

Brizio 1890, 284, 317–326, 338–340; Mansuelli 1963a: 45, n. 2; Tripponi 1967:396, n. 72; Tripponi 1971; Brizzolara et al. 1980:116–117; Mansuelli et al. 1982:110–111; Cristofani 1985a:160–161, n. 6.35; Colonna 1986:463–467; Sassatelli 1989a:62; Sassatelli 1991a:201, no. 33; Sassatelli 1994a:127–135; Jolivet 2011:74–75; Govi 2016:200–201.

Insula 3, northernmost sector, buildings excavated by the École Français de Rome:

Massa Pairault 1978; Brizzolara et al. 1980:115; Mansuelli et al. 1982:119–120; Malnati 1987; Sassatelli 1991a:203–204, no. 39–41; Sassatelli 1994a:137–140; Massa Pairault 1997; Lippolis 1998; Nijboer 1998:201; Gros 2001:34; Govi 2007, 37–38.

Insulae 3–4a–4b, southernmost sector, nineteenth-century excavations and latest surveys:

Brizio 1890:252, 284, 312–313, 322, 314–317, 334–335, 340–343; Mansuelli 1962b:27; Mansuelli 1963a:45, n. 2 and 60, n. 16; Mansuelli 1965:82; Mansuelli 1969b:80; Sassatelli 1991a: 191, no. 2–3, 197, no. 17, 200–201, no. 27–32; Sassatelli 1994a: 155–156; Nijboer 1998:201; Morpurgo 2009.

Insula 4b: southernmost sector, *strato del VI*:

Mansuelli 1962b:27; Mansuelli 1963b:145; Mansuelli 1965; Campagnano et al. 1970:67; Saletti 1970; Colonna 1974:15–17; Mansuelli et al. 1982:109–110; Malnati 1987; Sassatelli 1989a:31; Sassatelli 1994a:157–167.

Insula 5, the "Foundry":

Mansuelli 1962b; Gentili 1968; Mansuelli 1969b:70, 81; Campagnano et al. 1970:66–67; Brizzolara et al. 1980:111–112; Mansuelli et al. 1982:95; Cristofani 1985a:147, nn. 6.13 and 6.14; Malnati 1987; Sassatelli 1989a:62–67; Sassatelli 1990:68–74; Malnati and Manfredi 1991:192; Sassatelli 1991a:203, no. 38; Sassatelli 1994a:179–188; Lippolis 1997:53; Locatelli 1997; Nijboer 1998:196–199; Sassatelli 2002b; Locatelli 2005; Malnati and Locatelli 2006; Govi 2007:42–44; Morpurgo 2017.

Insula 5, building north of the "Foundry" excavated by the Archaeological Superintendence of Emilia-Romagna:
Baratti 2005.

Insula 5, northernmost sector, "House 1" excavated by the Archaeological Superintendence of Emilia-Romagna:
Malnati 1990a; Malnati 1990b:45–46; Malnati 1991; Sassatelli 1994a:169–177.

Insula 5, southernmost sector, structures near the modern escarpment of the plateau (19th-century excavations):
Gozzadini 1865: pl. II, 2, no. 13; Brizio 1890:252, 278, 312; Sassatelli 1991a:191, no. 1; Morpurgo 2009.

REGIO VI

Insula 1, structures near the modern escarpment of the plateau (19th-century excavations):
Gozzadini 1865: pl. II, 2, no. 13; Brizio 1890:252, 278, 312; Morpurgo 2009.

Insula 2, structures near the modern escarpment of the plateau (19th-century excavations):
Brizio 1890:284, 311, 313–314, 336–338; Sassatelli 1991a:198, 200, no. 25–26.

Insula 3, structures near the modern escarpment of the plateau (19th-century excavations):
Brizio 1890:284.

REGIO VII

Insula 2, structures near the modern escarpment of the plateau (19th century excavations):
Brizio 1890:284, 340–341, 385, 387, 391; Sassatelli 1991a:195, 196, nos. 15–16, 203, no. 36; Morpurgo 2009.

Insula 3, structures near the modern escarpment of the plateau (nineteenth-century excavations):
Brizio 1890:284, 317, 340; Sassatelli 1991a:201, 203, no. 34–35.

ACROPOLIS:

Sacred buildings:
Gozzadini 1854:3; Gozzadini 1865; Brizio 1890:257–262, 265–267; Slotty 1946–1947:197; Arias 1947; Arias 1949; Arias 1950–1951; Polacco 1952:82–84; Boethius 1953:172–186; Mansuelli 1960; Morini 1963:57; Colonna 1966:90–91; Castagnoli 1968:117–118; Schifone 1971; Vitali 1974; Pfiffig 1974:34, 57, 84–85; Boethius 1978:44; Cristofani 1978:107–108; Brizzolara et al. 1980:105–106; Massa Pairault 1981; Mangani, Rebecchi, and Strazzulla 1981:98–100; Mansuelli et al. 1982:102–109; Steingräber 1982; Vitali 1985b; Euwe-Beaufort 1985; Colonna 1986:473–474; Sassatelli 1986:38–42; Torelli and Gros 1988:42–45; Sassatelli 1989a:41–44; Sassatelli 1989–1990:599–610; Sassatelli 1991a:193, 195, no. 6–8; Lippolis 1997; Vitali, Brizzolara, and Lippolis 2001; Gottarelli 2003a; Gottarelli 2003b; Gottarelli 2005; Lippolis 2005; Govi 2007:20–22; Bentz and Reusser 2008:57–61; Pozzi 2009a; Gottarelli 2013; Govi 2014a; Gottarelli 2017; Gaucci 2017; Govi 2017b; Sassatelli 2017b.

Aqueduct:
Brizio 1885:228; Brizio 1890:308–309; Mansuelli et al. 1982:100–102; Sassatelli 1991a:183–188; Vitali, Brizzolara, and Lippolis 2001:71–76; Govi 2007:49–50; Pozzi 2009a.

Celtic tombs:
Brizio 1887a:502–532; Bertrand 1889:240, 348–355; Brizio 1890:276, 383–385; Kruta Poppi 1975; Brizzolara et al. 1980:118; Mansuelli et al. 1982:100; Vitali 1985a; Vitali, Brizzolara, and Lippolis 2001:78–92; Vitali 2005; Govi 2007:74–75; Bentz and Reusser 2008:104–109; Pozzi 2009a; Morpurgo 2016.

Water Shrine:
Mansuelli 1969a:230–231; Campagnano et al. 1970:61–62; Gualandi 1970; Mansuelli 1972; Gualandi 1973:332–341; Gualandi 1974; Gualandi 1975:110; Susini 1975; Gualandi 1976:96–97; Sassatelli 1979:117–118; Brizzolara et al. 1980:106–107; Mangani, Rebecchi, and Strazzulla 1981:95–96; Mansuelli et al. 1982:125; Gualandi 1983; Colonna 1985:113–115; Cristofani 1985b:23, 258–259; Massa Pairault 1986:360–361; Malnati 1987; Sassatelli 1989a:44–47; Sassatelli 1989–1990; Sassatelli 1994a:51–55; Govi 1995; Sassatelli 1998; Govi 2007:26–27; Bentz and Reusser 2008:61–62; Baldoni 2017.

Archaeological Superintendence of Emilia-Romagna excavations in the northeastern sector, the so-called *Terza Stipe*:
Brizio 1890:307–308; Malnati et al. 2005; Bentz and Reusser 2008:62–63; Desantis and Malnati 2009; Desantis and Malnati 2012.

NECROPOLEIS

Gozzadini 1865; Gozzadini 1867; Gozzadini 1870; Campagnano et al. 1970:55; Brizzolara et al. 1980:101–103; Mansuelli et al. 1982:117–118, 125–130; Sassatelli 1989a:47–48; Marchesi 2005; Govi 2007:67–72; Baldoni 2008; Bentz and Reusser 2008:66–77; Pozzi 2009b; Pozzi 2009c; Baldoni 2011; Baldoni 2012.

PLATEIAI (MAIN STREETS SEPARATING *REGIONES*)

Plateia A:

Gozzadini 1865:52, pl. II, 2, no. 13; Chierici 1883:147, n. 7; Brizio 1885:222; Brizio 1886:22; Brizio 1887b:301–304; Brizio 1890:252, 278, 280–281, 295–296; Arias 1951–1953:233; Arias 1952; Arias 1954; Mansuelli 1958; Mansuelli 1959b; Mansuelli 1962a; Mansuelli 1962b; Mansuelli 1963a:44–62; Saronio 1965: 386–390; Andrén 1967:25–27; Gentili 1968:116–117; Mansuelli 1969a; Campagnano et al. 1970:55–58; Grillini, Sassatelli, and Schiassi 1970:237; Mansuelli et al. 1982:83–86; Malnati 1990a; Malnati 1990b; Malnati 1991; Malnati 1991–1992; Sassatelli 1994a:169–178; Lippolis 2005:154; Govi 2007:45–48; Morpurgo 2009; Romagnoli 2010:246–248; Govi 2014a:94–95; Muzzarelli and Franzoia 2017.

Plateia B:

Chierici 1883:147, n. 7; Brizio 1885:222; Brizio 1890:253, 278, 280–281, 373; Arias 1953; Mansuelli 1959b; Mansuelli 1961; Mansuelli 1962a:16, 20, 26, n. 9; Mansuelli 1963a:44–62; Mansuelli 1965c; Grillini, Sassatelli, and Schiassi 1970:237; De Maria, Sassatelli, and Vitali 1978a:78–79; Mansuelli et al. 1982:86; Sassatelli and Brizzolara 1990:25–29; Sassatelli 1991a:23–30; Sassatelli and Brizzolara 1991a:389; Sassatelli and Brizzolara 1991b:14–15; Lippolis 1997:51–52; Sassatelli et al. 1997:11–13; Lippolis 2005:154; Govi 2007:45–48; Govi 2010a:21, 23–24; Romagnoli 2010:225–233, 248–249; Govi 2014a:94–95; Muzzarelli and Franzoia 2017.

Plateia C:

Brizio 1890:284–285; Mansuelli 1959b; Mansuelli 1963a: 44–62; Mansuelli 1965c; Mansuelli 1969a; Grillini, Sassatelli, and Schiassi 1970:237; Massa Pairault 1978:139; Mansuelli et al. 1982:94–95; Massa Pairault 1997:7–12; Lippolis 2005:154; Govi 2007:45–48; Romagnoli 2010:249; Govi 2014a:94–95; Muzzarelli and Franzoia 2017.

Plateia D:

Gozzadini 1865:52; Brizio 1887b:310; Brizio 1887b:301–304; Brizio 1890:254, 278–280, 284, 293–297, 387–388; Mansuelli 1960; Mansuelli 1963a:44–62; Mansuelli 1965c; Tripponi 1967; Grillini, Sassatelli, and Schiassi 1970:237–239; Gentili 1978; Brizzolara et al. 1980:116; Mangani, Rebecchi, and Strazzulla 1981:97–98; Mansuelli et al. 1982:110; Cristofani 1985a: 108, no. 3.18 and 158–160, no. 6.33; Massa Pairault 1986:340–343, 360–361; Sassatelli 1991a:182, 203, no. 37; Sassatelli and Govi 1992:128–130, 134–135; Sassatelli 1994a:189–190; Lippolis 2005:154–155; Govi 2007:45–48; Romagnoli 2010:249–250; Govi 2014a:94–95; Muzzarelli and Franzoia 2017.

STENOPOI (MINOR STREETS, SEPARATING *INSULAE* WITHIN *REGIONES*)

Stenopos a (separating *insulae* 3 and 4, preserved within *Regiones* II, IV):

Brizio 1890:286; Romagnoli 2010:250.

Stenopos b (separating *insulae* 2 and 3, preserved within *Regiones* II, IV):

Marchesi 1997:56; Mattioli 1997:270; Sassatelli et al. 1997: 11–13; Romagnoli 2010:236–246, 251.

Stenopos c (separating *insulae* 1 and 2, preserved within *Regiones* II, IV, VI):

Brizio 1890:286; Mansuelli 1963a:44–62; Sassatelli and Brizzolara 1990:25–29; Sassatelli 1991a:29–30; Sassatelli and Brizzolara 1991a:389; Sassatelli and Brizzolara 1991b:14–15; Sassatelli et al. 1997:11–13; Romagnoli 2010:233–236, 251.

Stenopos d (separating *insulae* 4b and 5, preserved within *Regiones* I, III, V):

Brizio 1890:286; De Maria, Sassatelli, and Vitali 1978a:68; Lippolis 2005:148; Romagnoli 2010:251–252.

Stenopos d' (separating *insulae* 4a and 4b, preserved within *Regiones* I, III, V):

Brizio 1890:312–313; Mansuelli 1969a:230; De Maria, Sassatelli, and Vitali 1978a:68; Lippolis 2005:148; Romagnoli 2010: 252.

Stenopos e (separating *insulae* 3 and 4, preserved within *Regiones* III, V, VII):

Brizio 1890:286; Tripponi 1967:401–402; Campagnano, et al. 1970; De Maria, Sassatelli, and Vitali 1978a:68, 72; Massa Pairault 1997:8, 11; Lippolis 2005:148; Romagnoli 2010: 252–253.

Stenopos f (separating *insulae* 2 and 3, preserved within *Regiones* III, V, VII):

Brizio 1890:286; Tripponi 1967:401–402; Campagnano et al. 1970:63–64; De Maria, Sassatelli, and Vitali 1978a:58–63, 79–80; Massa Pairault 1997:9–11; Lippolis 2005:148; Romagnoli 2010:253–254.

EASTERN GATE:

Tripponi 1967; Campagnano et al. 1970:67–69; Brizzolara et al. 1980:117; Mansuelli et al. 1982:111, 117; Sassatelli and Govi 1992:128–130; Sassatelli and Malnati 2008.

APPENDIX C

CHRONOLOGY OF KAINUA

Chronological framework		Etruria Padana	Kainua-Marzabotto.
Final Bronze Age	Eleventh century BCE		
Villanovan period	Tenth century BCE	–Re-occupation of the area near Bologna –Beginning of the formation process of Felsina and Verucchio	
	Ninth century BCE		–Earliest Villanovan evidences near Marzabotto: necropolis of Pian di Venola and Sperticano
	Eighth century BCE	–Ending of Felsina's formation process –Felsina's local aristocracy at its height	
Orientalizing period	Seventh century BCE	–Decline of the preurban center of Verucchio –Battle of Ticino	
Archaic period	Sixth century BCE	–Territorial reorganization of Etruria Padana –Refounding of Felsina	Marzabotto I phase: preurban settlement
			Marzabotto II phase: earliest urban formulation
Classic period	Fifth century BCE		Marzabotto III phase: the orthogonal city
Hellenistic period	Fourth century BCE	–Gaulish invasion of Italy and occupation of Felsina	
	Third century BCE	–Roman founding of Ariminum (268 BCE)	Celtic phase
Roman Republican period	Second century BCE	–Roman victory over the Boii (191 BCE), founding of Bononia (189 BCE), construction of the Via Aemilia (187 BCE)	The city is abandoned
	First century BCE	–The Gallia Cispadana becomes the *Regio* VIII Aemilia	Roman phase: Roman villas in the city area and at Sassatello
Roman Imperial period	First century CE		

BIBLIOGRAPHY

COMPILED BY STEFANO SANTOCCHINI GERG

Adam, J. P. 1984. *L'arte di costruire presso i Romani*. Milan.

Agusta Boularot, S., S. Huber, and W. Van Andriga. 2017. *Quand naissent les dieux. Fondation des sanctuaries antiques: Motivations, agents, lieux*. Rome.

Andrén, A. 1967. "Marmora Etruriae." *AP* 7:7–42.

Anzalone, R. M. 2019. "Il Museo Nazionale Etrusco Pompeo Aria." In *Kainua e Spina: Etruschi a confronto. Catalogo della mostra (Marzabotto 2019)*, 12–15. Bologna.

Anzalone, R. M., and A. Gaucci. 2019. "Il museo e la città etrusca di Marzabotto: Problemi e prospettive di ricerca e valorizzazione." *AnnFaina* 26:329–350.

Arias, P. E. 1947. "Marzabotto (Aemilia, Bologna)." *FA* 2: no. 261.

———. 1949. "Marzabotto (Aemilia, Bologna)." *FA* 4:214, no. 2293.

———. 1950. "Marzabotto (Aemilia, Bologna)." *FA* 5:208, no. 2321.

———. 1950–1951. "Scoperte archeologiche nel biennio 1949–1950 in Emilia e Romagna." *AttiMemBologna* n.s. 2:219–227.

———. 1951–1953. "Considerazioni sulla città etrusca a Pian di Misano (Marzabotto)." *AttiMemBologna* 4:221–234.

———. 1952. *RIA* 1:242–248.

———. 1953. "Marzabotto (Aemilia, Bologna)." *FA* 8:168–169, no. 2198.

———. 1954. "Marzabotto (Aemilia, Bologna)." *FA* 9:214, no. 2904.

———. 1955. "Una città etrusca presso Marzabotto." In *Mostra dell'arte e della civiltà etrusca. Catalogo della mostra (Milano 1955)*, 148–150. Milan.

———. 1958. "Marzabotto (Aemilia, Bologna)." *FA* 13: no. 2336.

Aurigemma, S. 1933. "Una città etrusca donata allo stato." *La rivista illustrata del popolo d'Italia* 7:43–50.

Baglione, M. P. 2013. "Le ceramiche attiche e i rituali del santuario meridionale." In Baglione and Gentili 2013:73–99.

Baglione, M. P., and M. Belelli Marchesini. 2015. "Nuovi dati dagli scavi dall'area a nord del santuario nella seconda metà del VI sec. a.C." *ScAnt* 21:133–152.

Baglione, M. P., and M. A. De Lucia Brolli. 2007–2008. "Le deposizioni infantili nell'agro falisco tra vecchio e nuovi scavi." *ScAnt* 14:869–893.

Baglione, M. P., and M. D. Gentili, eds. 2013. *Riflessioni su Pyrgi: Scavi e ricerche nelle aree del santuario*. Rome.

Bagnaresi, U., and C. Ferrari. 1987. *I boschi dell'Emilia Romagna*. Bologna.

Bagnasco Gianni, G. 2014. "Una nuova iscrizione dal 'complesso monumentale' della Civià di Tarquinia." In *Per Maristella Pandolfini cên zic ziχuχe*, ed. E. Benelli, 23–28. Pisa and Rome.

Bagnasco Gianni, G., and N. T. de Grummond. 2020. "Introducing the International Etruscan Sigla Project." In *Etruscan Literacy in Its Social Context*, ed. R. Whitehouse, 113–123. London.

Baldacci, P. 1983. "La celtizzazione dell'Italia settentrionale nel quadro della politica mediterranea." In *Popoli e facies culturali celtiche a nord e a sud delle Alpi. Atti del Convegno (Milano 1980)*, 147–155. Milan.

Baldassarra, D. 2013. *Dal Saronico all'Adriatico: Iscrizioni greche su ceramica del Museo archeologico nazionale di Adria*. Pisa.

Baldoni, V. 2008. "Nuovi dati sulle prime importazioni attiche a figure nere di Marzabotto: I materiali degli scavi ottocenteschi." *Hesperìa* 22:33–49.

———. 2009. *La ceramica attica dagli scavi ottocenteschi di Marzabotto*. Bologna.

———. 2011. "Stamnos attico a figure nere da una tomba tardo-arcaica di Marzabotto." In *Tra protostoria e storia. Studi in onore di Loredana Capuis*, 93–103. Rome.

———. 2012. "Forme, immagini e rituali: Osservazioni sulla ceramica attica dalle necropoli di Marzabotto." In *The Contexts of Painted Pottery in the Ancient Mediterranean World (Seventh–Fourth Centuries BCE)*, ed. D. Paleothodoros, 81–91. Oxford.

———. 2015. "Ceramiche greche da santuari urbani dell'Etruria padana: Marzabotto e Bologna." *StEtr* 78:115–142.

———. 2017. "Achille e Aiace che giocano ai dadi: Vecchie ipotesi e nuove letture." *ArchCl* 68:419–432.

———. 2022. "Marzabotto e La Quercia: Appunti sulla diffusione delle ceramiche di importazione greca." In Cappuccini and Gaucci 2022.

Bandelli, G. 2009. "Parma durante la Repubblica: Dalla fondazione della colonia a Cesare." In *Storia di Parma*, II: *Parma romana*, ed. D. Vera, 180–217. Parma.

Baratti, G. 2005. "Gli scavi 1971–1973 nella Regio V, 5: Proposta per una classificazione della ceramica depurata." In Sassatelli and Govi 2005:239–245.

Baronio, P. 2012. "Un architetto per il tempio di Tina a Marzabotto: Studio dell'antico procedimento geometrico-proporzionale utilizzato nel progetto del tempio urbano della città etrusca di Kainua." *Ocnus* 20:9–32.

———. 2017. "I caratteri dell'urbanistica etrusca ad assi ortogonali in area padana: Nuove considerazioni sull'impianto di Kainua-Marzabotto alla luce delle recenti indagini metrologiche." *Ocnus* 25:113–142.

Bar Oz, G. 2001. "An Inscribed Astragalus with a Dedication to Hermes." *Near Eastern Archaeology* 64.4:215–217.

Belfiore, V. 2010. *Il Liber linteus di Zagabria: Testualità e contenuto*. Pisa and Rome.

———. 2014. *La morfologia derivativa in etrusco: Formazioni di parole in -na e in -ra*. Pisa and Rome.

Belelli Marchesini, B. 2013. "Le linee di sviluppo topografico del santuario meridionale." In Baglione and Gentili 2013:11–40.

Bellelli, V. 2000. "Un disco fittile dall'area urbana dell'antica Caere." *RdA* 29:23–32.

———. 2010. "Il pasto rituale in Etruria: Qualche osservazione sugli indicatori archeologici." In *Cibo per gli uomini, cibo per gli dei: Archeologia del pasto rituale*, ed. D. Palermo, A. Pautasso, M. Cultraro, and R. Gigli, 16–26. Catania.

———. 2012. "Vei: Nome, competenze e particolarità cultuali di una divinità etrusca." In *Antropologia e archeologia a confronto: Rappresentazioni e pratiche del sacro*, ed. V. Nizzo and L. La Rocca, 455–478. Rome.

Bellelli, V., and E. Benelli. 2009. "Un settore 'specializzato' del lessico etrusco: Una messa a punto sui nomi di vasi." *Mediterranea* 6:139–152.

Bellelli, V., D. Mallardi, and I. Tantillo. 2018. "Cerveteri, area sacra del Manganello: L'organizzazione degli spazi, l'architettura, gli arredi di culto." *AnnFaina* 25:199–243.

Beltrami, F. 2010. "La ricostruzione virtuale della Casa 1: Una proposta." In Govi and Sassatelli 2010:283–287.

Benassai, R. 2004. "La necropoli capuana di IV–II sec. a.C." In *Carta Archeologica e Ricerche in Campania* 2, ed. L. Quilici and S. Quilici Gigli, 73–230. Rome.

Benelli, E. 2000. "Alfabeti chiusini di età arcaica." *AnnFaina* 7:205–217.

Bentini, L., M. Marchesi, L. Minarini, and G. Sassatelli, eds. 2019. *Etruschi: Viaggio nelle Terre dei Rasna*. Bologna.

Bentz, M., and Ch. Reusser. 2004. "Keramik aus Marzabotto, Haus IV, 1, 2: Die alten Grabungen." In *Attische Vasen in etruskischem Kontext: Funde aus Häusern und Heiligtümern, CVA Deutschland*, ed. M. Bentz and Ch. Reusser, 35–44. Munich.

———. 2008. *Marzabotto: Planstadt der Etrusker*. Mainz.

———, eds. 2010a. *Etruskisch-italische und römisch-republikanische Häuser*. Wiesbaden.

———. 2010b. "Das Haus der Hippokampen in Marzabotto (IV 1, 2)." In Bentz and Reusser 2010a:105–116.

Bérard, C. 1992. "Phantasmatique érotique dans l'orgiasme dionysiaque." *Kernos: Revue internationale et pluridisciplinaire de la religion greque antique* 5:13–26.

Bermond Montanari, G., ed. 1987. *La formazione della città in Emilia Romagna*. Bologna.

Berti, F., and P. G. Guzzo, eds. 1993. *Spina: Storia di una città tra Greci ed Etruschi*. Ferrara.

Bertrand, A. 1889. *Archéologie celtique et gauloise*. Paris.

Biagi, F., A. Camilli, T. Magliaro, M. Milletti, S. Neri, and F. Pitzalis. 2015. "Un'area di culto nella necropoli etrusca di San Cerbone a Baratti (Populonia, LI)." *ArchCl* 66:41–73.

Bini, M. P., G. Caramella, and S. Buccioli. 1995. *Materiali del Museo archeologico nazionale di Tarquinia*, 13: *I bronzi etruschi e romani*. Rome.

Boethius, A. 1953. "Die hellenisierte italische Stadt der römischen Republik." *Acta Inst. Athen. Regni Sueciae* 4.2:172–186.

———. 1978. *Etruscan and Early Roman Architecture*. London.

Bonamici, M. 1985. "L'uso del marmo nell'Etruria settentrionale: Le statue funerarie." In *Artigianato artistico in Etruria*, ed. A. Maggiani, 123–137. Volterra.

———. 1991. "Nuovi monumenti in marmo nell'Etruria settentrionale." *ArchCl* 43:795–817.

———. 2014. "Il 'viaggio' verso l'aldilà." In Sassatelli and Russo Tagliente 2014:45–52.

Bonansea, N. 2008. "Menade, baccante o ninfa? Uno studio sull'identità femminile dionisiaca nelle fonti letterarie e iconografiche tra VIII e V secolo a.C." *Mithos: Rivista di Storia delle Religioni* 2:107–129.

Bondé, F., A. Muller, D. Mulliez, and F. Poplin. 2003. "Οστά και ιεροτελεστίες: Μία τριττοία στη Θάσο Β-Α παρυφές της αγοράς." *Το αρχαιολογικό εργό στη Μακεδονία και Θράκη* 15:67–73.

Bondini, A., P. Desantis, F. Finotelli, and T. Trocchi. 2018. "Le Grotte di Labante tra geologia e archeologia." In *". . . Nel sotteraneo mondo": La frequentazione delle grotte in Emilia-Romagna tra archeologia, storia e speleologia*, ed. P. Boccuccia, R. Gabusi, C. Guardnieri, and M. Miari, 99–108. Bologna.

Bonghi Jovino, M., ed. 1993. *Produzione artigianale ed esportazione nel mondo antico: Il bucchero etrusco. Colloquio Internazionale (Milano 1990)*. Milan.

———. 2005. "Mini muluvanice—mini turuce: Depositi votivi e sacralità. Dall'analisi del rituale alla lettura interpretativa delle forme di religiosità." In *Depositi votivi e culti dell'Italia antica dall'età arcaica a quella tardo-repubblicana*, ed. A. Comella and S. Mele, 31–46. Bari.

———. 2007–2008. "L'ultima dimora: Sacrifici umani e rituali sacri in Etruria. Nuovi dati sulle sepolture nell'abitato di Tarquinia." *ScAnt* 14:771–793.

———. 2012. "I tampli arcaici e aspetti dell'architettura sacra a Tarquinia." In *Tarquinia: Il santuario dell'Ara della Regina. I templi arcaici (Tarchna IV)*, ed. M. Bonghi Jovino and G. Bagnasco Gianni, 41–51. Rome.

Boschi, F. 2016. "Reading Ancient Cities: The Contribution of the Non-invasive Techniques." In *Looking to the Future, Caring for the Past: Preventive Archaeology in Theory and Practice*, ed. F. Boschi, 85–100. Bologna.

Bottazzi, G. 1991. "Programmazione ed organizzazione territoriale nella pianura bolognese in età romana ed alcuni esiti alto-medievali." In *Romanità della Pianura. Atti delle Giornate di Studio (S. Pietro in Casale 1990)*, 43–112. Bologna.

Bouloumié, B. 1976. "La céramique locale de Marzabotto: Définition de quelques groups." *MÉFRA* 88:95–140.

Braga, R., M. Tirtei, and C. Trevisanello. 2022. "Ceramiche di impasto da Marzabotto: Studio archeologico e petrografico." In Cappuccini and Gaucci 2022.

Bragadin, M., ed. 2009. *Il castello Aria e la città etrusca di Marzabotto*. Granarolo dell'Emilia.

Briccola, N., M. Bertolini, and U. Thun Hohenstein. 2013. "Gestione e sfruttamento delle risorse animali nell'abitato di Spina: Analisi archeozoologica dei reperti faunistici." In *Spina: Scavi nell'abitato della città etrusca 2007–2009*, ed. C. Cornelio Cassai, S. Giannini, and L. Malnati, 178–199. Florence.

Brizio, E. 1885. "La provenienza degli Etruschi." *AttiMemBologna* 3:119–234.

———. 1886. *Guida alle antichità della Villa e del Museo Etrusco di Marzabotto*. Bologna.

———. 1887a. "Tombe e necropoli galliche della provincia di Bologna." *AttiMemRomagna* 5:457–493.

———. 1887b. "Una Pompei etrusca a Marzabotto nel Bolognese." *NAnt* 3, 7:290–310.

———. 1890. "Relazione sugli scavi eseguiti a Marzabotto presso Bologna dal novembre 1888 a tutto maggio 1889." *MonAnt* 1:249–426.

Brizzi, G. 2015. "Le operazioni belliche in Val Padana tra Annibale e la sconfitta di Boi e Insubri." In *Brixia: Roma e le genti del Po. Un incontro di culture III–I secolo a.C.*, ed. L. Malnati, V. Manzelli, and F. Rossi, 112–113. Milan.

Brizzolara, A. M. 2001. "I bronzetti delle stipi votive." In Vitali, Brizzolara, and Lippolis 2001:95–125.

Brizzolara, A. M., and V. Baldoni. 2011. "La ceramica attica figurata e a vernice nera." In Govi and Sassatelli 2010:9–44.

Brizzolara, A. M., G. Colonna, S. De Maria, G. Gualandi, G. A. Mansuelli, G. Sassatelli, D. Vitali, G. V. Gentili, and F. H. Pairault Massa. 1980. "Guida al Museo etrusco di Marzabotto." *Emilia Preromana* 8:97–120.

Brizzolara, A. M., and S. De Maria. 1980. "Un nuovo museo archeologico per Marzabotto." *Carrobbio* 6:59–78.

Bruni, S. 1996. "Ancora sull'iconografia di Dionysos in Etruria. Sul candelabro da Montechiaro presso Pontecchio (Sasso Marconi)." *Ocnus* 4:67–88.

———. 1998. *Pisa etrusca: Anatomia di una città scomparsa*. Milan.

———. 2014. "La Domus Nobilium de Balneo e la pera di San Lorenzo de Kinthica. Una nota sul reimpiego di materiali etruschi a Pisa." In *Concordi lumine maior: Scritti per Ottavio Banti*, ed. S. Bruni, 13–44. Pisa.

Bundrick, S. 2017. "Altars, Astragaloi, Achilles: Picturing Divination on Athenian Vases." In *Gods, Objects, and Ritual Practice*, ed. S. Blakely, 53–74. Atlanta, GA.

Burgio, R. 2009. "Gli aristoi della Valle del Samoggia e l'organizzazione del territorio felsineo." In Burgio, Campagnari and Malnati 2009:37–50.

Burgio, R., S. Campagnari, and L. Malnati, eds. 2009. *Cavalieri etruschi dalle Valli del Po: Tra Reno e Panaro, la Valle del Samoggia nell'VIII e VII secolo a.C.* Bologna.

Cahill, N. 2005. "Household Industry in Anatolia and Greece." In *Ancient Greek Houses and Households: Chronological, Regional, and Social Diversity*, ed. B. A. Ault and L. C. Nevett, 54–66. Philadelphia.

Calastri, C., C. Cornelio, R. Curina, P. Desantis, D. Locatelli, L. Malnati, and M. Miari. 2010. "L'architettura domestica in Cispadana tra VII e II secolo a.C.: Una rassegna alla luce delle nuove scoperte." In Bentz and Reusser 2010a:43–63.

Calastri, C., and P. Desantis. 2010. "Lo scavo di viale Aldini." In *Alla ricerca di Bologna antica e medievale: Da Felsina e Bononia negli scavi di via d'Azeglio*, ed. R. Curina, L. Malnati, and L. Pini, 191–208. Bologna.

Camilli, A. 2018. "Populonia tra necropoli e scorie; appunti topografici sulla conca di Baratti." *RassAPiomb* 26:87–132.

Camilli, A., and R. Meli, eds. 2015. *La scoperta archeologica di Populonia: Isidoro Falchi / La tomba delle Idrie di Meidias con un omaggio di Rodolfo Meli*. Florence.

Campagnano, L., A. Grillini, G. A. Mansuelli, and G. Sassatelli. 1970. "Nuove scoperte dal 1958 al 1969 a Marzabotto (Bologna)." *Emilia Preromana* 6:53–71.

Camporeale, G. 2004. "Purificazioni: Mondo etrusco." *ThesCra* 2:36–62.

———. 2016. "Dalle case dell'Accesa: Tra tradizioni aristocratiche e innovazioni democratiche." *AnnFaina* 23:319–341.

Cappers, R. T. J., R. M. Bekker, and J. E. A. Jans. 2012. *Digital Seed Atlas of the Netherlands*. Eelde.

Cappuccini, L. 2011. "Il bucchero dell'area mugellana e fiorentina: Riflessioni su una produzione orientalizzante." *AntK* 54:3–20.

———, ed. 2017. *Monte Giovi. "Fulmini e saette": Da luogo di culto a fortezza d'altura nel territorio di Fiesole etrusca.* Florence.

Cappuccini, L., and L. Fedeli. 2020. *Il "Principe" di Radicondoli: Un personaggio di rango dell'Orientalizzante etrusco nel territorio di San Piero a Sieve.* Florence.

Cappuccini, L., and A. Gaucci, eds. 2022. *Officine e artigianato ceramico nei siti etruschi dell'Appennino tosco-emiliano tra VII e IV sec. a.C.: I Convegno Internazionale di Studi sulla cultura materiale etrusca dell'Appennino (Arezzo-Dicomano 2019).* Bologna.

Carafa, P. 2007–2008. "Uccisioni rituali e sacrifici umani nella topografia di Roma." *ScAnt* 14:667–703.

Carandini, A., and P. Carafa. 1995. "Palatium e Sacra Via." *BdA* 31–34.

Carosi, S. 2002. "Nuovi dati dal santuario di Campetti a Veio." *ArchCl* 53:355–377.

Carra, M. 2018. "Nota archeobotanica relativa ai riempimenti delle olle votive di Marzabotto (Regio I, insula 4)." *AnnFaina* 25:637–643.

Castagnoli, F. 1968. "Note di architettura e di urbanistica." *ArchCl* 20:117–125.

Cattabriga, S., and A. Curci. 2007. "La caccia nell'Italia preromana: Tra sussistenza e prestigio." In *Atti del I Convegno Nazionale degli Studenti di Antropologia, Preistoria e Protostoria*, ed. U. Thun Hohenstein, 91–94. Ferrara.

Cattani, M. 1995. "Il sistema monetale di Marzabotto." *AIIN* 42:21–79.

Cattani, M., and E. Govi. 2010. "Gli antefatti dell'età del bronzo." In Govi and Sassatelli 2010:13–19.

Cerchiai, L. 2008a. "Gli Etruschi e i *pessoi*." In *Alba della città, alba delle immagini? Da una suggestione di Bruno D'Agostino*, ed. B. D'Agostino, 91–105. Athens.

———. 2008b. "La Campania: I fenomeni di colonizzazione." *AnnFaina* 15:401–421.

Cerchiai, L., and M. Menichetti. 2017. "La messa in scena della morte nell'immaginario della pittura tombale tarquiniese di età arcaica." In *OTIUM* 3:1–20.

Chellini, R. 2013. "Un'area di passaggio tra l'Etruria tirrenica e l'Etruria adriatica: Il territorio fiesolano (IX–III secolo a.C.)." *Journal of Ancient Topography* 23:129–154.

Chiaramonte Trerè, C. 2016. "Riti e offerte: Testimonianze di età orientalizzante e arcaica da Tarquinia." *Rivista di Storia dell'Agricoltura* 56.1–2:141–158.

Chiarantini, L., I. Giunti, M. Benvenuti, P. Costagliola, and G. Verdiani. 2010. "Indagine archeometrica di alcuni resti di lavorazione metallurgica." In Govi and Sassatelli 2010: 439–474.

Chierici, G. 1883. "Scavo su Monte Castagneto nella provincia di Reggio Emilia." *BPI*: 141–169.

Chiesa, F. 2005. "Un rituale di fondazione nell'area alpha di Tarquinia." In *Offerte dal regno vegetale e dal regno animale nelle manifestazioni del sacro. Atti dell'incontro di studi (Milano 2003)*, ed. M. Bonghi Jovino and F. Chiesa, 103–109. Rome.

Chiesa, F., and B. Binda. 2009. "Una possibile ricostruzione dei tetti arcaici." In *L'Ara della Regina di Tarquinia. Aree sacre. Santuari mediterranei*, ed. M. Bonghi Jovino and F. Chiesa, 65–91. Milan.

Ciaghi, S. 1999. "Le terrecotte." In *Tarquinia. Scavi sistematici nell'abitato. Campagne 1982–1988. I materiali, 1*, ed. C. Chiaramonte Trerè, 1–41. Rome.

Ciampoltrini, G. 2010. "Edilizia rurale fra Valdarno e Valle del Serchio: La colonizzazione etrusca tra VI e V secolo a.C. e le deduzioni coloniali d'età tardo repubblicana." In Bentz and Reusser 2010a:135–143.

Ciampoltrini, G., P. Rendini, and B. Wilkens. 1991. "L'alimentazione nell'abitato etrusco di Montecatino in Val Freddana (Lucca)." *StEtr* 56:271–284.

Cicala, V., A. Donati, and G. Susini. 2006. "La romanizzazione dell'Emilia Romagna." In *Regio VIII: Uomini, luoghi, percorsi dell'età romana in Emilia Romagna*, ed. F. Lenzi, 23–28. Bologna.

Cifani, G. 2008. *Architettura romana arcaica: Edilizia e società tra monarchia e Repubblica*. Rome.

Colina, M. 2006. "La iperostosi scheletrica idiopatica diffusa (D.I.S.H.)." In *Reumatismo* 58:104–111.

Colonna, G. 1966. "Nuovi elementi per la storia del santuario di Pyrgi." *ArchCl* 18:85–102.

———. 1970. *Bronzi votivi umbro-sabellici a figura umana*, I: *Periodo arcaico*. Florence.

———. 1974. "I Greci d'Adria." *RivStorAnt* 4:1–21.

———, ed. 1985. *Santuari d'Etruria*. Milan.

———. 1986. "Urbanistica e architettura." In *Rasenna: Storia e civiltà degli Etruschi*, ed G. Pugliese Caratelli, 371–532. Milan.

———. 1987. "I culti del santuario della Cannicella." *AnnFaina* 3:11–26.

———. 1989. "Etruschi ed Umbri a nord del Po." In *Gli Etruschi a nord del Po. Atti del Convegno (Mantova 1986)*, 11–26. Mantua.

———. 1999. "Felsina princeps Etruriae." *CRAI*: 285–292.

———. 2004. "Scrittura e onomastica." In de Marinis and Spadea 2004:299–307.

———. 2006. "Sacred Architecture and the Religion of the Etruscans." In de Grummond and Simon 2006:132–168.

———. 2016. "Ancora sulle lamine di Pyrgi." In *Le lamine di Pyrgi: Nuovi studi sulle iscrizioni in etrusco e in fenicio nel cinquantenario della scoperta*, ed. V. Bellelli and P. Xella, 157–171. Verona.

———. 2019. "The Sanctuary of Portonaccio." In *Veii*, ed. J. Tabolli, 117–125. Austin.

Cristofani, M., ed. 1985a. *Civiltà degli Etruschi*. Milan.

———. 1985b. "Il deposito votivo di Monteacuto Ragazza (Grizzana, Bologna)." In *I bronzi degli Etruschi*, ed. M. Cristofani, 257–259. Novara.

———. 2002. "I culti di Caere." *ScAnt* 10:395–425.

Csapo, E. 2006. "Cockfights, Contradictions, and the Mythopoetics of Ancient Greek Culture." In *Inaugural Lecture to the Arts Association*, 9–41. Sidney.

Cuomo di Caprio, N. 1971–1972. "Proposta di classificazione delle fornaci per ceramica e laterizi nell'area italiana." *Sibrium* 11:371–461.

———. 1981. "Rassegna di fornaci per ceramica e laterizi." *RdA* 6:90–97.

———. 2007. *Ceramica in archeologia 2: Antiche tecniche di lavorazione e moderni metodi di indagine*. Rome.

Curci, A. 2010. "I dati archeozoologici." In Govi and Sassatelli 2010:397–420.

Curci, A., M. Bigoni, and V. Ferrari. 2006. "Le nuove analisi archeozoologiche a Marzabotto: *Regio* IV, *Insula* 2, Casa 1." In Curci and Vitali 2006:197–204.

Curci, A., and S. Cattabriga. 2005. "Risorse animali a Monte Bibele (Monterenzio—BO): L'abitato di Pianella di Monte Savino nel quadro dell'Italia settentrionale preromana." *Quaderni del Museo Archeologico del Friuli Occidentale* 6: 273–283.

Curci, A., A. Penzo, and S. Cattabriga. 2006. "Animali a Monte Bibele: Sacrifici per gli dei, cibo per gli uomini." In Curci and Vitali 2006:111–125.

Curci, A., and S. Sertori. 2019. "Il cane in Etruria Padana: Usi domestici e valenze rituali." In *Atti dell'VIII Convegno Nazionale di Archeozoologia*, ed. J. De Grossi Mazzorin, I. Fiore, and C. Minniti, 297–306. Lecce.

Curci, A., and D. Vitali, eds. 2006. *Animali tra uomini e dei: Archeozoologia del mondo preromano*. Bologna.

Curina, R. 2015. "Bologna nel II–I secolo a.C." In *Brixia, Roma e le genti del Po: Un incontro di culture, III–I secolo a.C.*, ed. L. Malnati, V. Manzelli, and F. Rossi, 164. Milan.

Curri, C., and S. Sorbelli. 1973. "Note sulla tecnologia delle officine ceramiche etrusche e della scuola coroplastica di Veio." *StEtr* 41:245–266.

Dabas, M. 2009. "Theory and Practice of the New Fast Electrical Imaging System ARP®." In *Seeing the Unseen: Geophysics and Landscape Archaeology*, ed. S. Campana and S. Piro, 105–126. London.

de Albentiis, E. 1990. *La casa romana*. Milan.

Degli Esposti, M., P. Desantis, and P. Poli, eds. Forthcoming. *L'insediamento etrusco in loc. La Quercia: L'età del ferro lungo la Valle del Setta*. Florence.

De Grossi Mazzorin, J. 2005. "Introduzione e diffusione del pollame in Italia ed evoluzione delle sue forme di allevamento fino al Medioevo." In *Atti del III Convegno Nazionale di Archeozoologia (Siracusa 2000)*, 351–361. Rome.

———. 2006. "Il quadro attuale delle ricerche archeologiche in Etruria e nuove prospetive di ricerca." In Curci and Vitali 2006:77–96.

———. 2008. "L'uso dei cani nel mondo antico nei riti di fondazione, purificazione e passaggio." *Beni Archeologici– Conoscenza e Tecnologie* 6:71–81.

De Grossi Mazzorin, J., and C. Cucinotta. 2009. "Analisi archeozoologica di alcuni contesti dalla città antica di Veio." In *L'abitato etrusco di Veio. Ricerche dell'Università di Roma "La Sapienza"* I: *Cisterne, pozzi e fosse*, ed. G. Bartoloni, 125–138. Rome.

De Grossi Mazzorin, J., and C. Minniti. 2012. "L'uso degli astragali nell'antichità tra ludo e divinazione." In *Atti del VI Convegno Nazionale di Archeozoologia (Parco dell'Orecchiella 2009)*, 213–220. Lecce.

De Grossi Mazzorin, J., and N. Perrone. 2013. "Resti animali da alcuni contesti cultuali di Muro Leccese (LE), Loc. Cunella." In *Archeologia dei luoghi e delle pratiche di culto*, ed. L. Giardino and G. Tagliamonte, 205–214. Bari.

De Grossi Mazzorin, J., and A. Riedel. 1997. "La fauna delle terramare." In *Le Terramare: La più antica civiltà padana*, ed. M. Bernabò Brea, A. Cardarelli, and M. Cremaschi, 475–480. Milan.

de Grummond, N. T. 2016. "Dressing and Undressing the Goddess from the Cannicella Sanctuary, Orvieto." In *Forme e strutture della religione nell'Italia mediana antica*, ed. A. Ancillotti, A. Calderini, and R. Massarelli, 189–203. Rome.

de Grummond, N. T., and E. Simon, eds. 2006. *The Religion of the Etruscans*. Austin.

de La Genière, J., ed. 1997. *Hera: Images espaces cultes. Actes du colloque international, Lille 1993*. Naples.

De Lucia Brolli, A. M., ed. 2016. *Il santuario di Monte Li Santi–Le Rote a Narce. Scavi 1985–1996*. Pisa and Rome.

De Maria, S. 1985. "Marzabotto: Prime esplorazioni nell'area della fattoria romana di Pian di Misano." In *Scavi e ricerche archeologiche degli anni 1976–1979*, 90–93. Rome.

———. 1992. "Appunti sul popolamento antico e la viabilità nella Valle del Reno." In *La viabilità tra Bologna e Firenze nel tempo: Problemi generali e nuove acquisizioni*, ed. N. Alfieri, 217–230. Bologna.

De Maria, S., A. Grillini, U. Primiceri, and G. Sassatelli. 1972. "Nuovi contributi problematici per lo studio dell'urbanistica di Marzabotto." *StEtr* 40:313–317.

De Maria, S., G. Sassatelli, and D. Vitali. 1976. "Marzabotto: Scavi e scoperte." *StEtr* 44:389–391.

———. 1978a. "Marzabotto (Bologna): Scavi nella città etrusca di Misano (campagne 1969–1974)." *NSc* 1978:57–129.

———. 1978b. "Campagne di scavo a Marzabotto (Bologna): Anni 1974–1976." *RdA* 2:111–113.

de Marinis, R. 1977. "The La Tène Culture of the Cisalpine Gauls." *Keltske Studije*: 23–50.

———. 2007a. "Anfore greche da trasporto." In de Marinis and Rapi 2007:165–201.

———. 2007b. "Il Forcello nel quadro dell'Etruria padana." In de Marinis and Rapi 2007:265–270.

———. 2010. "Anfore greche da trasporto." In Govi and Sassatelli 2010:77–93.

de Marinis, R. C., and M. Rapi, eds. 2007. *L'abitato etrusco del Forcello di Bagnolo s. Vito (Mantova): Le fasi arcaiche.* Florence.

de Marinis, R. C., and G. Spadea, eds. 2004. *I Liguri: Un antico popolo europeo tra Alpi e Mediterraneo.* Milan.

Deriu, R., and L. Zamboni. 2008. "Aspetti tecnologici." In Neri and Malnati 2008:173–181.

Desantis, P. 2001. "Le anfore commerciali e le misure di capacità in Etruria padana." In *Pondera: Pesi e misure dell'antichità*, ed. C. Corti and N. Giordani, 103–110. Campogalliano.

———. 2009. "Il 'Signore dei Leoni' a Marzabotto: Coperchio di pisside orientalizzante in avorio dal pozzo della plateia D." In Burgio, Campagnari, and Malnati 2009:90–100.

———. 2014. "Un caso di committenza funeraria a Felsina: La tomba con stele della necropoli di via Saffi." In Govi 2015:101–125.

———. 2016. "Gli etruschi fra Reno e Setta: Il nuovo insediamento de La Quercia (Marzabotto–Bologna)." *AnnFaina* 23:377–397.

———. 2017. "La necropoli di Valle Pega: Note topografiche, aspetti cronologici e rituali." In Reusser 2017:85–98.

Desantis, P., and L. Malnati. 2009. "Il complesso sacro della 'terza stipe': Analisi dei documenti e ipotesi ricostruttive dell'area sacra nord-orientale di Marzabotto." In *Altnoi. Il santuario altinate. Strutture del sacro a confronto e i luoghi di culto lungo la via Annia*, ed. G. Cresci Marrone and M. Tirelli, 293–324. Rome.

———. 2012. "La signora di Marzabotto: Influenze elleniche nella bronzistica dell'Etruria padana." In *Francesco Nicosia: L'archeologo e il soprintendente. Scritti in memoria*, 163–179. Borgo S. Lorenzo.

Desantis, P., L. Manzoli, and P. Poli. 2022. "Un abitato etrusco in Val di Setta: L'insediamento de La Quercia e la sua ceramica di produzione locale." In Cappuccini and Gaucci 2022.

Devoto, G. 1948. *Le Tavole di Gubbio.* Florence.

Di Fazio, M. 2001. "Sacrifici umani e uccisioni rituali nel mondo etrusco." *RendLinc* 12.3:435–505.

Donati, L. 1993. "Dalla Plumpe- alla Schnabelkanne nella produzione ceramica etrusca." In *Atti del XVII Convegno di Studi Etruschi ed Italici*, 239–263. Florence.

———. 1994. *La Casa dell'impluvium: Architettura etrusca a Roselle.* Rome.

Donati, L., and L. Cappuccini. 2010. "Roselle, Poggio Civitella, Santa Teresa di Gavorrano: Realtà abitative a confronto." In Bentz and Reusser 2010a:158–172.

Durante, A. M., and L. Gervasini. 1987. "Marzabotto." In Bermond Montanari 1987:316–324.

Eliade, M. 1990. *I miti del costruire.* Milan.

Esposito, A. 2018. "La necropoli di Pontesanto a Imola." *Arimnestos* 1:187–206.

———. 2020. "Imola (Bologna), necropoli di Pontesanto: Scelta di oggetti dal corredo della tomba 4." In Bentini et al. 2019:394–397.

Esposito, A., and G. M. Sanidas. 2012. "La question des regroupements des activités économiques et le concept de 'quartier d'artisans': Quelle approche." In *Quartiers artisanaux en Grèce ancienne: Une perspective méditerranéenne*, ed. A. Esposito and G. M. Sanidas, 11–21. Lille.

Euwe Beaufort, J. 1985. "Altari etruschi." *BaBesch* 60:100–105.

Fabbri, M. 2017. "La regia di Gabii nell'età dei Tarquini." *BABesch* suppl. 29:225–239.

Fábry, N. B. 2008. "L'armilla da Bric San Vito nel quadro degli anelli a ovoli in Italia." In *Taurini sul confine: Il Bric San Vito di Pecetto nell'età del Ferro*, ed. F. M. Gambari, 127–132. Turin.

———. 2011. "Il costume degli anelli da caviglia ad ovoli cavi in età lateniana." In *Le grandi vie della civiltà: Relazioni e scambi fra il Mediterraneo e il centro Europa dalla preistoria alla romanità*, ed. F. Marzatico, R. Gebhard, and P. Gleirscher, 296–297. Trento.

Fai, S., T. Duckworth, K. Graham, and N. Wood. 2011. "Building Information Modelling and the Conservation of Modern Heritage." In *Proceedings of the 24th World Congress of Architecture*. Tokyo.

Farello, P. 1989. "Fiorano Modenese: Reperti faunistici." In *Rubiera: "Principi" etruschi in Val di Secchia*, ed. G. Ambrosetti, R. Macellari, and L. Malnati, 179–184. Reggio Emilia.

———. 1990. "Casale di Rivalta: Reperti faunistici." In *Vestigia Crustunei: Insediamenti etruschi lungo il corso del Crostolo*, ed. G. Ambrosetti, R. Macellari, and L. Malnati, 241–255. Reggio Emilia.

———. 1995. "L'Emilia dal VI al V secolo a.C.: Caccia e allevamento." *Padusa* 1:209–234.

———. 2006. "Caccia, pesca e allevamento nell'Etruria padana dall'VIII al IV secolo a.C." In Curci and Vitali 2006:97–109.

Ferrari, S., and D. Mengoli. 2005. "I materiali di età celtica dalla struttura 2 di Casalecchio (Bo), zona 'A.'" In *Studi sulla media e tarda età del ferro nell'Italia settentrionale*, ed. D. Vitali, 15–148. Bologna.

Fisher, K. D., and A. T. Creekmore III. 2014. "Making Ancient Cities: New Perspectives on the Production of Urban Places." In *Making Ancient Cities: Space and Place in Early Urban Societies*, ed. K. D. Fisher and A. T. Creekmore III, 1–31. Cambridge.

Foni, A. E., G. Papagiannakis, and N. Magnenat Thalmann.

2010. "A Taxonomy of Visualization Strategies for Cultural Heritage Applications." *Journal on Computing and Cultural Heritage* 3.1:1–21.
Forni, G., and A. Marcone, eds. 2002. *Storia dell'agricoltura italiana* I.1: *L'età antica. Preistoria*. Florence.
Forte, M. 1993a. "Qualche esempio di classificazione di immagini digitalizzate a proposito del bucchero di Marzabotto." In Bonghi Jovino 1993:73–86.
———. 1993b. "Le fasi arcaiche della città etrusca di Marzabotto." PhD diss., La Sapienza University of Rome.
Foschi, P. 2003. "Una nuova tappa di studi sulla via Flaminia Minore." *Carrobbio* 29:19–36.
Galestin, M. C. 1987. *Etruscan and Italic Bronze Statuettes*. Warfhuizen.
Gamba, M., and G. Gambacurta. 2011. "Le statue di Gazzo Veronese al confine tra Veneti ed Etruschi." In *Tra protostoria e storia. Studi in onore di Loredana Capuis*, 159–193. Rome.
Garagnani, S. 2017. "Archaeological Building Information Modeling: Beyond Scalable Representation of Architecture and Archaeology." *ACalc* 28.2:141–149.
Garagnani, S., and A. Gaucci. 2020. "The ArchaeoBIM Method and the Role of Digital Models in Archaeology." *ACalc* 31:181–188.
Garagnani, S., A. Gaucci, and E. Govi. 2016. "ArchaeoBIM: Dallo scavo al Building Information Modeling di una struttura sepolta. Il caso del tempio etrusco di Uni a Marzabotto." *ACalc* 27:251–270.
Garagnani, S., A. Gaucci, and B. Gruška. 2016a. "From the Archaeological Record to ArchaeoBIM: The Case Study of the Etruscan Temple of Uni in Marzabotto." *Virtual Archaeology Review* 7.15:77–86.
———. 2016b. "ArchaeoBIM: An Innovative Method for Archaeological Analysis of an Etruscan Temple in Marzabotto." In *Proceedings of the 8th International Congress on Archaeology, Computer Graphics, Cultural Heritage, and Innovation 'ARQUEOLOGICA 2.0' (Valencia 2016)*, 314–317. Valencia.
Garagnani, S., A. Gaucci, P. Moscati, and M. Gaiani. 2021. *ArchaeoBIM: Theory, Processes, and Digital Methodologies for the Lost Heritage*. Bologna.
Gaucci, A. 2010. "La ceramica etrusca figurata e a vernice nera." In Govi and Sassatelli 2010:45–76.
———. 2012a. "Le iscrizioni etrusche tardo-arcaiche di Adria: Nuove iscrizioni e analisi epigrafica e dei contesti." *Padusa* 48:143–179.
———. 2012b. "Alfabetari latini nell'Italia preromana." *Atti e Memorie della Accademia Petrarca di Lettere, Arti e Scienze* 72–73:59–83.
———. 2013. "I porti del delta padano nel IV secolo a.C." In *Ravenna e l'Adriatico dalle origini all'età romana*, ed. F. Boschi, 71–90. Bologna.
———. 2016. "Nuovi studi sull'isolato 'Mansuelli' di Marzabotto (*Regio* IV, *Insula* 1)." *AnnFaina* 23:243–299.
———. 2017. "Kainua Project: Principles, Theoretical Framework, and Archaeological Analysis." *ACalc* 28.2:99–112.
———. 2020. "Graffiti dai contesti abitativi e funerari della città etrusca di Adria: Il segno a croce." *Aristonothos* 16: 413–449.
———. 2021a. *Iscrizioni della città etrusca di Adria: Testi e contesti tra arcaismo ed ellenismo*. Bologna.
———. 2021b. "L'iscrizione (perduta) dalla Fonte Veneziana di Arezzo e l'epigrafia votiva su pietra di periodo tardo-arcaico." *StEtr* 84:163–184.
———. 2022. "Ceramiche figurate e a vernice nera di produzione etrusca nelle vallate appenniniche del Bolognese e del Fiesolano: Produzione, consumo e mobilità degli artigiani." In Cappuccini and Gaucci 2022.
Gaucci, A., and S. Garagnani, eds. 2017. *Knowledge, Analysis, and Innovative Methods for the Study and the Dissemination of Ancient Urban Areas. Proceedings of the KAINUA 2017 International Conference in Honour of Professor Giuseppe Sassatelli's Seventieth Birthday (Bologna 2017). ACalc* 28.2.
Gaucci, A., S. Garagnani, and A. M. Manferdini. 2015. "Reconstructing the Lost Reality: Archaeological Analysis and Transmedial Technologies for a Perspective of Virtual Reality in the Etruscan City of *Kainua*." In *2015 Digital Heritage. Proceedings of the 2015 Digital Heritage International Congress (Granada 2015)*, ed. G. Guidi, R. Scopigno, J. C. Torres, and H. Graf, 227–234. Granada.
Gaucci, A., E. Govi, and G. Sassatelli. 2021. "Le stele iscritte di Bologna." *StEtr* 83:163–207.
———. 2022. "Epigrafia e sacro a *Kainua*-Marzabotto: Questioni di metodo e analisi contestuale." In *Eqo Duenosio: Scritti offerti a Luciano Agostiniani*, ed. A. Calderini and R. Massarelli, 387–418. Perugia.
Gaucci, A., G. Morpurgo, and C. Pizzirani. 2018. "Ritualità funeraria in Etruria padana tra VI e III secolo a.C." *AnnFaina* 25: 653–692.
Gentili, G. V. 1968. "Esplorazione di una fonderia di bronzo (Nota preliminare)." *StEtr* 36:116–117.
———. 1970. "La recente scoperta di due tombe etrusche a Sasso Marconi (BO)." *StEtr* 38:241–249.
———. 1978. "Coperchietto d'avorio con quadriga dell'orientalizzante recente di Marzabotto." *Carrobbio* 4:255–262.
Gilmour, G. H. 1997. "The Nature and Function of Astragalus Bones from Archaeological Contexts in the Levant and Eastern Mediterranean." *OJA* 16.2:167–175.
Giontella, C. 2006. *I luoghi dell'acqua divina: Complessi santuariali e forme devozionali in Etruria e Umbria fra epoca arcaica ed età romana*. Rome.
Giorgetti, D. 2000. "La centuriazione nell'Emilia occidentale." In Marini Calvani 2000:64–72.
Giorgi, E., ed. 2009. *Groma 2: In profondità senza scavare: Metodologie di indagine non invasiva e diagnostica per l'archeologia*. Bologna.
Giudice, F. 2004. "La ceramica attica dall'Adriatico e la rotta

di distribuzione verso gli empori padani." *Hesperìa* 18: 171–210.

Giuliani, C. F. 2006. *L'edilizia nell'antichità*. Rome.

Giuliani Pomes, M. V. 1957. "Cronologia delle situle rinvenute in Etruria." *StEtr* 25:39–85.

Giusberti, G. 1990. "Resti faunistici, risorse alimentari e lavorazione dell'osso." In *I nuovi scavi dell'Università di Bologna nella città etrusca di Marzabotto*, ed. G. Sassatelli and A. M. Brizzolara, 44. Bologna.

Gottarelli, A. 2003a. "Auguraculum, sedes inaugurationis e limitatio rituale della città fondata: Elementi di analogia tra la forma urbana della città etrusca di Marzabotto ed il templum augurale di Bantia (I)." *Ocnus* 11:135–150.

———. 2003b. "Modello cosmologico, rito di fondazione e sistemi di orientazione rituale: La connessione solare (II)." *Ocnus* 11:151–170.

———. 2005. "*Templum* Solare e città fondata: La connessione astronomica della forma urbana della città etrusca di Marzabotto (III)." In Sassatelli and Govi 2005:101–138.

———. 2013. *Contemplatio. Templum solare e culti di fondazione, 1998–2013: Sulla regola aritmogeometrica del rito di fondazione della città etrusco-italica tra VI e IV secolo a.C.* Bologna.

———, ed. 2017. *Archaeology in the Upper Idice Valley*. Bologna.

Govi, E. 1994. "Un nuovo alfabetario etrusco dalla Romagna." *Ocnus* 2:67–77.

———. 1995. "Vasi attici a figure nere dal santuario per il culto delle acque di Marzabotto." *Ocnus* 3:61–76.

———. 1998. "Il sepolcreto etrusco della Certosa di Bologna: Rituale funerario e articolazione sociale." PhD diss., University of Padua.

———. 1999. *Le ceramiche attiche a vernice nera di Bologna*. Bologna.

———. 2001–2002. "La città etrusca di Marzabotto: L'ultima campagna di scavo nella *Regio IV, Insula* 2 e i nuovi scavi nella *Regio I, Insula* 5." *Ocnus* 9–10:231–234.

———. 2003. "Ceramiche etrusche figurate dal sepolcreto della Certosa di Bologna." *StEtr* 69:43–70.

———. 2005. "Le necropoli." In Sassatelli and Donati 2005: 264–282.

———. 2006. "L''ultima' Spina: Riflessioni sulla tarda etruscità adriatica." In *Rimini e l'Adriatico nell'età delle guerre puniche. Atti del Convegno Internazionale di Studi (Rimini 2004)*, ed. F. Lenzi, 111–135. Bologna.

———, ed. 2007. *Marzabotto, an Etruscan Town*. Bologna.

———. 2009a. "L'archeologia della morte a Bologna: Spunti di riflessione e prospettive di ricerca." In *Tra Etruria, Lazio e Magna Grecia: Indagini sulle necropoli. Atti dell'incontro di studio, Fisciano 2009*, ed. R. Bonaudo, L. Cerchiai, and C. Pellegrino, 21–36. Paestum.

———. 2009b. "Aspetti oscuri del rituale funerario nelle stele felsinee." In *Etruria e Italia preromana. Studi in onore di Giovannangelo Camporeale*, ed. S. Bruni, 455–463. Pisa-Rome.

———. 2010a. "L'analisi stratigrafica." In Govi and Sassatelli 2010:31–177.

———. 2010b. "L'analisi planimetrica e la ricostruzione delle fasi edilizie." In Govi and Sassatelli 2010:179–203.

———. 2010c. "Le tecniche di costruzione." In Govi and Sassatelli 2010:205–222.

———. 2011. "Rinascere dopo la morte: Una scena enigmatica sulla stele n. 2 del sepolcreto Tamburini di Bologna." In *Tra protostoria e storia. Studi in onore di Loredana Capuis*, 195–207. Treviso.

———. 2014a. "Etruscan Urbanism at Bologna, Marzabotto, and in the Po Valley." *JRA* 97:81–111.

———. 2014b. "Una nuova iscrizione dal tempio urbano di Tinia a Marzabotto." *StEtr* 78:109–147.

———. 2014c. "Lo studio delle stele felsinee: Approccio metodologico e analisi del linguaggio figurativo." *AnnFaina* 21:127–186.

———, ed. 2015a. *Studi sulle stele etrusche di Bologna tra V e IV sec. a.C.* Rome.

———. 2015b. "Etruscans in the Po Valley, Etruria: Urbanism and Domestic Architecture." In *Housing and Habitat in the Ancient Mediterranean: Cultural and Environmental Responses*, ed. A. A. Di Castro and C. A. Hope, 103–121. Leuven.

———. 2016. "L'architettura domestica di Marzabotto tra vecchi scavi e nuove indagini." *AnnFaina* 23:187–242.

———, ed. 2017a. *La città etrusca e il sacro: Santuari e istituzioni politiche. Atti del convegno (Bologna 2016)*. Bologna.

———. 2017b. "La dimensione del sacro nella città di Kainua-Marzabotto." In Govi 2017a:145–179.

———. 2017c. "Kainua-Marzabotto: The Archaeological Framework." *ACalc* 28.2:87–98.

———. 2017d. "Il progetto di ricerca sulla necropoli di Valle Trebba: Qualche spunto di riflessione." In Reusser 2017: 99–108.

———. 2017e. "Marzabotto: *Regio* I." *REE, StEtr* 79:294–312.

———. 2018a. "L'area sacra urbana di Marzabotto (R. I, 4–5): Culti e pratiche rituali." *AnnFaina* 25:613–651.

———. 2018b. "Museo Nazionale Etrusco 'P. Aria' di Marzabotto." In *Corpus Speculorum Etruscorum, Italia 8. Musei dell'Etruria Padana*, 21–34. Rome.

———. 2018c. "Marzabotto: *Regio* I, 4." *REE, StEtr* 80: 236–241.

———. 2019a. "Terrecotte architettoniche dal santuario urbano di Marzabotto." In *Deliciae Fictiles V: Networks and Workshops: Architectural Terracottas and Decorative Roof System in Italy and Beyond*, ed. P. Lulof, I. Manzini, and C. Rescigno, 541–549. Philadelphia.

———. 2019b. "L'Etruria padana." In Bentini et al. 2019: 357–361.

———. 2020. "Don Gaetano Chierici e Marzabotto." In *Attualità di don Gaetano Chierici, archeologo, museologo e maestro di impegno civile. Atti del Convegno di Studi (Reggio Emilia 2019). Bollettino di Paletnologia Italiana 100 (2015–2020): 79–88.

———, ed. 2021. *BIRTH: Archeologia dell'infanzia nell'Italia preromana*. Bologna.

Govi, E., I. Giunti, M. Benvenuti, L. Chiarantini, and E. Pecchioni. 2006. "La Casa 1 della Regio IV, insula 2 nella città etrusca di Marzabotto: Studio archeometallurgico di resti della lavorazione dei metalli rinvenuti nella *regio* IV, *insula* 2, casa 1." *Agoge* 3:333–346.

Govi, E., C. Pizzirani, and A. Gaucci. 2020. "Urbanism and Architecture in the Etruscan City of *Kainua*-Marzabotto: New Perspectives." In *Crossing the Alps: Early Urbanism between Northern Italy and Central Europe (900–400 BC)*, ed. L. Zamboni, M. Fernández Götz, and C. Metzner Nebelsick, 123–136. Leiden.

Govi, E., and G. Sassatelli. 2004. "Ceramica attica e stele felsinee." *Hesperìa* 18:227–265.

———, eds. 2010. *Marzabotto. La Casa 1 della Regio IV, Insula 2: 1, Lo scavo, 2: I materiali*. Bologna.

Gozzadini, G. 1854. *Di un sepolcreto etrusco scoperto presso Bologna / Relazione del conte Giovanni Gozzadini*. Bologna.

———. 1865. *Di un'antica necropoli a Marzabotto nel bolognese*. Bologna.

———. 1867. "Gruppo di bronzo rinvenuto nella necropoli a Marzabotto." *Bullettino dell'Instituto di Corrispondenza Archeologica* 39:152–154.

———. 1870. *Di ulteriori scoperte nell'antica necropoli di Marzabotto nel Bolognese*. Bologna.

———. 1881. *L'Appennino bolognese*. Bologna.

Grillini, A., G. Sassatelli, and A. Schiassi. 1970. "Verifica delle pendenze delle canalizzazioni." *StEtr* 38:237–239.

Gros, P. 2001. *L'architecture romaine*, II. Paris.

Gruška, B., G. Mancuso, and E. Zampieri. 2017. "Building Materials and Virtual Models of the Etruscan City of Kainua." *ACalc* 28.2:165–176.

Gualandi, G. 1970. "Problemi e testimonianze della città etrusca di Marzabotto: Il santuario fontile a nord della città." *StEtr* 38:217–223.

———. 1973. "Un santuario felsineo nell'ex Villa Casarini (Facoltà di Ingegneria)." *MemBol* 42:315–345.

———. 1974. "Santuari e stipi votive dell'Etruria padana." *StEtr* 42:37–68.

———. 1975. "Una processione 'riparatrice' e la scoperta di bronzetti etruschi a Monteacuto Ragazza." *Strenna Storica Bolognese* 25:101–122.

———. 1976. "La seconda età del ferro." In *Storia dell'Emilia Romagna*, 83–103. Bologna.

———. 1983. "Grecia ed Etruria: La monumentalizzazione della aree di culto." In *Studi sulla città antica: L'Emilia-Romagna*, 27–63. Rome.

Guarino, A. 2011. "Croce, crux interpretum: Alcune note sulla croce celeste etrusca, sull'orientamento dei templi etrusco-italici e sul fegato di Piacenza." In *Munuscula. Omaggio degli allievi napoletani a Mauro Cristofani*, ed. F. Roncalli, 183–235. Pozzuoli.

Guerra, L., T. Lejars, V. Poli, B. Vaccari, and D. Vitali. 2009. "Monterenzio Vecchio (Bologna)." *Ocnus* 17:192–198.

Guidi, F. 2004. "Il sepolcreto etrusco dei Giardini Margherita." PhD diss., University of Padua.

Guidi, F., and M. Marchesi. 2019. "Bologna metropoli dei Rasna." In Bentini et al. 2019:377–383.

Harari, M., and S. Paltineri. 2010. "Edilizia etrusca nella *chora* di Adria." In Bentz and Reusser 2010a:75–89.

Hedreen, G. 1994. "Silens, Nymphs, and Maenads." *JHS* 114:47–69.

Holmgren, R. 2004. "Money on the Hoof. The Astragalus Bone: Religion, Gaming, and Primitive Money." In *PECUS. Man and Animal in Antiquity*, ed. B. Santillo Frizell, 212–220. Rome.

Hostetter, E. 2001. *Bronzes from Spina*, 1: *The Figural Classes: Tripod, Kraters, Basin, Cista, Protome, Utensil Stands, Candelabra, and Votive Statuettes*. Mainz.

Howard, S., and E. P. Johnson. 1954. "The S. Valentin Class." *AJA* 58:191–207.

Iaia, C., and A. Moroni Lanfredini, eds. 2009. *L'età del ferro a San Sepolcro*. San Sepolcro.

Inglese, C., M. Docci, and A. Ippolito. 2019. "Archaeological Heritage: Representation between Material and Immaterial." In *Analysis, Conservation, and Restoration of Tangible and Intangible Cultural Heritage*, ed. C. Inglese and A. Ippolito, 1–22. Hershey, PA.

Isler-Kerenyi, C. 2001. *Dionysos nella Grecia arcaica: Il contributo delle immagini*. Pisa-Rome.

Izzet, V. 1997. "Putting the House in Order: The Development of Etruscan Domestic Architecture." In *From Huts to Houses*, ed. J. R. Brandt and L. Karlsson, 41–49. Rome.

———. 2007. *The Archaeology of Etruscan Society*. Cambridge.

Jolivet, V. 2011. *Tristes portiques. Sur le plan canonique de la maison étrusque et romaine des origines au principat d'Auguste (VIe–Ier siècles av. J.-C.)*. Rome.

Krider, R. G., and J. I. Messner. 2013. *The Uses of BIM: Classifying and Selecting BIM Uses, Version 0.9, September*. University Park, PA.

Kruta, V. 1980. "Les Boïens de Cispadane: Essai de paléoethnographie celtique." *EC* 17:7–32.

———. 1987. "L'Emilia Romagna tra IV e III secolo a.C." In Bermond Montanari 1987:313–315.

———. 2008. "Epilogo. L'abitato del Forte Urbano e la questione della presenza Celtica in Cispadana." In *Gli scavi di Castelfranco Emilia presso il Forte Urbano: Un abitato etrusco alla vigilia delle invasioni celtiche*, ed. L. Malnati and D. Neri, 225–228. Florence.

Kruta Poppi, L. 1975. "Les Celtes à Marzabotto (Province de Bologne)." *EC* 14:345–376.

———. 1981. "La sépolture de Casa Selvatica à Berceto (Prov. de Parme) et la limite occidentale du faciès boïens au IIIe siècle avant notre ère." *EC* 18:39–48.

———. 2009. "Le tombe di Casalecchio di Reno, via Isonzo: Una famiglia di maggiorenti di epoca orientalizzante." In Burgio, Campagnari, and Malnati 2009:195–217.

Kysela, J. 2010. "Italští Bojové a česká oppida / The Italian Boii and Bohemian Oppida." *ARozhl* 62:150–177.

Lambrinoudakis, V. 2002. "Rites de consécration des temples à Naxos." In *Rites et cultes dans le monde antique. Actes de la table ronde, Beaulieu-sur-Mer 2001*, 1–19. Paris.

———. 2005. "Consecration of Buildings: Foundation Rites." *ThesCRA* 3:337–346.

Lanzara, P. 1997. *Piante medicinali*. Milan.

Levi, S. T. 2010. *Dal coccio al vasaio: Manifattura, tecnologia e classificazione della ceramica*. Bologna.

Lewis, S. 2002. *The Athenian Woman: An Iconographic Handbook*. London.

Lezzi Hafter, A. 1976. *Der Schuwalow-Maler: Eine Kannenwerkstatt der Parthenonzeit*. Mainz.

———. 1988. *Der Eretria-Maler: Werke und Weggefährten*. Mainz.

Lippolis, E. 1997. "Marzabotto. Pian di Misano." *Archeologia dell'Emilia Romagna* I/2:48–53.

———. 1998. "Rezension zu 'F. H. Massa Pairault (edited by) Marzabotto.'" *Recherches sur l'Insula V,3*. *Ostraka* 7:211–216.

———. 2000. "Le importazioni greche in Emilia fra VII e VI secolo." *Hesperìa* 12:99–118.

———. 2001. "Scavi e restauri (1936–1961) e nuove scoperte (1995–2000)." In Vitali, Brizzolara, and Lippolis 2001:197–267.

———. 2005. "Nuovi dati sull'acropoli e sulla forma urbana di Marzabotto." In Sassatelli and Govi 2005:139–165.

Lippolis, E., L. Pini, and S. Sani. 1998. "L'insediamento pre-romano di Monte Acuto Ragazza." *Archeologia dell'Emilia Romagna* 2.1:75–89.

Lissarrague, F. 1995. "Identity and Otherness: The Case of Attic Head Vases and Plastic Vases." *Source: Notes in the History of Art* 15.1:4–9.

Locatelli, D. 1997. "Nuove ricerche sulla fonderia di Marzabotto (Regio V, Insula 5)." *Archeologia dell'Emilia Romagna* 1.1:53–62.

———. 2005. "La fonderia della Regio V, insula 5: Elementi per una definizione dell'attività produttiva." In Sassatelli and Govi 2005:213–237.

———. 2009. "Le comunità della Valle del Panaro nella prima Età del Ferro: Spunti di autonomia e influenze felsinee." In Burgio, Campagnari, and Malnati 2009:57–64.

Longo, F., and T. Tauro. 2016. "Costruire la città: Riflessioni sull'impianto urbano di Neapolis." In ΔPOMOI. *Studi sul mondo antico offerti a Emanuele Greco dagli allievi della Scuola Archeologica Italiana di Atene*, ed. F. Longo, R. Di Cesare, and S. Privitera, 189–212. Athens-Paestum.

Lo Sardo, P. 1999. "Verso il canone della polis." In *La città greca antica: Istituzioni, società e forme urbane*, ed. E. Greco, 83–96. Pomezia.

Lovejoy, C. 1985. "Dental Wear in the Libben Population: Its Functional Pattern and Role in the Determination of Adult Skeletal Age at Death." *American Journal of Physical Anthropology* 68:47–56.

Lunt, D. J. 2009. "The Heroic Athlete in Ancient Greece." *Journal of Sport History* 36:375–392.

Macellari, R. 2002. *Il sepolcreto etrusco nel terreno Arnoaldi di Bologna, 550–350 a.C.* Bologna.

———. 2008. "Rapporti fra Etruschi e mondo ligure." *AnnFaina* 15:365–400.

MacIntosh Turfa, J. 2006. "Votive Offering." In de Grummond and Simon 2006:90–115.

Mackay, A. 2010. *Tradition and Originality: A Study of Exekias*. Oxford.

Magagnini, E. 1953–1955. "Tracce della civiltà etrusca nella provincia di Reggio Emilia." *Emilia Preromana* 4:45–67.

Maggiani, A. 1990. "Alfabeti etruschi di età ellenistica." *AnnFaina* 4:177–217.

———. 1992. "Le iscrizioni di età tardo classica ed ellenistica." In *Populonia in età ellenistica. Atti del Seminario (Firenze 1990)*, ed. A. Romualdi, 179–190. Florence.

———. 1998a. "Sulla paleografia delle iscrizioni di Spina." In *Spina e il delta padano: Riflessioni sul catalogo e sulla mostra ferrarese. Atti del Convegno internazionale di studi Spina: Due civiltà a confronto (Ferrara 1994)*, ed. F. Rebecchi, 227–234. Rome.

———. 1998b. *Vasi attici figurati con dediche a divinità etrusche*. Rome.

———. 1999. "Culti delle acque e culti in grotta in Etruria." *Ocnus* 7:187–203.

———. 2004. "I Greci nell'Etruria più settentrionale." *AnnFaina* 11:149–180.

———. 2005. "Il cippo di Larth Cupures Veiente." *AnnFaina* 12:29–74.

———. 2009. "Une nouvelle attestation du mot 'sacniσa': Urne inédite de la Collection Consortini de Volterra." In *Ecritures, cultures, sociétés dans les nécropoles d'Italie ancienne*, ed. M. L. Haack, 441–448. Bordeaux.

———. 2012a. "Ancora sui sistemi ponderali in Etruria: Pesi di pietra dal territorio fiesolano." *MÉFRA* 124.2:393–405.

———. 2012b. "Le fontane nei santuari d'Etruria." *AnnFaina* 19:265–292.

———. 2013. "I santuari urbani." In *Gli Etruschi e il Mediterraneo: La città di Cerveteri*, 151–178. Paris.

———. 2017. "Cippi pisani." In *Cippi, stele, statue-stele e semata: Testimonianze in Etruria, nel mondo italico e in Magna Grecia dalla prima Età del Ferro fino all'Ellenismo*, ed. S. Steingräber, 81–98. Pisa.

Malavolti, F., and G. A Mansuelli. 1951–1952. "Scoperte e scavi paletnologici in Emilia 1951." *Emilia Preromana* 3:155–175.

Malkin, I. 1987. "La place des dieux dans la citè des hommes: La découpage des aires sacrées dans les colonies grecques." *RHR* 204.4:231–252.

Malnati, G. 1987. "Marzabotto: La fase arcaica." In Bermond Montanari 1987:125–137.

———. 1990a. "Marzabotto (Bologna). Località Pian di Misano. Scavi 1988–1989." *BA* 5–6:133–134.

———. 1990b. "Gli scavi della Soprintendenza Archeologica nella Regio V–La plateia." In Sassatelli and Brizzolara 1990: 45–46.

———. 1991. "Marzabotto. *Regio V–Insula 5*." *StEtr* 57:390–392.

———. 1991–1992. "Marzabotto." In *Studi e documenti di archeologia* 7:164–167.

———. 1993. "Il bucchero in Emilia: Elementi per una catalogazione preliminare." In Bonghi Jovino 1993:43–72.

———. 1994. "*Regio V–Insula 5*—Gli Scavi della Soprintendenza Archeologica dell'Emilia Romagna." In Sassatelli 1994:169–177.

———. 2004. "I Liguri in Emilia." In *Ligures Celeberrimi: La Liguria interna nella seconda età del Ferro. Atti del Convegno Internazionale (Mondovì 2002)*, ed. M. Venturino Gambari and D. Gandolfi, 159–164. Bordighera.

———. 2010. "I graffiti e le iscrizioni." In *Alla ricerca di Bologna antica e medievale: Da Felsina a Bononia negli scavi di via D'Azeglio*, ed. R. Curina, 118–120. Bologna.

Malnati, L., P. Desantis, A. Losi, and C. Balista. 2005. "Nuove testimonianze cultuali a Marzabotto: L'area sacra nord-orientale." In Sassatelli and Govi 2005:89–100.

Malnati, L., and D. Locatelli. 2006. "Ricerche sulla metallotecnica a nord degli Appennini: Un riesame della fonderia di Marzabotto-Kainua." *Agoge* 3:347–355.

Malnati, L., and V. Manfredi. 1991. *Gli Etruschi in Val Padana*. Milan.

Malnati, L., and G. Sassatelli. 2008. "La città e i suoi limiti in Etruria padana." In *La città murata in Etruria. Atti del XXV Convegno di Studi Etruschi ed Italici, Chianciano Terme-Sarteano-Chiusi 2005*, 429–469. Florence.

Malnati L., and A. Violante. 1995. "Il sistema urbano di IV e III secolo in Emilia-Romagna tra Etruschi e Celti (Plut. Vita Cam. 16, 3)." In *Europe celtique du Ve au IIIe siècle avant J.C.: Contacts, échanges et mouvements de populations*, ed. J. J. Charpy, 97–123. Sceaux.

Mancuso, G. 2019–2020. "L'isolato 'Mansuelli' di Marzabotto (Regio IV–Insula I): Studio dei materiali ed analisi architettonica delle abitazioni." PhD diss., La Sapienza University of Rome.

———. 2022. "Alcuni buccheri di importazione dall'Isolato 'Mansuelli' di Marzabotto." In Cappuccini and Gaucci 2022.

Mangani, E., F. Rebecchi, and M. J. Strazzulla. 1981. *Emilia. Venezie*. Rome and Bari.

Mannack, T. 2001. *The Late Mannerists in Athenian Vase-Painting*. New York.

Mansuelli, G. A. 1958. "Marzabotto (Aemilia, Bologna)." *FA* 13:128, no. 2337.

———. 1959a. "Il Museo etrusco Pompeo Aria di Marzabotto." *BdA* 44:180–182.

———. 1959b. "Marzabotto (Aemilia, Bologna)." *FA* 14:163–164, no. 2511.

———. 1960. "Marzabotto (Aemilia, Bologna)." *FA* 15:171–172, no. 2529.

———. 1961. "Marzabotto (Aemilia, Bologna)." *FA* 16: no. 2774.

———. 1962a. "La città etrusca di Misano (Marzabotto)." *ArtAntMod* 17:14–27.

———. 1962b. "Marzabotto (Aemilia, Bologna)." *FA* 17:196, no. 2728.

———. 1963a. "La casa etrusca di Marzabotto." *RM* 70: 44–62.

———. 1963b. "Lineamenti antropogeografici dell'Emilia Romagna dalla preistoria alla romanizzazione." In *Preistoria dell'Emilia e Romagna* 2:121–147. Bologna.

———. 1965a. "Una città etrusca dell'Appennino settentrionale." *Situla* 8:79–92.

———. 1965b. "Sulle testimonianze più antiche di Marzabotto." In *Studi in onore di Luisa Banti*, 241–248. Rome.

———. 1965c. "Contributo allo studio dell'urbanistica di Marzabotto." *PP* 20:314–325.

———. 1966. "Risultati urbanistici degli scavi di Marzabotto." *Rivista Ingegneri Architetti Costruttori* 04/04/66:1–8.

———. 1969a. "Problemi e testimonianze della città etrusca di Marzabotto: Nuovi risultati di scavo." *StEtr* 37:229–232.

———. 1969b. "Aspetti e problemi dei nuovi scavi di Marzabotto." *AttiMemBologna*, n.s., 20:69–86.

———. 1971. *Guida alla città etrusca e al Museo di Marzabotto*. Bologna.

———. 1970. "Marzabotto." *Enciclopedia dell'Arte Antica Classica e Orientale*, Supplemento: 436–463.

———. 1972. "Marzabotto: Dix années de fouilles et de recherches." *MÉFRA* 84.1:111–144.

Mansuelli, G. A., A. M. Brizzolara, S. De Maria, G. Sassatelli, and D. Vitali. 1982. *Guida alla città etrusca e al Museo di Marzabotto*. Bologna.

Mansuelli, G. A., L. Campagnano, A. Grillini, and G. Sassatelli. 1970. "Nuove scoperte dal 1958 al 1969 a Marzabotto (BO)." *Emilia Preromana* 6:53–71.

Maras, D. F. 2009. *Il dono votivo: Gli dei e il sacro nelle iscrizioni etrusche di culto*. Pisa-Rome.

———. 2014. "Note epigrafiche sulla stele di via Saffi." *AnnFaina* 21:336–342.

Marchesi, M. 1995–1996. "Le necropoli della città etrusca di Marzabotto." Specialization thesis in Archaeology, University of Bologna.

———. 1997. "Marzabotto, *Regio* IV, *Insula* 2." *Archeologia dell'Emilia Romagna* 1.2:54–56.

———. 2005. "Le necropoli: Dagli scavi ottocenteschi alla ricostruzione dei corredi." In Sassatelli and Govi 2005:191–212.

Marchesini, S. 1994. "*Etrusco* Niritalu: *Greco* Νήριτος." *AION ling* 16:273–281.

Marini Calvani, M. 2000. *Aemilia: La cultura romana in Emilia Romagna dal III secolo a.C. all'età costantiniana.* Venice.

Martelli, M. 1984. "Populonia: Cultura locale e contatti con il mondo greco." In *Atti del XII Convegno di Studi Etruschi ed Italici*, 161–172. Florence.

Marvelli, S., S. De Siena, E. Rizzoli, and M. Marchesini. 2013. "The Origin of Grapevine Cultivation in Italy: The Archaeobotanical Evidence." *Annali di Botanica* 3:155–163.

Marziali, V. 2019. "Pyrgi (Roma), santuario meridionale, scelta di oggetti dal deposito rho." In Bentini et al. 2019:173–174.

Mascelli, V. 2013. "I graffioni etruschi." *AttiFir* 77:167–184.

Massa Pairault, F. H. 1978. "Marzabotto (Bologna). Rapport préliminaire sur six ans de recherches (1971–1976) dans l'insula VIII (Brizio) o V, 3." *NSc* 1978:131–157.

———. 1981. "Deux questions religieuses sur Marzabotto." *MÉFRA* 93:127–154.

———. 1986. "Les expositions de 'L'année étrusque' en Toscane et Ombrie." *RA*: 335–369.

———, ed. 1997. *Marzabotto. Recherches sur l'Insula V, 3.* Rome.

Matheson, S. 2009. "Beardless, Armed, and Barefoot: Ephebes, Warriors, and Ritual on Athenian Vases." In *Archaeology of Representations: Ancient Greek Vase-Painting and Contemporary Methodologies*, ed. D. Yatromanolakis, 373–413. Athens.

Mattioli, C. 1997. "La città etrusca di Marzabotto: Le campagne di scavo del Dipartimento di Archeologia dell'Università di Bologna." *Ocnus* 5:269–272.

———. 2010. "I materiali ceramici di produzione locale (depurata, grezza e bucchero)." In Govi and Sassatelli 2010: 95–178.

———. 2013. *Atlante tipologico delle forme ceramiche di produzione locale in Etruria padana.* Bologna.

———. 2017. "The Craft Settings in Kainua-Marzabotto: Places and Archaeological Issues." *ACalc* 28.2:87–98.

———. 2022. "La produzione ceramica locale di Marzabotto." In Cappuccini and Gaucci 2022.

———. Forthcoming. *Atlante tipologico delle forme ceramiche di produzione locale in Etruria padana*, II: *Aggiornamento e integrazione: La città etrusca di Spina, abitato e necropoli di Valle Trebba.* Bologna.

Mattioli, C., G. Morpurgo, and C. Pizzirani. 2017. "The Craft Settings in Kainua-Marzabotto: Places and Archaeological Issues." *ACalc* 28.2:113–127.

Meiser, G., ed. 2014. *Etruskische Texte. Editio Minor*, I–II. Hamburg.

Melis, F., and A. Rathje. 1984. "Considerazioni sullo studio dell'architettura domestica arcaica." *Archeologia Laziale* 6: 382–395.

Menotti, E. M., and D. F. Maras. 2012. "Un'area sacra in Mantova etrusca." In *L'Etruria dal Paleolitico al Primo Ferro: Lo stato delle ricerche. Atti del 10° Incontro di studi preistoria e protostoria in Etruria (Valentano-Pitigliano 2010)*, ed. N. Negroni Catacchio, 875–888. Milano.

Miari, M. 2000. *Stipi votive dell'Etruria padana.* Rome.

Michelini, R. 2004. "Archeologia nella piana di San Lorenzo a Sasso Marconi." *Al Sâs* 10:141–144.

Michetti, L. M. 2013. "Riti e miti di fondazione nell'Italia antica: Riflessioni su alcuni contesti di area etrusca." *ScAnt* 19.2–3:333–357.

Millemaci, G. 1999. "Viabilità transappenninica etrusca (VI–V sec. a.C.)." *Rivista di Topografia Antica* 9:121–140.

Millemaci, G., and G. Poggesi. 2004. "Ceramica attica dall'abitato etrusco di Gonfienti." In *Attische Vasen im etruskischen Kontext. Funde aus Häusern und Heiligtümern, CVA Deutschland*, ed. M. Bentz and Ch. Reusser, 45–52. Munich.

Minto, A. 1954. "L'antica industria mineraria in Etruria e il porto di Populonia." *StEtr* 23:291–319.

Morandi, V., M. C. Nannetti, V. Minguzzi, S. Monti, M. Marchesi, and C. Mattioli. 1997. "Ceramiche e argille della città etrusca di Marzabotto." In *Il contributo delle analisi archeometriche allo studio delle ceramiche grezze e comuni. Il rapporto forma-funzione-impasto. Atti della I Giornata di archeometria della ceramica (Bologna 1997)*, ed. S. Santoro Bianchi and B. Fabbri, 40–45. Imola.

Morandi, V., M. C. Nannetti, V. Minguzzi, S. Monti, M. Marchesi, C. Mattioli, and F. Salvo. 1996. "Ceramics from the Etruscan City of Marzabotto: Geochemical-Mineralogical Approach and Connections with Raw Materials." *Mineralogica et Petrographica Acta* 39:341–350.

Morandi, V., M. C. Nannetti, V. Minguzzi, P. Trentini, M. Marchesi, and C. Mattioli. 1995. "Caratterizzazione minero-geochimica di varie tipologie di concotto di età etrusca (Marzabotto, Bo)." *Mineralogica et Petrographica Acta* 38:219–227.

Moretto, T. 1995. "Dati e considerazioni sulla metallurgia in Etruria padana." In *Agricoltura e commerci nell'Italia antica*: 65–71. *Atlante tematico di topografia antica*, Suppl. 1. Rome.

Morigi Govi, C., ed. 1994. *Il V Congresso di Antropologia e Archeologia Preistoriche a Bologna (1–8 ottobre 1871)*. Forlì.

Morigi Govi, C., and G. Sassatelli, ed. 1984. *Dalla stanza delle antichità al Museo civico: Storia della formazione del Museo civico archeologico di Bologna.* Bologna.

Morini, M. 1963. *Atlante di storia dell'urbanistica.* Milan.

Morpurgo, G. 2009. "Abitato." In Bragadin 2009:121–165.

———. 2016. "La fase tarda di Marzabotto." In *Il mondo etrusco e il mondo italico di ambito settentrionale prima dell'impatto con Roma (IV–II secolo a.C.). Atti del Convegno (Bologna 2013)*, 127–169. Rome.

———. 2017. "Luoghi di produzione urbani tra Bologna e Marzabotto." In *Gli artigiani e la città: Officine e aree produttive tra VIII e III sec. a.C. nell'Italia centrale tirre-*

nica. Atti del Convegno Internazionale (Roma 2016), 353–357. Rome.

———. 2018. *I sepolcreti etruschi di Bologna nei terreni De Luca e Battistini (fine VI–inizi IV secolo a.C.)*. Bologna.

Morpurgo, G., and A. Pozzi. 2009. "Documentazione degli scavi ottocenteschi." In Bragadin 2009:97–221.

Muffatti, G. 1967. "Ritrovamenti romani nell'area della città etrusca." *StEtr* 35:427–430.

———. 1968. "L'instrumentum in bronzo." *StEtr* 36:119–156.

———. 1969. "L'instrumentum in bronzo." *StEtr* 37:247–272.

Muzzarelli, A., and M. Franzoia. 2017. "The Ancient Digital Terrain Model and the Infrastructure of the Etruscan City of Kainua." *ACalc* 28.2:151–164.

Nannetti, M. C., V. Minguzzi, E. Zantedeschi, and E. Esquilini. 2010. "Le analisi archeometriche." In Govi and Sassatelli 2010:421–437.

Naso, A. 1996. *Architetture dipinte: Decorazioni parietali non figurate nelle tombe a camera dell'Etruria meridionale: VII–V sec. a.C.* Rome.

Natalucci, M. 2021. "The Rediscovery of Colors at Kainua-Marzabotto." *ACalc* 32.2:95–104.

Neri, D., and L. Malnati, eds. 2008. *Gli scavi di Castelfranco Emilia presso il Forte Urbano: Un abitato etrusco alla vigilia delle invasioni celtiche*. Florence.

Nijboer, A. J. 1998. *From Household Production to Workshops: Archaeological Evidence for Economic Transformations, Pre-Monetary Exchange, and Urbanisation in Central Italy from 800 to 400 BC*. Groningen.

Nocentini, A., S. Sarti, and P. G. Warden. 2018. *Acque sacre: Culto etrusco sull'Appennino toscano*. Florence.

Ortalli, J. 1994. "L'insediamento rurale in Emilia centrale. Il territorio bolognese. Assetto insediativo e fondiario della campagna emiliana tra prima e tarda romanità." In *Il tesoro nel pozzo: Pozzi-deposito e tesaurizzazioni nell'antica Emilia*, ed. S. Gelichi and N. Giordani, 169–222. Modena.

———. 1995a. "La necropoli celtica della zona 'A' di Casalecchio di Reno (Bologna). Note preliminari sullo scavo del complesso sepolcrale e dell'area di culto." In *Europe celtique du Ve au IIIe siècle avant J.-C.: Contacts, échanges et mouvements de populations*, ed. J. J. Charpy, 199–238. Sceaux.

———. 1995b. "Bonifiche e regolamentazioni idriche nella pianura emiliana tra l'età del ferro e la tarda antichità." In *Interventi di bonifica agraria nell'Italia romana: Atlante tematico di topografia antica* 4:58–86.

———. 1996. "La fine delle ville romane: Esperienze locali e problemi generali—1996." In *La fine delle ville romane: Trasformazioni nelle campagne tra tarda antichità e alto medioevo*, ed. G. P. Brogiolo, 9–20. Mantua.

———. 1997. "Archeologia topografica: La ricostruzione dell'ambiente e dell'insediamento antico nell'esperienza di Casalecchio di Reno." In *XLIII Corso di Cultura sull'Arte Ravennate e Bizantina (Ravenna 1997)*, 565–606. Ravenna.

———. 2002. "La 'rivoluzione' felsinea: Nuove prospettive dagli scavi di Casalecchio di Reno." *Padusa* 38:57–90.

———. 2004. "Precedenti locali e discrimine romano nell'urbanizzazione della Cispadana tra IV e II sec. a.C." In *Des Ibères aux Vénètes*, ed. S. Agusta Boularot and X. Lafon, 307–335. Rome.

———. 2005. "La città romana: Il paesaggio urbano." In Sassatelli and Donati 2005:479–514.

———. 2008. "L'insediamento celtico di Casalecchio di Reno (Bologna)." In *Tra mondo celtico e mondo italico: La necropoli di Monte Bibele*, ed. D. Vitali and S. Verger, 299–322. Bologna.

———. 2010. "Case dell'agro di Felsina: Un modello edilizio per il governo del territorio." In Bentz and Reusser 2010a:65–75.

Ossani, M. 2003–2004. "La grande fornace di Marzabotto (Regio II, Insula 1): I vani settentrionali." Postgraduate degree in archaeology, University of Bologna.

Östenberg, C. 1975. *Case etrusche di Acquarossa*. Rome.

Paleothodoros, D. 2010. "Light and Darkness in Dionysiac Rituals as Illustrated on Attic Vase Paintings of the Fifth Century BCE." In *Light and Darkness in Ancient Greek Myth and Religion*, ed. M. Christopoulos, E. Karakantza, and O. Levaniouk, 237–260. Lanham, MD.

Paoletti, O. 2004. "Purificazioni. Mondo greco." *ThesCra* 2: 3–35.

Paolucci, G. 2010. "Forme e tipi della ceramica etrusca con fregi ornamentali: A proposito della Tomba 162 di Chianciano Terme." *ArchCl* 51:33–83.

Parrini, A. 2008. "La ceramica a vernice nera." In *Tra mondo celtico e mondo italico: La necropoli di Monte Bibele*, ed. D. Vitali and S. Verger, 95–126. Bologna.

Pearsall, D. M. 2015. *Paleoethnobotany: A Handbook of Procedures*. Walnut Creek, CA.

Pelacci, C. 2017. "Ceramica etrusca dipinta a motivi ornamentali." In Cappuccini 2017:112–128.

Pellegrini, G., and G. Fogolari. 1958. "Iscrizioni etrusche e venetiche di Adria." *StEtr* 26:103–152.

Penzo, A. 2007. "Ricognizione dei reperti archeologici nel territorio di Sasso Marconi." In *Piano Strutturale Comunale: Quadro Conoscitivo* 2007:3–36.

Perazzi, P., and G. Poggesi, eds. 2011. *Carta archeologica della Provincia di Prato dalla preistoria all'età romana*. Florence.

Peyre, C. 1965. "Une récolte de céramique étrusque dans l'Appennin bolinais." *MÉFRA* 77:6–34.

———. 1987. "Felsina et l'organisation du territoire des Boïens selon l'historiographie antique." In *Celti ed Etruschi nell'Italia centro-settentrionale dal V sec. a.C. alla romanizzazione. Atti del Colloquio Internazionale (Bologna 1985)*, ed. D. Vitali, 101–110. Imola.

Pfiffig, A. J. 1974. *Religio etrusca*. Graz.

Philippaki, B. 1967. *The Attic Stamnos*. Oxford.

Pignatti, S. 2017. *Flora d'Italia*. 4 vols. Bologna.

Pintus, R., K. Pal, Y. Yang, T. Weyrich, E. Gobbetti, and

H. Rushmeier. 2016. "A Survey of Geometric Analysis in Cultural Heritage." *Computer Graphics Forum* 35:4–31.

Pizzirani, C. 2014. "Il mare nell'immaginario funebre degli Etruschi." In Sassatelli and Russo Tagliente 2014:71–80.

———. 2019. "Tecniche costruttive nell'edilizia domestica etrusca tra VI e IV secolo a.C." In *Alle origini del laterizio romano: Nascita e diffusione del mattone cotto nel Mediterraneo tra IV e I secolo a.C.*, ed. J. Bonetto, E. Bukowiecki, and R. Volpe, 335–344. Rome.

Pizzirani, C., and A. Pozzi. 2010. "Laterizi e materiali da costruzione." In Govi and Sassatelli 2010:285–313.

Polacco, L. 1952. *Tuscanicae Dispositiones: Problemi di architettura dell'Italia protoromana*. Padua.

Pontrandolfo, A., ed. 2009. *Fratte: Il complesso monumentale arcaico*. Milan.

Poppi, L. 1971. "Saggio stratigrafico nel centro urbano di Marzabotto." *Rivista di Scienze Preistoriche* 26.2:431–446.

Potts, Ch. R. 2015. *Religious Architecture in Latium and Etruria, c. 900–500 BC*. Oxford.

Pozzi, A. 2003–2004. "La grande fornace di Marzabotto (*Regio* II, *Insula* 1): I vani meridionali." Postgraduate degree in Archaeology, University of Bologna.

———. 2009a. "Acropoli." In Bragadin 2009:111–120.

———. 2009b. "Necropoli Nord." In Bragadin 2009:166–189.

———. 2009c. "Necropoli Est." In Bragadin 2009:190–210.

———. 2010. "Le fornaci e gli apprestamenti artigianali." In Govi and Sassatelli 2010:255-283.

Prayon, F. 1975. *Frühetruskische Grab- und Hausarchitektur*. Heidelberg.

———. 2009. "The Atrium as Italo-Etruscan Architectural Concept and Societal Form." In *Etruscan by Definition: The Cultural, Regional, and Personal Identity of the Etruscans*, ed. J. Swaddling and P. Perkins, 60–63. London.

———. 2010. "Frühetruskische Hausarchitektur—Bemerkungen zum Forschungsstand." In Bentz and Reusser 2010a:9–28.

Quilici, L. 2000. *Le strade dell'Emilia Romagna*. Pisa and Rome.

Ranieri, M. 2005. "La geometria della pianta del tempio urbano di Marzabotto (*Regio* I, *Insula* 5)." In Sassatelli and Govi 2005a:73–88.

Rapoport, A. 1990. "System of Activities and System of Settings." In *Domestic Architecture and the Use of Space*, ed. S. Kent, 9–20. Cambridge.

Reed, C. A. 1969. "Osteoarchaeology." In *Science in Archaeology*, ed. D. R. Brothwell and E. S. Higgs, 204–216. London.

Rendini, P., and M. Firmati. 2010. "Le case di Ghiaccio Forte, centro fortificato etrusco nella Valle dell'Albegna." In Bentz and Reusser 2010a:179–195.

Reusser, Ch. 2002. *Vasen für Etrurien: Verbreitung und Funktionen attischer Keramik im Etrurien des 6. und 5. Jahrhunderts vor Christus*. Zürich.

———. 2009. "Ein attisch Schwarzgefirnisster Askos aus Marzabotto." In *Etruria e Italia Preromana. Studi in onore di Giovannangelo Camporeale*, ed. S. Bruni, 781–787. Pisa and Rome.

———, ed. 2017. *Spina: Neue Perspektiven der archäologischen Erforschung. Tagung an der Universität Zürich 2012*. Rahden.

Ricciardi, L. 2003. "Il deposito votivo del santuario del Fontanile di Legnisina di Vulci." In *L'acqua degli dei*, ed. G. Paolucci, 125–132. Montepulciano.

Richardson, E. H. 1983. *Etruscan Votive Bronzes: Geometric, Orientalizing, Archaic*. Mainz.

Riedel, A. 1978. "Notizie preliminari sullo studio della fauna di Spina." *Atti dell'Accademia delle Scienze di Ferrara* 55:1–7.

———. 2002. *La fauna dell'insediamento protostorico di Vadena/ Die Fauna der vorgeschichtlichen Siedlung von Pfatten*. Rovereto.

Romagnoli, S. 2007. "The Roman Farm." In Govi 2007:76–77.

———. 2010. "Le sedi stradali e le canalizzazioni." In Govi and Sassatelli 2010:223–234.

———. 2014. *Il santuario etrusco di Villa Cassarini a Bologna*. Bologna.

Romualdi, A. 2000. "La Tomba delle hydrie di Meidias." *Ostraka* 9:351–371.

———. 2004. "Riflessioni sul problema della presenza di Greci a Populonia nel quinto secolo a.C." *AnnFaina* 11: 181–206.

———. 2010. "Populonia e il distretto minerario dell'Elba e del Campigliese." In *Gli Etruschi delle città: Fonti, ricerche e scavi*, ed. S. Bruni, 112–123. Milan.

Roncalli, F. 1990. "La definizione pittorica dello spazio tombale nella «età della crisi»." In *Crise et transformation des sociétés archaïques de l'Italie antique au Ve siècle av. J.-C. Actes de la Table Ronde (Rome 1987)*, 229–243. Rome.

Roversi, G. 2013. "Contributo alla conoscenza del popolamento antico nella Valle del Reno attraverso lo studio dei materiali del Sassatello (Marzabotto)." *Ocnus* 21:127–184.

———. 2015. "Ceramica tardoantica dal sito del Sassatello, Marzabotto (BO)." In *Le forme della crisi: Produzioni ceramiche e commerci nell'Italia centrale tra Romani e Longobardi (III-VIII sec. d.C.)*, ed. E. Cirelli, F. Diosono, and H. Patterson, 131–138. Bologna.

Russo, A. 2010. "Edilizia privata e società presso le genti indigene dell'Italia meridionale fra età arcaica ed ellenistica." In Bentz and Reusser 2010a:281–292.

Sacchetti, F. 2005. "I nuovi scavi del Dipartimento di Archeologia nella città etrusca di Marzabotto (*Regio* I, *Insula* 5): Le tecniche del rilievo." In Sassatelli and Govi 2005a:63–72.

———. 2012. *Les amphores grecques dans le nord de l'Italie: Échanges commerciaux entre les Apennins et les Alpes aux époques archaïque et classique*. Arles.

Saladino, V. 2004. "Purificazioni. Mondo romano." *ThesCra* 2:63–87.

Saletti, C. 1970. "Problemi artistici di Marzabotto: Le espressioni figurative e decorative." In *Studi sulla città antica. Atti del Convegno di Studi sulla Città etrusca e italica preromana (Bologna–Marzabotto–Ferrara–Comacchio 1966)*, 279–283. Bologna.

Salomone Gaggero, E. 2003. "Il territorio tortonese fra Liguri e Roma nel III–II secolo a.C.: La testimonianza delle fonti letterarie." In *Dertona Historia Patriae: Storia di Tortona dalla preistoria ad oggi. 1*, 121–152. Tortona.

Sani, S. 2009a. "Sulla via tra le due Etrurie: I principi della valle del Reno e il controllo degli scambi." In Burgio, Campagnari, and Malnati 2009:51–56.

———. 2009b. "Marzabotto, Pian di Venola, necropoli della prima età del Ferro." In Burgio, Campagnari, and Malnati 2009:180–195.

Sanidas, G. M. 2013. *La production artisanale en Grèce: Une approche spatiale et topographique à partir des exemples de l'Attique et du Péloponnèse du 7ᵉ au 1ᵉʳ siècle avant J.-C.* Paris.

Santocchini Gerg, S. 2012. "Riflessioni sui contatti fra Etruria settentrionale e padana: Motivi e tecniche decorative tra VII e V sec. a.C." *Ocnus* 20:223–252.

———. 2013. "L'apparato decorativo della ceramica dell'Etruria padana." In Mattioli 2013:495–535.

———. 2015. "Felsina villanoviana: 'Città visibile.' Strategie insediative tra Bronzo Finale e Primo Ferro." In *Le città visibili: Archeologia dei processi di formazione urbana*, I: *Penisola italiana e Sardegna*, ed. M. Rendeli, 13–58. Rome.

———. 2018. "L'Orientalizzante nel Bolognese: Ulteriori riflessioni su influssi e connessioni culturali." *StEtr* 80:23–60.

———. 2021. "L'Orientalizzante nel Bolognese." *Mediterranea* supp., n.s., 1 (2021):63–92.

———. 2022. "Il bucchero dell'Etruria padana e le sue relazioni con l'Etruria settentrionale fra VII e VI secolo a.C." In Cappuccini and Gaucci 2022.

Santocchini Gerg, S., E. Zampieri, B. Gruška, and G. Mancuso. 2017. "Topographical Survey and Digital Models." *ACalc* 28.2:129–139.

Saronio, P. 1965. "Nuovi scavi nella città etrusca di Misano a Marzabotto." *StEtr* 32:385–416.

Sassatelli, G. 1970. "Nuove scoperte dal 1958 al 1969 a Marzabotto (Bologna)." *Emilia Preromana* 6:53–71.

———. 1977. "L'Etruria padana e il commercio dei marmi nel V secolo." *StEtr* 47:107–118.

———. 1979. "Ancora sui marmi in Etruria nel V secolo: Confronti volterrani." *StEtr* 47:107–118.

———. 1980a. "Due segnacoli tombali etruschi al Museo di Pomposa." *Emilia Preromana* 8:47–50.

———. 1980b. "Ampliamento e nuova sistemazione del Museo etrusco di Marzabotto." *Musei e gallerie d'Italia* 25:51–66.

———. 1983. "Bologna e Marzabotto: Storia di un problema." In *Studi sulla città antica: L'Emilia-Romagna*, ed. G. A. Mansuelli, 65–127. Rome.

———. 1984. "Edoardo Brizio e la prima sistemazione storica dell'archeologia Bolognese." In Morigi Govi and Sassatelli 1984:381–400.

———. 1985a. "Tecnologia della ceramica." In Cristofani 1985a:161–162.

———. 1985b. "Matrici per la fusione del bronzo (e relativi calchi)." In Cristofani 1985a:147.

———. 1986. "Bologna etrusca: Nuovi dati e recenti acquisizioni." *AttiMemBologna* 36:9–56.

———. 1988. "Topografia e 'sistemazione monumentale' delle necropoli felsinee." In *La formazione della città preromana in Emilia Romagna. Atti del convegno (Bologna-Marzabotto 1985)*, 197–259. Bologna.

———. 1989a. *La città etrusca di Marzabotto.* Casalecchio.

———. 1989b. "Problemi cronologici delle stele felsinee alla luce dei rispettivi corredi tombali." In *II Congresso Internazionale Etrusco (Firenze 1985)*, 927–949. Florence.

———. 1989–1990. "Culti e riti in Etruria Padana: Qualche considerazione." *ScAnt* 3–4:599–617.

———. 1990. "La situazione in Etruria Padana." In *Crise et transformation des sociétés archaïques de l'Italie antique au V siècle av J.-C. (Actes Rome 1987)*, 51–100. Rome.

———. 1991a. "Opere idrauliche nella città etrusca di Marzabotto." In *Gli Etruschi maestri di idraulica. Atti del Convegno (Perugia 1991)*, 179–207. Perugia.

———. 1991b. "Marzabotto (Bologna). Località Pian di Misano. Nuovi scavi nell'isolato 2 della Regione IV. Campagne 1988–1991." *BdA* 9:27–31.

———. 1991c. "Nuovi dati epigrafici da Marzabotto e il ruolo delle comunità locali nella 'fondazione' della città." *ArchCl* 43:693–715.

———. 1993a. "La funzione economica e produttiva: Merci, scambi, artigianato." In Berti and Guzzo 1993:179–217.

———. 1993b. "Rappresentazioni di giochi atletici in monumenti funerari di area padana." In *Spectacles sportifs et scéniques dans le monde étrusco-italique. Actes de la table ronde, Rome 1991*, 45–67. Rome.

———. 1993c. "Marzabotto." *REE*, *StEtr* 58:276–286.

———, ed. 1994a. *Iscrizioni e graffiti della città etrusca di Marzabotto.* Bologna.

———. 1994b. "Gli scavi nella città etrusca di Marzabotto." *Ocnus* 2:247–254.

———. 1998. "Intervento." In *Spina e il Delta padano. Riflessioni sul Catalogo e sulla Mostra ferrarese. Atti del Convegno Internazionale di Studi (Ferrara 1994)*, 157–165. Rome.

———. 2002a. "Ricordo di Guido Achille Mansuelli." *StEtr* 65–68:9–13.

———. 2002b. "Marzabotto, *Insula* 5 della *Regio* IV (officina per la fusione del bronzo)." In *I lingotti con il segno del ramo secco*, ed. G. Colonna, N. Parise, and E. Pellegrini, 30–43. Rome.

———. 2003. "Celti ed Etruschi nell'Etruria padana e nell'Italia settentrionale." *Ocnus* 11:231–257.

———. 2004. "La città etrusca di Marzabotto (Bologna)."

In *Scoprire: Scavi del dipartimento di Archeologia. Catalogo della mostra (Bologna 2004)*, 10–11. Bologna.

———. 2005. "La fase felsinea." In Sassatelli and Donati 2005: 235–257.

———. 2006. "Guido Achille Mansuelli maestro di Etruscologia a Bologna." *Carrobbio* 32:5–13.

———. 2007. "Un nouveau temple de Tinia dans la cité étrusque de Marzabotto." *Dossiers d'Archéologie* 322:56–59.

———. 2008a. "Gli Etruschi nella Valle del Po: Riflessioni, problemi e prospettive di ricerca." *AnnFaina* 15:71–114.

———. 2008b. "Celti ed Etruschi nell'Etruria Padana e nell'Italia settentrionale." In *Tra mondo celtico e mondo italico: La necropoli di Monte Bibele. Atti della tavola rotonda (Roma 1997)*, ed. D. Vitali and S. Verger, 323–348. Bologna.

———. 2009a. "Il tempio di *Tinia* a Marzabotto e i culti della città etrusca." In *ALTNOI. Il santuario altinate. Strutture del sacro a confronto e i luoghi di culto lungo la via Annia*, ed. G. Cresci Marrone and M. Tirelli, 325–344. Rome.

———. 2009b. "Bologna etrusca e la sua espansione tra Reno e Panaro." In Burgio, Campagnari, and Malnati 2009:27–36.

———. 2011. "Città etrusca di Marzabotto. Una fornace per il tempio di Tinia." In *Corollari. Scritti di antichità etrusche e italiche in omaggio all'opera di Giovanni Colonna*, ed. D. F. Maras, 150–158. Pisa and Rome.

———. 2014. "La Bologna etrusca tra Grecia ed Etruria." In Sassatelli and Russo Tagliente 2014:99–109.

———. 2015. *Archeologia e preistoria alle origini della nostra disciplina: Il congresso di Bologna del 1871 e i suoi protagonisti*. Bologna.

———. 2017a. *Felsina vocitata tum qum princeps Etruriae esset: Raccolta di studi di Etruscologia e Archeologia italica*. Bologna.

———. 2017b. "La città e il sacro in Etruria padana: Riti di fondazione, culti e assetti urbanistico-istituzionali." In Govi 2017a:181–204.

———. 2017c. "Interazioni culturali tra Greci, Etruschi e indigeni." In *Percorsi: Scritti di archeologia di e per Angela Pontrandolfo*, ed. S. De Caro, F. Longo, M. Scafuro, and A. Serritella, 385–390. Paestum.

———. 2019. "Gli Etruschi oggi." In Bentini et al. 2019:17–27.

———. 2020. "Alle origini dell'Istituto Nazionale di Studi Etruschi: Ricerca, tutela e valorizzazione." In *Immaginare l'Unità d'Italia: Gli Etruschi a Milano tra collezionismo e tutela*, 201–216. Milan.

Sassatelli, G., and A. M. Brizzolara. 1990. *I nuovi scavi dell'Università di Bologna nella città etrusca di Marzabotto. Catalogo della mostra (Bologna 1990)*. Bologna.

———. 1991a. "Marzabotto (Scavi e scoperte)." *StEtr* 57:386–390.

———. 1991b. "La città etrusca di Marzabotto: Nuovi scavi dell'Università di Bologna nell'Isolato 2 della Regione IV." In *L'Alma Mater e l'antico. Scavi dell'Istituto di Archeologia, Catalogo della Mostra (Bologna 1991)*, 7–15. Bologna.

———. 1991–1992. "Gli scavi dell'Istituto d'Archeologia e dell'Università di Bologna nella città etrusca di Marzabotto." *Studi e Documenti di Archeologia* 7:160–163.

———. 1995. "Marzabotto. Regio IV–Insula 2. Scavi e scoperte." *StEtr* 60:501–505.

Sassatelli, G., A. M. Brizzolara, M. Marchesi, E. Govi, C. Mattioli, and C. Taglioni. 1997. "La città etrusca di Marzabotto: Scavi nell'isolato 2 della Regione IV." In *Scavi e ricerche del Dipartimento di Archeologia. Catalogo della Mostra (Bologna 1997)*, 9–28. Bologna.

Sassatelli, G., and A. Donati, eds. 2005. *Storia di Bologna* 1: *Bologna nell'Antichità*. Bologna.

Sassatelli, G., and A. Gaucci. 2010. "Le iscrizioni e i graffiti." In Govi and Sassatelli 2010:313–393.

Sassatelli, G., and E. Govi. 1992. "Testimonianze di età preromana: Strade e monumentalizzazione." In *Tecnica stradale romana. Atti dell'incontro di studio (Bologna 1991)*, 125–139. Rome.

———, eds. 2005a. *Culti, forma urbana e artigianato a Marzabotto. Nuove prospettive di ricerca. Atti del convegno di studi (Bologna 2003)*. Bologna.

———. 2005b. "Il tempio di Tinia in area urbana." In Sassatelli and Govi 2005:9–62.

———. 2010. "Cults and Foundation Rites in the Etruscan City of Marzabotto." *BABesch*, Supp. 16:27–36.

Sassatelli, G., E. Govi, and P. Baronio. 2014. "Kainua, 'città nuova.'" *Archeo* 357:39–45.

Sassatelli, G., E. Govi, A. Gaucci, and S. Garagnani. 2017a. "Marzabotto: Così reale, così virtuale." *Archeo* 386:34–45.

Sassatelli, G., E. Govi, A. Gaucci, S. Garagnani, and M. Tirtei. 2017b. "La realtà antica di Kainua: Nuove scoperte e ricostruzioni virtuali nella città etrusca di Marzabotto." *Al Sâs* 35–36:54–84.

Sassatelli, G., and G. Mancuso. 2017. "Marmi d'Etruria: Verso un quadro aggiornato del problema." In *Cippi, stele, statue-stele e semata: Testimonianze in Etruria, nel mondo italico e in Magna Grecia dalla prima Età del Ferro fino all'Ellenismo*, ed. S. Steingräber, 103–129. Pisa.

Sassatelli, G., and A. Russo Tagliente, eds. 2014. *Il viaggio oltre la vita: Gli Etruschi e l'aldilà tra capolavori e realtà virtuale*. Bologna.

Sassatelli, G., and C. Taglioni. 1991–1992. "Gli scavi dell'Istituto di Archeologia dell'Università di Bologna nella città etrusca di Marzabotto." *StDocA* 7:160–164.

———, eds. 2000. *Città etrusca di Marzabotto*. CD-Rom. Bologna.

Scagliarini Corlaita, D. 1978. "La villa romana e le ville della Regione VIII." In *La villa romana di Cassana: Documenti archeologici per la storia del popolamento rustico*, 3–31. Bologna.

———. 1989. "L'insediamento agrario in Emilia Romagna in epoca romana." In *Insediamenti rurali in Emilia Romagna Marche*, ed. G. Adani, 11–36. Cinisello Balsamo.

———. 2005. "Il suburbium di Bononia: Edifici pubblici, ville, fabbriche tra città e territorio." In Sassatelli and Donati 2005:535–557.

Scarani, R. 1963. *Repertorio di scavi e scoperte dell'Emilia e Romagna*. Bologna.

Schifone, C. 1971. "Antefisse fittili." *StEtr* 29:249–265.

Schwarz, S. 1979. "The Pattern Class Vases of the 'Gruppo di Orvieto' in the U.S. National Museum Collection, Smithsonian Institution, Washington, D.C." *StEtr* 47:65–84.

Schweingruber, F. H. 1990. *Anatomy of European Woods*. Stuttgart.

Sciortino, M. 2012. "Un nucleo inedito di anfore da trasporto dall'abitato di Spina." *LANX* 12:158–194.

Scopigno, R., and M. Dellepiane. 2017. "Integration and Analysis of Sampled Data: Visualization Approaches and Platforms." In *Sensing the Past: Geotechnologies and the Environment. From Artifacts to Historical Site*, ed. N. Masini and F. Soldovieri, 377–393. Cham.

Sertori, S. 2014–2015. "Offerte dal mondo animale nel santuario per il culto delle acque di Marzabotto." Specialization thesis in Archaeology, University of Bologna.

Servadei, C. 2005. *La figura di Theseus nella ceramica attica: Iconografia e iconologia del mito nell'Atene arcaica e classica*. Bologna.

Shefton, B. B. 1988. "Der Stamnos." In *Das Kleinaspergle: Studien zu einem Fürstengrabhügel der frühen Latènezeit bei Stuttgart*, ed. W. Kimmig, 104–152. Stuttgart.

Simon, E. 1998. "Apollo in Etruria." *AnnFaina* 5:119–128.

———. 2006. "Gods in Harmony: The Etruscan Pantheon." In de Grummond and Simon 2006:45–65.

Slotty, F. 1946–1947. "Etrusco 'manin.'" *StEtr* 19:176–247.

Smith, C. 2019. "Polis Religion, Lived Religion, Etruscan Religion: Thoughts on Recent Research." *Ocnus* 27:85–105.

Smith, M. E. 2007. "Form and Meaning in the Earliest Cities: A New Approach to Ancient Urban Planning." *Journal of Planning History* 6:3–47.

———. 2011. "Empirical Urban Theory for Archaeologists." *Journal of Archaeological Method and Theory* 18:167–192.

Soler, F., F. J. Melero, and M. V. Luzón. 2017. "A Complete 3D Information System for Cultural Heritage Documentation." *Journal of Cultural Heritage* 23:49–57.

Staccioli, R. A. 1967. "Sulla struttura dei muri nelle case della città etrusca di Misano a Marzabotto." *StEtr* 35:113–126.

———. 1970. "A proposito della casa etrusca a sviluppo verticale." In *Studi sulla città antica. Atti del Convegno di studi sulla città etrusca e italica preromana (Bologna–Marzabotto–Ferrara–Comacchio 1966)*, 129–133. Bologna.

Steingräber, S. 1982. "Uberlegungen zu etruskischen Altaren." In *Miscellanea archeologica T. Dohrn dedicata*, 102–116. Rome.

Stopponi, S., and A. Giacobbi. 2017. "Orvieto campo della fiera: Forme del sacro nel 'luogo celeste.'" In Govi 2017a:121–144.

Susenbeth, S., and K. Keitel. 1988. "Partition of Whole Body Protein in Different Body Fractions and Some Constants in Body Composition in Pigs." *Livestock Production Science* 20:37–52.

Susini, G. 1975. "Culti salutari e delle acque: Materiali antichi della Cispadana." *Studi Romagnoli* 26:321–338.

Taglioni, C. 1999. *L'abitato etrusco di Bologna*. Bologna.

Teichert, M. 1969. "Osteometrische Untersuchungen zur Berechnung der Widderisthohe bei Schafen." *KhunArchiv* 83:237–292.

Teržan, B. 1977. "Certoška Fibula." *AVes* 27:317–356.

Testa, A. 1989. "Considerazioni sull'uso del candelabro in Etruria nel V e IV sec." *MÉFRA* 95.2:599–616.

Tirtei, M. 2011–2012. "Il popolamento etrusco nelle valli bolognesi tra la metà del VI e la metà del IV secolo a.C." Graduation thesis, University of Bologna.

———. 2016–2017. "Il tratto settentrionale dello stenopos d della città etrusca di Marzabotto: Lo studio dello Scavo Mansuelli del 1968." Specialization thesis in Archaeology, Università di Bologna.

Torelli, M. 1986. "La religione." In *Rasenna: Storia e civiltà degli Etruschi*, ed. G. Pugliese Caratelli, 159–237. Milan.

———. Forthcoming. "Lo spazio centrale di *Marzabotto*: Qualche considerazione sulle agorai delle città etrusche." In *Giovannangelo Camporeale. Etruscologo e Antichista. A un anno dalla scomparsa (Firenze 29 maggio 2018)*.

Torelli, M., and P. Gros 1988. *Storia dell'urbanistica: Il mondo romano*. Rome and Bari.

Trentacoste, A. C. 2014. "The Etruscans and Their Animals: The Zooarchaeology of Forcello di Bagnolo San Vito (Mantova)." PhD diss., University of Sheffield.

Tripponi, A. 1967. "L'esplorazione della porta e del settore sud-est dell'area urbana." *StEtr* 35:389–425.

———. 1971. "Esplorazione di un edificio nella zona sud-orientale (Reg. V ins. 1)." *StEtr* 39:219–230.

Trocchi, T. 1999. "La Valle del Setta nell'Età del Ferro." *Ocnus* 7:127–138.

———. 2002. "La Valle del Samoggia nella prima Età del Ferro." In *Archeologia nella Valle del Samoggia. Atti del Convegno, Quaderni della Rocca 9*, 81–108. Bologna.

———. 2010. "Le fibule." In Govi and Sassatelli 2010:201–220.

Tsakirgis, B. 2005. "Living and Working around the Athenian Agora: A Preliminary Case Study of Three Houses." In *Ancient Greek Houses and Households: Chronological, Regional, and Social Diversity*, ed. B. A. Ault and L. C. Nevett, 67–82. Philadelphia.

Tsingarida, A. 2020. "Oversized Athenian Drinking Vessels in Context: Their Role in Etruscan Ritual Performances." *AJA* 124.2:245–274.

Vanzini, R. 2015–2016. "Un rituale sacrificale dall'area urbana di Kainua (Marzabotto)". Specialization thesis in Archaeology, University of Bologna.

Venturi, S., and M. Foschi. 1980. *Insediamento storico e beni culturali. Montagna bolognese*. Bologna.

Verger, S., and A. Kermovant. 1994. "Nouvelles données et hypothèses sur la topographie de la ville étrusque de Marzabotto." *MÉFRA* 106.2:1077–1096.

Vernet, J. L. 2001. *Guide d'identification des charbons de bois préhistoriques et récents*. Paris.

Vitali, D. 1974. "L'acropoli della città etrusca di Marzabotto. Problematica." *Ingegneri Architetti Costruttori* 342–343:157–167, 196–201.

———. 1982. "Il Villanoviano nella Valle del Reno: Due tombe inedite da Sperticano." In *Studi in onore di Ferrante Rittatore Vonwiller* 2, 777–792. Como.

———. 1984. "Il V Congresso di Antropologia e Archeologia Preistoriche a Bologna." In Morigi Govi and Sassatelli 1984:277–297.

———. 1985a. "Monte Bibele (Monterenzio). Und andere fundstellen der keltischen epoche im gebiet von Bologna." In *Kleine Schriften aus dem vorgeschichtlichen Seminar Marburg*, 16. Marburg.

———. 1985b. "L'Acropoli di Marzabotto." In Colonna 1985: 88–92.

———. 2001a. "L'acquedotto etrusco." In Vitali, Brizzolara, and Lippolis 2001:72–76.

———. 2001b. "I Celti a sud del Po." In *Celti nell'Alto Adriatico. Atti delle Giornate Internazionali di Studio (Trieste 2001)*, ed. G. Cuscito, 227–239. Trieste.

———. 2004. "La Cispadana tra IV e II secolo a.C." In *Des Hibères aux Vénètes*, ed. S. Agusta Boularot and X. Lafon, 277–292. Rome.

———. 2005. "L'arrivo dei Galli. Il territorio appenninico." In Sassatelli and Donati 2005:368–385.

———. 2006. "'Ligures perdomiti' dans l'Apennin bolonais." In *Nicolae Szabó anniversarium sexagesimum quintum. Acta archaeologica Academiae Scientiarum Hungaricae* 57:173–181.

———. 2007. *Les Celtes d'Italie*. Paris.

———. 2008. "Torquis e Boi cisalpini." In *Taurini sul confine: Il Bric San Vito di Pecetto nell'età del ferro*, ed. F. M. Gambari, 13–19. Turin.

———. 2009. "Celti e Liguri nel territorio di Parma." In *Storia di Parma*, II: *Parma romana*, ed. D. Vera, 146–179. Parma.

———. 2013. "Le témenos de Tinia dans la ville étrusque de Marzabotto: Entre données de fouilles, hypothèses et certitudes." In *L'âge du fer en Europe. Mélanges offerts à Olivier Buchsenschutz*, 583–594. Bordeaux.

———. 2014. "La vaisselle céramique 'celtique' des Boïens cisalpins (IVᵉ–IIIᵉ s. av. J.-C.): Quelques considérations générales." *AMosel* 9:295–314.

Vitali, D., A. M. Brizzolara, and E. Lippolis. 2001. *L'acropoli della città etrusca di Marzabotto*. Bologna and Imola.

Von den Driesch, A. 1976. *A Guide to Measurement of Animal Bones from Archaeological Sites*. Cambridge, MA.

von Eles, P. 1987. "Tombe villanoviane a Pontecchio, località S. Biagio." In Bermond Montanari 1987:102–112.

———. 2019. "Bologna, necropoli di via Belle Arti." In Bentini et al. 2019:388–389.

von Eles, P., M. Mazzoli, and C. Negrini. 2018. "La necropoli villanoviana e orientalizzante di via Belle Arti a Bologna." In *Atti della XLV riunione scientifica dell'Istituto italiano di Preistoria e protostoria*, ed. M. Bernabò Brea, 299–308. Modena.

Wallace Hadrill, A. 1997. "Rethinking the Roman Atrium House." In *Domestic Space in the Roman World: Pompeii and Beyond*, ed. R. Laurence and A. Wallace Hadrill, 219–240. Portsmouth, RI.

Wikander, Ö., ed. 1986. *Architettura etrusca nel viterbese. Ricerche svedesi a San Giovenale e Acquarossa 1956–1986*. Rome.

———. 1993. *Acquarossa, VI: The Roof-Tiles 2. Typology and Technical Features*. Stockholm.

Zaccaria Ruggiu, A. 2003. *More regio vivere: Il banchetto aristocratico e la casa romana di età arcaica*. Rome.

Zamboni, L. 2016. *Spina città liquida: Gli scavi 1977–1981 nell'abitato di Spina e i materiali tardo arcaici e classici*. Rahden.

Zannoni, A. 1876–1884. *Gli scavi della Certosa di Bologna*. Bologna.

Zanoni, V. 2011. *Out of Place: Human Skeletal Remains from Non-Funerary Context. Northern Italy during the I Millennium BC*. Oxford.

Zeidler, P. 2017. "Handwerk und Produktion in Marzabotto." In *Die Etrusker: Weltkultur im antiken Italien. Exhibition Catalogue Karlsruhe*, 170–171. Darmstadt.

Zohari, D., and M. Hopf. 1993. *Domestication of Plants in the Old World*. Oxford.

INDEX

Achilles, 156, 157 fig. 15.2, 172
Acquarossa, 7, 32, 59n32, 116–117, 124n12
acroterion, 81
Adria, xv, xx map 1, xxi map 2, 32, 44, 49n19, 58, 99, 102–103, 107, 111, 113n79, 113n91, 159
afterlife, 12, 31, 65, 76, 80, 82, 86, 97, 148–149, 152n44, 159, 165, 181, 187
agger, 38, 84
agora (*forum*), 8, 39, 88, 134n7, 143n56
Agrigento Painter, 161n29
Ajax, 156, 157 fig. 15.2
alabastron (pl. *alabastroi*), xix, 30, 161n26, 170–172, 185
Albagino, xxii map 3, 42
Alberti, Leandro, 3, 9
amber, 171, 174n34
amphoras, 44, 45 fig. 5.2, 49n20, 83–84, 93, 100, 102–106, 106 fig. 10.3, 112n11, 158, 161n10, 186, 209–210
antefixes, 76, 81, 88, 202
Aphrodite (Turan), 130
Aplu. *See* Apollo
Apollo (Aplu), 8, 81–82, 131, 172, pl. 4
Archetta, xxii map 3, 43, 49n17, 53
architectural slab, 85, 88, 90n87, 153n60, 171, 177–181, 194
Ardea, 85, 87
Arezzo, xx map 1, 3, 44, 80, 89, 143, 198, 200n38, 205
Aria, Count Giovanni, 3, 9–10
Aria, Count Pompeo, 9, 11
Aria Branca, Count Adolfo, 10
Ariadne, 159
Aria family, 3, 8n2, 9, 175
Arias, Paolo Enrico, 11–12, 142n10
Ariminum. *See* Rimini
Arno River and Arno Valley, maps 2–3, 42–46
atrium-house, 7, 37, 40n60, 87, 119–120, 125n24, 125n26
augur, 7, 33, 35, 105
auguraculum, 33, 35, 76, 122, 145

basins, mortar, 47, 81, 94, 102, 106, 151n1, 210, 212
beakers, 45, 47, 47 fig. 5.5
Bellerophon, 81
Bisenzio River and Bisenzio Valley, maps 2–3, 41–42, 54
Bologna (Felsina, Bononia), xiv, xv, xix, xxx–xxii maps 1–3, 3–4, 6, 9, 25n26, 32–33, 41, 43–44, 48, 49n35, 50n54, 51–52, 55, 59n30, 80, 86, 99–100, 102, 104–105, 107, 111, 112n33, 112n39, 112n47, 113n71, 113n91, 134n1, 140–141, 146 fig. 14.2, 147, 149, 151, 151n15, 152n26, 153n56, 155, 159, 160n6, 161n20, 161n27, 162n38, 166–167, 169–172, 173n17, 174n42, 175, 178–181, 181n5, 183–184, 186, 190, 193–194, 196, 198, 200n40, 201–202, 206, 206n11, 207n20, 217
Bononia. *See* Bologna
Brizio, Edoardo, 4, 5 figs. 1.2–3, 5–6, 9–10, 10 fig. 2.1, 30, 38, 54, 101, 140, 142n10, 143n33, 165, 167–168, 168 fig. 16.3, 173n9, 177, 180, 181n3, 194, 196
Bronze Age, 29, 64, 66–68, 80–81, 217
brooch. *See* fibula
bucchero, 12, 30, 39n13, 45, 46 fig. 5.4, 48, 77, 81, 83, 85, 91, 100–103, 105, 111, 140, 141, 209–212
Burzanella, xxii map 3, 41, 53

Caere (Cerveteri), xx map 1, 8, 39, 48, 66, 76–77, 79–80, 84, 86–88, 89n1, 93, 103, 105, 112n33
Calliope Painter, 187–188
Camugnano, xxii map 3, 41
candelabrum, 44, 172–173, 173 fig. 16.5, 174n62, 185–186, pl. 5
candleholder. *See candelabrum*
Cantaiola, 53, 53 fig. 6.2, 202
Capua, xx map 1, 88, 151
Carducci, Giosuè, 10
Casalecchio di Reno, xxi–xxii maps 2–3, 41, 51–52, 59n30, 196, 199, 200n43, 202, 206n11
Casale Marittimo, 149
Castagnoli, Ferdinando, 6

Castiglione dei Pepoli, 42, 53
Cath. *See* Persephone
Catha. *See* Persephone
Celts and Celtic culture, xxviii map 9, 9–10, 12–13, 29, 44, 47–48, 54–55, 59, 64, 81, 135, 142, 165, 191–199, 195–196 figs. 19.1–3, 200n11, 200n25, 200n40–41, 200n46, 201, 214–215, 217
centaurs, 187
Ceres. *See* Demeter
Cerveteri. *See* Caere
chalices, 45, 102, 211
Chia. *See* Uni
Chianciano Terme, 49n39, 80
Chierici, Gaetano, 9, 39n10, 173n9, 181n3
Chimaera, 3
Chiusi, xx map 1, 43–48, 103–105, 130, 170–172, 198
chthonic realm. *See* afterlife
cippus (pl. *cippi*), 6, 33, 35, 35 fig. 4.4, 41–42, 48, 54, 76, 81–82, 112n33, 148–149, 149 fig. 14.4, 152n31, 152n35, 168, 173, 190, 196
cista (pl. *cistae*), 52, 52 fig. 6.1, 169, 169 fig. 16.4, 171, 180
Civita Castellana, 80
civitas. *See* spura
clan. *See* gentilicium
columen, 123
commerce. *See* trade
compluvium, 16, 124, 125n26, 126n69
concotto (baked clay), 57–58, 128
Confienti, xxii map 3, 42, 49n48, 54–55, 59n15
Corinthian goods, 30, 44, 45 fig. 5.2, 49n20, 49n25, 49n28, 155
Cornelius Nepos, xvin1
crux, 6, 33, 35, 35 fig. 4.4, 76, 85
cups, 30, 45, 81–82, 91–94, 100–104, 107, 111, 142, 155–157, 157 fig. 15.2, 160 fig. 15.4, 161n10, 161n14–18, 162n41, 178, 185–190, 209–212

Daedalus (Taitale), 81, 88
decussis, 35. *See also crux*
Demeter (Ceres, Vei), 8, 77, 80, 85–86, 103, 112n43, 159, 209
Diomedes Painter, 160 fig. 15.4
Dionysus (Fuflufuns), 86, 91, 148–149, 152n40, 152n44, 158–160, 158 fig. 15.3, 160 fig. 15.4, 173, 186–187, 190
Dis Pater, 31, 76
dolium (pl. *dolia*), xix, 93, 102, 113n86, 137, 161n17, 180, 202, 210, 212

earthworks. *See* agger
Eastern Gate, 15, 30, 38, 147 fig. 14.3, 147, 169, 216–217
Eastern Necropolis, xxiv map 5, xxxii map 13, 9, 12, 76, 80, 147–148, 149 fig. 14.4, 151, 158, 158 fig. 15.3, 165, 167–173, 168 fig. 16.3, 173 fig. 16.5, 175–181, 182n17, 215, pl. 3, pl. 8
Etrusca Disciplina, 6, 32, 35, 127
Etrusco-corinthian ceramics, 30, 44–45
Etruscus ritus, 7, 33
exchange. *See* trade
Exekias, 156, 161n10
ex-votos, 9, 12, 30–31, 37, 41–43, 42 fig. 5.1, 53–54, 76–77, 79–84, 83 fig. 8.6, 89, 91, 93, 99, 102–104, 106–107, 112n24, 113n92, 130–132, 131–132 figs. 12.3–4, 136, 145–148, 146 fig. 14.2, 150–151, 151n10, 151n14–15, 152n16–18, pl. 4

Falerii, 90n68
Fat Boy Group, 162n41
Felsina. *See* Bologna
Ferrara T. 585 Group, 198
Festus, 33
fibula (brooch), 39n6, 49n28, 195 fig. 19.1, 185, 187
Fiesole, xx–xxii maps 1–3, 42, 44, 47–48, 54, 103
Forcello di Bagnolo San Vito, xxi map 2, 32, 44, 64–65, 99, 140, 143n27
forum. *See* agora
foundation rite, xiii, 27, 32–33, 34 fig. 4.3, 39, 40n40, 76, 82–85, 97, 145
"Foundry" of *Regio* V (5), 38, 102, 128–133, 130 fig. 12.2, 133 fig. 12.5, 134n4, 160n4, 211, 214–215
Fratte, xx map 1, 7, 117
Fuflufuns. *See* Dionysus
furnaces. *See* kilns and furnaces

Gabii, 85
Gaelic culture. *See* Celts and Celtic culture
Gate, Eastern. *See* Eastern Gate
Gate, Northern. *See* Northern Gate
gentilicium (clan), 84, 104–106, 113n65, 113n73, 133, 142
glass, 10, 171, 174n34, 185–186
gold, 10, 83–84, 171–172, 185, pl. 1
Gonfienti (Prato), xxi–xxii maps 2–3, 40n17, 42, 44, 49n13, 54, 161n28
Gozzadini, Giovanni, 4, 9, 54, 83, 101–102, 133, 165, 170–171, 173n9, 173n16, 175, 193
Granaglione, xxii map 3, 41
Gravisca, 88
"Great Furnace/Great Kiln," 15, 38, 101, 106, 111, 136 fig. 13.1, 135–142, 142n57, 210, 213
Grizzana Morandi, xxii map 3, 43

healing. *See* sanatium
Helen, 159, pl. 9

Hera (Juno, Uni, Chia), 7–8, 13, 77, 79–80, 79 fig. 8.2, 82, 85–86, 90n73, 90n79, 103, 209
Heracles (Hercle), 159–160, 160 fig. 15.4, 172, 186
Hercle. *See* Heracles
Hermes (Turms), 62, 148
Herodotus, 62
Hippodamus of Miletus, 6
hut, 29–30, 32, 39n8, 39n13, 85, 124n6

Idice River and Idice Valley, maps 2–3, 42, 47, 51, 55, 196–198, 202
impluvium, 16. *See also* compluvium
inauguratio, 33, 35, 84
Ionian ceramics, 155, 160n1
ivory *pixis*, 30, 44, 45 fig. 5.3

jars, 10, 45, 91–94, 97, 100, 102, 209
jugs, 12, 47, 47 fig. 5.5, 49n40, 81, 93, 102, 161n35, 185–187, 207n28, 209–210, pl. 7
Juno. *See* Hera
Jupiter. *See* Zeus

Kachrylion Potter, 156
kantharos (pl. *kantharoi*), xix, 45, 81, 102, 159, 161n35, 172, 185–187, 190, 198, 211, pl. 9
kilns and furnaces, 20, 37, 55, 58, 58 fig. 6.4, 77, 101, 117, 135–138, 139 fig. 13.4, 140, 142n14, 143n23, 143n27, 143n40, 203–204, 206, 207n18
kioniskos (pl. *kioniskoi*), 91
kore (pl. *korai*), 42, 42 fig. 5.1, 130–131, 131 fig. 12.3, 159
kouros (pl. *kouroi*), 42, 42 fig. 5.1, 79, 79 fig. 8.3, 81, 130, 130 fig. 12.2, 131
krater, 30, 82, 158–159, 160n1, 161n17, 171–172, 185–187, 198
kyathos (pl. *kyathoi*), 44–45, 53, 53 fig. 6.2, 185–187
kylix (pl. *kylikes*), 45, 91, 124n11, 156–159, 166, 198

Laconian ceramics, 30, 44, 49n25, 82, 155, 160n1
ladle. *See* simpulum
La Quercia, xxi–xxii maps 2–3, 42, 54–55, 56 fig. 6.3, 58 fig. 6.4, 58–59, 59n19, 161n28
Lasa, 198, 198 fig. 19.4
Legnisina, 77, 80, 87
Limentra River and Limentra Valley, maps 2–3, 41, 43, 53
limitatio, 5–6, 35
Little Masters Group, 30, 45, 82, 124n11, 155, 160n8
Liver of Piacenza, 35, 83, 174n27
Livy, Titus Livius, xv, 35, 201–202

louterion (pl. *louteria*), 80
Louvre G 456 Painter, 190n21, 190n29

maenads, 88, 158 fig. 15.3, 159, 161n21, 187
Mansuelli, Guido Achille, 6–7, 9n5, 11–12, 38, 129, 140, 143n40, 181
Manth (Mantus), 31
Mantova. *See* Mantua
Mantua (Mantova), xv, xx–xxi maps 1–2, 6, 31, 86, 104, 140
Mantus. *See* Manth
marble, 15, 43–44, 49n16, 79, 79 fig. 8.3, 130, 146, 148–149, 151, 151n1, 152n33, 153n60, 169, 179, 183, 186, 190n35, 206, pl. 8
Mars, 85
Marzabotto Group, 41–43, 53, 81, 131, 152n20
Medelana, xxii map 3, 43
Melpum, xviii1, 197
Memnon, 172
Menelaos, 159, pl. 9
Menerva. *See* Minerva
Minerva (Menerva), 3, 82, 88
Modena, xxi map 2, 42, 201
Monteacuto Ragazza, xxii map 3, 42, 42 fig. 5.1, 49n48, 52, 54–55, 103–104
Monte Bibele, xxii map 3, 47, 55, 64, 66, 196–197, 200n39, 200n43
Monte della Croce, 52
Monterenzio, xxi–xxii maps 2–3, 42, 47
Montese, xxii map 3, 42
Montese Group, 42
Monteveglio, xxii map 3, 42
Montorio (Monzuno), xxii map 3, 42, 53
Montovolo, 52, 153
Monzuno. *See* Montorio
Mugello, 42, 49n35, 55
mundus (*munth*), 31–32, 76, 80, 84, 100 fig. 10.1, 209
munth. *See* mundus
mutulus (pl. *mutuli*), 23, 88, 123

Neapolis, xix, 37, 39
Necropolis, Eastern. *See* Eastern Necropolis
Necropolis, Northern. *See* Northern Necropolis
Nethuns (Poseidon), 80
New York 96.18.51, class of, 161n19
Niobid Painter, 161n29, 172, 190n19
Nocera, xix
Nola, xix, xx map 1
Northern Gate, 38, 80, 213
Northern Necropolis, xxiv map 5, xxxii map 13, 3, 4 fig. 1.1, 9, 12, 77, 80, 148, 149 fig. 14.4, 149, 151n14, 159, 165–166,

Northern Necropolis (*continued*)
167 fig. 16.2, 169 fig. 16.4, 169–173, 174n62, 175–181, 176 fig. 17.1, 182n37, 215
Numa Pompilius, 35
nymphs, 158–159, 161n21. *See also* maenads

oil, 44, 49n20, 70, 85, 206, 207n14
oinochoe (pl. *oinochoai*), 47, 49n42, 84, 159, 161n35, 170, 185–186, 188
olla (pl. *ollae*), 47, 47 fig. 5.5, 79, 81, 85, 100, 102, 111, 209
olpe (pl. *olpai*), xix, 79, 102, 209
Ombrone River and Ombrone Valley, xxi–xxii maps 2–3, 41, 44, 53
Ops, 85
Orchard Painter, 161n29, 172
Orestes Painter, 187
Orvieto (Volsini), xx map 1, 45–48, 86, 88–89, 90n87, 99, 105, 130, 169, 175

Panaro River and Panaro Valley, xxi–xxii maps 2–3, 42, 51, 59n4
Panico, xxii map 3, 43
patera (pl. paterae), 86, 169–172, 174n42, 185
Pausanias, 62
Pegasus, 81
Penthesilea Painter, 190n21
Persephone (Cath, Catha), 80, 148, 169, 174n27
Perugia, xx map 1, 3, 77
Pian di Venola, xxii map 3, 43, 52, 52 fig. 6.1, 202, 217
Pisa, xx–xii maps 1–3, 43–44, 48, 148, 152n34, 152n41
Pistoia, xxii map 3, 41–43, 52–53, 207n20
plinth, 88, 123, 146, 152n31
Pliny the Elder, xvi, 197
Podium-altar B, 31–32, 31 fig. 4.2, 76, 215, pl. 12
Podium-altar D, 76–77, 145, 146 fig. 14.1, 147, 215, pl. 11
Poggio della Gaggiola, 41, 52
Polybius, 201
Pompeii, xiii, xx map 1, 5, 10
Pontecagnano, xx map 1, 8, 31, 84
Populonia, xx map 1, 39, 44, 64, 66, 169–170, 172, 174n24, 174n42, 174n49, 176, 178–181, 181n13, 182n36
Po River and Po Valley, xv, xviii1, xix, xxi map 2, 6, 30, 32, 41–42, 44, 47, 49n35, 51, 130, 140, 198, 201, 205–206
Poseidon. *See* Nethuns
Prada, xxii map 3, 53
Praeneste, 198, 200n40
praenomen, 82, 104, 133
Prato. *See* Gonfienti
priest-augur. *See* augur

Proitos, 81
puteal. See well
Pyrgi, 8, 76, 79, 83–84, 87–88, 90n87, 96–97, 174n37

Reno River and Reno Valley, xv, xix, maps 2–3, 9, 12–13, 20, 27, 32–33, 35, 41–43, 47, 51–55, 58, 75, 127, 140, 150, 175, 181n3, 183, 194, 197, 202–203, 205–206, 206n11, 207n15, 212
R Group, 159
Rhodes Group, 30, 156, 157 fig. 15.2
Rimini (Ariminum), xxi map 2, 103, 201
Riola, xxii map 3, 43, 53
Roman culture, xvi, xix, xxiii map 4, 5, 8, 10, 12–13, 16, 29, 64, 66, 82, 96, 105, 111, 123, 125, 127, 165, 179, 191, 193, 201–206, 100–101 figs. 10.1–2, 207n27, 213–214, 217
Rome, xx map 1, 42, 76, 84, 87, 193, 201
Roselle, xx map 1, 39, 64, 66
Rubiera, xxi map 2, 112n33

Samoggia River and Samoggia Valley, 42, 51–52, 59n3
sanatium, 80, 82, 131, 199
San Polo d'Enza, xxi map 2, 86
Sansoni, Filippo, 165–166, 167 fig. 16.2, 170, 173, 175, 179–180, 193
Sassatello, 205–206, 205 fig. 20.2, 207n20, 217
Sasso Marconi, xxi–xxii maps 2–3, 12–13, 43, 51, 53, 55, 148, 149 fig. 14.4, 153n55, 173, 183–184, 184–185 figs. 18.1–2, 188–189 figs. 3–4, 202, 206n11
Satricum, 85, 88
Satyr, 158–159, 158 fig. 15.3, 187, pl. 9
Secchia River and Secchia Valley, xxi map 2, 49n35
Serchio River and Serchio Valley, xxi map 2, 49n35
Serravalle, xxii map 3, 42
Serravalle Group, 42
Servius, Maurus Honoratus, 31
Setta River and Setta Valley, xxi–xxii maps 2–3, 41–42, 47, 49n48, 53–55, 56 fig. 6.3, 57–58, 183, 202, 206n11
Shuvalow Painter, 188, 190n20
Siana cup, 30, 45, 82, 155, 160n8
Sibano, xxii map 3, 43, 153n55, 202
Sienese Workshop, 198
Sillaro River and Sillaro Valley, xxii map 3, 42
silver, 185, 194
simpulum, 44, 186–187
situla (pl. *situlae*), 44, 48, 81, 170–171, 185–187
Sokra Group, 198
spectio, 35
Sperticano, xxii map 3, 43, 52, 217

Spina, xv, maps 1–2, 6, 24n2, 32, 44, 49n20, 50n54, 65–66, 70, 99, 102, 104–105, 107, 111, 113n91, 140–141, 158–160, 161n27, 170–172, 174n46, 190, 200n30

spura (*civitas*), 7, 39, 43, 48, 83–84, 79 fig. 8.2, 87, 92, 100 fig. 10.1, 103, 106, 209

stamnos (pl. *stamnoi*), 44, 47, 158, 161n20, 171, 174n57, 174n60, 180, 185–186

statuettes (bronze), 42, 42 fig. 5.1, 44, 53–54, 77, 79, 81–82, 83 fig. 8.6, 89, 91, 130, 172–173, 173 fig. 16.5, pls. 4–5

stele (pl. *stelae, stelai*), 41, 48, 50n51, 76, 80, 102, 104–105, 111n3, 112n47, 113n56, 113n66, 113n71, 147 fig. 14.3, 147–148, 151, 152n26, 153n56, 169, 174n24

Śuri, 31

symposium, 12, 44–45, 47, 158–159, 161, 186–187

Taitale. *See* Daedalus

Tarquinia, xx map 1, 8, 39, 64, 84–85, 87–88, 90n79, 93, 123

temenos (pl. *temene*), 77, 85, 92, 100, 103, 145, 209

Temple A, 32, 76, 86, 215

Temple C, 32, 76, 86–87, 215

Temple E, 76, 86–87, 215

Temple of Tinia, xiv, xxiv map 5, 7–8, 21 fig. 3.4, 24 fig. 3.8, 25n21, 30, 32, 37–38, 67, 77, 78 fig. 8.1, 79–80, 83–84, 86–88, 91, 92 fig. 9.1, 93, 97, 103–104, 120, 122, 136, 140–141, 145, 150, 151n1, 153n54, 157, 165, 204, 209, 213

Temple of Uni, xxiv map 5, 7–8, 21–24, 22 fig. 3.5, 23 fig. 3.7, 33, 37, 39, 40n60, 69, 77, 78–79 figs. 8.1–2, 79–80, 82–88, 91–92, 92 figs. 9.1–2, 97, 100, 103, 122–123, 145, 150, 152n53, 157, 209, 213

templum, 8, 16, 33, 35, 36 fig. 4.5, 38, 76, 80, 83, 145, 147

"*Terza Stipe,*" 83, 83 fig. 8.6, 145, 152n16, 153n54, 215

Thefarie Velianas, 84

Tiber River and Tiber Valley, 44, 47, 49n35, 198

Tin, Tins. *See* Zeus

Tinia. *See* Zeus

trade, xxii map 3, 12, 32, 41, 44–45, 45 fig. 5.2, 51–54, 57, 70, 127, 129–130, 151, 158–160, 161n18, 172, 183, 197–199, 206

travertine, 10, 80, 82, 86, 118, 123–124, 125n53, 131, 145–146, 149–151, 151n7, 151n14, 152n16, 152n31, 152n53, 153n55, 181, 186, 194, 197

Turan. *See* Aphrodite

Turms. *See* Hermes

Tuscania, 190n25

underworld. *See* afterlife

Uni. *See* Hera

Vei. *See* Demeter

Veii, Veio, xx map 1, 42, 49n8, 65, 79–80, 82, 93, 112n46, 190n21, 197

Veii Painter, 190n21

Vergato, xxii map 3, 43, 53

Verucchio, xxi map 2, 103, 217

Vetulonia, xx map 1, 44

Vienna Group, 162n41

Villa Giulia Painter, 161n29

Villanovan period, 10, 39n13, 41, 45, 180, 217

Vimignano, 43, 53

Vitruvius, Marcus Pollio, 16, 22, 77, 87, 121, 123

Volsinii. *See* Orvieto

Volterra, xx map 1, 43–44, 47–48, 77, 84, 86, 89, 130, 170, 198, 200n38

votives. *See* ex-votos

Vulci, xx map 1, 44, 47–48, 77, 80, 87, 105, 132

Water Shrine, xxiv map 5, 15, 30, 61–63, 62 fig. 7.1, 70n1, 70n6, 75, 80, 81 figs. 8.4–5, 82–83, 88, 102, 104, 106, 112n47, 131, 132 fig. 12.4, 145, 152n17, 155, 157 fig. 15.2, 160n4, 160n8, 161n11, 199, 212, 215, pl. 4

well, 30–33, 37–38, 39n13, 42, 44, 54, 76–77, 79–80, 101, 106, 113n86, 140, 169, 193, 197, 200n24, 203, 206, 207n28, 211–212, 214, pl. 8

wine, 44, 49n20, 84, 93, 102, 106, 158, 186

wood, 12, 21, 23, 44, 52, 55–57, 66–69, 123, 131, 136, 177–178, 181, 187, 203

workshop-house, 38, 117, 121, 124n17, 128–129

Zeus (Jupiter, Tinia, Tins), 8, 13, 38, 79, 83, 86, 91, 103, 106–107, 112n46, 107 fig. 10.4, 125n32, 130, 136, 209